The Lyotard Reader and Guide

Edited by

KEITH CROME AND JAMES WILLIAMS

Edinburgh University Press

Edinburgh University Press Ltd
22 George Square, Edinburgh

Typeset in 10.5/12.5 Bembo
by Servis Filmsetting Ltd, Manchester, and
printed and bound in Great Britain by
Antony Rowe Ltd, Chippenham, Wilts

A CIP record for this book is available from the British Library

ISBN 0 7486 2057 5 (hardback)
ISBN 0 7486 2058 3 (paperback)

Published with the support of the
Edinburgh University Scholarly Publishing Initiatives Fund.

Contents

Acknowledgements

Keith Crome: I would like to express my gratitude to Mark Sinclair for his help and advice. The translations we worked on together owe their fluency to his skills alone, and those parts of the book I have written have benefited greatly from his acute comments and constructive criticism.

James Williams: I would like to thank the Arts and Humanities Research Board and the Carnegie Trust for grants that have allowed me to complete the research for this book.

The editors and publisher would like to thank the following for permission to include the material collected here: every effort has been made to trace the copyright holders, but if any have been inadvertently overlooked, the publisher will be pleased to make the necessary arrangements at the first opportunity.

'Taking the Side of the Figural', originally appeared in *Discours, figure* (Éditions Klincksieck, 1971), pp. 9–23.

'The Great Ephemeral Skin', from *Libidinal Economy* (Continuum and Indiana University Press, 1993), pp. 1–20.

'Presentation' from *The Differend* by Jean-François Lyotard. © 1988 by The University of Minnesota. Originally published in French as *Le Différend*. © 1983 by Les Éditions de Minuit. Reprinted by permission of Georges Borchardt, Inc., for Les Éditions de Minuit.

The Postmodern Condition, pp. 37–53; English translation and foreword © 1984 the University of Minnesota and Manchester University Press, Manchester, UK. Original French-language edition © 1979 Les Éditions de Minuit.

'The Affect-phrase' from the *Journal of the British Society for Phenomenology*, Vol. 32, No. 3, October 2001, pp. 234–41. Originally published as 'La phrase-affect: d'un supplement au Différend' in *Misère de la philosophie*, © 2000 Editions Galilée, Paris, pp. 43–54.

'Answering the Question: What is Postmodernism?', from Ihab Hassan, *Innovation/Renovation* © 1983. Reprinted by permission of the University of Wisconsin Press.

'Return upon the Return', from *Toward the Postmodern*, ed. Robert Harvey & Mark S. Roberts (Amherst, NY: Humanity Books), © 1999 Robert Harvey & Mark S. Roberts. Reprinted with permission.

Soundproof Room: Malraux's Anti-Aesthetics, trans. Robert Harvey, pp. 24–50. © 1993 Éditions Galilée; English translation © 2001 by the Board of Trustees of the Leland Stanford Jr University.

'Sendings' from *The Confession of Augustine*, trans. Richard Beardsworth, pp. 65–77. © 1998 Éditions Galilée; English translation © 2000 by the Board of Trustees of the Leland Stanford Jr University.

'The State and Politics in the France of 1960', originally appeared in *La guerre des Algériens*, (Paris, Éditions Galilée, 1989). English translation © 1993 by the Regents of the University of Minnesota.

'A Short Libidinal Economy of a Narrative Set-up' originally appeared in *Des dispositifs pulsionnels* © Paris, Éditions Galilée, 1994.

'A Memorial of Marxism', from *Peregrinations: Law, Form, Event*. English translation © 1988 Columbia University Press.

'The Communication of Sublime Feeling', from *Lessons on the Analytic of the Sublime*, trans. Elizabeth Rottenberg © 1991 Éditions Galilée; English translation © 1994 by the Board of Trustees of the Leland Stanford Jr University.

'Time Today' from *The Inhuman*. Reprinted by permission of Polity Press Ltd.

Jean-François Lyotard, 'The connivances of desire with the figural' from *Driftworks*, Roger McKeon, ed., pp. 57–68. New York, Semiotext(e) Foreign Agents series, 1984.

'Newman: the instant', trans. David Macey, in *The Lyotard Reader*, ed. A. Benjamin (Oxford: Blackwell, 1989).

'Painting as a Libidinal Set-up' originally appeared in *Des dispositifs pulsionnels*. The editors thank Mme Lyotard for permission to reproduce this extract.

'On what is "art"', from *Toward the Postmodern*, ed. Robert Harvey & Mark S. Roberts (Amherst, NY: Humanity Books), © 1999 Robert Harvey & Mark S. Roberts. Reprinted with permission.

List of Translators

Part 1: Philosophy
1. Taking the Side of the Figural   Mark Sinclair
2. The Great Ephemeral Skin   Iain Hamilton Grant
3. Presentation   Georges Van Den Abbeele
4. *The Postmodern condition*   Geoffrey Bennington & Brian Massumi
5. The Affect-phrase   Keith Crome

Part 2: Literature
6. Answering the Question   Régis Durand
7. Return upon the Return   Robert Harvey & Mark S. Roberts
8. *Soundproof Room*   Robert Harvey
9. Sendings   Richard Beardsworth

Part 3: Politics
10. The State and Politics in the France of 1960   Bill Readings & Kevin Paul Geiman
11. A Short Libidinal Economy of a Narrative Set-up   Keith Crome & Mark Sinclair
12. A Memorial of Marxism   Cecile Lindsay
13. The Communication of Sublime Feeling   Elizabeth Rottenberg
14. Time Today   Geoffrey Bennington & Rachel Bowlby

Part 4: Art
15. The Connivances of Desire with the Figural   Anne Knab
16. Painting as a Libidinal Set-up   Keith Crome & Mark Sinclair
17. Newman: The Instant   David Macey
18. On What is 'Art'   Robert Harvey

Abbreviations

Hegel
PhG   *Phenomenology of Mind*, trans. J. B. Baillie, New York: 1967

Kant
KPV   *Critique of Practical Reason*, trans. Lewis White Beck, New York: 1956
KRV   *Critique of Pure Reason*, trans. N. Kemp Smith, New York: 1929
KU   *Kant's Critique of Judgement*, trans. J. C. Meredith, Oxford: 1952

Malraux
AM   *Anti-Memoirs*, trans. T. Kilmartin, New York: 1968
JE   'D'une jeunesse européenne' in *Écrits par André Chanson [sic], André
       Malraux, Jean Grenier, Henri Petit, suivis de Trois Poèmes de J. P. Jouve,
       129–153*, Paris: 1927
Laz   *Lazarus*, trans. T. Kilmartin, New York: 1977
MF   *Man's Fate*, trans. H. M. Chevalier, New York: 1961
RW   *The Royal Way*, trans. S. Gilbert, New York: 1935
VS   *The Voices of Silence*, trans. S. Gilbert, Garden City, New York: 1953

Wittgenstein
TB   *Notebooks*, ed. & tr. G. E. M. Anscombe & G. H. von Wright, Oxford:
       1979
TLP   *Tractatus Logico-Philosophicus*, tr. D. Pears & B. McGuinness, London:
       1961

Introduction

Jean-François Lyotard is one of the key intellectual figures of our time. He achieved wide renown in the early 1980s as the author of *The Postmodern Condition (La Condition Postmoderne)*, which quickly became a central text in postmodern theory. Yet, notwithstanding the importance of the analyses it offered of contemporary society and science, *The Postmodern Condition* was a short, occasional piece, commissioned by the *Conseil de Universités* of the government of Quebec, and Lyotard was doubtless somewhat embarrassed by its success. Informing the text, but largely eclipsed by it — at least outside of Lyotard's native France — there lay thirty years of profound engagement with the central philosophical and political problems of the latter part of the twentieth century. Thus whilst the popularity of *The Postmodern Condition* cast a shadow over Lyotard's other work, through it that work fundamentally influenced, and continues to influence, thinking in the humanities, arts and sciences, often in subtle and unacknowledged ways. For this reason alone an understanding of the full range of Lyotard's work is indispensable to anyone seeking to appreciate current thinking and practice in these three central areas of human life.

Beyond the success and influence of *The Postmodern Condition*, Lyotard's other work is important in its own right. Lyotard is acknowledged to be one of the major philosophers and political theorists of the twentieth century, and his writings have transformed our philosophical and political understanding of ourselves in numerous and profound ways. For anyone seeking to grasp our contemporary cultural, social and political situation, Lyotard is necessary reading. Moreover, it is certain that his significance will continue to grow as this century strives to come to terms with the artistic, intellectual and political legacy of the previous century.

For these reasons we felt that there was a need to collect, and make readily accessible, an up-to-date selection of Lyotard's writings covering the full range of his concerns, and displaying the breadth, depth and provocation of his thought. Since the publication of the last major English-language anthology of Lyotard's writings in 1989, much new work by Lyotard has appeared. In addition, scholarly and critical appreciation of his work has advanced considerably, substantially enriching and complicating the understanding of his importance as a philosopher and literary, cultural and political theorist. Our choice of material is a reflection of this: we have included selections from Lyotard's most recent work, from his three main books, and also some earlier writings, the importance of which has become increasingly apparent in the light of recent studies, and some of which are available here in translation for the first time.

In addition to this general introduction, in which we set out the development of Lyotard's work and outline his most abiding concerns, we have provided a detailed introduction to each of the four major sections of this volume. In each of these sections we identify Lyotard's principal contributions to philosophy, literature, politics and art respectively, and critically situate the writings included therein. This division into separate areas is our own: even in those essays and texts where he deals with the work of a particular visual artist, literary author, philosophical movement or political issue, Lyotard nearly always introduces concerns and raises problems that are taken from these other areas. We hope the deliberate artificiality of our arrangement will encourage rather than impede reflection on the interrelations between these areas in Lyotard's thought.

We have also included a select bibliography listing Lyotard's principal writings in both French and in English translation, and some of the more important studies of his work. Thus, whilst this volume is primarily for students looking for an introduction and guide to Lyotard's work, we hope that it will also be of some use to scholars seeking to understand better Lyotard's contribution to contemporary thought in general.

The most immediately striking aspect of Lyotard's work as a whole, and one which scholars have been quick to note, is its heterogeneity. In addition to the great range of his writings, covering disciplines such as art history and theory, literary theory, political theory, psychoanalysis, and philosophy, Lyotard's work is marked by abrupt shifts in tone, style, form and thematic concerns. Most often these shifts occur between different books or groups of books, but they are sometimes present within the individual works themselves. They have exercised Lyotard's commentators, some of whom have inclined towards identifying a single trajectory underlying Lyotard's thought as a whole, whilst others have sought to resist such readings, stressing instead the differences between the various works, and suggesting that it is only the proper name 'Lyotard' that confers anything like a unity on this complex patchwork of writings. In order to give an overall impression of the nature and scope of Lyotard's work, here we shall give an account of the main stages of its development. The headings under which we have arranged this account are intended only to suggest something of that development; they are not definitive. We will afterwards outline what we consider are the central issues and concerns raised by that work.

Marxism

Lyotard was born in Versailles, France on 10 August 1924. He was educated at the Sorbonne where he studied philosophy. Among his classmates were Michel Butor and Roger Laporte, both of who went on to become important literary authors. In 1948 Lyotard published his first essay, 'Nés en 1925' (translated as 'Born in 1925', in *Political Writings*), in the journal founded by Jean-Paul Sartre, *Les Temps modernes*. Addressing the philosophical and political situation of France's youth immediately after the Second World War, the essay evinces many of Lyotard's later concerns. It evokes a Europe tortured by the nihilism intrinsic to it: in the face of the horrors of the war Europe no longer knows how to behave and has ceased to understand itself; communism, the last great political project of the West, has declined, Lyotard writes, into mere orthodoxy; and the fate of Western humanity has been abandoned to economic management.

The significance of these claims for any understanding of Lyotard's work should not be overlooked. Certainly, they marked Lyotard out among his contemporaries. If 'Born in 1925' manifested Lyotard's acutely critical political and philosophical intelligence, it also bore witness to the intellectual and personal courage that allowed him to look clear-sightedly at his own age, and to his taste for difference and dispute. For in the immediate postwar period in France intellectual life was dominated by Marxism, and for many of Lyotard's contemporaries the declaration of a decline of communism would have been anathema. That is not the essay's only significance, however; 'Born in 1925' announces and evokes the historical and existential predicament that informs Lyotard's life and work. Deeply affected by the catastrophic breakdown of the political projects of the West that surrendered Europe, if not the world, to bureaucratic management and economic exploitation, Lyotard wrestled for the rest of his life with the collapse of Marxism and the ever-increasing nihilism of European culture.

On passing the *agrégation* examination – a competitive examination for teachers – Lyotard took a position teaching philosophy at a lycée in Constantine, at that time the capital of the French department of East Algeria, where he taught from 1950–2. Whilst there, Lyotard met Pierre Souyri, with whom he forged an important friendship. As 'Born in 1925' had shown, Lyotard was already possessed of a sharp political sensibility; in Souyri, whose political commitment appeared to Lyotard to come from the very core of his being, Lyotard encountered a Marxist who was no mere dogmatist, and a Marxism that was more than a doctrine in decline. For Souyri, Marxism was both the profound expression of the need to articulate and resist the radical wrong suffered by the working class under capitalism, and a resolve, which could never be abandoned, to transform the world. Lyotard's friendship with Souyri marked a period of militant, if unorthodox, Marxism: in 1954 Lyotard, along with Souyri, was admitted to the radical Marxist group *Socialisme ou Barbarie* (Socialism or Barbarism), whose most prominent members were Claude Lefort and Cornelius Castoriadis. Lyotard would remain affiliated to the group for a decade.

In the same year Lyotard published his first book, *La Phénoménologie*. This short monograph testified to Lyotard's early philosophical interest in phenomenology. In the book Lyotard acknowledged the richness of phenomenological analyses, stressing its opposition to the objectivism of the human sciences, and its re-insertion of philosophy into existence. However, his account was not entirely uncritical. His enthusiasm for phenomenology was tempered by a critique: phenomenology, he argued, refuses to restore truth's material reality, and in this respect it is far behind the philosophies of Hegel and Marx.

From 1955 until 1963 Lyotard devoted himself to political writing. He published almost exclusively with *Socialisme ou Barbarie*'s journal, for the most part producing analyses of French colonialism and the dynamics of the class struggle in Algeria. In 1964 *Socialisme ou Barbarie* splintered under the pressure of a tendency which, on the basis of Castoriadis' analyses of the development of capitalism, attempted to reorient the group's political direction. Despite some sympathy with Castoriadis' position, Lyotard affiliated himself with one of the resulting factions, *Pouvoir Ouvrier* (Worker's Power), which was to continue to devote itself to building a proletarian organisation capable of initiating the overthrow of capitalism. However, this affiliation was somewhat short-lived. As a result of intellectual and political differences with Marxism as such – differences he had already felt, if not felt himself able to articulate, before leaving *Socialisme ou Barbarie* – Lyotard resigned from *Pouvoir Ouvrier* after two years, in 1966.

Libidinal Driftworks

Almost immediately Lyotard began to publish work of an ostensibly quite different nature to the rigorous political analyses of the Algerian situation that he had devoted himself to more or less exclusively over the previous twelve years. There ensued a period that Lyotard has sometimes described as one of 'drifting' with and away from Marx (see, in particular, the essays published as a collection in 1973 under the title *Dérive à partir de Marx et Freud*). What Lyotard meant by 'drift' was a movement that was not motivated by a single aim and which would progress towards a particular goal, hence not a movement driven or directed by reason; rather, to 'drift' was to be pulled and pushed by one or more currents – affective, impulsive currents – whose motion remains opaque to, and thus exceeds, reason's comprehension.

Lyotard was not merely adrift with and from Marx; he was also drifting along with another of the so-called 'masters of suspicion', Freud. In the mid-1960s Lyotard had attended the now famous seminars of the psychoanalyst Jacques Lacan in Paris; in 1968 he published an essay entitled 'Le Travail du rêve ne pense pas' ('The Dream Work Does Not Think') in *Revue d'Esthétique* that was concerned with Freud's *Interpretation of Dreams*. The essay gave theoretical expression to the resistance Lyotard felt at the time to Lacan. Opposing the structuralist and semiotic reading of Freud that the latter influentially propounded, Lyotard argued that the dream is not the speech of desire, but its work, a work in which desire figures itself as a force of distortion and transgression. By taking issue with Lacan, Lyotard once more placed himself in the very midst of the intellectual concerns of the time whilst agitating at their margins.

'Le Travail du rêve ne pense pas' was included as part of Lyotard's doctoral thesis. This was published in 1971 as *Discours, figure*, and is widely regarded as Lyotard's first major work. Principally a reflection on the practice and experience of art, and of profound importance for aesthetics, *Discours, figure* is, nonetheless, a fractured work within which many currents of thought wash and struggle against one another. As the title suggests, Lyotard is interested in the functions of language and the activity of vision, saying and seeing, how they differ and how, as a result of their difference, they interact.

The first chapters of the book are phenomenological in orientation. They draw on Lyotard's early interest in phenomenology, and in particular on his engagement with the work of the great French phenomenologist, Maurice Merleau-Ponty. In the later chapters, however, the importance accorded phenomenology declines, and it is criticised and displaced not by Marxism, as had been the case in *La Phénoménologie*, but by analyses indebted to the psychoanalytic account of desire. However, as alien as *Discours, figure* is in terms of its tone and subject matter from the political analyses of *Socialisme ou Barbarie*, it is nonetheless underpinned by political concerns. In the introduction to the book (translated here as 'Taking the side of the figural'), Lyotard himself claims, in terms that cannot be entirely detached from Marxism, that *Discours, figure* is intended to lead to 'the practical critique of ideology'.[1]

That critique had been presaged some three years before the publication of *Discours, figure*, in and through the political activities that took place in France in May 1968. On 22 March of that year, 150 students at the left-wing University of Paris at Nanterre, protesting against the arrest of six members of an anti-Vietnam movement, occupied the university's administrative block. In response, the government closed courses at the university. This action in turn sparked further protests on the part of students, which then inflamed the whole of France, provoking a popular and spontaneous uprising that threatened to bring down the French government. By mid-May ten million workers were on strike, and France was at a standstill. At the time of the student uprising, Lyotard was a lecturer (*maître de conférence*) at Nanterre and so was at the very heart of the protests. He played a prominent role in the radical left-wing *Mouvement du 22 Mars*, formed upon the occupation of the administrative tower at Nanterre.

The student-sparked revolt was, for Lyotard, of the order of what he would call an *event* in *Discours, figure*: what was unleashed by the protesters was an unforeseen, unpredictable plurality of desires and passions, a galvanising current of intensities coursing through the body politic, transgressing established social and political structures. What May 1968 announced, for Lyotard, was not a political protest in the sense of a demand for the restitution of rights denied within a certain social framework; it was the expression of a desire for something different, a desire for a different society, for different relations between people.

If there was a practical critique of ideology at stake in these events, and in particular in the political activities of the *Mouvement du 22 Mars*, it was because they entailed what Lyotard called, in an introduction to an unfinished book on the *Mouvement*, 'a critique of *representation*'.[2] In a sense, every critique of ideology is a critique of representation. As it is classically understood, ideology is identified with false consciousness or the misrepresentation of social relations, interposing a screen between people and the real conditions of their existence. On this view, ideology is a system of ideas or representations that are believed, but which do not correspond to reality, and hence are not true. In this sense, the critique of ideology is a critique of illusory representations in the name of truth. Nevertheless, it remains intrinsically tied to the idea of representation: it puts into question particular representations of reality, but not representation as such. Simply put, truth, as opposed to ideology, is what corresponds to, and thus represents, reality. The critique of representation identified by Lyotard as at stake in the events of May 1968 exceeds the parameters of this classical account of ideology, since it is a critique directed at representation *as such*.

Supposing that ideology distorts or veils a true state of affairs implies that all criticism of ideology must be hermeneutic; events, actions, and practices all harbour a truth that is not apparent, or not entirely apparent, to those implicated in them. That truth is discovered through interpretation. The passion and delirium of the events of May 1968 were not, however, phenomena to be understood; they were events that 'caught everything established and all thought (including revolutionary thought) off guard, offering a figure of what this society represses or denies, a figure of its unconscious desire':[3] they were a mutation of desire in relation to the existing socio-political system, and every attempt to represent them on the political stage, resulted in their disintensification. (The role of the traditional left-wing parties in the events of May 1968 bore this out. The established organs of the French left failed to realise the potential of the events unfolding before them: whilst the protests were against political power, the trade unions exacted only minimal reforms from the government.)

What was important, then, about these events was not what they meant, but how they worked, how they unleashed energies and intensities that disfigured the body politic. The practical critique of ideology that Lyotard saw in the actions of May 1968 showed that politics did not pose its problems in terms of meaning, and thus could no longer be conceived in terms of representation. Since every form of representation was a channelling, a directing and even damming-up of the flood of potentially critical energies, the political instead showed itself to pose its problems in terms of energy and the transformation of energy. In short, the critique of ideology that was at play in May 1968 was not a contestation of representations but an exposure of representation as such as a set-up for regulating, conducting and transforming desire. Thus, the political practices of May 1968 were a type of political intervention that worked to disrupt the very forms of political activity itself.

The essays collected together in *Des dispositifs pulsionnels* (1973), which were written between 1970 and 1973, and the book *Libidinal Economy* (1974) develop and extend the description and delimitation of social, political and aesthetic set-ups in terms of their energetic functioning – their capacity to release, channel or bind desire. *Libidinal Economy*, which Lyotard regarded as his second 'real book', quickly gained notoriety for the virulence of its account of Marxism, and has been seen by some to mark the furthest point in Lyotard's drift away from Marx. However, despite the extremity and violence of its account of Marx, *Libidinal Economy* does not so much mark a break with Marx's account of capitalism as mark a further complication of it. It is important to note that that relationship would continue, with varying intensity, throughout Lyotard's work.

Paganism

Almost immediately after the publication of *Libidinal Economy*, Lyotard's work found a new centre of gravity in what he called the pagan. In 1977 he published two books in which this displacement was apparent: *Instructions païennes* (*Lessons in Paganism*) and *Rudiments païens* (*Pagan Rudiments*), the latter a collection of essays published separately between 1974 and 1976.

As Lyotard saw it in *Libidinal Economy*, the critique of representation is not only a critique of ideology and politics but also a critique of religion, because in the West – proclamations of its atheism notwithstanding – politics and religion are fundamentally intertwined. The belief in a meaning implicit in events is essentially theological. It supposes that behind the scenes, so to speak, and occupying a position of transcendence, there is that which gives meaning to everything. Following Nietzsche, Lyotard argues that because this belief is theological it is nihilistic. By distinguishing between events and that which, lying outside of them, gives them their meaning, it negates or devalues the former in favour of the latter.

What exceeds the sphere of religion, Lyotard says, is not science, as many might suppose, but paganism. Paganism is not opposed to religion and theology by its atheism, at least not in a straightforward sense, because, as Lyotard reminds us, for the pagans, 'the least hiccup, the least scandal, a copulation without issue, a birthing, a pee, a military decision'[4] were all attended by several gods and goddesses. What distinguishes paganism is that it is affirmative and not nihilistic. For the pagan, the divine is the affirmation of the singularity of events, and not their negation.

Events are conceived of here as energetic intensities that resist recuperation into utilities. A utility is, we say, something that is good for something and which can be used or used up. Thus, a utility belongs to a totality of relationships; it is something that has a certain function within a given system. The energetic intensity of what Lyotard calls 'events' makes them unpredictable and unstable, and hence they cannot be incorporated into a system: they are, in other words, of no use. As a consequence of its usefulness, a utility disappears into its function. In other words, the being of a utility is always already inhabited by negation. For example, a tree is useful insofar as it can be turned into something else – its being a tree is negated and from that negation a table or a chair is made. These things are useful in turn insofar as they are directed towards a certain task and absorbed in it – writing or eating for the table, sitting for the chair – or, given this general utility, insofar as they can be sold (and the money generated from the sale of a utility is itself useful since it can be exchanged for labour or other goods). In contrast to a utility, which calls for negation, an event calls for affirmation and can only be affirmed, since it is singular and un-exchangeable.

Although *Libidinal Economy* appealed to paganism, the pagan works themselves mark a break with the framework of the former book. Whilst both *Instructions païennes* and *Rudiments païens* continue the concern with delimiting and describing the functioning of representative apparatuses, the role accorded to libido and a libidinal energetics in the description of such apparatuses recedes; instead, there is a more rhetorical description of their workings, an analysis of how discourses position what they speak about, and how they position and affect those that speak and listen to them.

Such an analysis is pagan in that an attention to the rhetorical effects of a discourse implies a certain disregard for its meaning in the sense of its truth. As Lyotard points out, pagans – and here he includes the rhetoricians and sophists of Greece – are not concerned with truth; for them, the referential function of language is a minor consideration; they use their words to win over, to disguise themselves, to trap and trick their adversaries, and to transform an unpromising situation to their advantage. Even their religious rites, ceremonies and prayers harbour a certain impiety. Pagans talk to their gods as they talk to one another: they ruse with them; they seek to sway them, sweet-talk them, and seduce them using words that are openly duplicitous. Far from itself being nihilistic – a charge sometimes made against such a view which accords truth and meaning a minor role in language – such a way of looking at language is essentially affirmative; it does not refer language back to something independent of it, a transcendental truth in which its meaning grounds, but considers it simply in terms of what it does.

As a consequence of the move away from the privilege accorded to the libido, the way in which Lyotard conceives the event changes. In the pagan works, it is rhetorical utterances themselves that are events. What matters for the pagan is not the exemplary value or universal significance of their speech–acts – it is of little or no importance whether what they say is true, or whether it will become canonical – but the disruptive effects that such acts have at the moment they are spoken, their transformative potential and the possibilities for thinking and speaking that they open up.

In *Au juste* (translated as *Just Gaming*), a series of conversations with Jean-Loup Thébaud that took place in 1977–8, Lyotard appears to further specify the sense in which rhetorical acts are events. He writes: 'paganism . . . is a name, neither better nor worse than others, for the denomination of a situation in which one judges without criteria'.[5] For example, the ruses employed by the sophists and those associated with them are used either when there exists no established way of speaking or judging, or in order to confute stable systems that guide speaking and judging, and thus incite thought or speech to proceed in advance of established criteria. When Eubulides of Megara says 'I lie', this statement disrupts any established framework for judging it true or false: it destabilises the instituted ways in which we normally consider statements that supposedly make a truth claim about something. It is thus an event in that it refuses to be placed in the frame within which we normally judge affirmative statements to be meaningful. However, the way in which paganism is now described signals a new period in Lyotard's thought. By characterising paganism in terms of judgement, Lyotard ushers in a period in which the work of the German philosopher Immanuel Kant becomes an important resource, and in which the emphasis on paganism recedes. That period centres around Lyotard's third major book, *The Differend* (published in French as *Le Différend* in 1983).

The Differend

This capacity to destabilise the established systems that guide speech and judgement, which Lyotard had named pagan in *Just Gaming*, is thought by him to have a political sense: what is at stake is the reversal of instituted forces, undermining the strong and revealing a certain strength of the weak. It is thus a matter of upsetting the balance of power within a given area or field. Such reversals are political through and through, and not only when they intervene in the established arena of politics. This sense of the political significance of paganism informs both Lyotard's account of the postmodern and what he calls 'the differend'.

In *The Postmodern Condition: A Report on Knowledge* (1979), Lyotard argued that contemporary science has changed the way in which knowledge must itself be conceived. Contemporary scientific knowledge can no longer be thought as proceeding towards a single goal, nor can it be unified in a single great system of knowledge. Taking contemporary mathematics and physics as his guide, Lyotard claims that, far from seeking to augment existing knowledge, contemporary science seeks to articulate claims that destabilise existing models of explanation, promulgating new norms for understanding and establishing new axioms. Rather than proceeding consensually, science progresses through disagreement and dissent, fragmenting fields of knowledge rather than unifying them.

If this analysis has a political significance, it is because Lyotard detects in the transformation of science a capacity to resist the commodification of knowledge in contemporary societies. As Lyotard sees it, in the most highly developed contemporary societies knowledge has become a commodity bought and sold on the market. Knowledge is no longer regarded as an end in itself, nor as something that contributes to the development of humanity or its freedom; rather, its value is as a productive tool used to improve economic performance, that is, to increase efficiency and maximise profits. Only knowledge that can contribute to profit is liable to attract support; all other forms of knowledge are subject to threat. However, as Lyotard points out, contemporary science does not develop in an efficient, orderly way. It proceeds as a search for instabilities that develops in a highly unpredictable way, and thus resists incorporation within a framework that wants to invest in what it predicts it can put to profitable use.

The recourse to Kant, evident in *Just Gaming*, was less directly apparent in The *Postmodern Condition*; with the publication of *The Differend*, however, the influence of Kant became explicit. The idea of judging without criteria that Lyotard had linked to paganism in *Just Gaming*, is a formula that is, in fact, Kantian. It describes what, in the *Critique of Judgement*, Kant calls 'reflective judgement'. Reflective judgements are opposed by Kant to what he calls 'determinant judgements'. According to Kant, we make determinant judgements when we fit our experience under an existing conceptual structure, thus determining it. In contrast, we are called upon to make reflective judgements when we cannot subsume our experience under any pre-given conceptual frame, and we instead have to look for a way of conceptualising that experience, thereby inventing the criteria by which to judge something.

What, in *The Differend*, Lyotard names a differend calls upon such a capacity to judge reflectively. The differend names a conflict between at least two parties which, lacking any common ground, cannot be settled by recourse to any determinant standard of judgement without wronging at least one of the parties to the dispute. A differend occurs, then, when someone 'is divested of the means to argue and becomes for that reason a victim'.[6] For example, suppose you were told of a situation that was so traumatic that those who witnessed it were unable to speak about it. According to the accepted and instituted ways of verifying the existence of something, it is necessary to have someone testify to it: this was the situation, I was there, I saw it. However, if the situation was of the nature that is claimed, then no such testimony can be forthcoming, since either those who were there will not be able to speak about what they saw, or if they can, then the situation was not so traumatic as to prevent it being spoken about. The demand for first-hand testimony provokes a differend.

In order to hear the differend, in order to give it its due, it is necessary to discover a new rule or criterion by which to judge. Since the established way of regarding matters makes it impossible to testify to a differend, what provokes this recourse to reflective judgement is, Lyotard says, a feeling: when something asks to be said that cannot be said, there is a feeling of pain that accompanies the silence, whilst the invention of a new rule of judgement, and the institution of a new idiom in which the differend can be stated, is accompanied by pleasure. The description is again quite deliberately Kantian and evokes the latter's description of the sublime, in *The Critique of Judgement*. This notion of the sublime becomes an important and insistent element in Lyotard's thought; it is one to which he devotes an entire study, *Lessons on the Analytic of the Sublime* (published in French in 1991 as *Leçons sur l'analytique du sublime*).

Late Writings

Although *The Differend* is widely held to be Lyotard's last major work, he nevertheless went on to produce a considerable body of important work. Most notable amongst this work were two collections of essays: *L'Inhuman* (1988), translated as *The Inhuman*, and *Lectures d'enfance* (1991); two books on Kant, called *L'enthousiasme: La critique kantienne de l'histoire* (1986) and *Lessons on the Analytic of the Sublime*; and two books on the French writer André Malraux (1901–76): called *Signé Malraux* (1996), translated as *Signed, Malraux*, and *Chambre sourde: L'antiesthétique de Malraux* (1998), translated as *Soundproof Room*. After Lyotard's death there followed two further works: an unfinished and highly experimental work on the medieval Christian theologian Saint Augustine (AD

354–430), *La Confession d'Augustin* (1998), translated as *The Confession of Augustine*, and a collection of essays entitled *Misère de la philosophie* (2000).

As outwardly varied as this work is, it continues and extends the concerns of *The Differend*, significantly inflecting it in the direction of aesthetics. In an interview published in 1994, Lyotard declared that his task in the future would be to 'try to elaborate what could be called *The Differend II*'. That elaboration, he continued, would concern everything left out of *The Differend*, namely 'the body, the sexual, space and time, the aesthetic',[7] classically all topics related to aesthesis. Although *The Differend II* was never written as such, the publications that postdate *The Differend* are all fruits of that project. In particular, Lyotard attends to the aesthetic sensibility that a sensitivity to the differend demands. To become sensitive to the differend, to that which does not give itself directly, which holds itself back in the given and thus is unpresentable, demands a certain impoverishment of the mind, a disarming of the intellect's mastery. It is this sensitivity, this disarming of the mind that Lyotard attempts to locate in his attention to literature, art, Judaism and Augustinian confession.

Although at first glance the themes, influences and import of Lyotard's writings appears to change radically, throughout his work Lyotard was concerned to bear witness to the indeterminacy of thinking itself. In his many writings on art, he often suggested that what was at stake in painting – particularly in modern painting – was not a question of an adequation between vision and the world, but a fidelity to the enigma of vision and the visible. By paradoxically attesting to that which renders visible – 'the unpresentable in presentation' as he called it – the artwork testifies to the capacity of thought to be affected by that which escapes the determination of thinking itself. The same might be said of Lyotard's own work. Its various stages are indications not so much of a thought trying to elaborate a system and to establish itself, so to speak; rather, they are a series of attempts, necessarily renewed, to remain open to events, to find lines of resistance to the miserable indolence of our time, and to make trial of, and thus displace, the dominant political discourses and powers of contemporary life.

Lyotard and Post-structuralism

Lyotard is a post-structuralist thinker, but it is important to determine how his contribution to post-structuralism differs from those of others (from Derrida, Foucault, Kristeva and Deleuze, for instance). The first remark to make is that this difference does not imply radical divergence. Lyotard shares historical, political and philosophical concerns with many other post-structuralist thinkers. Deleuze taught with and held joint seminars with Lyotard. His metaphysics bears a strong resemblance to Lyotard's work in *Discours, figure* and *Libidinal Economy*. Lyotard's thought is also strongly influenced by Derrida's deconstruction, though he also sought to distance himself from it. He worked closely with other key figures in deconstruction such as Jean-Luc Nancy and Philippe Lacoue-Labarthe, producing important books on Kant and judgement, and participating in influential debates, notably around Derrida's work, for example, on the ends of man. Like Derrida, Foucault and Deleuze, Lyotard returned to Kant, in particular in relation to aesthetics and politics. Similarly, like many other post-structuralist thinkers Freud plays a crucial role in Lyotard's work, as do Nietzsche and Hegel (if more negatively). Finally, a constant engagement with Levinas defines his ethical concerns.

Lyotard's distinctiveness can be organised around two factors: the central role of aesthetics in his critique and development of the notion of structure, and his philosophy of the event. He describes aesthetic, that is, sensual events at work within structures. These events question the reliability and truthfulness of structures, replacing notions of structures as models, representations, maps or closed systems of relations, with notions of structures as more mobile and intricate interactions of many structures with the intense events that occur within them and across them.

In *Discours, figure*, the destabilising work of events in structures (for example, in any given discourse) allows for a form of deconstruction that opens up structure to the energy and emotional charge of events. But we cannot 'have done' with structure and hence turn strictly to intensity and events; rather, we can deconstruct it in order to render it more mobile. This mobility is both a matter of changing structures and multiplying them, and a matter of introducing intense feelings and desires into them. The two processes cannot be separated, since the multiplicity of structures rests on desires and feelings that they cannot reduce and that work in different ways in different structures. This failure of structures invites them to change in relation to one another and in relation to desires.

The idea that structures are always prey to aesthetic events that destabilise and undermine them, as well as taking them beyond themselves, links Lyotard to post-structuralist critiques of the self and of the subject. The self cannot be thought of as a reliable structure of differences and of boundaries. Instead, it is also determined by its significant events and by an openness to future events. These undermine any identity ascribed to the subject, since that identity will always be incomplete and open. Furthermore, any identity will only be meaningful and effective (in the sense of driving change) on the basis of the events that generate its desires and thoughts. There can be no satisfactory self-knowledge, therefore, from Lyotard's point of view, unless this knowledge is also set with sensations and with the events that carry them. These hold the self in abeyance, for example, in ethical relations to others, or in relation to language since, following Lyotard's work on language in *The Differend*, there is no fixed sense that runs reliably from one sentence to another. Though sense works within established structures, for example, in terms of what constitutes know-ledge, we must also be open to the ways in which this work can be disrupted and, more importantly, to its intrinsic failure both to show the events that have constituted it and those that it attempts to exclude.

Similarly, the subject cannot be defined as a free decision-making and reflect-ing capacity, since such decisions and reflections are always incomplete with respect to events and in their thrall. One of the most attractive aspects of Lyotard's thought is his description of the kind of chance encounters that deter-mine a life beyond its conscious decisions and beyond what it thought it knew of itself. Our memories and actions are records not only of historical causal effects, allied to supposedly free acts. They are also traces of the occurrence of events that have shaped us, but in ways that could never be fully accounted for in representations of ourselves or definitions of key free decisions. There are always latent energies and emotional intensities that can erupt again, or be countered by different events, or that are working in unforeseeable ways in the background.

In *Libidinal Economy*, Lyotard describes this relation of structure and event in the subject through the image of the labyrinth. We are but interconnected labyrinths that fail to resolve into a single one, with its united laws and keys, because each labyrinth connects to others through events and not through pas-sages that belong to one or to the other. So the event changes us and our labyrinths, but without reducing them to one another and without providing us with a final image or sense to our lives and acts:

> When my Roman friend passes from one labyrinth to another, he is not moving through a spatio-temporal grid. The labyrinths which for convenience's sake (in the inevitable tribute paid to the order of the reasonable) I called first, second, etc., in no way form an ordered series. They do not belong to a structure of carrying over; nothing of the one is rediscovered in the other, at least as long as each is formed as a sort of cyclone around a heart which is the encounter, whose effects he prolongs and which he flees. Each of these mazes is closed, at the same time as it is in undecid-able expansion; closed, in that it has no cross-over point, nor any part in common, with the other terrifying cyclones; as to its expansion, this would be in proportion to the effective force of the encounter.[8]

If we are such labyrinths, then philosophy cannot base itself on the self or on the subject, even as relatively stable foundations. Instead, Lyotard's philosophy of the event develops strategies to do justice to the nature of encounters and to their positive effect on the energy that runs through lives defined as labyrinths. This is why he avoids closing on traditional philosophical injunctions 'to know ourselves' or to 'dare to know'. Instead, we must find ways of inviting events into our lives in order to disrupt and set such known structures in movement.

He seeks an openness and passivity with respect to events, not in order to reach a peaceful state of absence of will, but in order to create and to sense with renewed vigour and in greater touch with the former events that fed into structures that must necessarily decay, if they are built on identity and on a corresponding denial of radically new events.

In order to maintain this positive sense of passivity in his own philosophy, Lyotard's post-structuralism turns away from forms of thought that cannot do justice to definitions of truth that go beyond sense and reference. He insists on the relation of matter to feeling and desire, rather than to scientific laws. He is concerned to preserve a realm that cannot be accounted for according to traditional divisions (subject/object, sense/reference, structure/reality) and according to accepted forms of knowledge – even if these are defined as open and falsifiable. Events cannot be a matter of objective truth and the structuralist hope for such truth is curtailed and balanced by Lyotard's insistence on the role of events.

The term 'figural', from *Discours, figure*, explains the capacity of the event to remain outside the grasp of structures and yet to work within them. For Lyotard, a painting is figural in the way it always goes beyond descriptions of it and theories about it. It is neither an objective figure or shape, nor a figure in a language: it is a process between the two. The figural is the association of the intensity of desires and feelings with the openness and ambiguity of matter; where matter is not defined according to the physical sciences, but in terms of a special interaction with sensations. The special aspect lies in the open-endedness and inexhaustibility of matter when it works through feelings that defy knowledge and understanding. This is not the matter of laws and fact, but matter as that which always exceeds any description of it as fact or as subject to law. The art-work is not a closed figure, but an open matter associated with feelings. It has a figural sense that is neither meaning, nor a referent, but an effect of disturbance and transformation.

Language (signification) and things (designation) cannot account for this disturbing association of feeling and event. This is because the event defies description and cannot be the referent of a designation. This failure of language and of our capacity to designate must be understood as a failure to account for the extra emotional intensity that occurs with events. This intensity demands different terms, the figural and the event, to explain how language and things evolve and how they acquire a special, changeable and dynamic meaning for us. But this imposes a new way of approaching events: the figural must be responded to laterally or obliquely owing to the limits of significance, knowledge and reference. It must be expressed anew, rather than shown, defined or explained. If the figural could be approached in direct ways, then it would collapse onto an objective reference or a subjective meaning, there would be full knowledge of the figural, or a capacity to refer to or point to it in objects.

Lyotard's interest in art and aesthetics comes from a desire to go beyond knowledge and to invoke feelings that cannot be captured or identified. Painting is both an event and a sideways, expressive approach to events. A work does not represent or show the event; it is an event in itself that testifies to other events, but without revealing them in full. As a figural event, painting must be a process that creates and destroys discourse and referents − knowledge and objective reality. It unleashes feelings and desires into systems that need them, but that also resist them. So the art-work is an association of intensity and of structure that then transfers its intensity into other structures − revealing their limits, but also their openness to change and difficult connections to other structures.

Styles

Lyotard's works are highly inventive in terms of style. It is helpful to view him as a writer–philosopher, in the sense of a literary creator, rather than as a purely technical or academic thinker. This variation in styles and great attention to each one is double-edged for the reader, since it adds to the difficulty of his works, but also adds to their depth and beauty. At his best, for example in his last works, Lyotard can achieve a rare kind of philosophical prose, close to poetry in its sensual quality and carefully crafted rhythms.

The variation of styles through his oeuvre reflects different stages and dom-inant ideas and concerns. This is because Lyotard adapts his writing to suit the material and the feelings he wants to communicate. He has used shock, humour, irony, sensibility, ellipsis, dialogue, fragments, aphorisms and careful scholarly exposition at different times. Each attempt is designed to unite philo-sophical reflection and material, but also to make sure that this unity is inter-nally complex and contradictory, in the sense of not being reducible to a single theory or set of propositions.

This means that Lyotard must be read with great care. We should always be looking beyond any given interpretation or conclusion, to see how it feeds into paradoxes and how it is given a singular twist through his association of ideas with the physical. We should experiment with interpretations of his works and try to take them to their limits and into new spheres and new possibilities. We should also treat his work as an aesthetic event, something to be felt rather than thought upon. His style is an invitation to such experimentation. It is not a revelation of his biography, of a series of historical facts, but of a sensual and intellectual life that crosses over with ours and that has the power to enrich them (but also to make them seem thin or abandoned).

Four of the most important tones to keep close to the surface in reading him are fear, laughter, passion and irony. Lyotard's fear is deeply physical and connects with his concern with nihilism throughout his intellectual life. There is a strong sense of a connection between morbidity, of an incapacity to value and of the destructive power of ideas in his view of nihilism. These are articulated through the ways in which the body can fail us and through a deep fear of that failure. Yet, surprisingly, these failures have a revelatory power, as if they are something we can emerge out of, driven by new capacities to affirm and to create. His texts can seem to run out of energy, or to reach dead-ends or points of great bitterness or cynicism, only to suddenly depart in a new and tangential direction.

There is, then, a connection between Lyotard's laughter and his fear, as if joy were not full until it had risen out of despair and out of the fear of a final nihilistic absence of will. It is, again, a mistake to read joy without fear, as it is a mistake to separate the paradoxical connection of pleasure and pain in his interpretation of the sublime. He is not a lugubrious and heavy thinker, but neither is he an irresponsible one. Both such interpretations depend on missing the way his style relates distant ideas and emotions in order to reveal their necessary interactions. This sense of a thrust and parry with distant connections can be traced to his reading of Freud and of Lyotard's sense that the unconscious and our desires demand creative forms of working through that release new drives and free us of blockages. But, equally, these trials with the unconscious are the site for a deep responsibility to memory and to an otherness that defies knowledge and representation and yet that we are still obligated to.

So Lyotard's irony, though stylistically light, has the high ethical role of testifying to that which we can never know, but only sense as unknowable. It is, then, not an irony of contradictory propositions or positions, but one of paradoxical obligations without release. The irony is not one of sneering asides or clever mind-games, it is one of profound ethical lessons, where we learn of the limitations of even our most powerful and valuable ideas in the face of feelings and demands that we can only testify to and never fully articulate. So, when his writing appears to settle on a given light or insufficient conclusion, it is as well to look for the material signs of its lack or insufficiency. These will re-launch it and save us from the illusion of answers that are not also failures.

Lyotard writes alongside art-works, not in order to comment on them, but in order to allow for a cross-over from his philosophical art to theirs. He does not judge or draw conclusions on other works, but interacts with features and powers, with how things work or fail to work. This indication can only be done through a collaboration, rather than through a pointing and description. That is why art and literature, film and architecture are interleaved into his works, rather than catalogued or simply referred to externally. Any such reference could not account for what Lyotard wants to show, that is, that the work and its materiality are always more than the conceptual meanings we associate with them. In his experimentation with philosophical styles, he shows this even at the heart of the most dispassionate and clear-set subject.

A poignant example of this desire to live with other works and other people without extinguishing their unreachable value, yet contributing to it, can be found in the closing sections of *Libidinal Economy*. There, Lyotard mocks the way theory must capture its prey and exhibit it, much as butterfly hunters and taxidermists do. He then sets himself the challenge of writing philosophy free of the requirement to identify and to represent. The book is not irresponsible, but open to a different sense of responsibility, perhaps one that is also found in his later work on the differend. We should never settle for grasping and capturing, when that which we frame in this way becomes lifeless. A theory that is not also a creation and an aesthetic event is a theory about nothing at all, or nothing living. It is a failure to be open to an ethical and political demand hidden under the illusion of listening to others by speaking in their place.

Like irony, shock is not to be understood in any traditional or banal role in Lyotard's work. His desire to shock and his love of the shocking are not an interest in the extreme for its own sake, but an interest in the ways in which dominant patterns of thought can be revealed in their contingency and in terms of what they conceal beneath them. Shock is not something that comes from outside, but from a denied and unspeakable interior. Lyotard knows that this shock is ultimately less manageable than even the most powerful external one, since it questions management itself. This management is a facet of capitalism that he despises perhaps almost as much as the demand to increase profit and accelerate time. In *The Differend*, he defines them as interdependent: there is no acceleration without measurement and classification, and no point to measurement and classification without acceleration.

So Lyotard's interest in shocks through sex and violence is again neither irresponsible nor malevolent. It is attention to the connections and collaborations between forms that claim to be able to judge and to reprehend, but that draw their power from what they pass judgement over, indeed that replicate what they seek to ban or to classify within themselves. He does not show the shocking in the abstract, as a reprehensible or desirable object, but as something that only works through the implication of different and apparently separate structures within one another. The shock is political and revolutionary. It is mobile and ever-changing in form and location. That is why the subject of shock varies so much through Lyotard's work, from gender in *Discours, figure*, to sexual events in his work on artists in the 1970s, to an aesthetic, followed by a political, then an ironic sublime in the 1980s and, lastly, to an intricate bodily sublime in his last works (the shock of the grating of one's own voice in an emotionally affected throat, for example – how we sound through our own sobs).

Truth can therefore never be separated from style in Lyotard's work and the truth of that work is in its style, not exclusively but unavoidably. In his last posthumous work on Augustine, he shows how passion and truth can only be physical events, if they are to be given their full power without a dishonest and self-destructive denial. Lyotard's invention of the term 'soul-flesh' is the central idea in this association of truth and physical passion. It is not that the soul cannot be separated from the body that matters to him, but rather, that the highest truths of both lie in their relation to one another. The soul can only rise to truth through feeling; feeling only rises above tame perception when it sets ideas in motion and drives them forward with greater intensity.

Lyotard, Today

Writers are sometimes associated with ideas and epochs so strongly that, when the ideas and times pass away and lose all sense of topicality, the writers also fall into irrelevance. Could this be the fate of Lyotard as commentators become weary of the 'postmodern'?

We have already argued that the following selection of texts shows that there is much more to Lyotard than *The Postmodern Condition*. The guiding principles, style and main ideas of his works are not linked to an epoch or to a single idea or invention. On the contrary, his thought is characterised by a richness that makes it one of the most rewarding reference points in terms of new ideas and uncommon thoughts. His style is designed not to close off possibilities and narrow down reflection to core truths and dominant theories. On the contrary, Lyotard writes to provoke, to energise and to transform his readers, not through their adoption of any given idea, but through a transfer of enthusiasm and of varieties of directions and impulses.

This enthusiasm is an important moment in Lyotard's reading of Kant's political philosophy. It is the point where we realise that Lyotard's sublime is not simply a halt in front of otherness or in the grip of something that cannot be expressed. Instead, it is a series of actions that respond to, but do not contain events that demand political action. But these feelings and actions fail if they fix the object of enthusiasm and the sublime, or if they build a politics of certainty and promised ends on the open vagaries of the event and its emotional signs:

> In its periodic unbridling, however, enthusiastic pathos conserves an aesthetic validity, it is an energetic *sign*, a tensor of *Wunsch*. The infinity of the Idea draws to itself all the other capacities, that is, all the other faculties, and produces and *Affekt* 'of the vigorous kind,' characteristic of the sublime.[9]

Lyotard's works seek to be such signs, that is, aesthetic moments that connect different ideas, but without providing a meta-narrative, external logic or synthesis that would resolve productive tensions. The term 'tensor' comes from Lyotard's libidinal work and reappears fleetingly in the later book on the differend; it means a sign that brings together different drives and ideas in a single and tense place. The fact that it does, though, is important because it reminds us of the importance of feelings and affects (of transforming emotions): they arise out of the impossibility of relating different ideas and structures fully, but force us to transfer their value into new structures. According to this definition of the sign and of the tensor, Lyotard's work is therefore a new and valuable critical and creative moment in philosophy. It is new because his critique does not put forward alternative foundational views, or a single critical method. Instead, it makes series of multi-faceted moves designed to transform situations, not in view of specific goals, but against any settled opinion or theory. In that sense, his work launches thought anew and in different directions. This explains its difficulty, in particular for a reading that searches for fixed conclusions and for categories to fit each thinker.

This preference for problems and paradoxes, for irony and humour, over solutions and settled positions does not betray an error-prone philosophy, happy to reside in contradictions. Rather, it is the sign of a philosopher wary of making claims to truth or commitments to methods that curtail thought and stunt our capacity to feel and to think differently. As such it is an invitation to us to think along with Lyotard, after Lyotard.

Notes

(Full bibliographic references for all Lyotard's work can be found in the bibliography at the end of this book.)
1. Lyotard, 'Taking the Side of the Figural', in *The Lyotard Reader and Guide*, p. 43.
2. Lyotard, 'March 23', in *Political Writings*, p. 61.
3. Ibid. p. 63.
4. Lyotard, 'The Great Ephemeral Skin', in *The Lyotard Reader and Guide*, p. 53.
5. Lyotard, *Just Gaming*, p. 16.
6. Lyotard, *The Differend*, p. 9.
7. Lyotard, 'Nietzsche and the Inhuman', p. 92.
8. Lyotard, *Libidinal Economy*, p. 36.
9. Lyotard, *The Differend*, p. 167.

Part I

Philosophy

Introduction: Philosophy

The five texts included in this section provide an overview of the development of Lyotard's central philosophical concerns through the key stages of his thought. Three are chapters from what are widely considered to be Lyotard's principal publications: 'Taking the Side of the Figural' is the introductory chapter of Lyotard's first major work, *Discours, figure* (1971); 'The Great Ephemeral Skin' is the first chapter of *Libidinal Economy* (1974); 'Presentation' is the third chapter of *The Differend* (1983). The fourth text comprises chapters 10–12 of what is perhaps still Lyotard's most famous work, *The Postmodern Condition* (1979). The fifth text, 'The Affect-phrase', is taken from the important posthumous collection of articles, *Misère de la philosophie* (*The Poverty of Philosophy*) (2000).

As will be apparent from this selection, Lyotard's philosophical writings are of great stylistic and thematic variety, and they manifestly refuse the attempt to draw from them a unified philosophical system. For some of Lyotard's critics, this is a flaw, a failure to develop methodically and coherently a philosophical position. However, far from being a weakness, this aspect of Lyotard's work is integral to its philosophical significance and manifests its openness and capacity to respond critically to the world of which it is a part and from which it arises.

As Lyotard often argues, that world is one that has been fundamentally shaped by philosophy. Consequently, in seeking to respond to it, Lyotard is always drawn to an engagement with the work of other philosophers. By thinking with them and against them he attempts to explore the limits of philosophy and thus the horizons of our times. It would be wrong, however, to think that as a result Lyotard looks to bring the contemporary world under the mastery of philosophical knowledge. Rather, what he seeks to bear witness to is that which within our world exceeds our ability to know it. This incapacity, which for Lyotard is irremediable, does not signal the defeat of thinking. It leads to another idea of thinking, one that is not characterised by the mind's mastery over itself and what it thinks about, but by an ability to be affected by what is not knowable.

In the following sections we consider some of the main concerns of Lyotard's philosophy as exemplified in his three major books, *Discours, figure*, *Libidinal Economy* and *The Differend*.

Phenomenology and the Figure

As well as being Lyotard's first major work, *Discours, figure* is the fulcrum of an important turning in his thinking. In 1954 Lyotard had published a short monograph on phenomenology. The opening chapters of *Discours, figure* are in large part informed by phenomenology, and in particular Maurice Merleau-Ponty's phenomenology of perception. However, as Lyotard remarks in the introduction, the importance accorded to perception declines,[1] and in its place there emerges an engagement with Freud and the psychoanalytic account of desire. Thus the latter part of *Discours, figure* points towards *Libidinal Economy* and the essays grouped around it, most of which are included in two collections, both published in 1973: *Dérive à partir de Marx et Freud* and *Des dispositifs pulsionnels*.

Yet despite its radically fractured nature, *Discours, figure* is held together by its criticism of what is sometimes called Platonism, or what Lyotard calls simply *metaphysics*. Following Plato, philosophy has drawn a distinction between the visible (or the sensible) and the intelligible. The visible, the sensible is placed on the side of mere appearance: in itself it is very little, almost nothing, and what meaning and truth it has are considered to have come from an intelligible order distinct from it. This Platonic distinction is *metaphysical* in that in distinguishing between the sensible and the intelligible it holds the latter to be in some sense beyond (*meta*) the physical world.

It is as part of its criticism of metaphysics that 'Taking the Side of the Figural' opens with Lyotard remarking the difference between word and world. The world, he insists, is not set out before us like a book: it 'is not a text, there is a density to it . . . which is not to be read, but to be seen.'[2] The word is held to be essentially intelligible, since ordinarily its sensible aspect barely figures as in reading or speaking it withdraws in favour of the idea or meaning it conveys. Thus, likening the world to a book is an essentially Platonic metaphor: the world, like the word, gives way to the meaning that underlies it.

Lyotard's insistence on the difference between reading and seeing disturbs this traditional, Platonic view of things. The visible world, he protests, is sensibly profound, and its depth, its thickness is not offered to the intellect but to perception. The visible world only shows itself to a being that is part of it; it is not apprehended by an intellect that knows no location, separated from things, but by a vision that takes place within a *bodily* experience. Sight is always situated, and that is to say, it is always limited and partial, never wholly able to possess either its object or itself. What we see, we see from a certain point of view, which hides as much as it reveals, and that is constituted at its fringes by half-glimpsed lateralities, as much a part of the visual field as its focus. Vision contains, then, an ineliminable opacity. This opacity is not, however, equivalent to mere obscurity and rending, the darkness of a perception waiting to be illuminated by intellection; rather, it is constitutive of vision and contains its own truth.

Having affirmed the rights of the sensible, having shown that it cannot be collapsed into the intelligible and that seeing is of a different order to reading, Lyotard is able to reveal how the sensible inhabits the intelligible in what he calls the *figure*. Initially defined by Lyotard as 'a spatial manifestation' that language 'cannot incorporate without being shaken',[3] the figure is not opposed to language, but is ambiguously located on both the edge and the interior of discourse, thereby disrupting the hold of the intellect over its own realm.

This figural inhabitation of language is perhaps best exemplified in the first main part of *Discours, figure*, entitled 'Signification and Designation', where Lyotard exposes this ambiguous location of figurality by engaging with those elements of language that linguists and grammarians call designators or deictics. These are words whose use it is to point something out, terms such as *here, now, there, then, this* and *that*. Lyotard argues that such words derive their meaning not simply from their place in the system of language − as structuralist linguistics claims of linguistic terms in general − but from the immediate context of their use. Whereas a term such as 'coat' is charged with significance through its relation to, and thus difference from, other terms within a given language, and has that significance whether it is spoken or not, the meaning of a deictic is created by its being pronounced. As Lyotard puts it, deictics 'await their "content" in their actualisation in a discursive act' and thus 'open language onto an experience that it cannot stock in its inventory since it is the experience of a *hic et nunc*, of an *ego* . . .'[4] Irreducible to merely significant terms, deictics − as their name suggests − have a sort of 'gestural extension . . . which far from being signifiable in words, stretches out their edges'.[5] Deictics are figural in that they introduce visible space, or the perceptual field, into the domain of language.

More generally, Lyotard claims that 'all discourse has something opposite it, an object of which it speaks'.[6] Indeed, whilst it is more or less possible to account for the signification of words by appealing only to the differential play of linguistic terms amongst themselves, such an account does nothing to explain the fact, which we experience for ourselves whenever we speak, that our discourse is cast in the direction of something, that it aims at something. This openness and opening-onto the opacity of the perceived world is, for Lyotard, an essential aspect of language; not only is it impossible to explain how this would be possible if, as structuralism argued, language is to be conceived as a closed and sufficient totality shut in on itself, but it is also impossible to see how being entirely shut up in a language reduced to the mere play of conceptual terms, we would ever have anything to say. In other words, Lyotard recognises that without that which resists conceptuality, without that which cannot be reduced to a possession of the intellect, experience becomes empty and meaningless.

As we noted above, this analysis draws its inspiration from Merleau-Ponty's phenomenology of perception. However, for all that a phenomenological attention to perceptual experience reveals an original ontological order, for Lyotard it too is limited. There is in phenomenology, he claims, a withdrawal of emotion in favour of perception, in favour of an intimate bond between body and world. Beyond the co-ordination of perception and world, Lyotard seeks to bring to light an affective order, troubling and untying the links maintained between body and world, drawing on the very uncertainty that always inhabits our bodily hold on things. We are not always in the world, immersed in perception and meaning; that immersion is interrupted, for example, in deep sleep and in orgasm. At the very heart of the perceived world and at the very heart of language, there are 'insane events':[7] operations, occasions, which dis-*figure* perception and intellection, world and word alike.

Freud (I)

For Lyotard the figural is a force of figuration or dis-figuration. In the latter part of *Discours, figure*, he identifies this force with desire. This identification marks what we have above called a turning in Lyotard's thought in which the phenomenology of perception recedes and psychoanalysis comes to the fore. In particular, Lyotard draws on Freud's account of dreams to show that desire is in essence a work of (dis)figuration.

Lyotard's interpretation of Freud, and in particular his reading of the central operations of the dream-work – namely those of condensation, displacement, figurability and secondary revision – has deservedly attracted much attention. In essence, Lyotard argues that the dream is not the disguised language of desire; rather, it comprises of a seeing which has 'taken refuge amidst words', and which is 'irreducible to "saying"'.[8] For example, the process of condensation, in which according to Freud the dream 'thoughts' are compressed into the brief, laconic content of the dream, is likened by Lyotard to the physical process of condensation in which the volume of an object is reduced. Thus, in the dream thoughts *figure*; they are like things and it is thus that they can be folded and crumpled up. To be sure, this process is one of distortion, but Lyotard cautions that it should not be thought that it is one in which desire disguises itself; contrary to the usual understanding, Lyotard argues that desire is not hidden behind the dream thoughts, but it is the force that compresses them. It is an 'energy which folds, which crumples and creases the text [of the dream] and makes a work from it'.[9]

By affirming that desire does not speak and that the dream is not the language of desire but its work, Lyotard pursues further his critique of the metaphysical

opposition of appearance and reality. Desire cannot be thought as a second discourse within discourse; it does not constitute a second world behind the scenes
that forms the prior condition and 'truth' hidden behind the manifest discourse
of the dream. Rather, the dream is to be understood as the work of desire in
which desire actively dis-*figures* itself, in which it makes itself manifest, whilst
simultaneously resisting all cognitive appropriation: desire *is* nothing other than
this activity of dis-figuration. Here, then, the figure is thought beyond its
traditional determination as mere appearance (either in the sense of a rhetorical figure that clothes a true meaning or as the outward and visible aspect of
something), it is the very play of presencing and absencing in which desire
figures itself forth. It is an event that is itself of the order of truth inasmuch as
it is something that makes itself manifest, that is figured or felt as a certain
violent disfiguration or disruption of discourse.

A Libidinal Philosophy

The first paragraphs of *Libidinal Economy* describe the opening-up of the body
to the polymorphous diversity of the multiple intensities that pass across and
constitute it. They make explicit the degree to which Lyotard has distanced
himself from the phenomenology of perception that informed the early chapters of *Discours, figure* and the prominence accorded to desire in the work of this
period. This body is nothing like the situated, oriented, well-formed body that
Lyotard finds in Merleau-Ponty's phenomenology; it is a body charged with
desires, a body that is barely a body, a body without limits, with no frontier, no
interior or exterior; less a body than a libidinal patchwork or skin.

The intensities that Lyotard describes as constituting this libidinal body also
constitute *Libidinal Economy* itself. In this sense it is a disconcerting book, disorienting its reader with its violent shifts of register and apparently abrupt tran-
sitions in subject matter. It is, perhaps, the 'good book' that Lyotard speaks of in
'Taking the Side of the Figural', a book in which the disruption of order, of
structure, system and knowledge is not only signified, but directly operative.

It is sometimes alleged that because of its violent style, its disruption of
theoretical discourses and positions, *Libidinal Economy* represents the height of
post-structuralist irresponsibility, abandoning any and all claims to consistency
and truth. This is a mistake, and it is worth pointing out that such criticisms
are more violent than the book they denounce, since they entirely overlook
the philosophical sense of what Lyotard does. Through its attention to the
intensity of what Lyotard calls libidinal 'events', *Libidinal Economy* offers a rad-
icalisation of the delimitation of Platonism that ran throughout *Discours, figure*.
It is this delimitation that we will concentrate on here, not only because of the

continuity it establishes between the two texts, but because the critique of Platonism is essentially a critique of what Lyotard, following Nietzsche, calls *nihilism*.

The seeds of nihilism are to be found in the distinction which we have seen Plato make between the sensible and the intelligible. In making this distinction Plato institutes a division between appearances and what appears in them. Behind the world that appears – the immediate world of sensible experience – are what Plato calls the *ideas*, which form the prior condition and transcendental truth of those appearances. For example, when Plato says all beautiful things are beautiful because they partake in, and are illuminated by, the *idea* of beauty, he is saying that we see the former as an appearance of the latter. For the Lyotard of *Libidinal Economy*, this division between true being and its appearance is *theatrical*, posing the illusion of a world behind the scenes. Essential to this theatre of representation is the staging of a spectacle and the screening it implies. There is what is seen on the stage itself, and unseen there is the whole mechanics of its production, just as in the Platonic cave pictured in Book VII of *The Republic* there is the shadow-show on the wall of the cave which captivates the cave-dwellers' attentions, whilst behind their back, and thus unseen, artefact-bearers pass in front of fire, producing the shadows that are thrown onto the cave wall.

Posed in this way, representation is always the representation of an absence: there is always something outside the space of representation that is the pre-condition of what is seen, that produces the spectacle, whilst effacing itself. Yet this is more than just a description of the theatrical apparatus implied by representation, since the absence or lack – which Lyotard sometimes calls *Alterity*, sometimes the *Great Zero*, sometimes the *Other*, depending on what is represented as lacking – has traditionally always been held to call up and determine desire. Desire desires what is lacked, because only what is lacking can be wanted.

From Plato onwards such a determination of desire has been central to the philosophical tradition. For that tradition, what is distinctive about human desire is that it can be put to work and something made from it. For example, for Plato, human desire is purposive: in contrast to the blind striving of brute, animal life, a life ensnared in itself, human desire is a force that goes beyond life itself aiming towards the *ideas*. In particular, human desire strives towards the *idea* of the beautiful, which for Plato is what is radiant and allows us to see the world, and towards that of the good, which grants to everything its unity and purpose, and this is what makes it possible to know the world and thus act in it. However, whilst such a determination of desire accounts for the possibility of the human world, it also entails a violence and negation of that world. Driven beyond itself, human desire looks towards a certain transcendent absence that devalues the world at the same time as it renders it knowable, and it is this that constitutes its nihilism.

It is important to understand that for Lyotard, such an account of desire is not simply false; rather, it is a limitation of desire and thus activity. Basically, the problem is that desire is reduced to its 'positive' side, that is, the knowledge that arises from it, and the consequence of this reduction is played out in history as nihilism. The world that is rendered knowable is one that the human being can change and develop insofar as it knows it. Generally, we think of this as a positive thing, something good. However, in return for being rendered knowable, the world becomes something that is simply 'there', a purely passive presence to be acted upon. Commonly this is represented as the scientific and technological mastery of nature – the overcoming of its secrets and thus of its resistance. But by mastering the world and ultimately ourselves, knowledge ultimately becomes good for nothing. What knowledge we have is increasingly ineffective when it comes to maintaining a meaningful existence, since it treats all actual existence, including human existence, as a mere utility, something that can be calculated, manipulated and profited from. It is for this reason that Lyotard seeks to recover another sense of desire – an active passivity – that would allow us to be responsive to what is other than knowledge, and which would allow us to be open to and affected by the world in a way that does not devalue it and reduce it to a mere utility.

Freud (II)

As part of Lyotard's elaboration of a different way of picturing desire, he draws once more on Freud. This time Lyotard concentrates on what he sees as the two meanings of 'desire' operative in Freud's work. On the one hand, there is *Wunsch-desire*, wish-desire; on the other, there is *libido-desire*, or what Freud otherwise calls the *primary processes*. The former, *wish-desire*, supposes that a drive, frustrated in reality, is represented in a phantasy scene – a dream or game, for example – and there meets with a surrogate fulfilment. On this account, desire is pictured as directed teleologically towards an absence, a lost object, which it models. This is desire thought in quite traditional terms as ordered by negativity. The latter, *libido-desire*, is an intensive force, and it is primarily characterised by its mobility, investing various regions and zones with energy. In *Libidinal Economy*, Lyotard links this latter sense of desire to Freud's description of the 'polymorphous perversity' of the child or infant, in which there is simply a diverse, endlessly displaced flow of libidinal intensity, over a surface that is lacking nothing. Consequently, Lyotard is able to claim that it is not lack that produces desire, but a certain organisation and disintensification of desire, of libidinal energy, which produces a set-up, a *dispositif*, dominated by absence.

Just such a disintensification of desire is at stake for Lyotard in Freud's analysis of a game played by his grandson in *Beyond the Pleasure Principle*. According to Freud, the game, in which his grandson throws away a cotton reel and retrieves it, is the symbolic enactment by the child of the loss of the original libidinal involvement with the mother. Through its being symbolised, the separation from the mother is mastered by the child; the menacing masses of displaceable libidinal energy, displeasurable and distressing to the child, are channelled and bound, set up on the sign-substitute of the cotton reel. Here, Lyotard observes, Freud produces a traditional account in which absence orders desire, and produces signification and meaning. Yet, in this instance, the account presupposes the very ordering of desire it seeks to explain, since the symbolic representation can only be instituted by pain and lack if the mother is already perceived as a person, a something separate from the child; and for that the child, too, must already be a totalised unity, an organised body, rather than the polymorphously perverse flux of libidinal energies that, elsewhere, Freud claims it is. In this account, then, the intense libidinal energies and connections between mother and child, incomparably fierce and singular events, have already become instead 'so many common, universal signs of a lost origin'.[10]

The other desire that Lyotard locates, in part through Freud's description of *libido-desire*, is not opposed to desire ordered by absence and subjugated to knowledge. Rather, it inhabits it and disrupts it, and consequently discloses possibilities that cannot be reduced to the order of knowing, and the activity of the human being founded on it. This is why Lyotard links such an account of desire to the idea of the child. Despite being promised to the adult world, the child is the place of an openness to the world that cannot completely be assimilated to rational activity and reasonable desire. In his later work, particularly the essays collected in *Lectures d'enfance* and *The Inhuman*, and also in 'The Affect-phrase', Lyotard returns again to the idea of childhood, and the ambiguous place it occupies in Western thought.

The Differend

In his third major work, *The Differend*, Lyotard turned more directly than in any of his previous works to another of the principal concerns of philosophy: language. In contrast to the exuberance of *Libidinal Economy*, Lyotard adopts what he calls 'a zero-degree style' in *The Differend*,[11] and apparently dispenses with the arguments and preoccupations of the earlier works, particularly the analysis of desire. Consequently, the temptation is to see it as constituting a major break in Lyotard's work, manifesting a shift in philosophical direction, and posing questions and responding to problems excluded by his earlier commitments.

Perhaps for this reason, and also because the idea of the differend was used by Lyotard in many of his subsequent writings, it is easy to see *The Differend* as marking an advance over the earlier work, and it is frequently claimed that it is Lyotard's most important philosophical book. Some have suggested that it provides the positive philosophical underpinnings of the pragmatic analysis of narratives and language games used in Lyotard's best-known work, *The Postmodern Condition*. Others have found in the idea of the differend a novel, linguistic-based account of argumentation eschewing the traditional argumentative ideal of consensus. Whilst not entirely wrong, these views nevertheless overlook the fact that in *The Differend* Lyotard does not so much offer a positive account of language, as seek to link the phenomenon of nihilism to the way in which we understand language and argumentation. Thus, in this respect *The Differend* has an important continuity with the earlier work.

According to Lyotard, a differend names a situation in which someone is divested of the means to argue and for that reason becomes a victim. The first of the numbered paragraphs that form the main text of *The Differend* gives an example of such a situation. Lyotard writes: 'You are told that human beings endowed with language were placed in a situation such that none of them now can tell you what it was'.[12] Such a claim becomes a differend when positive proof, in the form of first-hand testimony, is demanded. On the one hand, should someone attempt to speak of the situation in order to testify to it, then that testimony cannot be accorded any credibility because it would give the lie to its own claim, namely that it cannot be talked about. On the other, should they say nothing, then the situation cannot be shown to have existed. Thus, and simply, the judgement is that: 'either the situation did not exist as such. Or it did exist, and thus the testimony of your informant is false'.[13]

What is immediately at issue here is revealed in the second paragraph. The strikingly indeterminate situation of the first paragraph refers to the Holocaust. The inability to speak which Lyotard invokes is the inability felt by many of the survivors to talk about what happened; the differend to which they are subject, and the discrediting of the reality of the situation, is effected by the so-called revisionist historians, and in particular by Robert Faurisson, who sought to deny the existence of the Holocaust by alleging that there is no-one able to establish the reality of what was said to have happened there. Lyotard is scathingly critical of Faurisson, yet his concern is not with Faurisson alone. Rather, he is concerned with the ability of which Faurisson avails himself to make his voice heard, and to silence the silence of the Holocaust survivors.

Lyotard characterises Faurisson's argument as nihilistic. It is nihilistic in the sense that Faurisson seeks, through argument, to annihilate the reality of the gas chambers, and thus denies what we regard as ethically important to remember: in the usual understanding, this is nihilism as the negation of the highest ethical imperatives, the cynical belief in nothing. For Lyotard, however, it is nihilistic in another and perhaps more philosophically important and far-reaching sense, since it reduces reality – or what is – to what can be established by the strict protocols of verification, and language to the mere transfer of information. Certainly, Faurisson's attempts to deny the reality of the Holocaust on grounds of insufficient empirical verification can – and have – been refuted on similar grounds. Yet, as Lyotard argues, to answer Faurisson in this way is to reduce the reality of the Holocaust, treating it like any other historical event which we can come to understand in terms of arguments bearing on positive facts. Yet it is not what can be established by facts and communicated in language that is important here. To seek to establish the reality of the Holocaust in this way is, in a certain sense, to perpetuate the differend, since that reality is lost to us when it becomes a matter of fact. What is important here is what exceeds cognition. The reality of the Holocaust is signalled by its inability to be put into words, and thus, for Lyotard, in order to recognise this it is necessary to break with the monopoly granted to cognition when it comes to reality, or what is.

Broadly speaking, then, what Lyotard addresses with the idea of the differend is, the reduction of what is to what can be said, and the simultaneous reduction of language to an instrument by which information or facts are communicated. The silence that surrounds the Holocaust, and that resists being put into words, impugns such an understanding of language. In the chapter from *The Differend* reprinted here, Lyotard argues that there is in language itself something that holds out against such a reduction.

Speaking not of language but of particular linguistic acts, which he calls *phrases*, Lyotard says that a phrase *presents* a universe that comprises what is signified, what it is signified about, to whom and by whom it is signified. However, the presentation entailed by a phrase is not, and cannot be, presented in the universe presented by that phrase itself. It can be presented as an instance in another phrase. The presentation of phrase (1) can become the referent of phrase (2). In being presented in phrase (2), the presentation entailed by phrase (1) is removed from the currentness of its presenting: in being situated in another phrase it ceases to be an event; instead, it is something present, an existent, of the order of what is given by a phrase. Similarly, a phrase that presents the presentation of another phrase itself entails a presentation which it does not present. In order to be presented it is necessary to call on another phrase (3). In short, whilst a phrase presents something, it cannot present its own act of presentation.

It is this excess of presentation over what is presented that is important to Lyotard. Every attempt to say what a phrase presents is constitutively inadequate to the event of presentation that the phrase is. Consequently, it cannot be grasped by the intellect, cognitively appropriated or known. Since there is no incontrovertible evidence for it – any attempt to present it must fail – it is easy enough to ignore it. However, if it cannot be known or presented, it can nevertheless be felt. Perhaps the most common experience we have of this is in literature, in the surprise or astonishment we feel when we read a poem, for example, and in the resistance the poem offers to any attempt to say what it means. For Lyotard, that surprise and astonishment is nothing other than the registration that there is a phrase, that there are phrases, and that in those phrases something calls to us that cannot itself be put into words.

The recognition of this moment of excess in the phrase, and thus of what defeats cognition, is a recognition of the limits of an understanding that reduces all being to what can be known. As Lyotard was aware, the apparent limitlessness of our capacity to know is what imperils philosophy in our age: for a world that can be mastered by knowledge, a world reduced to positive facts, philosophy is a discipline of thought that is increasingly redundant and pointless. This is, however, one of the most telling symptoms of the nihilism of our age, since by turning its back on philosophy it turns away from one of its founding moments. By wilfully blinding itself to its own origin it necessarily becomes ignorant of its own nature. Lyotard's work is nothing less than the attempt to dislodge such ignorance, recalling us to the need for philosophy.

Notes

1. See Lyotard, 'Taking the Side of the Figural', in *The Lyotard Reader and Guide*, p. 43.
2. Ibid. p. 34.
3. Ibid. p. 37.
4. Lyotard, *Discours, figure*, p. 39.
5. 'Taking the Side of the Figural', in *The Lyotard Reader and Guide*, p. 38.
6. Ibid, p. 37.
7. Lyotard, *Discours, figure*, p. 138.
8. Ibid. p. 239.
9. Lyotard, 'Taking the Side of the Figural', in *The Lyotard Reader and Guide*, p. 39.
10. Lyotard, *Libidinal Economy*, p. 23.
11. Lyotard, *The Differend*, p. xiv.
12. Ibid. §1.
13. Ibid.

Chapter 1

Taking the Side of the Figural

The Figural as Opacity

That 'the eye listens', as Claudel said, signifies that the visible is readable, audible, intelligible. The 'second logic' that he opposed to classical logic, which determined the nature and the function of words, 'teaches the art of assembling them'; it is 'practised before our eyes by nature herself',[1] 'there is knowledge, there is an obligation of one [party] to the other, and thus a bond between the different parts of the world, just as there is one *between the elements of discourse for it to be possible to form a readable phrase*'.[2]

This book protests: the given is not a text, there is a density to it, or rather a difference, a constitutive difference, which is not to be read, but to be seen; this difference, and the immobile mobility which reveals it, is what is continually forgotten in signifying it. 'Long ago in Japan as I was going up from Nikko to Chuzenji, I saw, though far in the distance, juxtaposed by the alignment of my eyes, the greenness of a maple tree accepting the harmony suggested by a pine. These pages comment on this forest text'.[3] Without going beyond perception: is what speaks only when the eye has found 'the point of view', when my regard has become the regard to which things are 'due',[4] a text? A text does not have a physical depth; we do not have to move before it or inside it in order for it to accomplish its harmonies; if we do, it is only metaphorically. Yet the sensible world, the world of the forest, appears to be the absolute frame of reference of all *analoga*: here we move, seeking the composition, constituting the space of the scene, working on that plastic extension wherein the eye, the head, the body move or bathe, carried as in a tank of mercury. It is the alignment of the eye that produces the harmony of the pine and the maple; an accomplished, since complete, harmony of silhouette, tone, value, position, desire that is fulfilled in an instant. An alignment of the eye; Claudel does not say an alignment of the pine and the maple. The two trees are 'distant'; nevertheless the line of sight threads and sticks them together upon an indeterminate background or canvas. Very well: but this flattening constitutes 'the scene'[5] [*tableau*] and not a page of writing which is a sort of table. A scene is not read; it is not understood. Sitting before a table, one identifies, one recognises linguistic unities; standing before a representation one seeks plastic, libidinal events.

The idea that the world is readable signifies that an Other, on the other side, writes the things, and that from the right point of view I could, in principle, decipher them. This is, again, to grant much to things, and it is what constitutes Claudel's paganism. He was not unaware of it; indeed, he had to dissociate poetry and prayer. All of his work emanates from the drama, for a Christian, of being able to be almost calmed by the harmony of a pine and a maple, of experiencing a sanguine faith, desire and pleasure, in the sensible. The road to Chuzenji is the Calvary of an absolution of the sensible; in going to Chuzenji, it is the other side of the scene that Claudel wants to see, but he wants to take this side with him from Nikko, toward the other side. Such is the imaginary: to possess both this side and the other. Such is sin and pride: possessing both the text and the illustration. This hesitation is that of Christianity itself, of the *de facto* Christianity that occupies the subsoil of the problematic proper to us as Westerners: the hearing of the Word, but a philosophy of creation. The former demands that we deliver ourselves from the thickness of flesh, that we shut our eyes, and that we are all ears; for the latter, it is necessary that the movement of things, which constitutes them as worldly, that their shimmeringness, their appearance, and the depth that provides it, are in some way or other absolved, if it is true that they proceed from what can do everything and what can love everything. A hesitation that marks the history not only of Western thought, but also of painting, born from Writing, daring to illustrate it, badly held in check, always coming back to submit to it and yet escaping it.

Otherwise it is necessary to leave Creation behind, crudely supporting the radicality of the ethical, challenging the transcendence of the sensible – the transcendence in immanence of which Merleau-Ponty spoke following the painters – placing depth on the side of false transcendence, of temptation, even rejecting it as the false text of the world, no longer wanting to understand it correctly, and perhaps even less than this. In its radicality, this return to Writing understood as allocution of the Other and as promise, in which Jewish thought and demythologised Christian thought meet, renounces the idea that the eye listens. Let them be shut tight and even pulled out, like those of Oedipus: master of illusion, slave of illustrations, always the 'evil eye'. First and last philosophy is morality, as Emmanuel Levinas says; it is the face-to-face of the face [*le vis-à-vis du visage*] because the face is the presence of the absolutely Other, the only *Gegenstand* worthy of this name; one which we cannot walk around and survey, which does not belong to the sensible, which announces something that I am unable to thematise as the reverse of what is present to me from my perspective, like the noema of a noesis. The face is the presence of speech. It is not the thickness of the sensible that is spread out between it and me listening to it, but the opening of the absolute, absolute disequilibrium, true irreversibility, which comprises not only the things and my look, as Claudel believed, but the infinite and the finite. This suffering that knows the infinite in the face is said to be good; the action of the eye, on the contrary, would be passion, perversion.

This book is a defence of the eye, its localisation. It has shadow for its prey. It is interested in that penumbra which, following Plato, speech has cast like a grey veil over the sensible that it has ceaselessly thematised as less-than-being; the sensible whose side has only very rarely been truly taken, taken in truth, because it was understood that the side of the sensible is that of falsity, of scepticism, of the rhetorician, the painter, the condottiere, the libertine, the materialist – it is this penumbra that is the concern of this book. 'The eye', André Breton says, 'exists in a savage state';[6] the sensible, says Merleau-Ponty, is the place of the chiasm, or rather the chiasm is where place takes place; there is no absolutely Other, but there is the element which splits itself, overturns itself, that constitutes the face-to-face and the sensible at the same time; there is the 'there is' which is not initially heard speech, but the work [*oeuvre*] of a sort of drift-work [*travail de dérive*], splitting the single element into two sides and leaving them in this disequilibrium of which ethical life speaks, but that is the disequilibrium of the seer and the visible, which is unheard speech.

Such at least was what Merleau-Ponty resolved: to descend as far as this original chiasm without crushing its disequilibrium with the phenomenological reduction, without overcoming its exteriority with the immanence of the transcendental sphere. Consequently he sought a language that could signify what is the very root of signification itself. It took nothing less than making language itself a gesture in order to make it consubstantial with the chiasmic space that it is charged with articulating. But we know what happens as a consequence of mixing speech and gesture, of dissolving saying in seeing: either speaking is silenced, or the seen is necessarily already like speaking. Has not Hegel challenged sense-certainty to speak without falling into the anguish of uncertainty? And even when leaning over its shoulder, condescending to its silence, Hegel takes pains to follow its index finger designating the Here, in drawing out the mediation of discerning from this supposedly immediate faith, has he not made a movement which is, as he says, a discourse, having the same negativity as that of language? In sum, then, depth appears empty; in its shadow all cows become black, and the truth is that it is necessary to begin right where one is: in the midst of words.

Let us begin, then, from this point and take up such a challenge; let us enter into this place. We have to attack the sufficiency of discourse. It is easy enough to dissipate the current prestige of the system, of closure, in which the partisans of language believe themselves capable of imprisoning all meaning. Here we find ourselves once again with the text, but this time nobody has written it and it reads itself. Meagre advantages, no doubt. The impertinence remains, which is such a negligence regarding the sensible that it is as if humans had become bi-dimensional beings, with nothing to feel, but instead moving along the gaps in the network. Could one break this closure by postulating an absolute excess of meaning in the initial phrase and the necessary finitude of endless interpretation? This infinity, this opening, that we find in Paul Ricoeur's hermeneutics, marks a certain reservation with regard to Hegelianism, but remains in its sphere; because it is above all Hegel who fails to conceive the symbol otherwise than as an object of thought; he saw it as a moment to be overcome, whilst fundamentally he entirely failed to see it, wanting to hear the voice of its silence.[7] Once this is assumed, hermeneutics is content to leave open the passage of consciousness towards listening. It thus appears to respect the transcendence of the symbol to all commentary, and the infinity of its task. Yet its relationship with the dialectic is not in doubt; it lies in this: the symbol, the starting point is not taken as a thing, but as confused speech. The transcendence of the symbol is the transcendence of a discourse emanating from an Other. This is not Creation as something thick which marks, or which collects together, alterity; it is being deaf to revelation; the visible is not what manifests itself by hiding itself in its verso, it is only a screen of appearances; it is not appearance, but noise drowning out a voice.

What is savage is art as silence. The position of art is a refutation of the position of discourse. The position of art indicates a function of figure, which is not signified, and this functions both at the edge of and within discourse. It indicates that the transcendence of the symbol is the figure, that is, a spatial manifestation that linguistic space cannot incorporate without being shaken, an exteriority that cannot be interiorised as *signification*. In its alterity, art is posed as plasticity and desire, curved extension, opposed to invariability and reason, diacritical space. Art wants the figure; 'beauty' is figural, non-related and rhythmic. The true symbol makes us think, but first it makes itself 'seen'. And the amazing thing is not that it makes us think, at least if every object is signifiable, able to enter into discourse, once language exists, thus falling into the pan where thought shakes and sorts everything; the enigma is that it remains to be 'seen' at all, that it remains sensible, that there is a world which is a store of 'views', or an inter-world which is a store of 'visions', and that all discourse exhausts itself before exhausting it. The absolutely other would be this beauty or difference.

Is it necessary, then, to be quiet in order to make it manifest? But the silence of beauty, of feeling, silence before speech, silence of the breast, is impossible; it is not a matter of passing across to the other side of discourse. Only from the interior of discourse can we pass to and into the figure. We could pass across to the figure by making it apparent that all discourse has something opposite it, an object of which it speaks, which is over there, as what it designates in a horizon: a view bordering discourse. And we could pass across to the figure without leaving language behind because it is lodged in it; it is enough to let oneself fall into the well of discourse in order to find the eye that it has at its centre, the eye of discourse in the sense that in the midst of a cyclone there reigns an eye of calm. The figure is outside and inside; that is why it possesses the secret of connaturality, but also reveals it as an illusion. Language is not a homogenous milieu; it is divisive because it exteriorises the sensible opposite itself, as an object; and it is divided because it interiorises the figural in what is articulated. The eye is in speech both because there is no articulated language without the exteriorisation of a 'visible', and also because there is at the very least a gestural, 'visible', exteriority at the heart of discourse, which is its expression. In pursuing this twofold exteriority, we could take up the challenge that language presents to the visible, the ear to the eye, and show that the gestural extension which gives depth or representation, far from being signifiable in words, stretches out on their edges as their power of designation and also as the cradle of their power of expression, and thus that it accompanies them, that it is their shadow, in one sense as their end, and in another as their beginning. For one cannot be immersed in language if one is to speak; the 'absolute' object, language, cannot speak. What speaks is something that must be outside of language and that does not cease to remain so even when it speaks. Silence is the contrary of discourse, it is violence and simultaneously beauty; but it is the condition of discourse because it is on the side of things *which* are to be spoken about and *that* it is necessary to express. No discourse without attempting to undo and restore this opacity, this inexhaustible thickness. Silence results from the splitting in which a discourse and its object are placed opposite one another, and from which the work of signification begins; and it results from the splitting built into speech, where the work of expression is effectuated.

Such violence belongs to the very essence of language, it is its starting point, since we speak in separation and since the object must be both constituted and lost in order to be able to be signified. It thus forms the birth certificate of the problem of knowledge, it forces us to desire the true as the interiorisation (the fulfilled signification) of the exteriority (of the object). The cognitive function contains in itself this death which produces the opposition, the desire which produces the thickness of reference. But the expressive function also contains it, only differently; it introduces it into discourse itself, because the violence of the rending does not place an absolutely pure object on one side, and an absolutely pure subject on the other, the whole giving rise to our cherished exercises concerning the possibility of truth; this violence makes the object a sign; but, symmetrically, it makes discourse a thing, it puts thickness in it, it sets out a scene, in the articulation and the limpidity of signification, at the same time that on the side of the object it hollows out its other face, its wings.

The eye is force. To make the unconscious a discourse is to neglect energetics. It is to make ourselves complicit with the entirety of Western reason, which kills art at the same time as the dream. We do not in the least break with metaphysics by putting language everywhere; on the contrary, we complete it; we complete the repression of the sensible and of *jouissance*. The opposition is not between form and force, or else we confuse form and structure! Force is never anything other than energy which folds, which crumples and creases the text and makes a work from it, a difference, that is to say, a form. A painting is not readable, as contemporary semiologists suggest; Klee said that it is to be browsed, it shows itself, it offers itself to the eye as an exemplary thing, as a naturing nature, Klee would again have said, since it shows what seeing is. Now it shows that seeing is a dance.[8] Looking at the painting is tracing out paths, co-tracing paths at least, since in painting it the painter has arranged imperiously (although laterally) the paths to follow, and his work is this movement deposited between four wooden struts, which an eye sets in motion and enlivens once again. The 'convulsive' beauty lucidly demanded by *l'amour fou*.

And you believe that this [i.e. painting] is discourse? Cold prose almost does not exist, except at the lowest point of communication. A discourse is thick. It does not merely signify, it expresses. And if it expresses, it is because there is also movement and force deposited in it, which cause the table of significations to erupt through a quake which produces meaning. It also gives itself over to browsing, and not merely to comprehension. It also appeals to the eye, it is also energetic. If we trace the passage of the eye in the linguistic field, if we seize the fixed-movement, espouse the undulations of metaphor, which is the fulfilment of desire, then we will see how exteriority, force, formed space can be present in interiority, in closed signification.

The Figural as Truth

But is it not the case that taking this side is siding with illusion? If I show that beneath the surface of all discourse there is a form in which energy is captured and in relation to which its surface is agitated; if I show that discourse is not only signification and rationality, but also expression and affect, do I not destroy the very possibility of truth? The door would be opened to a sophistry through which one could always assert that the manifest signification of discourse does not exhaust its meaning, and that far from holding the latter to be wholly drawn together in the signified, discourse receives it unconsciously, passively, from a source exterior to it, which does not belong to the structure of the language in which it is spoken, that its other is contained in it, and that consequently the one who speaks does not know what he says. The door is opened to a sophistry, to a 'terrorism', since from the moment that we neglect the common appeal to signification that is made by all discourse; from the moment that the implicit or explicit reference that all speakers make to a universality and to a possible understanding is interrupted, and their words are taken as mere things that have arrived from elsewhere, there remains only violence in order to decide exactly where they come from. If I can no longer speak with you, that is, if I cannot accept that you and I respectively and reciprocally take seriously the sense of what we say, referring it to a commonly agreed geometry which will allow us to decide what is right and what is wrong; if I speak about you, grasping your words as if delivered in the third person, as if they came from an absent speaker – words that would no longer be explicitly significative but rather implicitly expressive speech – then communication collapses, and along with it the possibility of truth, and it would no longer even be a question of *knowing* what your words 'mean', since this *knowledge* is in turn constructed with words, both my words and yours. We would have to decide, and for that, to have postulated that there is a sort of expressive rationality, a causal order of the unsaid, another discourse speaking in your discourse, that I myself could know, or that in any case someone could know. We would have to imagine this 'non-sense': that this other discourse that you do not speak, but which speaks in your own, is nevertheless signifiable except by and for you; that I or someone else could say it, that we could speak about you, but not to you. Such is its violence or seduction. It is said that philosophy ends here.

Is it this reductive way that we seek here? I would like to show the opposite. I would like to show that this alternative – either communicative discourse, good will and dialogue or war and schizophrenia – is not in itself radical. The common reference to an instance that the two interlocutors recognise, for want of a judge or a third party, equipped with sufficient guarantees, is not truth; this common reference makes possible the construction of knowledge. The configuration of discourse as interlocution, as a potential universality, by reflection on the rules that will serve as an index of the dialogue at the same time as it elaborates them; in short those rules that through Socrates the West has received as its distinctive position of speech, presuppose the end of truth [*la fin de la vérité*]. It is not only Nietzsche who teaches us this; there are the works of semantic history to confirm it.[9] Not that the alternative is between the well-intentioned dialogue and Callicles; we must understand that these two opposites themselves belong to a world of speech that has broken with another world, that of ἀλήθεια, and that truth is not at stake in the alternative, but at play outside of it; that the alternative is itself constructed when truth as such withdraws, when truth is neglected, covered over by discourse and the desire for knowledge. Consequently sophistry, trickery, the illusion of εἰκόνες is certainly made possible, but so is philosophy, the dialogue and the illusion of knowledge. Illusion, since truth is foreclosed to it right from the beginning. 'Truth', Braque says, 'does not have a contrary'.[10]

It will be said that it no longer falls to anyone to restore this presence of truth. It is obvious that when they are linguistic, these restorations are in general unsubtle reconstructions. Nietzscheans labour like thesis writers . . . Either we will all be 'artists' together, or no-one will be; those who believe it to be on their side already, those who have adopted Nietzsche and the truth in order to ridicule the others, are not the least discursive [*discoureurs*]. They only continue philosophy as a separate activity, and the manipulation of discourse as the stamp of knowledge. Nobody today could speak *for* the truth; all *prosopopoeia* is mockery, all those who 'officiate', far from snatching us away from the alternatives of knowledge and ignorance, plunge us once more into the clericalism which rests on it. Nevertheless, it is necessary to hold that truth is possible and it is probable that many of those who appear to be ridiculous pedants or charlatans devote themselves to it. How can it be otherwise?

Freud has taught us what utopia is; utopia strictly defined.[11] Utopia is that truth never appears where it is expected. This means many things, including at least the following two that will serve us as guides. First, truth shows itself as an aberration when measured by signification and knowledge. Truth is out of tune. To be out of tune in discourse is to deconstruct its order. Truth in no way passes through a discourse of signification, its impossible *topos* cannot be located by the co-ordinates of the geography of knowledge. Rather, it makes itself felt on the surface of discourse by its effects, and this presence of meaning is called expression. Only not every expression is truth. And here again Freud teaches us some rules of judgement. Not that we could ever grasp the truth as one picks a flower after having separated it from the weeds that surround it. Truth and error occur together, not like contraries in a system, but a little like depth which has its recto and verso together. Nevertheless, truth must struggle in order for its effects to appear on the surface, for its monsters of meaning to be openly apparent in discourse, in the order of signification. To learn to distinguish not the true from the false, both defined either in terms of the internal consistency of a system or an operation upon a referential object; but rather to learn to distinguish between two expressions: the one which is there in order to elude the look (in order to capture it) and the one which is there to dislocate it, to give it the invisible to see. The latter requires the work of the artist, free-floating attention, and a principled disregard for established principles; the former is produced by the dream work. One aims at deceiving, the other at averring. However, they are identical in operation, excepting a supplementary inversion in the former, which makes its product a work [*oeuvre*].

Second, if truth does not appear where we expect it, and if no discourse can present it in its absolute meaning because it does not belong to its area, then this book is not true, inasmuch as it obviously tries to produce articulated meanings. Despite this it is not learned, since it does not seek to construct a unitary theory, even as its horizon. Rather, it is a dislocated body, where speech inscribes fragments that can in principle be joined in diverse ways, but which the constraints of typographic composition, those of meaning and ratio, oblige us to present in an immutable order. This order is certainly determined and determining – it is not arbitrary in any case – but it is arbitrarily privileged (by the constraints in question) in relation to others. A good book, in order to let truth appear in its aberration, would be a book in which linguistic time (the time in which meaning develops, the time of reading) would itself be deconstructed; a book that the reader could pick up at any point, and in any order; a book for browsing. (And which would also be marked by the aphorism as a literary genre; I say this in thinking of Nietzsche who had a great fondness for this genre.) This particular book is not such a good book, it is still attached to signification; it is not an artist's book; deconstruction does not operate directly in it, but it is *signified*. This is still a book of philosophy. Certainly, its sense is fragmentary; there are lacunae and, I hope, rebuses. Nevertheless that only makes for an uncertain, intermediate object, which I should like to be able to call, in order to excuse it, an inter-world, like Klee, or a transitional object, like Winnicott; but which it is not really, because this status only belongs to the figural things of the game, of painting, and because here again we do not allow the figure to come into words playing its own game; but we want words to *say* the pre-eminence of the figure, we want to *signify* the other of signification. We still want too much, we are still only the last men, and the space of this book is no more than baroque. But all the same, and it is necessary to say it to exonerate ourselves, this too much is very little.

We have renounced the madness of unity, the madness of supplying a first cause in a unitary discourse, the fantasy of the origin. The Freudian utopia maintains us under the rule dictated by the so-called death drive, which is that the unification of diversity, even in the unity of discourse (even in that of Freudian theory), is always repelled, always forbidden. Just as from out of consideration of this rule, it is necessary to renounce the Ego as an unitary constituted instance, so it is time for philosophers to renounce the production of a unitary theory as the last word upon things. There is no *arche*,[12] but nor does the Good appear as an unitary horizon. We never touch the thing except metaphorically, but this laterality is not, as Merleau-Ponty believed, that of existence, which is much too close to the unity of the subject, as he finally recognised;[13] rather, it is that of the unconscious or of expression, which in one and the same movement opens and reserves all content. This laterality is difference or depth. But whilst Merleau-Ponty formulated it as the possible movement of going over there at the same time as remaining here, as a ubiquitous opening, as continuous mobility, and in having seen its model in the perceptual chiasm, thus succumbing to the illusion of a unitary discourse,[14] we produce weapons for figural space, with Cézanne and Mallarmé, with Freud, with Frege: depth greatly exceeds the power of the reflection that would like to signify it, to place it in its language, not as a thing, but as a definition. Meaning is present as the absence of signification; yet signification takes hold of it (and it can, one can say everything), and it is exiled on the borders of a new speech act. Here, the death-drive is always intertwined with Eros-Logos. The construction of meaning is only ever the deconstruction of signification. There is no assignable model for this evasive configuration. It will be said that violence is at the beginning like castration, and that the silence or the death that our words could drive out is the offspring of this initial terror that has given rise to desire. Very well, but the place of this desire being utopia, let it be known that we have to give up situating it.

This is of great importance for practice, for the practical critique of ideology. This book is itself only a detour intended to lead to this critique, and if we had to wait a long time for our own resistance to writing it to recede, then this is certainly (amongst other things) for fear of being seduced, turned away from this end, hypnotised by language. What its practical function is, what remains active or warm in it, is not for me to judge.

The Figural as Event

A word after the fact: there is an evident decadence in the course of this string of sections. The reader will have become aware of it. He will protest that my thought is uncertain. What decreases, in the passage from the first to the final lines, is the importance accorded to perception. We first explore the order of discourse so as to disentangle what is properly signification from designation, thus isolating a phenomenological or visual space whose properties are reputedly entirely other than those of linguistic signification, without truly analysing them, leaving this to the phenomenology of the visible that Merleau-Ponty undertook. Then we pass from vision to seeing, from the world to fantasy; and the responsibility for constituting the object, its standing over and against us, initially determined from the point of view of discourse, is transmitted to, and restored to, the action of desire. In parallel fashion the figure is displaced: no longer is it only the image of presence or of representation, but the form of the staging, the form of discourse itself, and more profoundly still, a phantasmic matrix. Freud's teaching takes over from that of Husserl.

The point of transition is the point of deception *par excellence*; this is the category of continuity. If it is true that the gesture is meaning or sense, it must be so in opposition to linguistic signification. The latter constitutes itself only as a network of discontinuities, it gives rise to an immobile dialectic where who is thinking and what is thought never merge, and where the elements of thought itself never encroach upon each other. The gesture on the contrary, such as Merleau-Ponty understood it, is the experience of a sense where the sensing and the sensed are constituted in a common rhythm, like the two edges of one furrow, and where the constituents of the sensible form an organic and diachronic totality. Only the gesture comes back, if not to a subject, then at least to a type of subjectivity that would be anonymous or, as Mikel Dufrenne says, nature: it is felt, experienced [*vécu*], or in any case it structures experience. It derives from an unconscious which is not an object of repression, but the subject of constitution.

At first sight the meaning of which the psychoanalyst speaks equally is presented as continuity; it is legitimate to oppose to it linguistic signification just as the plastic extension of displacements, condensations and distortions are opposed to the discrete and transparent space where significations are formed by ordered differentiation. By together standing against linguistic signification, libidinal meaning and sensible meaning seem to overlap. It is this overlapping which finds itself, in the end, undone in this book, the phenomenological mask sliding upon not the face of the unconscious that no-one has seen or will see, but upon the mask of desire. The decline is that of phenomenology.

What is to be transformed is reflection on difference, reflection on the organisation of sensible space. The idea that the latter cannot be reduced to a geometric organisation entirely thinkable by concepts, was underlined by phenomenology itself. *Eye and Mind* has gone as far as it was able in the direction indicated by the description of passivity, of the passivity of the perceptive synthesis, that was already contained in the work of Husserl. By opposing Cézanne's space to that of the *Dioptrique*, Merleau-Ponty wanted to say that an articulated, discontinuous, active, logical conception of sense and space can only lack the fact [*donnée*] or rather the donation of the visible; that the latter was invisible to such a conception, as it is in our constituted experience of extended things; that it necessitated the enormous immobility of Cézanne in order to go beyond the rationalisation of perceptive space and to make visible the original donation in its obliqueness and ubiquity, in its lateral transgression of the rules of optical geometry. Cézanne desires that Mont Sainte-Victoire cease to be an object of vision in order to become an event in the visual field; it is this that the phenomenologist hopes to comprehend, and which I believe he cannot comprehend.

His ultimate concept, his most subtle concept for the purpose of taking hold of the eventuality [*événementialité*] of the given is certainly not intentionality; it is passivity. But this concept can operate only in the field delineated by phenomenology, as the correlate or the contrary of intentional activity, as its support. Seeing as an act rests upon a passive synthesis which is the very donation of that which is seen. This passivity is thus still thought as a supposition of the seeing subject, as an immanence presupposed in its transcendent relation with the object; the subject finds itself in a sense disposed (dispossessed) there, but it is also posed there. It is thus that Merleau-Ponty would pass from the I to the One. But note the distance that still exists between the One and the Id.

The One, on the contrary, does not constitute an event in relation to an I. What would we find in following the direction of this anonymous One? At best the organisation of the forms of sensibility, a space-time that is certainly more secret than that which is experienced, and less tributary to properties of physical knowledge than those that Kant described, but finally a space and a time which form the framework wherein the given is given, where the event leaps forth, but which cannot be the principle of any event. A preconceptual system, as one might describe it, but like every system it is able to give an account not of the fact that there are events (in the visual field or elsewhere), but of the fact that the event (donation) is absorbed, received, perceived, integrated in the world (or into history, etc.). The enigma of the event will remain entire even in attempts to descend as far as the One. It is not the search for the condition, impersonal or not, of the given which immobilised Cézanne before his mountain; it is the search for its donation. Phenomenology cannot reach donation because, faithful to the philosophical tradition of the Occident, it is still a reflection on *knowledge*, and the function of such a reflection is to absorb the event, to recuperate the Other into the Same.

Now the event in its initial alterity cannot arise from the world, to whose meaning we are attuned. Discordance cannot come from speech, which insofar as it is understood is articulated signification constituting the object of a form of knowledge; but no more can it come from a world with which one's own body [*le corps propre*] co-operates in order to produce the *sensoria* which are its element. Certainly the worldly body can constitute an event in the order of discourse, since it is evident that sense is not disposed in it as signification is in language. And this is why one could understand the presence of figures in discourse according to the model of the insertion of gestural operations, impressed on a continuous space, in a field that tolerates transformations only between discrete elements. It is in this way that the Merleau-Pontyian notions of 'encroachment' and 'laterality' are to be situated. These effects are relevant in order to define the poetic or rhetorical order in general. But to what are they to be attributed?

What must serve as a guide here is the fact that this discord in the order of signification has always been thought, in myths, tragedies and philosophies as culpable. Imputing this culpability to one's own body alone is impossible. This body is not a privileged place of the discord and the event; there is a subterranean silence in the life of the flesh, its ὑγίεια, and it is true, as Merleau-Ponty thought, that it is only a chiasm in the milieu of the world, comprised by it and comprising it. It is upon this euphoria that this philosopher attempted to construct a pagan philosophy. But his paganism remains caught in the problematic of knowledge; this makes a philosophy of the flesh wise, which is fortunate, and misjudges disempowerment [*dessaisissement*]. The event as discord is always what defies knowledge; it can defy articulated knowledge in discourse; but it can also shake the quasi-comprehension of one's own body and render it disharmonious with itself and with things, as in emotion. There is as much culpability and inconvenience contained in a look or a pallor as there is in a lapsus. It is not the body which troubles language; it is something else able to trouble both language and the body. To accept the body as the place of the event, is to adopt the defensive displacement, the vast rationalism, operated by the Platonic-Christian tradition with the aim of masking desire.

The event cannot be posed somewhere other than in the vacant space opened by desire. This vacancy of space is precisely the chosen place of donation. This shows itself immediately in the anguish which subtends all the emotions,[15] but also in the presence in discourse of words, of turns of phrase which signal the regions of turbulence where the one who speaks receives. Such a vacancy is not an ethical 'attitude' to be recommended, in the way, for example, of the paradox of the knight of faith according to Kierkegaard or of an–archy in Levinas.[16] To want to make oneself a partisan of the event, an official of the event, is again an ethical illusion. Donation has the character of disempowering us; we cannot appoint ourselves to this disempowering; the event does not arrive where one expects it; even a non–expectation would be disappointed. One cannot pass to the side of the primary process: this is a secondary illusion. Desire has its rejection in itself, which is the principle of the disempowering of its effects. Desire is truly unacceptable, one cannot appear to accept it; to accept it is again to reject it, and it will become an event elsewhere.

In truth, the event cannot be situated if one begins by taking it out of the space left empty by repression or rejection in general. Neither discourse nor the body has in itself this crossed out, distorted disposition that *allows* for the donation precisely because it *forbids* the recognition or understanding of what is donated. Cézanne's prayer: that the familiar mountain disempower him, that it appear somewhere other than where the eye expects it and that in this way it seduce him. A prayer of deconciliation; an anti–prayer. It joins the visible neither to the I–You of language nor to the One of perception, but rather to the Id of desire. And not to the immediate figures of desire, but to its operations.

Such, then, is the displacement or the rotation that will be felt in this book. It will be able to be localised more precisely once we reflect on opposition and difference. One will ask: since you say that the order of the perceptive One masks that of the Id, why have you not discarded the mask in effacing the former? I will reply in saying that this displacement is precisely what makes this book an event for me. For in accordance with what order, which supposed function of the book, what sort of prestige of discourse, are we to efface it?

Notes

1. P. Claudel, *Art poétique* (Paris: Mercure de France, 1941), pp. 50–1.
2. Ibid. pp. 74–5; emphasised by me.
3. Ibid. p. 50.
4. Ibid. p. 74.
5. Ibid. p. 74.
6. A. Breton, *Le surréalisme et la peinture*, (Paris: Gallimard, 1965), p. 1.
7. Compare the definition of the 'hermeneutic circle', which unites belief and comprehension, religion and philosophy (*Finitude et culpabilité*, Paris: Aubier, 1960, t. II, p. 325ff.); and notably this: 'the symbol is already in the sphere of speech; we have often said that it drags feeling and fear away from silence and confusion: it gives a language to confession; by its means humanity, through and through, remains wholly in language. That is not the most important thing. No part of symbolic language exists without hermeneutics; where one man dreams and hallucinates, another man arises who interprets: what was already discourse, albeit incoherent discourse, is raised to coherency by hermeneutics' (pp. 325–6). Compare this with these passages from Hegel's introduction to the *Lessons on the History of Philosophy* (Berlin: 1823–4): 'philosophy has an identical object, universal reason which is in and for-itself absolute substance; by way of philosophy, spirit wants to appropriate this object. Religion executes this reconciliation by means of meditation (*Andacht*) and the cult, that is, by means of feeling; but philosophy wants to execute it by thought, the knowing which thinks. Meditation is the *feeling* of the unity of the divine and the human, but a feeling *which thinks*; the expression 'meditation' (*Andacht*) already contains thinking (*denken*); it leads us to think, this is an aspiration towards thought, a "to think about", a "thinking towards something" (*ein Daranhindenken, Sichherandenken*). But philosophy's form is a pure thinking, a knowing; this is the point at which it begins to differentiate itself from religion [. . .] When someone says to us that what is revealed should not have been able to be discovered by human reason, it is necessary to remark that the truth, the knowledge of divine nature, it is true, reaches men only by an external means, that the consciousness of truth as sensible object is in a general manner the first form of consciousness; it is thus that Moses perceived God in the burning bush and the Greeks have represented their gods in marble statues or other images, such as one finds in the poets. It is in this external way that thought generally begins; thus content appears first as given, coming to the spirit from the exterior: we see it, understand it, etc. But we do not remain in this exteriority, and we must not, neither from the point of view of religion nor from the point of view of philosophy. These fantastic images or this historical matter must not remain in exteriority, but become – for the spirit – of the spiritual order, they must lose this exterior existence, which has precisely nothing spiritual about it [. . .] The universality of Spirit, to which both philosophy and religion are related, is an absolute universality, not external; an universality which penetrates everything, is present in everything. We ourselves come to represent spirit as free; the freedom of spirit signifies that it is

close to itself, that it understands itself. Its nature consists in encroaching upon the Other, rediscovering itself, reuniting with itself, possessing and playing with itself' (this quotation is a slightly modified version of J. Gibelin's French translation (Paris: Gallimard, 1954)). There are few texts in which the function of *the effacement of difference* assigned to the dialectic, the 'tautegoric' character (as Schelling and Ricouer say), the recuperative character (we say) of the interpretative discourse, and the Odyssean narcissism of knowledge (as Levinas says) are more explicit. I thank Serge Boucheron for having indicated this to me.

8. Georg Muche relates this: 'In 1921, when Klee entered into the Bauhaus, he moved into a workshop next to mine. One day, I heard a strange noise, as if someone was rhythmically tapping his or her foot. Meeting Klee in the corridor I asked if he had heard anything. Ah! You heard? Excuse me, he said to me. I was painting, I was painting, and then all of a sudden – it was stronger than me: I started dancing. You heard me. How upsetting! Normally I never dance.' ('Paul Klee', *Frankfurter Allgemeine Zeitung*, 30 June 1956).

9. Cf. M. Détienne, *Les maîtres de vérité dans la Grèce archaïque* (Paris: Maspero, 1966).

10. G. Braque, *Le jour et la nuit* (Paris: Gallimard, 1952), p. 38.

11. J. B. Pontalis, 'L'utopie freudienne', in *L'Arc*, no. 34, 1965 special edition on Freud.

12. E. Levinas, 'Humanisme et anarchie', *Revue internationale de philosophie*, 1968, pp. 85–6.

13. M. Merleau-Ponty, *Le visible et l'invisible* (Paris: Gallimard, 1964), pp. 229, 253.

14. And it is prepared when he renounced what there was of the philosophy of the Cogito in the *Phenomenology of Perception*, maintaining unitary philosophy by putting Being in the place of the I.

15. Which Pierre Kaufmann shows at the end of the first chapter of *L'expérience émotionnelle de l'espace* (Paris: Vrin, 1967).

16. See in particular E. Levinas, 'Humanisme et anarchie'.

Chapter 2

The Great Ephemeral Skin

Opening the Libidinal Surface

Open the so-called body and spread out all its surfaces: not only the skin with each of its folds, wrinkles, scars, with its great velvety planes, and contiguous to that, the scalp and its mane of hair, the tender pubic fur, nipples, nails, hard transparent skin under the heel, the light frills of the eyelids, set with lashes – but open and spread, expose the labia majora, so also the labia minora with their blue network bathed in mucus, dilate the diaphragm of the anal sphincter, longitudinally cut and flatten out the black conduit of the rectum, then the colon, then the caecum, now a ribbon with its surface all striated and polluted with shit; as though your dressmaker's scissors were opening the leg of an old pair of trousers, go on, expose the small intestines' alleged interior, the jejunum, the ileum, the duodenum, or else, at the other end, undo the mouth at its corners, pull out the tongue at its most distant roots and split it; spread out the bats' wings of the palate and its damp basements, open the trachea and make it the skeleton of a boat under construction; armed with scalpels and tweezers, dismantle and lay out the bundles and bodies of the encephalon; and then the whole network of veins and arteries, intact, on an immense mattress, and then the lymphatic network, and the fine bony pieces of the wrist, the ankle, take them apart and put them end to end with all the layers of nerve tissue which surround the aqueous humours and the cavernous body of the penis, and extract the great muscles, the great dorsal nets, spread them out like smooth sleeping dolphins. Work as the sun does when you're sunbathing or taking grass.

And this is not all, far from it: connected onto these lips, a second mouth is necessary, a third, a great number of other mouths, vulvas, nipples. And adjoining the skin of the fingertips, scraped by the nails, perhaps there should be huge silken beaches of skin, taken from the inside of the thighs, the base of the neck, or from the strings of a guitar. And against the palm, all latticed with nerves,

Translator's note: The great ephemeral skin (La grande pellicule éphémère). Lyotard later refers to the pellicule in the technical sense, meaning *film*; I have chosen, in keeping with the imagery here, to take slight liberties and translate *pellicule* as 'skin'.

and creased like a yellowed leaf, set potter's clays, or even hard wooden handles encrusted with jewels, or a steering wheel, or a drifter's sail are perhaps required. Don't forget to add to the tongue and all the pieces of the vocal apparatus, all the sounds of which they are capable, and moreover, the whole selective network of sounds, that is, the phonological system, for this too belongs to the libidinal 'body', like colours that must be added to retinas, like certain particles to the epidermis, like some particularly favoured smells to the nasal cavities, like preferred words and syntaxes to the mouths which utter them and to the hands which write them. It is not enough, you see, to say, like Bellmer, that the fold in the armpit of the child, dreamily intent, her elbow on the table and chin in her hand, could *count as* [*valoir pour*] the folds of her groin, or even as the juncture of the lips of her sex. The question of 'counting as', don't urge us to ask it, far less to resolve it. It is not a part of the body, of what body? – the organic body, organized with survival as its goal against what excites it to death, assured against riot and agitation – not a part which comes to be *substituted* for another part, like, for example, in the case of this little girl, the fleshiness of the arm for that of the thighs and its faint fold for the vaginal slit; it is not this displacement of parts, recognizable in the organic body of *political economy* (itself initially assembled from differentiated and appropriated parts, the latter never being without the former), that we first need to consider. Such displacement, whose function is representation, substitution, presupposes a bodily unity, upon which it is inscribed through transgression. There is no need to begin with transgression, we must go immediately to the very limits of cruelty, perform the dissection of polymorphous perversion, spread out the immense membrane of the libidinal 'body' which is quite different to a frame. It is made from the most heterogeneous textures, bone, epithelium, sheets to write on, charged atmospheres, swords, glass cases, peoples, grasses, canvases to paint. All these zones are joined end to end in a band which has no back to it, a Moebius band which interests us not because it is closed, but because it is one-sided, a Moebian skin which, rather than being smooth, is on the contrary (is this topologically possible?) covered with roughness, corners, creases, cavities which when it passes on the 'first' turn will be cavities, but perhaps on the 'second', lumps. But as for what turn the band is on, no-one knows nor will know, in the eternal turn. The interminable band with variable geometry (for nothing requires that an excavation remain concave, besides, it is inevitably convex on the 'second' turn, provided it lasts) has not got two sides, but only one, and therefore neither exterior nor interior.

It is certainly not a libidinal theatre then, no density, intensities running here and there, setting up, escaping, without ever being imprisoned in the volume of the stage/auditorium. Theatricality and representation, far from having to be taken as libidinal givens, *a fortiori* metaphysical, result from a certain labour on the labyrinthine and Moebian band, a labour which prints these particular folds and twists, the effect of which is a box closed upon itself, filtering impulses and allowing only those to appear on the stage which come from what will come to be known as the *exterior*, satisfying the conditions of interiority. The representative chamber is an energetic *dispositif*. To describe it and to follow its functioning, that's what needs to be done. No need to do a critique of meta-physics (or of political economy, which is the same thing), since critique pre-supposes and ceaselessly creates this very theatricality; rather *be inside and forget it*, that's the position of the death drive, describe these foldings and gluings, these energetic vections that establish the theatrical cube with its six homoge-nous faces on the unique and heterogeneous surface. To go from the pulsion to representation, but without allowing oneself, in order to describe this implant-ation, this sedentarization of the influxes, without allowing oneself the suspect facility of lack, the trick facility of an empty Alterity, of a Zero whose silence is about to be shattered by the demand which disturbs it (demand, already speech then? and addressed already, and to something? yes, to this Other; and by something, which is therefore already able to speak? yes, whether in gestures, tears, fury, the infatuated suckling's torpor, interjections, as they say), so that with this trick of the demand and the Zero's silence, well, it remains only to inaugurate the theatre and power, and set them to work, the theatre of power where satisfactions will dupe the desire originating from this alleged lack itself. Quite the contrary, it is necessary, we will come to this later, to describe the business of the cube starting with the opened and exposed band of the libidinal body, according to the unique face without verso, the face which hides nothing.

We should not continue to confuse the closure of representation, that sarcastic discovery, that sham dropping of the scales from our eyes, by those thinkers who come and tell us: what is outside is really inside, there is no outside, the exteriority of the theatre is just as much its interiority – don't mix up this sad piece of news, this cacangelism which is only the other side of evan-gelism, this wretched news that the artefact-bearers running along their little wall behind the backs of slaves who are bound and seated at the bottom of their cave, do not even exist, or what amounts to the same: that they themselves are only shadows in the cave of the sunlit world, reduplication of sadness – don't go confusing this crestfallen message and this representation of an entirely closed theatre with our Moebian-labyrinthine skin, single-sided patchwork of all the organs (inorganic and disorganized) which the libido can traverse: for however well it is closed upon itself, it too, like a good Moebius band, is not at all closed in the sense of a volume, it is infinite, and contrary to the representative cube, intensities run in it without meeting a terminus, without ever crashing into the wall of an absence, into a limit which would be the mark of a lack, there is nothing the libido lacks in reality, nor does it lack regions to invest, the slender and very dark finger of her left hand which, in a conversation, the young woman, anxious because she is afraid of what she believes to be your erudition, passes over her eyebrow, while in the other hand she pulls at a cigarette – here is a real region to invest, one can die for it, one can give all one's organicity, one's ordered body, one's functional arrangement of organs, one's memory of organs, one's socio-professional status, one's supposed past and one's supposed future, one's agenda and one's intimate theatre, one can feel like paying very dearly, exorbitantly, for this finger which is like an engraver's stylus and the whole orbital space, cranial, vaginal, that it engenders around the eye. And it is not because it is prohibited that it is invested, not because it is represented, beyond a stage-set and because one hasn't the right to climb onto the stage – but because one desires to climb up there and *seize it!* The libido never fails to invest regions, and it doesn't invest under the rubric of lack and appropriation. It invests without condition. Condition is rule and knowledge. But the passage of emotion on the hand stroking the eyelid, what does it matter if it obeys rules, laws of emotion and other nonsense, what does it matter what causes the woman's shyness before your supposed personage (obviously paternal . . .), what does all this matter, this hotchpotch of words which will give an account and do the accounts? It is these words, which set about representing the gesture and produce it in the exteriority internal to all discourse, and the law that they invent in order to *explain* exteriority and the spectacle, it is their own law as knowledge.

Far from taking the great Zero as the ontological motif, imposed on desire, forever deferring, re-presenting and simulating everything in an endless post-ponement, we, libidinal economists, affirm that this zero is itself a figure, part of a powerful *dispositif*, wise like the god of the Jews and pale like the void of Lao-tzu, a concentratory *dispositif* [*dispositif de circonversion*] where, of course, several libidinal positions are affirmed together, which we make merry in dis-intricating and demonstrating with tact, in disengaging without shock, like Japanese, like blades enmeshed in a fencing match – and we will show not only that it is not necessary to pass through it in order to follow the course of inten-sities on the labyrinth, but moreover that the passage through the zero is itself a particular libidinal course, that the position of the Signifier or of the Other is, in the concentratory *dispositif*, itself an enjoyable [*jouissive*] position, that the 'rigour of the law' gives more than one person a hard-on, and that this Nothing is not a matter of ontological necessity, but of a religious fantasy, libidinal then, and as such, moreover, quite acceptable, that is, if it were not, alas, terroristic and deontic. We must model ourselves an affirmative idea of the Zero.

So we rebegin the critique of religion, so we rebegin the destruction of piety, we still seek atheism, terribly intelligent, we have understood that the reintro-duction of the Zero, that is to say, of the negative, in the economy of desire, is quite simply that of accountancy in libidinal matters; it is political economy, that is, capital, carried even into the sphere of passions, and with this economy of capital, necessarily, and yet again, we have understood that it is piety that comes to take its course, the pulsional and passionate *dispositif* of religiosity, inasmuch as this is identified as the *force of lack*, capitalist religiosity, which is that of money engendering itself, *causa sui*. And therefore we 'are doing politics', we desire that the force of lack collapse, that it degenerate, we love and we want all that affirms that this zero not only does not engender itself, and no more is it engendered by another force (the force of labour, Marx supposes, but once again, exactly as lacking, effaced 'on the surface' of the social stage), but most of all that questions of engenderment are trapped, they bear within them knowledge and its 'answers', all of which strikes you as incredibly funny – no, we do not subordinate our anti-religious, that is to say, anti-capitalist, politics to knowing what the origin of meaning, that is to say, what surplus-value really is, not even to know that there really is no origin and that it does not lack any this or that, but is lacking as an origin, we want and do a dismembered, unaccountable politics, *godless* for politicians, and it is in this way that the *critique* of religion which we rebegin is no longer a critique at all, no longer remains in the *sphere* (that is to say, note, the theatrical volume) of what it critiques, since critique rests in turn on the force of lack, and that *critique is still religion.*

Pagan Theatrics

We desire the atheism of the libidinal band, and if it cannot be critical, that is to say religious, then it must be pagan, that is to say affirmative. We have therefore to leap over two frontiers, that which separates the political from the apolitical, but also that which separates the religious from the secular, we have to say, for example, that there is perhaps more atheism (affirmative) in that religion of the Low Empire which Augustine detested and ridiculed, this religion in which for the least hiccup, the least scandal, a copulation without issue, a birthing, a pee, a military decision, there was a god, a goddess, several gods and goddesses *attending* the act, the patient and the agent, not to double them in a pointless spectacle, as Augustine appeared to believe, and no more to divest the alleged subject, implied in the act in question, of his responsibility, but because in this way all these gestures, all these situations, in the life (ever since) called the everyday (as if there were another) on the one hand were valued as intensities, could not decay into 'utilities', and on the other hand did not have to be connected by a paradoxical, dialectical, arbitrary, terrorist link to an absent Law or Meaning, but on the contrary, being self-sufficient in their self-assertion, never failed to be affirmed as singularities. The *divine* was simply this self-assertion. Perhaps nothing is closer to what happens on the libidinal band than the *parody* that 'theatrical theology' makes of this popular religion, half sceptic, half stoic, of late

Rome. It is in any case, even if we are unjust in its favour, much more atheist than the discourses of science, of politics and critique, of our contemporary liberators of desire, women, children, Blacks, Indians, spaces and the proletariat – liberators whom we love, and who, moreover, we *too* are.

Between theatrical theology and the Judaeo-Christian who today still governs the critique of religion and political economy, there is no opposition between a eulogy to the divine in the world and a hymn to God at the expense of the world and *in absentia*, there is the difference between two *dispositifs* of pathos. This is where Klossowski begins. On his advice, let us listen to Augustine discussing the disjunction made by Varro between a fabulous or mythic theology and a civil or political theology. The Christian takes the example of the nuptial coupling:

> And if Virginensis is among those present, to see to the untying of the virgin's girdle, and Subigus, to see that the bride is subdued to her husband, and Prema, to make sure that, when subdued, she is pressed tight, to prevent her moving – if they are there, what is the function of the goddess Pertunda? She should blush for shame and take herself off! Let the bridegroom have something to do for himself! It would be most improper for anyone but the husband to do what her name implies. But it may be that she is tolerated just because she is a goddess, not a god . . . But what am I talking about? Priapus is there as well, that all-too-male divinity. And the newly wed bride used to be told to sit on his phallus, that monstrous obscenity, following the most honourable and most religious custom of Roman matrons. So let our friends go and try to use all their subtlety to make a distinction between 'civil' and 'fabulous' theology, between the city and the theatre, the temple and the stage, priestly ceremonies and poets' verses – a supposed distinction between decency and obscenity, truth and falsehood, solemnity and frivolity, the serious and the farcical, between what is to be desired and what is to be rejected.[1]

And Augustine continues with a good apostle's argument: if Varro works in such a way that the respective representations of the divine on the theatrical stage and the social stage are after all indiscernible, it is because already the certainty fills this pagan that only natural theology is true, that of the philosophers, meaning Plato, and therefore that of Augustine, meaning Christ. All these simulacra, whether of actors or of priests, come to fall together on one side, on the side of the false, of the illusory, of the impure; the new limit is set up to separate all that, which is appearance, from the essential, which is pure and veridical. What is Augustine thereby doing? He believes he has finished with the theatre, he invents it, reinvents it after Plato and the others, restores what the adherents of Subigus, Prema and Pertunda had demolished, that is to say the devaluation of the here and now, its subordination to the Other, he reforms voluminous theatricality and repeats the *dispositif* by which the auditorium is ignored, in favour of the stage and the stage devoted to the representation of an Exteriority left behind at the doors to the theatre, and then judged non-theatrical once and for all.

But popular, Varronian theatrics did not present this distribution of functions in its scenography at all. If the young bridegroom provoked Virginensis to strip the girdle from the young woman he was about to deflower, how can it be imagined that it could be by indecency, foolishness and falsehood? Is it not obvious that Virginensis is the name borne by the impatience of the *vir desiderans* and the *virgo*, equally astonished and expectant, yet full of amazement; also the untying of the girdle in order that it be released, and superimposed, the formation of another knot in the process of being tied between her arms, her shoulders, stomach, thighs, her *introitus* and her *exitus*? Virginensis is a cry forced out by all this at once, a cry made of several incompossible cries: she opens up, he takes me, she resists, he squeezes, she gets loose, he starts and stops, she obeys and commands, this could happen, happen impossibly, supplication and order, oh the most powerful thing of all flowing through them, do what desire desires, be its slave, connect, I give you a name.

And for each connection, a divine name, for each cry, intensity and multiplication brought about by experiences both expected and unexpected, a little god, a little goddess, which has the appearance of being useless when one looks at it with globulous, sad, Platonic-Christian eyes, which in fact is of no use, but which is a name for the passage of emotions. Thus every experience gives rise to a divinity, every connection to an inundation of affects. But Augustine passed into the camp of the great Zero, and so already understands nothing of all this, he wants and calls for resignation, abandon the libidinal band, he says, only one thing merits affect, it is my own Zero, my Other, it is through him that all your emotions come, you must give them to him, go, leave them with him, render them unto him, he will buy them back from you, the redeemer. What does the Christian want? To bring connection into disrepute and almost to disconnect it: the *next*, what a joke of a word! The other is put into the atmosphere of an affective distance, then brought much nearer again by a particular and paradoxical effort, named *caritas*★ because it is expensive (one gives without return, one gives distances from a distance, it is the Zero who perceives them and fructifies them). As a result of this disconnection, more singularities. *Caritas* has an answer to everything. And that is why everything which became the ancient god finds itself devalued, divided into its appearance, Virginensis, Priapus, fool, and into its essence, the new god, the central Zero, the stage-director [*metteur en scène*].

In its appearance, delirium or madness, and in its essence, divine intentions. Listen to the Father of the Church attempting to cleave intensities:

> They want to derive the name Liber from *Liberamentum* (deliverance), on the ground that through his assistance males are 'delivered' from semen in coition . . . Besides this they have women, as well as wine, assigned to Liber, with a view to provoking sexual

★ TN: *Caritas* (L.): Christian love and charity: gift or payment: dearness, high price, esteem, affection.

desire, and in this way Bacchanalia were celebrated with all their limitless insanity; Varro himself admits that the Bacchants could not have performed their feats if their minds had not been deranged (*nisi mente commota* . . .). One thing is certain; such performances would never have taken place in the theatre; they had entertainment there, not raving madness. And yet to have gods who delight in such entertainments is similar to a kind of lunacy (*simile furoris*).[2]

That is how the excellent Father prepares the generalized closure of appearances under the name of symptoms. The devaluation of the given functions fully, that is to say emptily: the movement of forces becomes commotion of the spirit, and soon *dementia* and *amentia*. The pagans called it Dionysus and Bacchus, names of inestimable singularity. And note Augustine's paralogism, his faltering way of paying tribute, nevertheless, to the force of their theatrics: the Bacchants were prey to rage and madness; this cannot be seen in the theatre where one only acts; although theatre plays are such that they could please only the gods who were also seized by *furor*. The implication is direct, and pagan: *furor* is divine, the divine is *furor*, as much in sacred rites as in stage plays, there is nothing that does not enter the tracks of the impulses, under a singular name, and there is nothing that keeps itself outside this passage. We catch Augustine; here in the act of folding the libidinal band onto itself in order to produce within it a volume and a chamber of presence/absence. Intensities will need to be filtered and imparted to the active voice of the Zero, in order to balance all the accounts. And we see how he cannot succeed in doing this, how the difference between play and madness, simulacrum and truth, clowning and seriousness, is not succesfully set up.

This, this affirmation of the band, this banditism, is written in a pain which makes the hand tremble. Let's listen to it, this is certainly more important than what is said. This pain is not a sadness or a loss of force, but the opposite. It is stamped with an expenditure of important quantities of energy, employed to make something bearable which is not bearable, perhaps this same accumulation of forces [*puissances*]. Crying, yelling are within the hand's capabilities. Figures – meanwhile the hand continues to advance its pen through Dionysus' groves – figures of life and death are accumulated, figures which are this same energy fixed for a moment and for an eternity, and which devour it, mistresses of wild beasts. Egyptian face, Negev hair, bistre-coloured androgyne, unmanageable girl-child.

With this pain, perhaps at the centre, this new event, truly awful: this same Egyptian face, staring into space with its impassive gaze, it has become yesterday evening, a *black* night. The figure of the young woman has become the death mask of a young man the cops had kept watch over and beaten up two years ago in an island prison bordering the African seaboard, and whose body had been buried after his father refused, having examined it, to admit their version of death by suicide. It is this same face, this same narrow forehead, big nose, a little crooked, and the third great identifying feature of the Abyssinian type, the same fineness of the jaw. And he spoke, all the time, while she kept silent, he yielded, escaping to his death and looking for it through floods of words, speaking like a Negro, multiplying the ambushes of words: but his speech was so soft and imperious that it was followed by visible effects, just like physical actions. If his death could have exploded as his words exploded, into palpable transformations, when he was his body! To make of his death his active body again, transformer. The anagrams of his *nomen* were Roma, Amor.

And this tension, above all difficulty and intolerance, is associated with the incompossibility of all these simultaneous figures. You would need to be one hundred per cent Christian and stupid to think that these Romans and Negros are libidinal idiots, innocents plunged in debauchery. This suffering through excess is that of the Bacchants, it proceeds from the *incompossibility* of figures, of masks which together occupy the same space-time and thereby reveal the libidinal band; for such an incompossibility where several parts, however different, of the alleged organic body, are affirmed at the same time, or even, if you prefer, where sections of the psychic and social apparatus which must only be affirmed separately or successively, are affirmed at the same time; it is unbearable. Is this because it is the dissolution of unity, of the supposed synthesis? What is engulfed in theatrical theology, for we who come long afterwards, having centuries, almost two millennia of disfiguring traditions upheld by religion, religions, metaphysics, capital, is identity. Is it possible that all intensity is suffering only because we are religious, are clergy of the Zero? Even to say this is perhaps a consolation.

Our danger, we libidinal economists, lies in building a new morality with this consolation, of proclaiming and broadcasting that the libidinal band *is good*, that the circulation of affects *is joyful*, that the anonymity and the incompossibility of figures *are great and free*, that all pain is reactionary and conceals the poison of a formation issuing from the great Zero – what I have just said. But it is not an ethics, this or another, that is required. Perhaps we need an *ars vitae*, young man, but then one in which we would be the artists and not the propagators, the adventurers and not the theoreticians, the hypothesizers and not the censors.

We do not even have to say: this great Zero, what crap! After all, it is a figure of desire, and from what position could we assume to deny it this quality? In what other, no less terrorist Zero? *One cannot assume a position* on the twisted, shock-ridden, electrified labyrinthine band. One's got to get this into one's head: the instantiation of intensities on an original Nothing, on an Equilibrium, and the folding back of complete parts onto the libidinal Moebian band, in the form of a theatrical volume, does not proceed from an error, from an illusion, from malice, from a counter-principle, but again from desire. One must realize that representing [*la mise en représentation*] is desire, putting on stage, in a cage, in prison, into a factory, into a family, being boxed in are desired, that domination and exclusion are desired; that extreme intensities are instantiable in these assemblages too. That the black Pharoah face has died, that the metamorphosis he was looking for had been the death that he was. We must succeed in hearing that without any rejection, for it is rejection, the exteriorization, which prolongs theatricality like a shadow cast over the libidinal band. This rejection is necessarily concomitant with the setting-up of a point of view on the Zero, on the empty centre, the place where everything is supposed to be visible and intelligible, the place of knowledge.

Turning of the Bar

Thus there is the pain of incompossibility. This pain is much older than the word incompossibility can indicate. This word could tend to produce the belief that the origin of pain is logic, the violation of the compossible, the simultaneous affirmation of the this and the not-this. There is certainly a bit of suffering, which the most acute mathematicians and logicians are well aware of, in these occupations of spaces previously reputed to be exclusive and carefully distinguished: one should recall the matter of imaginary numbers, of fuzzy sets, of the logic of individuals. Same thing with the painters, when Klee, for example, opens the perspectivist cube onto the plastic support as one, as ten dislocated boxes presented together from five or six points of view. A bit of suffering, but it is not, however, this pain, it is like its negative, it is this pain announced *a contrario* in the spaces of non-pain. Exactly where the concept had produced the strict delimitation of the this and the not-this, had crossed the limit, had thus determined a zone of points that were neither this nor not-this, neutralized points forming a frontier and forbidding confusion, a new 'labour' (as they say) of the concept displaces this series of points, unbound and rebound in another way, provoking the panic of a square negative, of a trivalent logic, or, in Lesnievski's hypothesis, the truth of a proposition like *the edge of the book is the book.*

Brief panic, one settles down again, one sedentarizes in another way, at least when we are in the grip of an obsession with the great Zero, when, at any cost, one wants to produce a discourse of so-called knowledge, when therefore one never ceases, after all these disturbances, to proclaim that now, this is it, one holds the true *dispositif* of the logic of propositions, of the theory of numbers, of whatever. The true, that is to say what the great Zero itself produces, and assumes. One soon stops nomadizing, one occupies and cultivates the earth, under the security of the True. But these disfigurations rarely take place, thank god, even today's scientists are starting out on the road to pain, letting their little sufferings subside, their little scandals, the petty dialectic and the wretched 'labour of the concept'. They know that this is deception itself, that what works is not the concept, that the concept is capital which pretends to work, but which determines the conditions of labour, delimits the outsides and insides, the authorized and the prohibited, selects and valorizes, invests, realizes, that the concept is trade, but that the movement, the strength of trade is not the concept, this wretched little suffering of the academic radical–socialist.

Our great mathematicians, those whom we love, our brothers in pain and joy, know very well that it is not even correct, that it is futile and almost base to say with a last smile: yes, all that we do is only a game, yes we quite understand that there is only the great Zero and that one can only turn about it, like a vast spectacle. They know as well as we do that it is *not at all* a question of a game, that one never leaves the sham seriousness of the concept for the facsimile of the game. Roman pain and joy, pagan and stoic, are not games. The stage plays that Augustine despises (and adores) are in no way simulacra of another reality, the stage masks could not be the popular and political version of serious divinity; the Nothing with which the philosophers and priests have furnished us as the maximum and optimum of consciousness or knowledge or wisdom, and thanks to which the vivacious and deadly intensities that shoot across us shall be *discredited*, this Nothing, it is their desire that produces it, it is not it that produces their desire. These intensities do not in any way proceed from illusions of changing investment on the immobile circle that surrounds the Nothing; but on the contrary, they can engender this as the centre of a concentratory disposition also called the proper body, ego, society, universe, capital, the good lord. The thought of the game, of the great Game, game of desire and game of the world, is still a little sad thought, that is to say, a thought. It remains entirely instantiated on the Zero, and from there it makes this effort, supreme for thought, to say to itself: this, all that happens on the periphery, on the circle, is nothing but the transit of intensities, turn and eternal return; it says to itself: I am nothing but thought, that is, the Nothing and nothing, what is turns around outside, and so, to be, I have only to place myself as well on the circumference, turn with the intensities, act *as if* I loved, suffered, laughed, ran, fucked, slept, shat and pissed, I, thought. May this supreme effort of thought die, such is our wish as libidinal economists.

The pain of incompossibility does not refer to a delimiting, selective, orientating zero. Thought does not precede it. More often than not, what is called thought is what escapes it, is produced as a way out of it. The *dispositif* of confinement, that is to say of delimitation and conception, which will produce the exterior and the interior, which will enclose the extension of the concept, which will define *places* (of art, of culture, of production, of politics, of sexuality), this *dispositif* with its zero can only be engendered by disintensification.

The operator of disintensification is exclusion: either this, or not-this. Not both. The disjunctive bar. Every concept is therefore concomitant with negation, exteriorization. It is this exteriorization of the not-this that will give rise to theatricization: the outside 'will have to' *be conquered*, the concept 'will will' its own extension, to master what it had left at the gates of its territory, it will set off for war and for labour with Hegel, as previously with Augustine, towards the outside, in order to annex it. In reality it is pushed into this not only by the demon of confusion, by synchretism, by the *jouissance* of overthrowing, by the quest for intensities, but by flight in the face of this pain of incompossibility that we are talking about. What anguish in these limits, in these devaluations followed by exclusions! How they are loved, these exteriorities! Hence voyages, ethnology, psychiatry, pediatrics, pedagogy, the love of the excluded: enter, beautiful Negresses, charming Indians, enigmatic Orientals, dreamers, children, enter my work and the spaces of my concepts. All this is theatre; it is the white innocence of the West in expansion, base cannibalistic imperialism.

The little suffering is only the displacement of the disjunctive bar. The little suffering carried to the second degree, is the consciousness that this displacement is the rule, that there is always displacement. Little suffering that attains its acme in the thought of metaphor and of difference [*écart*]. But the pain we speak of is in no way bound to the displacement of the bar of the concept. This pain is not the depression that follows from the position of having one foot here and one foot there, one foot inside and one foot outside, of being *divided*. This pain has no relation to the little suffering of castration, which is the suffering of the concept, fissure and disfiguration ceaselessly deferred. Instead, this is how to imagine it, perfumed Mane of hair.

Take this bar which separates the this from the not-this. That is to say any segment at all. Place it in a neutral space, say three-dimensional to facilitate the imagination's highly crude intuition. Subject it to a movement of rotation around a point belonging to this segment, a movement yielding the following three properties: the rotation takes place on all the axes without exclusion, the central point is itself displaced over the segment in an aleatory way, finally it is equally displaced in the supposed neutral space. Thus a surface is engendered, which is nothing other than the labyrinthine libidinal band which was in question: this surface always has as its breadth the length of the segment, etc. But to describe the properties of the band is not the important thing. This segment which 'passes over' the whole landscape of 'corporeal' surfaces joined end to end as has been said (which in fact *engenders* this landscape point by point in the ungraspable time of its passage), the more quickly it turns on itself, the more energy it employs and expends, and heats the travelled zone. This passage may be absolutely immobile, the black sun of so-called hysterical *conversions*, or the so-called obsessional or paranoiac *fixations*, or conversely fulminating or ephemeral *ideas* of art, of science, of love. The ice that it leaves behind it is in proportion to the energy sucked up: extremely cold intensities. And every intensity, scorching or remote, is always *this and not-this*, not at all through the effect of castration, of repression, of ambivalence, of tragedy due to the great Zero, but because intensity pertains to an asynthetic movement, more or less complex, but in any event so rapid that the surface engendered by it is, at each of its points, at the same time *this and not-this*. Of no point, of no region, however small, can one say what either is, because this region or this point has not only already disappeared when one claims to speak of it, but, in the singular or atemporal instant of intense passage, either the point or the region has been invested in from both sides at once.

When one says *at the same time*, one says *both together* (or *n* together), but one also says *one at a time*, in the singularity of the time, *della volta*. Only one turn, full of drifting affects. Not a matter of separation, but on the contrary, of move-ment, of displaceability on the spot. It is even necessary to imagine the mono-face band as produced by this aleatory rotation, this mad segment acting as a matrix whose properties never stop changing and so unravelling the unpre-dictable ribbon of libidinal marks in its 'printout' [*sortie*]. But even this image needs to be corrected for it is modelled on an industrial machine, for example a wire drawing machine or a rolling mill, and with this model, it implies the category of an accumulation, of a stock-piling, of a material memory, and, what amounts to the same, of a diachrony. For example, you could, I think, modify in an incessant and arbitrary way the norms of extrusion or rolling, and you would still obtain bars or wires with necessarily variable properties. The fact remains that they *remain*, that the marks of variations are inscribed on these objects and transform them into monuments of a past activity, into means of determining an activity to come, they thus open the space of an upstream and a downstream in production, of a cumulative diachronic time, of a capitalizing history. And beware, because with the instrument, the machine, you are already right in the zero. When the whirls of the disjunctive segment in its libidinal journey, being singular, produce no memory, this segment only ever being where it is in an ungraspable time, *a tense*, and therefore what was 'previously' journeyed through does not exist: acephalia,[3] time of the unconscious.

Duplicity of Signs

See at once, grey-eyed Unkind One, where, once again, we intend to break off, we libidinal economists: we will no longer speak of *surfaces of inscription* (except inadvertently, count on it), of regions to invest, and other similar things. We are suspicious of the separation allowed between inscription and its site. It is nec-essary (very different, Nietzsche says, this *it is necessary* from the *you must*), it is necessary that we strengthen our imagination, our palpative potential [*puissance*] until – rather than to think, we are not thinkers – until we forge the idea of an intensity which far from setting itself up on a producer-body, determines it; the idea of a passage over nothing, which produces, one instant beyond countable time, the being of its proper passing, its *passage* (speaking like some others, but in quite another way). Therefore not a surface first, then a writing or inscription over it. But the libidinal skin of which, *after the event*, one will be able to say that it is made up of a patchwork of organs, of elements from organic and social bodies, the libidinal skin initially like the *track* of intensities, ephemeral work, useless like a jet trail in the thin air at an altitude of 10,000, with the exception that it be, as opposed to the trail, completely heterogeneous. But like it, being at the same time the surface crossed and the crossing. You will say: 'crossed' is a past, it is not the passage which produces the skin, but the past of the passage, not the intensity, but what it will have been [*son après coup*]: and the surface, the libidinal skin is thus already a memory of intensities, a capitalization, a localization of their passages, there is the intensity and what *remains* of it, and your comparison doesn't count since there is a *caput*,* a surface of inscription, a register, when its function was to render the acephalus visible.

I see you, Unkind One, smiling at the hoax played on me by the words of knowledge and capital, before I had even begun to speak. Let us love this farce, let us not fear it, let us say yes each time it *requires* us to (and it will require us to, and require us again) say what we have to say as libidinal economists, this farce will stuff our words with its old hash of nihilist sadness. Between the libidinal skin and a register of inscription, confusion will always be possible, as between Christ and the Antichrist, between matter and anti-matter. We haven't the *power*, thank god, to dissociate them, to isolate a region, precisely, a domain, precisely! which would be a good representation, precisely, of the libidinal band and would escape the management of the concept, its hard scepticism and its nihilism. There is no *affirmative region*, words which cancel each other out.

Freud said, marvellously: the death drives work in silence in the uproar of Eros. Eros and the death drives, incompossibles, are indissociable. And so it is, all things being equal, for the passage of intensities and the surface of inscription. For this operates like memory, preserving the passage, it is that by means of which effervescence is recorded and conserved, it is the means of transforming the singular sign of nothing, which is intensity, into terms of presence/absence, the position, and thereby the value, of which will be assigned as the presence/absence of other terms, functioning as their recording, their place in a form, *Gestalt*, or composition. The surface of inscription is then the means of recording. And from the means of recording to the means of production there is but one thing to do, which the despot accomplishes, as Deleuze says, which the great Gestaltist accomplishes. We well know that this surface is

---

* TN: *Caput* (L): a freeman as opposed to a slave: the head, the seat of the intellect: source (of a river): origin, beginning in time.

at the same time, indiscernibly, the libidinal skin 'engendered' by the mad bar and the wise flat sheet of the account book. At the same time the juxtaposition of singular effects named Sarah, Birgit, Paul, faith, the left eye, the cold, hard neck, juxtaposition of punctual intensities, never assembled as a body, merely adjoined in the impossible idea of the pulsional band, which cannot be one surface of inscription, but rather *several* explosions, not even necessarily successive, ephemeral explosions of libidinal intensities – therefore at the same time this, and the index-sheet where, in the form of *lists*, of words, of registery offices, of notebooks, of indexes, under the double law of paradigm and syntagm, of the column and the line, where what remains of intensity is recorded, its trace, its writing.

There is the farce that words play with us, that intensities play with us and that our passion itself will play with us from one end to the other of this book: this fit of passion, reader, Unkind one, will reach you at *second hand*, reported, this sheet on which I write and which is in one moment, in bewilderment and impatience, a woman's skin caressed or the sheet of water in which I lovingly swim, this sheet, you receive it printed, the same thing repeated, reduplicated, you receive a recording sheet. Words burning the point of the pen, whipped like an inert herd by this point, making them run and trapping the most noble, the fastest, the strongest amongst them, in flight, you receive them as a lexicologist. And all the comparisons which may come to mind, they are damned in advance by the accumulation (*cum*) which they comprise and which subject them to procedures of weighing, thought, commensurability, good for the register and accountability, for ever incapable of yielding intensity in its *event*.

Do you believe that the gloomy declaration of this *differing* [*différer*] of writing dismays and depresses us? It interests us acutely and gives us new impetus. If there is a secret, it is this, its own: how does the impossible juxtaposition of intense singularities give way to the register and recording? How does the differing-displacement, beyond space-time, of the affective singularity give space and time to multiplicity, then to generality, then to universality, in the concept, in the frozen whole of the register, how does it give space-time to the differing-composition or co-placing? How does *force* [*puissance*] give rise to *power* [*pouvoir*]? How does searing affirmation become circumscribed around a zero which, inscribing it, annihilates it and assigns it meaning?

This is our great interest (political interest amongst others, since this is the entire political question). And the hows that we address to it are not *whys*. The *why* is galling, nostalgic, treacherous, always nihilistic. We do not deny the *reality*, libidinal of course, of this zero, of this register, we haven't the least intention of devaluing it *ex hypothesi*, to start saying: this zero is an evil despot, this zero represses us, this is what it is made for, etc., all *ressentiments* which are often used as a political means and which we take no part in. Once again, what interests us: the sign in the Klossowskian-Roman sense of *Subigus* and of *Pertunda*, the singular tensor with its mad multiplicity of directions, not contemplating its disintrication from the 'bad' nihilist sign, from Plato right up to Peirce and Saussure, with a view to placing it apart in a good place where one would be at last in the shelter of the great semiotic-semiotician's Zero, not therefore to dissociate and exteriorize it in relation to the bad sign, or – not even – to exteriorize the latter in relation to the former, to separate them and so ourselves become the Just, the Blessed, Sages, Equals, Brothers, Comrades; no, none of these settlements interests us, rather this: to become sufficiently refined where we are, in order to feel, *in* the baseness of exchangeable signs, the unrepeatable singularities of the passages of affect, sufficiently discriminatory and – I will say it as a provocation – sufficiently *Jesuitical* to seize, *in* the general movement of smoothing down and inscription on this Zero of capital, of the Signifier, the *this-sides* or the *beyonds* of this movement, the immobilities or the excitations which trail and betray this movement, to love inscription not because it communicates and contains, but through what its production necessitates, not because it channels, but because it drifts.

There is our problem, political and otherwise, there, at least, is its position: theatricality without reference, masks revealing no face unless it is a mask in its turn. Names (beware the capital letter!) from a history which is not societies' memories, names which would be their amnesia – but always inseparable from this excess of the Apollinian appearance, the Dionysus inseparable from the great light, not as its opposite but as its nuclear night, the singularity always placed in the paranoiac order of the universal. And in this sense, it is not a revolution we need, it is one revolution, and one, and one more . . . *permanent* revolution if you like, but on condition that this word cease to denote continuity and mean: we will never be sufficiently refined, the (libidinal) world will always be *too beautiful*, there will always be too great an excess of mute vibrant trembling in the most ordinary nonsense or depression, we will never stop becoming disciples of its affects, the routes of the affects ceaselessly crossing and recrossing the signs of representation and tracing the most unheard of, the most audacious, the most disconcerting itineraries on them. And on condition that *permanent* also mean: we do not seek to produce a cartography, a memory, a register of our efforts at refinement, an organization, a party of the refined, an anti-society, a school for a framework of affects, an apparatus of refinement's officials, the permanence in question is not something that persists throughout a time identical to itself and from which could be distilled out of acquisitions, attainments, experiments and results, a knowledge in matters of intensities, on the contrary, all will be gradually lost (of what?), and will be so lost that in one sense we will never be able *to will* continually, to will in the sense of a sustained resolution, this refinement in the (dispossessing) seizures of signs, because power [*puissance*] (*Macht*) cannot be willed (*Willkür*), because desire cannot be assumed, accepted, understood, locked up in names = nomenclatured, because these intensities we desire horrify us, because we flee them, because we forget them. And it is in just such a way that there is a different revolution in each libidinal event, different to all others, incomparable (and always already comparable and still compared, as in the very words I have just employed); and no permanence at all: in fleeing *jouissance-death*, we *meet* it head on, unrecognizable, immediately recognized, *unheimlich* because *heimisch*, different, not willed by a deliberate decision, on the contrary avoided, fled from in panic and nostalgic terror, and therefore truly desired (*Wille*), unassumable. It will have to be forgotten every time, because it is unbearable, and then this forgetting means that it will be 'willed' in the sense of the *Wille*, produces displacement, the voyage of intensities, their return beyond identity. Our politics is of flight, primarily, like our style.

Notes

1. St Augustine, *City of God*, trans. H. Bettenson (Harmondsworth: Penguin, 1972), Bk VI, ch. 9, p. 246.
2. Ibid. p. 244.
3. *Acéphalie*: the Acephallus, from a drawing by André Masson, was taken up by Georges Bataille, to some extent as an answer to the Nietzschean problematic of the Overman and the Death of God: 'The acephalic man mythologically expresses sovereignty committed to destruction and the death of God, and in this the identification with the headless man merges and melds with the identification of the superhuman, which IS entirely "the death of God"'. See Georges Bataille, 'Propositions', in *Visions of Excess*, trans. A. Stoekl, C. R. Lovitt and D. M. Leslie (Manchester: Manchester University Press, 1985), pp. 199–200. – TN.

Chapter 3

Presentation

94. It is not the thinking or the reflective I that withstands the test of universal doubt (Apel 1981), it is time and the phrase. It does not result from the phrase, *I doubt*, that I am, merely that there has been a phrase. Another phrase (the one we just read: *There has been a phrase*) has linked onto the first one by presenting itself as what follows it. And a third one, the one we just read, */ There has been a phrase / follows / I doubt /*, has linked onto the first two by presenting their linkage in the form of a temporally ordered series (*There has been . . ., follows . . .*).

95. *I doubt* is not a first phrase, no more than *I think* or *Es denkt* or *Cogitatur* or *Phrazetai*. There are two reasons for this. First reason: *I doubt* presupposes *I* and *doubt* or *I* and *think*, and so on. And each of these 'terms' presupposes in turn other phrases: definitions, examples of 'usage.' It presupposes language, which would be the totality of phrases possible in a language. Like all totalities, language is the referent of a descriptive phrase, a referent whose reality cannot be established for want of an ostensive phrase (the phrase descriptive of the whole is a phrase of the Idea, in the Kantian sense). One can, in fact, describe, *Language is this and that*, but not show, *And this is language*. The totality is not presentable. Second reason: to verify that *I doubt* or any other phrase presumed to be the first in position is in fact there, one must at least presuppose the ordinal series of events, from which the predicate *first* derives its sense. Now, this series itself results, as Wittgenstein explains about propositions, from a 'general form of passage [*Uebergang*] from one proposition to another' (*TLP*: 6. 01). This form is an operation by means of which the series of whole numbers takes place (*TLP*: 6. 02). This operation must always be able to be applied to its result. Now, with this always, which connotes the principle of the recursivity of the application of the operation to its result, it is succession itself which is already presupposed. Such is the operator of the series: *And so on* (*TLP*: 5. 2523). So, the affirmation that a phrase is first presupposes the temporal series of phrases of which this phrase presents itself as the first.

96. It should be added that the phrase *I doubt* presupposes not only language and the serial operator (succession) but also a prior phrase onto which it links by transforming the regimen according to which the prior phrase presented its universe. The 'same' universe that had been asserted is now problematical. Apart from this presupposed prior phrase, there is understood [*on*

sous-entend](Ducrot 1977: 33–43) a question which is applied to it: *What is not doubtful?*

97. But the phrase that formulates the general form for operating the passage from one phrase to the next can be presupposed as an *a priori* for the formation of the series. It nonetheless still takes place after the phrase that formulates the passage. This at least is the case for No. 94, where the phrase which formulates the form of the passage from the first to the second phrase, which formulates the series under the circumstances, comes in third position. Shouldn't we distinguish between a logical or transcendental priority and a chronological priority? – One always can and undoubtedly always must if what is at stake is that the passage from one phrase to the other be effectuated under the logical or cognitive regimen (especially that of implication). One rule of this regimen is then to disregard the fact that *a priori* propositions or definitions and axioms are themselves presented by phrases in ordinary language which are chronologically prior to them. One rule is to disregard even the chronologism- be it a meta–chronologism–that remains unexamined in the idea of logical priority (for example, in the operator *if, then*). As opposed to the logician or the theoretical linguist, the philosopher has as his or her rule not to turn away from the fact that the phrase formulating the general form for operating the passage from one phrase to the next is itself subject to this form of operating the passage. In Kantian terms, the synthesis of the series is also an element belonging to the series (*KRV*, Critical Solution of the Cosmological Conflict: 444). In Protagorean terms, the debate over the series of debates is part of this series (Protagoras Notice). In Wittgensteinian terms, 'the world is the totality of facts,' 'a picture is a fact,' and 'logical pictures can depict the world (*die Welt abbilden*)' (*TLP*: 1. 1, 2. 141, 2. 19). (But a phrase should not be called a 'picture' Wittgenstein later renounces this) (No. 133).

98. Philosophical discourse has as its rule to discover its rule: its *a priori* is what it has at stake. It is a matter of formulating this rule, which can only be done at the end, if there is an end. Time can therefore not be excluded from this dis- course without it ceasing to be philosophical. On the other hand, time is in principle excluded from logical discourse. Kant asks that the clause *at one and the same time* be excluded from the statement of the principle of contradiction. The validity of the principle of contradiction is not subordinate to a condition of the possibility of experience, since this principle extends to every possible (intelligible) object, whether given or not (*KRV*, Highest Principle of all Analytic Judgments: 191). Heidegger, on the contrary, observes that the clause should be maintained because, according to him, the issue is not that of an iden- tity of an object (an existent) in time (its intratemporal identity), but of the very possibility of the identification of an object. Whatever the latter might be, its identification as an object requires a synthesis of pure recognition (Heidegger 1929: §§ 33c, 34). This assures that it is one and the same object which was and

will be in question. Heidegger thus situates the principle of contradiction in a transcendental, and not in a formal, logic. The problem for the former is the constitution of an object identical to itself across different views (he writes, 'aspects') at different nows. That is why Heidegger identifies primordial time with the faculty of having ideas in general, the transcendental (productive) imagination or faculty of presentation (*Darstellung*). But is it possible to admit faculties, when the idea of faculties presupposes a subject whose organs they are?

99. What escapes doubt is that there is at least one phrase, no matter what it is. This cannot be denied without verifying it *ideo facto*. *There is no phrase* is a phrase, *I lie* is a phrase, even if it is not a well-formed expression (Koyré 1947; Wittgenstein, *Zettel*: §§ 691, 692). *What do I know?* is a phrase. *The phrase currently phrased as a phrase does not exist* is a phrase (Burnyeat 1976; Salanskis 1977). The phrase considered as occurrence escapes the logical paradoxes that self-referential propositions give rise to. These paradoxes reveal themselves when we apply to them the regimen to which well-formed expressions are subject, in particular the rule of consistency with regard to negation (or the principle of contradiction). This regimen forbids that a propositional function can be its own argument (*TLP*: 3. 332, 3. 333). But phrases are not propositions. Propositions are phrases under the logical regimen and the cognitive regimen. Their formation and linking are subject to the stakes of speaking true. The logically true proposition is devoid of sense (*sinnlos*) (*TLP*: 4. 461, 6. 1, 6. 11, 6. 113) the cognitively true proposition is endowed with sense (subjected to the rule of ostension by a *This is the case*). But the self-referentiality of a negative phrase prohibits a decision concerning its truth or falsehood (Russell, 1959: 74–85): and the self-referentiality of an affirmative phrase allows any statement to be demonstrated (Curry in Schneider). But phrases can obey regimens other than the logical and the cognitive. They can have stakes other than the true. What prohibits a phrase from being a proposition does not prohibit it from being a phrase. That there are propositions presupposes that there are phrases. When we are surprised that there is something rather than nothing, we are surprised that there is a phrase or that there are phrases rather than no phrases. And we are right. Logic 'is prior to the question "How?", not prior to the question "What?" ' (*TLP*: 5. 552). A phrase is a 'what'.

100. The phrase that expresses the passage operator employs the conjunction *and* (*and so forth, and so on*). This term signals a simple addition, the apposition of one term with the other, nothing more. Auerbach (1946: ch. 2 and 3) turns this into a characteristic of 'modern' style, paratax, as opposed to classical syntax. Conjoined by *and*, phrases or events follow each other, but their succession does not obey a categorial order (*because; if, then; in order to; although* . . .). Joined to the preceding one by *and*, a phrase arises out of nothingness to link up with it. Paratax thus connotes the abyss of Not-Being which opens between phrases, it stresses

the surprise that something begins when what is said is said. *And* is the conjunction that most allows the constitutive discontinuity (or oblivion) of time to threaten, while defying it through its equally constitutive continuity (or retention). This is also what is signaled by the *At least one phrase* (No. 99). Instead of *and*, and assuring the same paratactic function, there can be a comma, or nothing.

101. 'The phrase survives the test of universal doubt.' But what in the phrase? Its reality, its sense? And is *the* phrase this 'current' one or phrases in general? I note that *reality, sense, current, in general* are instances or quantities which are taken as referents in the phrase universes that constitute these questions. One phrase calls forth another, whichever it may be. It is this, the passage, time, and the phrase (the time in the phrase, the phrase in time) that survives the test of doubt. Neither the sense of a phrase nor its reality are indubitable. Its sense, because it is suspended to a link with another phrase which will explain it. Its reality, because its assertion is subject to the rules for establishing reality which entail the test of doubt (Referent Section). But for there to be no phrase, that is impossible.

102. For there to be no phrase is impossible, for there to be *And a phrase* is necessary. It is necessary to make linkage. This is not an obligation, a *Sollen* [an ought to], but a necessity, a *Müssen* [a must]. To link is necessary, but how to link is not (No. 135).

103. The necessity of there being *And a phrase* is not logical (the question '*How?*') but ontological (the question '*What?*'). It is nonetheless not founded upon any evidence (Apel). Evidence requires that a witness–subject independent of the linking of phrases be able to certify that this linking always takes place. The aporia is a triple one: 1° the object's evidence to a witness (namely, the ostensive phrase whose addressor he or she would be: *This is the case*) does not suffice to establish that object's reality (Nos 61–4); 2° the idea of an 'absolute witness for a reality' is inconsistent (No. 70); and 3° *And a phrase* is not an object for which one can bear witness, it is a presupposition for 'objects,' for their 'witnesses' and so on.

104. By *A phrase*, I understand the phrase which is the case, *der Fall*, the phrase *token*, the phrase event. A phrase-type is the referent of a phrase-event. For a phrase to survive the test of universal doubt stems neither from its being real nor from its being true (No. 101), but from its being merely what happens, *what is occurring, ce qui arrive, das Fallende*. You cannot doubt that something happens when you doubt: it happens that you doubt. If *It happens that you doubt* is a different phrase than *You doubt*, then another phrase is happening. And if it is found that it is not happening, but that it has happened, then it happens that this is found. It is always too late to doubt the 'what'. The question already has its answer: another question.

105. For *And a phrase* to be necessary signifies that the absence of a phrase (a silence, etc.) or the absence of a linkage (the beginning, the end, disorder, nothingness, etc.) are also phrases. What distinguishes these particular phrases from

others? Equivocality, feeling, 'wishes' (exclamation), etc. (Nos. 22, 23, and Gertrude Stein Notice).

106. Give a definition of what you understand by *phrase*. – By such a pre-scription, you are presupposing an object called a *phrase*, a phrase-type. You are also presupposing, are you not, that a complete description of it should be given in order for us to be able to debate and to arrive at an agreement on the nature of this object? Let me show you that 1° the substitution of a phrase-type (or of the object, *phrase*) for a phrase event is required by a phrase regimen, the definitional regimen (only terms taken as objects of a metalanguage and for which definite descriptions have been established are introduced into dis-course), and by a genre of discourse, the dialogical genre. Your prescription is one of the rules of this regimen and this genre. Does this hold a preeminent authority (Plato notice)? 2° It does not seem that the genre of discourse (if there is one) which is obeyed by the phrases that compose the present book privi-leges the definitional regimen. The question is: How to define definition? By an endless regression in the logical order, unless recourse is made to a decision or to a convention. Or an endless progression in the succession of phrase events, and here there is no exception, only time (Descombes 1981a).

107. Give a definition of what you understand by *phrase*. – A definition is a phrase that obeys logical and cognitive rules. But your *Give a definition . . .*, for instance, is a prescriptive that does not obey these rules. – Agreed. That does not at all prohibit you from giving a definition of this prescriptive. There is no need for the definition and what is defined to arise from the same phrase regimen – Indeed, but it is necessary that the value of a phrase that is the object of a definition (which is taken as the referent of a definitional phrase) be trans-formed on account of its being taken as the referent of another phrase, the def-initional one, which is metalinguistic (Nos. 43, 45, 46). In order to validate the command *Give a definition of the phrase*, a definition of the phrase must be given. If we answer by observing that this command is a phrase that does not obey the regimen of logical and cognitive phrases, that command is situated as the refer-ent of the 'current' phrase, it is turned into a counter-example of a logical or a cognitive phrase. This command is not validated, it is used, in its capacity as the referent of an ostensive phrase (*Here is a case of a noncognitive phrase*), to val-idate another phrase, a descriptive one (*Certain phrases are under a noncognitive regimen*) (Kant Notice 2, § 1). Now you are carrying out the same metalinguis-tic operation with *A phrase*. You are taking the expression *A phrase* as if it were a phrase. You are depriving it of its 'currentness' (I wouldn't say of its context, cf. No. 141). of its referential and 'pragmatic' import as an event, which calls forth many kinds of possible phrases. You command me to link onto it with a metalinguistic definitional phrase. You have the right to do so. But know that you are making a command.

108. Lacking a definition of *phrase*, we will never know what we are talking

about, or if we are talking about the same thing. And in talking about phrases, aren't you also using a metalanguage yourself? – It's not easy to know what one is phrasing about (Antisthenes Notice), but it is indubitable that 'one is phrasing' be it only in order to know this. As for the metalanguage at play in 'my' phrases here, it has no logical status, its function is not to fix the sense of a term. It calls upon the capacity of ordinary language to refer to itself: *I've had enough of your/maybe's/; /Mary/is a proper name; His/I love you/was a lot of playacting* (Rey-Debove 1978).

109. Here are some phrases (for once, we'll drop the italics which are supposed to signal their autonymical value): It's daybreak; Give me the lighter; Was she there?; They fought till their last round of ammunition; May he escape the heavy weather!; Is the phrase/There is a phrase/denotative?; $ax^2 + bx + c = 0$; Ouch!; But I just wanted to . . .; Perhaps you thought that I . . .?; There is a phrase; This is not a phrase; Here are some phrases.

110. The young Scythians had orders to beget children with those good warriors, the Amazons. One of them unexpectedly comes upon one of these combatants right when she is squatting to relieve her bowels. 'She nothing loth, gave him what he wanted' and asked him to return on the following day: *Phônèsai mén ouk éikhé, tè dé khéiri éphrazé* (Herodotus IV, 113): 'Unable to express her meaning in words (as neither understood the other's language), she phrased this to him by hand.' French *Aïe*, Italian *Eh*, American *Whoops* are phrases. A wink, a shrugging of the shoulder, a taping of the foot, a fleeting blush, or an attack of tachycardia can be phrases. – And the wagging of a dog's tail, the perked ears of a cat? – And a tiny speck to the West rising upon the horizon of the sea? – A silence (Nos. 24, 26)? – *Ei d'axunèmôn ousa mè dékhei logon/su d'anti phônès phrazé karbanôi khéri* (Aeschylus, *Agamemnon*: 1060–1). Back from Troy, Agamemnon has just entered the palace of Atreus, leaving Cassandra, his captive, motionless in the chariot. Clytemnestra entreats her to come in too. Frozen by her vision of the impending crime, Cassandra neither hears nor answers: 'She bears herself like a wild creature newly captured' (1063). The queen grows impatient: 'But if failing to understand our language, you do not catch my meaning, then instead of speech, make sign [phrase] with thy barbarian hand.' – Silence as a phrase. The expectant wait of the *Is it happening?* as silence. Feelings as a phrase for what cannot now be phrased. The immediate incommunicability of desire, or the immediate incommunicability of murder. The phrase of love, the phrase of death. 'Femininity' or 'bestiality' as a blank in the argument (*logos phônè*). The suspense of the linking. Comic: the Amazon on the stool; as well as tragic: the queen about to kill.

111. A phrase presents at least one universe (Nos. 18, 25). No matter which regimen it obeys, it entails a *There is* [*Il y a*]. There is what is signified, what it is signified about, to whom and by whom it is signified: a universe. *At least* one universe, because the sense, the referent, the addressor, or the addressee can be equivocal (Nos 137–40).

112. The expression *There is* is a mark of presentation in a phrase. Are there other marks of presentation?

113. Could the presentation entailed by a phrase be called *Being*? But it is *one* presentation, or what in a phrase-case is the case. Being would be a case, an occurrence, the 'fact' that it happens to 'fall,' that it 'comes running' (*Fall, occurrence*). Not Being, but one being, one time, [*un être, une fois*].

114. A presentation can be presented as an instance in the universe of a phrase. Thus Being can be presented, as an existent. But the phrase that presents the presentation itself entails a presentation, which it does not present. Can we even say that this presentation slips away or is deferred? That would be to presuppose that it is the same for several phrases, an identicalizing effect of the definite article, *the* presentation.

115. A presentation is that there is at least one universe. A situation is that at the heart of a universe presented by a phrase, relations indicated by the form of the phrases that link onto it (through the phrase's regimen, which calls forth certain linkings) place the instances in relation to each other. *I saw it* is a phrase that situates three of the instances (the addressee instance is not indicated by the phrase), and this situation consists in particular in the determination of a tense. *It's there that I saw it* determines in particular a space-time in which the same three instances are situated. *I tell you that it's there that I saw it* situates in particular the place of the addressor thanks to the 'constative' *I tell you that* . . . (Habermas 1971: 111ff.). The forms of phrases indicate the situations of the instances with regard to each other. The set of these situations forms the presented universe.

116. The presentation entailed by a phrase-case is not presented in the universe that this phrase presents (but it may be marked in the phrase, for example by *There is*). It is not situated. But another phrase-case can present it in another universe and thereby situate it.

117. The categories of Aristotle, Kant, and others are families or species of situations, that is, families or species of relations between the instances presented in a phrase universe. It would be a mistake to call them genres or modes of presentation (or of Being) (Aubenque 1966, 176–80). The presentation of a phrase allows itself to be determined by genres only if it is situated in the universe of another phrase, that is, as a presented presentation. That is why genres of presentation, if there are any, are presentable only as genres of situation.

118. Let's admit for the sake of convenience two phrases (1) and (2), linked in the following way: phrase (1) presents a universe, it entails a presentation; phrase (2) signifies something about the presentation of phrase (1); it presents a universe in which the presentation of phrase (1) is in the situation, shall we say, of referent. The presentation (1) that is presented is not entailed in (2); the presentation (2) that is entailed is not presented in (2). A presented presentation and an entailed presentation do not therefore make two presentations. A set of

two presentations is formed by two presentations presented by a single phrase, which is some phrase (3). The presentation entailed by the latter is not part of the set of presentations (1) and (2) that it presents, or: the synthesis of the series of presentations presented by a phrase-case entails a presentation which does not enter into the series presented by this phrase-case. It is presentable, though, in another phrase-case. And so on.

119. The universe presented by a phrase is not presented to something or to someone like a 'subject'. The universe is there as long as the phrase is the case. A 'subject' is situated in a universe presented by a phrase. Even when the subject is said not to belong to the world, qua addressee or addressor of the presentation – thinking I in Descartes, transcendental Ego in Husserl, source of the moral law in Kant, subject in Wittgenstein (*TLP*: 5. 632; *TB*: 7. 8. 1916ff.), – this subject is nevertheless situated in the heart of the universe presented by the philosophical phrase that says it does not belong to the world. What is not in the 'world,' the subject, is presented in a phrase universe where it is situated under the relation of transcendence, but transcendence is a situation immanent to the universe presented by the phrase that states it.

120. There wouldn't be any space or time independent of a phrase.

121. If asked from where you hold this notion that space and time are like kinds of situations, it may be answered that it is held from phrases like *The marquise went out at five,** It had happpened, He had arrived,*** Get out of here, Asleep! Already?*, etc. But above all from the phrase *From where do you hold . . .?* which presupposes space and time. And it may be added that I do not hold it, phrases can so hold themselves, that is, they can situate their instances so and situate themselves so in relation to others. Space and time are headings that group the situational effects produced in phrase universes by expressions like *behind, much later, just below, was born, in the beginning*, etc. (and *etc.*). There are phrases whose regimen requires these marks (such as narratives), others which exclude them as an assumption (such as mathematics, or logic, even if there is a logic of time).

122. There are as many universes as there are phrases. And as many situations of instances as there are universes. – But you say that there are families of instantial situations such as space and time (No. 121)? Then, there are phrase universes that are at least analogous to each other? – A metalinguistic phrase has several of these different phrases as its referent, and it states their resemblance. This resemblance removes none of their heteogeneity (Bambrough 1961: 198–9).

---

* TN: *La marquise sorit à cinq heures*; since Paul Valéry, this sentence has served as *the* example of cliché in the French novel. Cf. English: *Twas a dark and stormy night.*

** TN: *Il était arrivé:* By itself, the French remains ambiguous and could mean either the impersonal 'it had happened' or the personalized 'he had arrived' depending on whether the pronoun *il* is understood to be impersonal or to refer to someone.

Space or time or space-time are family names attributed to these situations. No element is common to all – Are you a nominalist? – No, resemblance may be established by the procedure for establishing the reality of a referent (Nos 63ff.) but not by 'use,' as Wittgenstein thinks, prey to anthropological empiricism. – But among the kinds of phrases required by this procedure, there is the ostensive, which makes use of spatio-temporal deictics, *over there, then*, etc.! – That only shows that metalanguage is part of ordinary language (Desclès and Guentcheva Descès 1977: 7).

123. Isn't your way of partitioning phrase universes anthropocentric and pragmatic? From where do you hold it that they entail four instances? – From the ways to link. Take the phrase *Ouch!* You link onto the addressor with *Are you in pain?*; onto the addressee with *I can't do anything about it*; onto the sense with *Does it hurt?*; onto the referent with *The gums are always very sensitive*. The instances are valences of linkage. – For human language perhaps, but what about a cat's tail? – You link onto the raised tail of a cat by, respectively: *What do you want?; You're bothering me; Hungry again?; They have very expressive tails*. I'm purposively choosing phrases where neither the instances nor their situation is marked. The partitioning is not pragmatic if the presupposition or prejudice of pragmatics is that a message goes from an addressor to an addressee each of whom would 'exist' without it. Nor is it humanist: try to come up with nonhuman entities who could not occupy one or another of these instances! It is rare perhaps for all of the instances to be marked. (Many modern literary techniques are tied to the de-marcating of instances: the addressor in *In Remembrance of Things Past*, the addressee in Butor's *La modification*, both addressor and addressee in Derrida's *La carte postale*, the referent in Claude Simon's *Les Géorgiques*, the sense in Robert Pinget's *L'apocryphe*, to mention recent French examples alone. And the presumed author (Puech 1982). This de-marcating has the effect of making the phrases take place *sponte sua:* a critique of the prejudice that it is 'man' who speaks. 'Love of phrases, unlove of people.' 'His having always loved phrases is not, as far as I'm concerned, to his credit but I don't know my judgment to be infallible' (Pinget 1980: 149, 57).)

124. The presentation entailed by a phrase is forgotten by it, plunged into the river Lethe (Detienne 1967: 126–35). Another phrase pulls it back out and presents it, oblivious to the presentation that it itself entails. Memory is doubled by oblivion. Metaphysics struggles against oblivion, but what is whatever struggles for oblivion called?

125. Augustine's God or Husserl's Living Present is presented as the name borne by the instance that synthesizes the nows. It is presented, though, by means of the phrases in which it is presented, and the now of each of these phrases then remains to be synthesized with the others, in a new phrase. God is for later, 'in a moment'; the Living Present is to come. These only come by

not arriving. Which is what Beckett signifies. Time is not what is lacking to consciousness, time makes consciousness lack itself.

126. You qualify presentation, entailed by a phrase, as *absolute*. By qualifying it in this way, you are presenting it. Its quality as absolute is situated in the universe presented by your phrase, and is relative to it. This is why the absolute is not presentable. With the notion of the sublime (and on the condition that *Darstellung* be understood as we have here), Kant will always get the better of Hegel. The *Erhabene* persists, not over and beyond, but right in the heart of the *Aufgehobenen*.

127. What is not presented is not. The presentation entailed by a phrase is not presented, it is not. Or: Being is not. One could say that when an entailed presentation is presented, it is not an entailed but a situated presentation. Or: Being grasped as an existent is non-Being. This is how the first chapter of the *Wissenschaft der Logik [Science of Logic]* should be understood. What Hegel calls determination and which is the mainspring of the passage from Being to non-Being is the situation of Being (or of presentation) in a phrase universe, that is, the passage from the presentation entailed by the first phrase to the presentation (of the first phrase) presented by the second phrase. This 'disintegration' (the passage from Being to existent or non-Being) only works, however, if the stakes of the second phrase are to present the presentation; that is, if the stakes of this second phrase are those of the genre of ontological discourse. One of the rules constitutive of the genre prescribes a linkage of this kind and the resulting passage or disintegration: the rule of the *Resultat* (Hegel Notice). There are many genres of discourse, though, whose stakes as prescribed by their rules do not involve presenting the presentation, and where 'disintegration' is consequently not necessary.

128. This is why negation is needed to present the entailed presentation. It is only presentable as an existent, that is, as non-Being. This is what the word *Lethe* means.

129. The argument 'that the unknown can be known, on the ground that it can be known to be unknown' (*Epistèton to agnôston, ésti gar épistèton to agnôston hoti agnôston*) is classed by Aristotle (*Rhetoric*: 1402 a) among the apparent enthymemes. He says it is a paralogism in which the absolute and the relative are confused (through a mistake or a ruse that he attributes to Antisthenes). The argument in effect resorts to insisting upon the presentation ('can be known,' the absolute) all the way up to asserting what is unpresented (what is unsignified, 'the unknown'), which is presented by the phrase *that the unknown . . .*, and which is therefore relative to it. To call this linkage a paralogism, though, is a decision constitutive of the genre of logical discourse, which is not concerned with the *quod* (No. 91).

130. The faculty of presenting for a single referent, its sense and the contrary (negation) of its sense (for the unknown, the sense of the unknown and the sense

of the known; for Being, the sense of Being and the sense of non-Being) should not be called *die ungeheure Macht des Negativen*, the portentous power of the negative, as Hegel does (*PhG*, Preface: 93). If there is a power, where is it? In a phrase's ability to present a property as lacking in its referent? That's (only. . .) 'the mystery of negation' (Wittgenstein, *TB*: 9, 15. 11. 1914) (No. 90). – In a phrase's ability to present a property as simultaneously present and absent? But such is not the case: one phrase presents it as present, another phrase presents it as absent. This is not 'at one and the same time.' – In the ability of two phrases relating to the same referent to say something and its contrary about it? But it needs to be established that this concerns the same referent (Nos. 68, 80). In this last case, what is portentous does not come from the negative, but from the *Ereignis*. For it could be that there were no 'second' phrase. The impossible, nothingness would be possible. What is portentous is that it is not so.

131. 'Every phrase is' Is everything which is, a phrase? *Is* is not *which is*. Nor is *is*, for that matter, *is real*. It cannot be said that *Every phrase is real*. Even less so, that *Everything rational is real*. Reality is a property of a referent that remains to be established (Referent Section), it is not. This includes the reality of a phrase. That everything real is rational, yes, that can be said if *rational* signifies: in conformity with the procedure for establishing the reality of a referent. – In *Every phrase is*, *every phrase* signifies *everything which happens*; *is* signifies *there is, it happens*. But *It happens* is not what happens, in the sense that *quod* is not *quid* (in the sense that the presentation is not the situation). *Is* does not therefore signify *is there*, and even less so does it signify *is real*. *Is* doesn't signify anything, it would designate the occurrence 'before' the signification (the content) of the occurrence. It would designate it, but it does not designate it, since by designating it it situates it ('before' signification), and thereby occults *nun* in *hústeron protéron* (Aristotle Notice). Rather *is* would be: *Is it happening?* (the *it* indicating an empty place to be occupied by a referent).

132. In sum, there are events: something happens which is not tautological with what has happened. Would you call what happens *the case*? – The case, *der Fall*, would be that something happens, *quod*, rather than what happens, *quid*. – Would you say that 'the world is all that [which] is the case (*alles, was der Fall ist*),' as Wittgenstein does? – We could if we distinguished between *the case* and *that which is the case*. Wittgenstein also calls a fact (*Tatsache*) that which is the case (*TLP*: 2). He can then write that 'the world is the totality (*die Gesamtheit*) of facts' (1. 1), or that 'the sum-total of reality (*die gesamte Wirklichkeit*) is the world' (2. 063). *Totality* and *all* are not themselves cases. They are referents of Ideas in the Kantian sense. Or else logical quantifiers. One cannot proceed to test the reality of the whole. – But the case is not that which is the case. The case is: *There is, It happens*. That is to say (No. 131): *Is it happening?*

133. There is no 'picture of the world' that 'we' would 'make' for ourselves (*TLP*: 2. 1). But the world as the whole of reality can be situated as an instance

in a universe presented by a (cosmological) phrase. It gives rise to the antinomies described by Kant. These reveal that the referent *world* is not an object of cognition, it eludes the test of reality. The concept of a picture (*Bild, eikón*) of facts condenses within itself the metaphysical illusion, the reversal or prejudice that phrases come after facts. In this sense, there is no representation. − By *world* (No. 60), I understand a network of proper names. No phrase can exhaust this network. No phrase can substitute a complete description for every name: 'For it seems—at least so far as I can see at present—that the matter is not settled by getting rid of names by means of definitions' (*TB*: 13. 5. 15).

134. 'You can't say everything' (Descombes, 1977). − Disappointed? Did you desire it? Or at least did something − 'language' − want it? Wanted to unfurl its full powers? A will? A 'life'? A desire, a lack? These are so many teleologies of fulfillment, or melancholias for the unfulfilled. − But you certainly accept (No. 23) that 'something asks to be put into phrases'? − This does not imply that *everything* ought to or wants to be said. This implies the expectant waiting for an occurrence, for the 'portentousness,' that indeed everything has not been said (No. 130). The vigil. This waiting is in the phrase universe. It is the specific 'tension' that every phrase regimen exerts upon the instances.

135. 'What we cannot speak about we must pass over in silence' (*TLP*: 7). − Is the *must* (*Il faut, muss man*) addressed to man? To Spirit? It is not in their power to pass over in silence what they cannot speak about. Insofar as it is unable to be phrased in the common idioms, it is already phrased, as feeling. The avowal has been made. The vigil for an occurrence, the anxiety and the joy of an unknown idiom, has begun. To link is not a duty, which 'we' can be relieved of or make good upon. 'We' cannot do otherwise. Don't confuse necessity with obligation. If there is a *must* (*Il faut*), it is not a *You ought to* (*Vous devez*) (No. 102).

136. To link is necessary, but a particular linkage is not. This linkage can be declared pertinent, though, and the phrase that does the stating is a rule for linking. It is a constitutive part of a genre of discourse: after such and such a kind of phrase, here are those phrases that are permitted. The *Analytics* circumscribe in this way the genre of linkages for classical logic, the *Science of Logic* for modern dialectics, and the *Vorlesungen uber neuere Geometrie* [*Lectures in the New Geometry*] for modern axiomatics (Pasch in Blanché 1955: 20–2). There are many genres of discourse whose rules for linking are not stated.

137. A phrase can be formulated in such a way that it co-presents several universes. It can be equivocal, not only with regard to the sense, but also with regard to the referent, the addressor, or the addressee. For example: *I can come by your place.* Equivocation can affect *I, come by*, or *your*. Restricting ourselves to the modal *can*, here are some co-presented universes:

1.1 I have the ability to do it.
1.2 I have the time to do it.

1.3 You have a place and I know the address.
2   It's possible that I'll do it.
3.1 I desire to do it.
3.2 I desire that you tell me to do it.
4   I have permission to do it.

Ability (1), eventuality (2), wish (3), right (4). Description (1, 2, 4); representation (3.1) (in the sense of Habermas' 'representative' phrases (1971: 112):
I want, I fear, I desire that . . .); regulation (3.2) (as in: *I order you, I beg you, I promise
you to . . .*). Not only is the sense of *I can* equivocal, but its equivocalness is
passed on to the other instances: *your* is not the same if it is part of the described
referent or if it is the addressee of a prescription; the same goes for *I*.

138. A linkage may reveal an equivocalness in the previous phrase. *The door
is closed* can give rise to *Of course, what do you think doors are for?*, or to *I know,
they're trying to lock me in*, or to *All the better, I have to talk to you*, etc. In these
linkages, the closed door ceases to be a state of things to be discussed or verified.
It verifies the functionalist definition of doors given by an obsessive neurotic;
it confirms the tale a paranoiac tells about them, etc. Are we dealing with the
same door? With the same addressee, etc.? Let's suppose two interlocutors.
They talk about the closed door. One says: *Of course*, etc.; the other: *I know*, etc.
Here is a differend. The logician who would put order into their obscure
contention by saying, *It's only a matter of a simple description*, would merely add
to the differend. Some vignettes of these disorders along with their juridico-
political impacts can be found in La Fontaine's *Fables*. Which is the pertinent
linkage?

139. We suppose that the addressor of the subsequent phrase is 'the same' as
the addressee of the prior phrase. Couldn't it be said that the linkage is pertinent at least if the universe of the second phrase presents or co-presents anew,
and therefore re-presents, one of the universes presented by the first phrase?
For example, if you linked onto *I can come by your place* (No. 137) in version
(1.1) with *Can you walk?, Your car is fixed?*, or *You think so?* (= You really have
the ability of movement to do so?). In version (1.2) with *No, you won't have time,
Yes, it's very close to your place, You think so?* (= You really have the availability of
time to do so?). In version (1.3) with *But I was thrown out*. In version (2) with
That would surprise me, You think so? (= Is it even possible?). In version (3.1)
with *So you say* (= I don't believe in your desire to do so), *You think so?* (= Do
you have the desire?). In version (3.2) with *There's no need to* (= It's not my
desire), *As you wish* (= I don't have any desires about this matter). *You think so?*
(= Do you really want to know my desire?). In version (4) with *Oh good!, You
think so?* (= Was this permission really given to you?). This makes for a lot of
pertinences.

140. The addressee of the first phrase may link onto *I can come by your place*

with *How is Chantal?* Would we say that this is not a pertinent linkage? Ducrot would say (1977) that it is not pertinent if we stick to the presuppositions just examined; but it may be pertinent if we also admitted something understood [*sous-entendu*]: *I can come by your place, Chantal isn't there.* Pertinence supposes a 'good' rule for linking. There are a number of good rules for linking onto an equivocal phrase. It is here that the pragmatician (Engel 1981) gets tangled up in the question of the speakers' intentions, in order to save communication from its wreckage. The metaphysics of consciousness runs aground, though, upon the aporia of otherness: Husserl's fifth *Cartesian Meditation*. No matter what he or she says, the addressor of the linking phrase is situated in the universe presented by 'his' or 'her' phrase in a nonarbitrary way with relation to the phrase 'of the other.' Even *You think so?* is a way of linking without resolving the equivocalness: it is a question, and it suits every version of the first phrase. This way of linking is not entirely haphazard, it resorts to the interrogative at least.

141. But the context at least should allow us to decide what the addressor of the first phrase wanted to say and what the addressee, who is the addressor of the second phrase, would have had reason to understand . . . − The context needs to be presented, by means of phrases. This is what I have sketched out by presenting the co-presented universes. Or else, in invoking the context, your phrase situates you as the addressee in a cognitive universe in which the context is the addressor and informs you about itself. Why should you judge this addressor to be more credible than the addressor of the first phrase?

142. For example, the phrase *The meeting is called to order* is not performative because its addressor is the chairperson of the meeting. The addressor is the chairperson of the meeting to the extent that the phrase in question is performative. The equation chairmanship-performativity is independent of the context. If the phrase is performative and the addressor is not the chairperson, he or she becomes the chairperson; if it is not performative and the addressor is the chairperson, he or she ceases to be the chairperson. − Doesn't this alternative, though, at least depend upon the context? − The context is itself made of phrases linked onto the phrase in question. Onto a phrase like *The meeting is called to order*, such phrases as the following can be linked: *Okay, you chair the meeting* in the first case, or *No way*, or *By what right?*, in the second. − But doesn't the occurrence of these phrases depend, in turn, upon the context? − What you are calling the context is itself but the referent of cognitive phrases, those of the sociologist for example. The context is not an addressor. Positivism, in particular the positivism of the human sciences in general, resides in this confusion between context and referent and between context and addressor. With the notion of context, the floor is turned over to the object of the 'scientist' next door, as if this referent were an addressor.

143. Won't we know, though, anyway after the fact which universe was the

one really presented by the initial phrase? Won't the subsequent series of phrases decide the regimen of the first phrase? – The subsequent series will decide nothing (no more than 'history will tell if . . .'). If there is a decision, it comes from the genre of discourse wherein this series is 'led'. Imagine two opposite poles between which all the genres would be distributed. One of them, the discourse of cognition, stakes itself on leading the series toward clearing up the initial equivocation. The other, the discourse of the unconscious, stakes itself on maintaining this equivocation to the greatest extent possible. This is not to say that one of them is more or less faithful than the other to the 'essence' of language, nor that one is 'originary' and the other secondary. In the order of discourses, they are like tautology and contradiction in the order of propositions: the rational phrase presents the universe that it presents, the phrase of the passions co-presents incompossible universes.

144. You call them incompossible (No. 143) because you are signifying them in relation to the discourse of cognition. Take Freud's analysis of the female fantasy which he entitles by the phrase '*Ein Kind wird geschlagen* [A child is being beaten].' The woman, that is to say, her name, is an addressee in the universe presented by this phrase (a troubled addressee: when the phrase takes place, there is masturbation). But she is also the referent: she is the beaten child. The instance of the referent, however, is also occupied by 'another child' beaten by the father. As for the father, he is instantiated as a reference, but he is also not instantiated at all (he is effaced). And who is the addressor presented in these mixed universes? That addressor is never marked in the phrase or phrases. Would it be the big Other, according to Lacanian metaphysics? The incompossibles, as you see, coexist marvelously. – Yes, but they form a symptom. – They form an idiolect, to speak the language of Wittgenstein. – And the masturbating? – A mode of the simultaneous occurrence of the incompossibles, like a dream, a blush, a cramp, an oversight, an illness, a silence, a feeling, alcohol, or drugs. Agitation, in other words, a leaping from one version to another within a single instant: Pierre Guyotat's *Prostitution* (1975).

145. But isn't the body real? – The body 'proper' is a name for the family of idiolects. It is, moreover, the referent of phrases obeying various regimens. *My teeth hurt*: this is a descriptive, paired with a co-presented request: *Relieve me of this*. The dentist turns your suffering into a case that verifies a cognitive phrase (by the three-phrase procedure: there it is; that there is called the neck of the tooth; chances are, it is a cavity in the neck of the tooth). In relation to this case, and by way of an answer to your request, the dentist prescribes certain actions proper to re-establishing your health (health being itself the object of an Idea). The same goes for other professionals of the 'body' *mutatis mutandis*: for the sports coach, for the sex therapist, for the culinary artist, for the dance or singing teacher, for the military instructor, the body is a set of symptoms read and treated on the basis of an Idea of the good body. – But the toothache is painful,

it's a lived experience, etc.! – How can you verify that it is lived experience? You are the exclusive addressee of this pain. It is like the voice of God: 'You can't hear God speak to someone else, you can hear him only if you are being addressed' (*Zettel:* § 717). Wittgenstein adds: 'That is a grammatical remark.' It circumscribes what an idiolect is: 'I'am alone in hearing it. The idiolect easily falls beneath the blows of the dilemma (No. 8): if your lived experience is not communicable, you cannot testify that it exists: if it is communicable, you cannot say that you are the only one able to testify that it exists.

146. At least grant that while phrases from ordinary language are equivocal, it is a noble task to seek out univocality and to refuse to entertain equivocation. – That's Platonic, at the very least. You are preferring dialogue to differend. You are presupposing, first of all, that univocality is possible; and second, that it constitutes the healthiness of phrases. But what if the stakes of thought (?) concerned differend rather than consensus? In its noble as well as in its ordinary genre? In its best of 'health' and at its most vigilant? This does not mean that equivocation is entertained. But, at the far end of univocality, something announces itself (through feeling) which that 'unique voice' cannot phrase.

147. From one phrase regimen (descriptive, cognitive, prescriptive, evaluative, interrogative . . .) to another, a linkage cannot have pertinence. It is not pertinent to link onto *Open the door* with *You have formulated a prescription*, or with *What a beautiful door!* This impertinence may be opportune, though, within a genre of discourse. A genre of discourse determines what is at stake in linking phrases (Nos 178ff.): to persuade, to convince, to vanquish, to make laugh, to make cry, etc. It may be opportune to link onto the chain in a non-pertinent way in order to achieve one or another of these effects. Teleology begins with genres of discourse, not with phrases. Insofar, though, as they are linked together, phrases are always caught up in one (or at least one) genre of discourse.

148. The stakes bound up with a genre of discourse determine the linkings between phrases. They determine them, however, only as an end may determine the means: by eliminating those that are not opportune. One will not link onto *To arms!* with *You have just formulated a prescription*, if the stakes are to make someone act with urgency. One will do it if the stakes are to make someone laugh. But there are many other means to achieve an end. The idea of seduction needs to be extended. A genre of discourse exerts a seduction upon a phrase universe. It inclines the instances presented by this phrase toward certain linkings, or at least it steers them away from other linkings which are not suitable with regard to the end pursued by this genre. It is not the addressee who is seduced by the addressor. The addressor, the referent, and the sense are no less subject than the addressee to the seduction exerted by what is at play in a genre of discourse.

149. An offense is not an impertinence, just as a wrong is not the damages

(No. 41). An offense is the hegemony of one phrase regimen over another, the usurpation of its authority. *Open the door.* – You said to open the door, you have thus formulated a prescription. A discussion ensues in order to know if this is the case (the definition of a prescription, the conformity of the command with this definition, etc.), Suppose that it is the case. *You have formulated a prescription* is then a validated phrase. It attributes a property to *Open the door*, that of being a prescription. Impertinence is to link onto the command by a commentary on the command, and not by its execution. An offense would be for the commentator of the command, who is also the addressee of the command, to say: 'I have under stood which phrase family *Open the door* belongs to, and I am by that fact therefore acquitted of this command.' This is the speculative, and in general the metalinguistic, offense (No. 45).

150. The wrong implied in the last judgment: *After what I have just said, there is nothing else to say.* – But you are saying it! What are you adding to what has previously been said by declaring that there is nothing more to add? You are adding either that the preceding phrase was the last phrase, or else that the phrases to come after your 'last' phrase will be tautologies of prior phrases. The first explanation is non-sense (the after-the-last); the second requires demonstrating that there is no new phrase to come. As for this demonstration, two things come down to one: either the demonstration is not made of tautologies of prior phrases, or else it is. In the first case, it refutes *de facto* what it establishes *de jure*; in the second, the demonstration has then already been done before it has been done. – And how do you know that it hasn't already been done? – I know only that what has not already been done is to demonstrate that it has already been done. And this demonstration will then refute *de facto* what it establishes *de jure*.

151. How can a phrase offend a phrase, or do it wrong? Do phrases have honor, or pride? An anthropomorphism: now, it's your turn? – In simple terms you never know *what* the *Ereignis* is. A phrase, in which idiom? In which regimen? The wrong is still in anticipating it, that is, in prohibiting it.

EN: For reason of space we have here omitted the Kant, Gertrude Stein and Aristotle 'notices' from this chapter of *The Differend*. In the original they occur after paragraphs 98, 104 and 119 respectively. We have preserved Lyotard's references (e.g. (April 1981)), as they are an essential philosophical aspect of the text. Full bibliographic details are given in *The Differend*.

Chapter 4

The Postmodern Condition, chapters 10–12

10. Delegitimation

In contemporary society and culture – postindustrial society, postmodern culture[1] – the question of the legitimation of knowledge is formulated in different terms. The grand narrative has lost its credibility, regardless of what mode of unification it uses, regardless of whether it is a speculative narrative or a narrative of emancipation.

The decline of narrative can be seen as an effect of the blossoming of techniques and technologies since the Second World War, which has shifted emphasis from the ends of action to its means; it can also be seen as an effect of the redeployment of advanced liberal capitalism after its retreat under the protection of Keynesianism during the period 1930–60, a renewal that has eliminated the communist alternative and valorized the individual enjoyment of goods and services.

Anytime we go searching for causes in this way we are bound to be disappointed. Even if we adopted one or the other of these hypotheses, we would still have to detail the correlation between the tendencies mentioned and the decline of the unifying and legitimating power of the grand narratives of speculation and emancipation.

It is, of course, understandable that both capitalist renewal and prosperity and the disorienting upsurge of technology would have an impact on the status of knowledge. But in order to understand how contemporary science could have been susceptible to those effects long before they took place, we must first locate the seeds of 'delegitimation'[2] and nihilism that were inherent in the grand narratives of the nineteenth century.

First of all, the speculative apparatus maintains an ambigious relation to knowledge. It shows that knowledge is only worthy of that name to the extent that it reduplicates itself ('lifts itself up;' *hebt sich auf;* is sublated) by citing its own statements in a second-level discourse (autonymy) that functions to legitimate them. This is as much as to say that, in its immediacy, denotative discourse bearing on a certain referent (a living organism, a chemical property, a physical phenomenon, etc.) does not really know what it thinks it knows. Positive science is not a form of knowledge. And speculation feeds on its suppression. The Hegelian speculative narrative thus harbors a certain skepticism toward positive learning, as Hegel himself admits.[3]

A science that has not legitimated itself is not a true science; if the discourse that was meant to legitimate it seems to belong to a prescientific form of knowledge, like a 'vulgar' narrative, it is demoted to the lowest rank, that of an ideology or instrument of power. And this always happens if the rules of the science game that discourse denounces as empirical are applied to science itself.

Take for example the speculative statement: 'A scientific statement is knowledge if and only if it can take its place in a universal process of engendering.' The question is: Is this statement knowledge as it itself defines it? Only if it can take its place in a universal process of engendering. Which it can. All it has to do is to presuppose that such a process exists (the Life of spirit) and that it is itself an expression of that process. This presupposition, in fact, is indispensable to the speculative language game. Without it, the language of legitimation would not be legitimate; it would accompany science in a nosedive into nonsense, at least if we take idealism's word for it.

But this presupposition can also be understood in a totally different sense, one which takes us in the direction of postmodern culture: we could say, in keeping with the perspective we adopted earlier, that this presupposition defines the set of rules one must accept in order to play the speculative game.[4] Such an appraisal assumes first that we accept that the 'positive' sciences represent the general mode of knowledge and second, that we understand this language to imply certain formal and axiomatic presuppositions that it must always make explicit. This is exactly what Nietzsche is doing, though with a different terminology, when he shows that 'European nihilism' resulted from the truth requirement of science being turned back against itself.[5]

There thus arises an idea of perspective that is not far removed, at least in this respect, from the idea of language games. What we have here is a process of delegitimation fueled by the demand for legitimation itself. The 'crisis' of scientific knowledge, signs of which have been accumulating since the end of the nineteenth century, is not born of a chance proliferation of sciences, itself an effect of progress in technology and the expansion of capitalism. It represents, rather, an internal erosion of the legitimacy principle of knowledge. There is erosion at work inside the speculative game, and by loosening the weave of the encyclopedic net in which each science was to find its place, it eventually sets them free.

The classical dividing lines between the various fields of science are thus called into question – disciplines disappear, overlappings occur at the borders between sciences, and from these new territories are born. The speculative hierarchy of learning gives way to an immanent and, as it were, 'flat' network of areas of inquiry, the respective frontiers of which are in constant flux. The old 'faculties' splinter into institutes and foundations of all kinds, and the universities lose their function of speculative legitimation. Stripped of the responsibility for research (which was stifled by the speculative narrative), they limit themselves to the transmission of what is judged to be established knowledge, and through didactics they guarantee the replication of teachers rather than the production of researchers. This is the state in which Nietzsche finds and condemns them.[6]

The potential for erosion intrinsic to the other legitimation procedure, the emancipation apparatus flowing from the *Aufklärung*, is no less extensive than the one at work within speculative discourse. But it touches a different aspect. Its distinguishing characteristic is that it grounds the legitimation of science and truth in the autonomy of interlocutors involved in ethical, social, and political praxis. As we have seen, there are immediate problems with this form of legitimation: the difference between a denotative statement with cognitive value and a prescriptive statement with practical value is one of relevance, therefore of competence. There is nothing to prove that if a statement describing a real situation is true, it follows that a prescriptive statement based upon it (the effect of which will necessarily be a modification of that reality) will be just.

Take, for example, a closed door. Between 'The door is closed' and 'Open the door' there is no relation of consequence as defined in propositional logic. The two statements belong to two autonomous sets of rules defining different kinds of relevance, and therefore of competence. Here, the effect of dividing reason into cognitive or theoretical reason on the one hand, and practical reason on the other, is to attack the legitimacy of the discourse of science. Not directly, but indirectly, by revealing that it is a language game with its own rules (of which the a priori conditions of knowledge in Kant provide a first glimpse) and that it has no special calling to supervise the game of praxis (nor the game of aesthetics, for that matter). The game of science is thus put on a par with the others.

If this 'delegitimation' is pursued in the slightest and if its scope is widened (as Wittgenstein does in his own way, and thinkers such as Martin Buber and Emmanuel Lévinas in theirs)[7] the road is then open for an important current of postmodernity: science plays its own game; it is incapable of legitimating the other language games. The game of prescription, for example, escapes it. But above all, it is incapable of legitimating itself, as speculation assumed it could.

The social subject itself seems to dissolve in this dissemination of language games. The social bond is linguistic, but is not woven with a single thread. It is a fabric formed by the intersection of at least two (and in reality an indeterminate number) of language games, obeying different rules. Wittgenstein writes: 'Our language can be seen as an ancient city: a maze of little streets and squares, of old and new houses, and of houses with additions from various periods; and this surrounded by a multitude of new boroughs with straight regular streets and uniform houses.'[8] And to drive home that the principle of unitotality − or

synthesis under the authority of a metadiscourse of knowledge – is inapplicable, he subjects the 'town' of language to the old sorites paradox by asking:
'how many houses or streets does it take before a town begins to be a town?'[9]

New languages are added to the old ones, forming suburbs of the old town:
'the symbolism of chemistry and the notation of the infinitesimal calculus.'[10]
Thirty-five years later we can add to the list: machine languages, the matrices
of game theory, new systems of musical notation, systems of notation for non-
denotative forms of logic (temporal logics, deontic logics, modal logics), the
language of the genetic code, graphs of phonological structures, and so on.

We may form a pessimistic impression of this splintering: nobody speaks all
of those languages, they have no universal metalanguage, the project of the
system-subject is a failure, the goal of emancipation has nothing to do with
science, we are all stuck in the positivism of this or that discipline of learning,
the learned scholars have turned into scientists, the diminished tasks of research
have become compartmentalized and no one can master them all.[11] Speculative
or humanistic philosophy is forced to relinquish its legitimation duties,[12] which
explains why philosophy is facing a crisis wherever it persists in arrogating such
functions and is reduced to the study of systems of logic or the history of ideas
where it has been realistic enough to surrender them.[13]

Turn-of-the-century Vienna was weaned on this pessimism: not just artists
such as Musil, Kraus, Hofmannsthal, Loos, Schönberg, and Broch, but also the
philosophers Mach and Wittgenstein.[14] They carried awareness of and theoretical and artistic responsibility for delegitimation as far as it could be taken.
We can say today that the mourning process has been completed. There is no
need to start all over again. Wittgenstein's strength is that he did not opt for the
positivism that was being developed by the Vienna Circle,[15] but outlined in his
investigation of language games a kind of legitimation not based on performativity. That is what the postmodern world is all about. Most people have lost
the nostalgia for the lost narrative. It in no way follows that they are reduced to
barbarity. What saves them from it is their knowledge that legitimation can only
spring from their own linguistic practice and communicational interaction.
Science 'smiling into its beard' at every other belief has taught them the harsh
austerity of realism.[16]

11. Research and Its Legitimation through Performativity

Let us return to science and begin by examining the pragmatics of research. Its
essential mechanisms are presently undergoing two important changes: a multiplication in methods of argumentation and a rising complexity level in the
process of establishing proof.

Aristotle, Descartes, and John Stuart Mill, among others, attempted to lay down the rules governing how a denotative utterance can obtain its addressee's assent.[17] Scientific research sets no great store by these methods. As already stated, it can and does use methods the demonstrative properties of which seem to challenge classical reason. Bachelard compiled a list of them, and it is already incomplete.[18]

These languages are not employed haphazardly, however. Their use is subject to a condition we could call pragmatic: each must formulate its own rules and petition the addressee to accept them. To satisfy this condition, an axiomatic is defined that includes a definition of symbols to be used in the proposed language, a description of the form expressions in the language must take in order to gain acceptance (well-formed expressions), and an enumeration of the operations that may be performed on the accepted expressions (axioms in the narrow sense).[19]

But how do we know what an axiomatic should, or does in fact, contain? The conditions listed above are formal conditions. There has to be a metalanguage to determine whether a given language satisfies the formal conditions of an axiomatic; that metalanguage is logic.

At this point a brief clarification is necessary. The alternative between someone who begins by establishing an axiomatic and then uses it to produce what are defined as acceptable statements, and a scientist who begins by establishing and stating facts and then tries to discover the axiomatics of the language he used in making his statements, is not a logical alternative, but only an empirical one. It is certainly of great importance for the researcher, and also for the philosopher, but in each case the question of the validation of statements is the same.[20]

The following question is more pertinent to legitimation: By what criteria does the logician define the properties required of an axiomatic? Is there a model for scientific languages? If so, is there just one? Is it verifiable? The properties generally required of the syntax of a formal system[21] are consistency (for example, a system inconsistent with respect to negation would admit both a proposition and its opposite), syntactic completeness (the system would lose its consistency if an axiom were added to it), decidability (there must be an effective procedure for deciding whether a given proposition belongs to the system or not), and the independence of the axioms in relation to one another. Now Gödel has effectively established the existence in the arithmetic system of a proposition that is neither demonstrable nor refutable within that system; this entails that the arithmetic system fails to satisfy the condition of completeness.[22]

Since it is possible to generalize this situation, it must be accepted that all formal systems have internal limitations.[23] This applies to logic: the metalanguage it uses to describe an artificial (axiomatic) language is 'natural' or 'everyday' language; that language is universal, since all other languages can be translated into it, but it is not consistent with respect to negation – it allows the formation of paradoxes.[24]

This necessitates a reformulation of the question of the legitimation of knowledge. When a denotative statement is declared true, there is a presupposition that the axiomatic system within which it is decidable and demonstrable has already been formulated, that it is known to the interlocutors, and that they have accepted that it is as formally satisfactory as possible. This was the spirit in which the mathematics of the Bourbaki group was developed.[25] But analogous observations can be made for the other sciences: they owe their status to the existence of a language whose rules of functioning cannot themselves be demonstrated but are the object of a consensus among experts. These rules, or at least some of them, are requests. The request is a modality of prescription.

The argumentation required for a scientific statement to be accepted is thus subordinated to a 'first' acceptance (which is in fact constantly renewed by virtue of the principle of recursion) of the rules defining the allowable means of argumentation. Two noteworthy properties of scientific knowledge result from this: the flexibility of its means, that is, the plurality of its languages; and its character as a pragmatic game – the acceptability of the 'moves' (new propositions) made in it depends on a contract drawn between the partners. Another result is that there are two different kinds of 'progress' in knowledge: one corresponds to a new move (a new argument) within the established rules; the other, to the invention of new rules, in other words, a change to a new game.[26]

Obviously, a major shift in the notion of reason accompanies this new arrangement. The principle of a universal metalanguage is replaced by the principle of a plurality of formal and axiomatic systems capable of arguing the truth of denotative statements; these systems are described by a metalanguage that is universal but not consistent. What used to pass as paradox, and even paralogism, in the knowledge of classical and modern science can, in certain of these systems, acquire a new force of conviction and win the acceptance of the community of experts.[27] The language game method I have followed here can claim a modest place in this current of thought.

The other fundamental aspect of research, the production of proof, takes us in quite a different direction. It is in principle part of an argumentation process designed to win acceptance for a new statement (for example, giving testimony or presenting an exhibit in the case of judicial rhetoric).[28] But it presents a special problem: it is here that the referent ('reality') is called to the stand and cited in the debate between scientists.

I have already made the point that the question of proof is problematical since proof needs to be proven. One can begin by publishing a description of how the proof was obtained, so other scientists can check the result by repeating the same process. But the fact still has to be observed in order to stand proven. What constitutes a scientific observation? A fact that has been registered by an eye, an ear, a sense organ?[29] Senses are deceptive, and their range and powers of discrimination are limited.

This is where technology comes in. Technical devices originated as prosthetic aids for the human organs or as physiological systems whose function it is to receive data or condition the context.[30] They follow a principle, and it is the principle of optimal performance: maximizing output (the information or modifications obtained) and minimizing input (the energy expended in the process).[31] Technology is therefore a game pertaining not to the true, the just, or the beautiful, etc., but to efficiency: a technical 'move' is 'good' when it does better and/or expends less energy than another.

This definition of technical competence is a late development. For a long time inventions came in fits and starts, the products of chance research, or research as much or more concerned with the arts (*technai*) than with knowledge: the Greeks of the Classical period, for example, established no close relationship between knowledge and technology.[32] In the sixteenth and seventeenth centuries, the work of 'perspectors' was still a matter of curiosity and artistic innovation.[33] This was the case until the end of the eighteenth century.[34] And it can be maintained that even today 'wildcat' activities of technical invention, sometimes related to *bricolage*, still go on outside the imperatives of scientific argumentation.[35]

Nonetheless, the need for proof becomes increasingly strong as the pragmatics of scientific knowledge replaces traditional knowledge or knowledge based on revelation. By the end of the *Discourse on Method*, Descartes is already asking for laboratory funds. A new problem appears: devices that optimize the performance of the human body for the purpose of producing proof require additional expenditures. No money, no proof – and that means no verification of statements and no truth. The games of scientific language become the games of the rich, in which whoever is wealthiest has the best chance of being right. An equation between wealth, efficiency, and truth is thus established.

What happened at the end of the eighteenth century, with the first industrial revolution, is that the reciprocal of this equation was discovered: no technology without wealth, but no wealth without technology. A technical apparatus requires an investment; but since it optimizes the efficiency of the task to which it is applied, it also optimizes the surplus-value derived from this improved performance. All that is needed is for the surplus-value to be realized, in other words, for the product of the task performed to be sold. And the system can be sealed in the following way: a portion of the sale is recycled into a research fund dedicated to further performance improvement. It is at this precise moment that science becomes a force of production, in other words, a moment in the circulation of capital.

It was more the desire for wealth than the desire for knowledge that initially forced upon technology the imperative of performance improvement and product realization. The 'organic' connection between technology and profit preceded its union with science. Technology became important to contemporary knowledge only through the mediation of a generalized spirit of performativity. Even today, progress in knowledge is not totally subordinated to technological investment.[36]

Capitalism solves the scientific problem of research funding in its own way: directly by financing research departments in private companies, in which demands for performativity and recommercialization orient research first and foremost toward technological 'applications'; and indirectly by creating private, state, or mixed-sector research foundations that grant program subsidies to university departments, research laboratories, and independent research groups with no expectation of an immediate return on the results of the work — this is done on the theory that research must be financed at a loss for a certain length of time in order to increase the probability of its yielding a decisive, and therefore highly profitable, innovation.[37] Nation-states, especially in their Keynesian period, follow the same rule: applied research on the one hand, basic research on the other. They collaborate with corporations through an array of agencies.[38] The prevailing corporate norms of work management spread to the applied science laboratories: hierarchy, centralized decision making, teamwork, calculation of individual and collective returns, the development of saleable programs, market research, and so on.[39] Centers dedicated to 'pure' research suffer from this less, but also receive less funding.

The production of proof, which is in principle only part of an argumentation process designed to win agreement from the addressees of scientific messages, thus falls under the control of another language game, in which the goal is no longer truth, but performativity — that is, the best possible input/output equation. The State and/or company must abandon the idealist and humanist narratives of legitimation in order to justify the new goal: in the discourse of today's financial backers of research, the only credible goal is power. Scientists, technicians, and instruments are purchased not to find truth, but to augment power.

The question is to determine what the discourse of power consists of and if it can constitute a legitimation. At first glance, it is prevented from doing so by the traditional distinction between force and right, between force and wisdom — in other words, between what is strong, what is just, and what is true. I referred to this incommensurability earlier in terms of the theory of language games, when I distinguished the denotative game (in which what is relevant is the true/false distinction) from the prescriptive game (in which the just/unjust distinction pertains) from the technical game (in which the criterion is the efficient/inefficient distinction). 'Force' appears to belong exclusively to the last game, the game of technology. I am excluding the case in which force operates by means of terror. This lies outside the realm of language games, because the efficacy of such force is based entirely on the threat to eliminate the opposing player, not on making a better 'move' than he. Whenever efficiency (that is, obtaining the desired effect) is derived from a 'Say or do this, or else you'll never speak again,' then we are in the realm of terror, and the social bond is destroyed.

But the fact remains that since performativity increases the ability to produce proof, it also increases the ability to be right: the technical criterion, introduced on a massive scale into scientific knowledge, cannot fail to influence the truth criterion. The same has been said of the relationship between justice and performance: the probability that an order would be pronounced just was said to increase with its chances of being implemented, which would in turn increase with the performance capability of the prescriber. This led Luhmann to hypothesize that in postindustrial societies the normativity of laws is replaced by the performativity of procedures.[40] 'Context control,' in other words, performance improvement won at the expense of the partner or partners constituting that context (be they 'nature' or men), can pass for a kind of legitimation.[41] *De facto* legitimation.

This procedure operates within the following framework: since 'reality' is what provides the evidence used as proof in scientific argumentation, and also provides prescriptions and promises of a juridical, ethical, and political nature with results, one can master all of these games by mastering 'reality,' That is precisely what technology can do. By reinforcing technology, one 'reinforces' reality, and one's chances of being just and right increase accordingly. Reciprocally, technology is reinforced all the more effectively if one has access to scientific knowledge and decision-making authority.

This is how legitimation by power takes shape. Power is not only good performativity, but also effective verification and good verdicts. It legitimates science and the law on the basis of their efficiency, and legitimates this efficiency on the basis of science and law. It is self-legitimating, in the same way a system organized around performance maximization seems to be.[42] Now it is precisely this kind of context control that a generalized computerization of society may bring. The performativity of an utterance, be it denotative or prescriptive, increases proportionally to the amount of information about its referent one has at one's disposal. Thus the growth of power, and its self-legitimation, are now taking the route of data storage and accessibility, and the operativity of information.

The relationship between science and technology is reversed. The complexity of the argumentation becomes relevant here, especially because it necessitates greater sophistication in the means of obtaining proof, and that in turn benefits performativity. Research funds are allocated by States, corporations, and nationalized companies in accordance with this logic of power growth. Research sectors that are unable to argue that they contribute even indirectly to the optimization of the system's performance are abandoned by the flow of capital and doomed to senescence. The criterion of performance is explicitly invoked by the authorities to justify their refusal to subsidize certain research centers.[43]

12. Education and Its Legitimation through Performativity

It should be easy to describe how the other facet of knowledge – its transmission, or education – is affected by the predominance of the performativity criterion.

If we accept the notion that there is an established body of knowledge, the question of its transmission, from a pragmatic point of view, can be subdivided into a series of questions: Who transmits learning? What is transmitted? To whom? Through what medium? In what form? With what effect?[44] A university policy is formed by a coherent set of answers to these questions.

If the performativity of the supposed social system is taken as the criterion of relevance (that is, when the perspective of systems theory is adopted), higher education becomes a subsystem of the social system, and the same performativity criterion is applied to each of these problems.

The desired goal becomes the optimal contribution of higher education to the best performativity of the social system. Accordingly, it will have to create the skills that are indispensable to that system. These are of two kinds. The first kind are more specifically designed to tackle world competition. They vary according to which 'specialities' the nation-states or major educational institutions can sell on the world market. If our general hypothesis is correct, there will be a growth in demand for experts and high and middle management executives in the leading sectors mentioned at the beginning of this study, which is where the action will be in the years to come: any discipline with applicability to training in 'telematics' (computer scientists, cyberneticists, linguists, mathematicians, logicians . . .) will most likely receive priority in education. All the more so since an increase in the number of these experts should speed the research in other learning sectors, as has been the case with medicine and biology.

Secondly, and still within the same general hypothesis, higher learning will have to continue to supply the social system with the skills fulfilling society's own needs, which center on maintaining its internal cohesion. Previously, this task entailed the formation and dissemination of a general model of life, most often legitimated by the emancipation narrative. In the context of delegitimation, universities and the institutions of higher learning are called upon to create skills, and no longer ideals – so many doctors, so many teachers in a given discipline, so many engineers, so many administrators, etc. The transmission of knowledge is no longer designed to train an elite capable of guiding the nation towards its emancipation, but to supply the system with players capable of acceptably fulfilling their roles at the pragmatic posts required by its institutions.[45]

If the ends of higher learning are functional, what of its addressees? The student has changed already and will certainly change more. He is no longer a youth from the 'liberal elite,'[46] more or less concerned with the great task of social progress, understood in terms of emancipation. In this sense, the 'democratic' university (no entrance requirements, little cost to the student and even to society if the price per student is calculated, high enrollment),[47] which was modeled along the principles of emancipationist humanism, today seems to offer little in the way of performance.[48] Higher education is in fact already undergoing a major realignment, dictated both by administrative measures and by social demands (themselves rather uncontrolled) emanating from the new users; the tendency is to divide the functions of higher learning into two broad categories of services.

In its function of professional training, higher education still addresses itself to the young of the liberal elite, to whom it transmits the competence judged necessary by each profession. They are joined through one route or another (for example, institutes of technology) – all of which, however, conform to the same didactic model – by the addressees of the new domains of knowledge linked to the new techniques and technologies. They are, once again, young people who have yet to become 'active.'

Aside from these two categories of students, who reproduce the 'professional intelligentsia' and the 'technical intelligentsia,'[49] the remainder of the young people present in the universities are for the most part unemployed who are not counted as job seekers in the statistics, though they outnumber the openings in their disciplines arts and human sciences). Despite their age, they do in fact belong to the new category of the addressees of knowledge.

For in addition to its professionalist function, the University is beginning, or should begin, to play a new role in improving the system's performance – that of job retraining and continuing education.[50] Outside the universities, departments, or institutions with a professional orientation, knowledge will no longer be transmitted *en bloc*, once and for all, to young people before their entry into the work force: rather it is and will be served 'a la carte' to adults who are either already working or expect to be, for the purpose of improving their skills and chances of promotion, but also to help them acquire information, languages, and language games allowing them both to widen their occupational horizons and to articulate their technical and ethical experience.[51]

The new course that the transmission of knowledge is taking is not without conflict. As much as it is in the interests of the system, and therefore of its 'decision makers,' to encourage professional advancement (since it can only improve the performance of the whole), any experimentation in discourse, institutions, and values (with the inevitable 'disorders' it brings in the curriculum, student supervision and testing, and pedagogy – not to mention its sociopolitical repercussions) is regarded as having little or no operational value and is not given the slightest credence in the name of the seriousness of the system. Such experimentation offers an escape from functionalism; it should not be dismissed lightly since it was functionalism itself that pointed the way.[52] But it is safe to assume that responsibility for it will devolve upon extrauniversity networks.[53]

In any case, even if the performativity principle does not always help pinpoint the policy to follow, its general effect is to subordinate the institutions of higher learning to the existing powers. The moment knowledge ceases to be an end in itself – the realization of the Idea or the emancipation of men – its transmission is no longer the exclusive responsibility of scholars and students. The notion of 'university franchise' now belongs to a bygone era. The 'autonomy' granted the universities after the crisis of the late 1960s has very little meaning given the fact that practically nowhere do teachers' groups have the power to decide what the budget of their institution will be;[54] all they can do is allocate the funds that are assigned to them, and only then as the last step in the process.[55]

What is transmitted in higher learning? In the case of professional training, and limiting ourselves to a narrowly functionalist point of view, an organized stock of established knowledge is the essential thing that is transmitted. The application of new technologies to this stock may have a considerable impact on the medium of communication. It does not seem absolutely necessary that the medium be a lecture delivered in person by a teacher in front of silent students, with questions reserved for sections or 'practical work' sessions run by an assistant. To the extent that learning is translatable into computer language and the traditional teacher is replaceable by memory banks, didactics can be entrusted to machines linking traditional memory banks (libraries, etc.) and computer data banks to intelligent terminals placed at the students' disposal.

Pedagogy would not necessarily suffer. The students would still have to be taught something: not contents, but how to use the terminals. On the one hand, that means teaching new languages and on the other, a more refined ability to handle the language game of interrogation – where should the question be addressed, in other words, what is the relevant memory bank for what needs to be known? How should the question be formulated to avoid misunderstandings? etc.[56] From this point of view, elementary training in informatics, and especially telematics, should be a basic requirement in universities, in the same way that fluency in a foreign language is now, for example.[57]

It is only in the context of the grand narratives of legitimation – the life of the spirit and/or the emancipation of humanity – that the partial replacement of teachers by machines may seem inadequate or even intolerable. But it is probable that these narratives are already no longer the principal driving force behind interest in acquiring knowledge. If the motivation is power, then this aspect of classical didactics ceases to be relevant. The question (overt or implied) now asked by the professionalist student, the State, or institutions of higher education is no longer 'Is it true?' but 'What use is it?' In the context of the mercantilization of knowledge, more often than not this question is equivalent to: 'Is it saleable?' And in the context of power-growth: 'Is it efficient?' Having competence in a performance-oriented skill does indeed seem saleable in the conditions described above, and it is efficient by definition. What no longer makes the grade is competence as defined by other criteria like true/false, just/unjust, etc. – and, of course, low performativity in general.

This creates the prospect for a vast market for competence in operational skills. Those who possess this kind of knowledge will be the object of offers or even seduction policies.[58] Seen in this light, what we are approaching is not the end of knowledge – quite the contrary. Data banks are the Encyclopedia of tomorrow. They transcend the capacity of each of their users. They are 'nature' for postmodern man.[59]

It should be noted, however, that didactics does not simply consist in the transmission of information; and competence, even when defined as a perform-ance skill, does not simply reduce to having a good memory for data or having easy access to a computer. It is a commonplace that what is of utmost import-ance is the capacity to actualize the relevant data for solving a problem 'here and now,' and to organize that data into an efficient strategy.

As long as the game is not a game of perfect information, the advantage will be with the player who has knowledge and can obtain information. By defin-ition, this is the case with a student in a learning situation. But in games of perfect information,[60] the best performativity cannot consist in obtaining addi-tional information in this way. It comes rather from arranging the data in a new way, which is what constitutes a 'move' properly speaking. This new arrange-ment is usually achieved by connecting together series of data that were previ-ously held to be independent.[61] This capacity to articulate what used to be separate can be called imagination. Speed is one of its properties.[62] It is possible to conceive the world of postmodern knowledge as governed by a game of perfect information, in the sense that the data is in principle accessible to any expert: there is no scientific secret. Given equal competence (no longer in the acquisition of knowledge, but in its production), what extra performativity depends on in the final analysis is 'imagination,' which allows one either to make a new move or change the rules of the game.

If education must not only provide for the reproduction of skills, but also for their progress, then it follows that the transmission of knowledge should not be limited to the transmission of information, but should include training in all of the procedures that can increase one's ability to connect the fields jealously guarded from one another by the traditional organization of knowledge. The slogan of 'interdisciplinary studies,' which became particularly popular after the crisis of 1968 but was being advocated long before that, seems to move in this direction. It ran up against the feudalism of the universities, they say. It ran up against more than that.

In Humboldt's model of the University, each science has its own place in a system crowned by speculation. Any encroachment of one science into another's field can only create confusion, 'noise' in the system. Collaboration can only take place on the level of speculation, in the heads of the philosophers.

The idea of an interdisciplinary approach is specific to the age of delegitimation and its hurried empiricism. The relation to knowledge is not articulated in terms of the realization of the life of the spirit or the emancipation of humanity, but in terms of the users of a complex conceptual and material machinery and those who benefit from its performance capabilities. They have at their disposal no metalanguage or metanarrative in which to formulate the final goal and correct use of that machinery. But they do have brainstorming to improve its performance.

The emphasis placed on teamwork is related to the predominance of the performativity criterion in knowledge. When it comes to speaking the truth or prescribing justice, numbers are meaningless. They only make a difference if justice and truth are thought of in terms of the probability of success. In general, teamwork does in fact improve performance, if it is done under certain conditions detailed long ago by social scientists.[63] In particular, it has been established that teamwork is especially successful in improving performativity within the framework of a given model, that is, for the implementation of a task. Its advantages seem less certain when the need is to 'imagine' new models, in other words, on the level of their conception. There have apparently been cases where even this has worked,[64] but it is difficult to isolate what is attributable to the team setup and what derived from the individual talent of the team members.

It will be observed that this orientation is concerned more with the production of knowledge (research) than its transmission. To separate them completely is to fall into abstraction and is probably counterproductive even within the framework of functionalism and professionalism. And yet the solution toward which the institutions of knowledge all over the world are in fact moving consists in dissociating these two aspects of didactics – 'simple' reproduction and 'extended' reproduction. This is being done by earmarking entities of all kinds – institutions, levels or programs within institutions, groupings of institutions, groupings of disciplines – either for the selection and reproduction of professional skills, or for the promotion and 'stimulation' of 'imaginative' minds. The transmission channels to which the first category is given access can be simplified and made available on a mass scale, the second category has the privilege of working on a smaller scale in conditions of aristocratic egalitarianism.[65] It matters little whether the latter are officially a part of the universities.

But one thing that seems certain is that in both cases the process of delegitimation and the predominance of the performance criterion are sounding the knell of the age of the Professor: a professor is no more competent than memory bank networks in transmitting established knowledge, no more competent than interdisciplinary teams in imagining new moves or new games.

Notes

1. Certain scientific aspects of postmodernism are inventoried by Ihab Hassan in 'Culture, Indeterminacy, and Immanence: Margins of the (Postmodern) Age' *Humanities in Society* 1 (1978), 51–85.
2. Claus Mueller uses the expression 'a process of delegitimation' in *The Politics of Communication* (New York: Oxford University Press, 1973), p. 164.
3. 'Road of doubt . . . road of despair . . . skepticism,' writes Hegel in the preface to the *Phenomenology of Spirit* to describe the effect of the speculative drive on natural knowledge.
4. For fear of encumbering this account, I have postponed until a later study the exposition of this group of rules. [See 'Analyzing Speculative Discourse as Language-Game,' *The Oxford Literary Review* 4, no. 3 (1981), 59–67.]
5. Nietzsche, 'Der europäische Nihilismus' (MS. N VII 3); 'der Nihilism, ein normaler Zustand' (MS. W II 1); 'Kritik der Nihilism' (MS. W VII 3); 'Zum Plane' (MS. W II 1), in *Nietzsches Werke kritische Gesamtausgabe*, vol. 7, pts 1 and 2 (1887–9) (Berlin: De Gruyter, 1970). These texts have been the object of a commentary by K. Ryjik, *Nietzsche, le manuscrit de Lenzer Heide* (typescript, Département de philosophie, Université de Paris VIII [Vincennes]).
6. 'On the future of our educational institutions,' in *Complete Works* (note 35), vol. 3.
7. Martin Buber, *Ich und Du* (Berlin: Schocken Verlag, 1922) [Eng. trans. Ronald G. Smith, *I and Thou* (New York: Charles Scribner's Sons, 1937)], and *Dialogisches Leben* (Zürich: Müller, 1947); Emmanuel Lévinas, *Totalité et Infinité* (La Haye: Nijhoff, 1961) [Eng. trans. Alphonso Lingis, *Totality and Infinity: An Essay on Exteriority* (Pittsburgh: Duquesne University Press, 1969)], and 'Martin Buber und die Erkenntnis theorie' (1958), in *Philosophen des 20. Jahrhunderts* (Stuttgart: Kohlhammer, 1963) [Fr. trans. 'Martin Buber et la théorie de la connaissance,' in *Noms Propres* (Montpellier: Fata Morgana, 1976)].
8. *Philosophical Investigations*, sec. 18, p. 8.
9. Ibid.
10. Ibid.
11. See for example, 'La taylorisation de la recherche,' in *(Auto) critique de la science* (note 26), pp. 291–3. And especially D. J. de Solla Price, *Little Science, Big Science* ((New York: Columbia University Press, 1963), who emphasizes the split between a small number of highly productive researchers (evaluated in terms of publication) and a large mass of researchers with low productivity. The number of the latter grows as the square of the former so that the number of high productivity researchers only

really increases every twenty years. Price concludes that science considered as a social entity is 'undemocratic' (p. 59) and that 'the eminent scientist' is a hundred years ahead of 'the minimal one' (p. 56).

12. See J. T. Desanti, 'Sur le rapport traditionnel des sciences et de la philosophie,' in *La Philosophie silencieuse, ou critique des philosophies de la science* (Paris: Seuil, 1975).

13. The reclassification of academic philosophy as one of the human sciences in this respect has a significance far beyond simply professional concerns. I do not think that philosophy as legitimation is condemned to disappear, but it is possible that it will not be able to carry out this work, or at least advance it, without revising its ties to the university institution. See on this matter the preamble to the *Projet d'un institut polytechnique de philosophie* (typescript, Département de philosophie, Université de Paris VIII [Vincennes] 1979).

14. See Allan Janik and Stephan Toulmin, *Wittgenstein's Vienna* (New York: Simon & Schuster, 1973), and J. Piel, (ed.), 'Vienne début d'un siècle,' *Critique*, 339–40 (1975).

15. See Jürgen Habermas, 'Dogmatismus, Vernunft unt Entscheidung – Zu Theorie und Praxis in der verwissenschaftlichen Zivilisation' (1963), in *Theorie und Praxis* [*Theory and Practice*, abr. ed. of 4th German edn, trans. John Viertel (Boston: Beacon Press, 1971)].

16. 'Science Smiling into its Beard' is the title of ch. 72, vol. 1 of Musil's *The Man Without Qualities*. Cited and discussed by J. Bouveresse, 'La Problématique du sujet' (note 54).

17. Aristotle in the *Analytics* (ca. 330 BC), Descartes in the *Regulae ad directionem ingenii* (1641) and the *Principes de la philosophie* (1644), John Stuart Mill in the *System of Logic* (1843).

18. Gaston Bachelard, *Le Rationalisme appliqué* (Paris: Presses Universitaires de France, (1949); Michel Serres, 'La Réforme et les sept péchés,' *L'Arc* 42, Bachelard special issue (1970).

19. David Hilbert, *Grundlagen der Geometrie* (1899) [Eng. trans. Leo Unger, *Foundations of Geometry* (La Salle: Open Court, 1971)]. Nicolas Bourbaki, 'L'architecture des mathématiques,' in Le Lionnais, (ed.), *Les Grands Courants de la pensée mathématique* (Paris: Hermann, 1948); Robert Blanché, *L'Axiomatique* (Paris: Presses Universitaires de France, 1955) [Eng. trans. G. B. Keene, *Axiomatics* (New York: Free Press of Glencoe, 1962)].

20. See Blanché, *L'Axiomatique*, ch. 5.

21. I am here following Robert Martin, *Logique contemporaine et formalisation* (Paris: Presses Universitaires de France, 1964), pp. 33–41 and 122ff.

22. Kurt Gödel, 'Über formal unentscheidbare Sätze der Principia Mathematica und verwandter Systeme,' *Monatshefte für Mathematik und Physik* 38 (1931) [Eng. trans. B. Bletzer, *On Formally Undecidable Propositions of Principia Mathematica and Related Systems* (New York: Basic Books, 1962)].

23. Jean Ladrière, *Les Limitations internes des formalismes* (Louvain: E. Nauwelaerts, 1957).

24. Alfred Tarski, *Logic, Semantics, Metamathematics*, trans. J. H. Woodger (Oxford: Clarendon Press, 1956); J. P. Desclès and Z. Guentcheva-Desclès, 'Métalangue,

métalangage, métalinguistique,' *Documents de travail* 60–1 (Università di Urbino, January–February 1977).

25. *Les Eléments des mathématiques* (Paris: Hermann, 1940–). The distant points of departure of this work are to be found in the first attempts to demonstrate certain 'postulates' of Euclidian geometry. See Léon Brunschvicg, *Les Etapes de la philosophie mathématique*, 3rd edn (Paris: Presses Universitaires de France, 1947).

26. Thomas Kuhn, *Structure of Scientific Revolutions*.

27. A classification of logico-mathematical paradoxes can be found in F. P. Ramsey, *The Foundations of Mathematics and Other Logical Essays* (New York: Harcourt & Brace, 1931).

28. See Aristotle, *Rhetoric* 2. 1393a ff.

29. The problem is that of the witness and also of the historical source: is the fact known from hearsay or *de visu?* The distinction is made by Herodotus. See F. Hartog, 'Hérodote rapsode et arpenteur,' *Hérodote* 9 (1977), 55–65.

30. A Gehlen, 'Die Technik in der Sichtweise der Anthropologie', *Anthropologische Forschung* (Hamburg: Rowohlt, 1961).

31. André Leroi-Gourhan, *Milieu et techniques* (Paris: Albin-Michel, 1945), and *Le Geste et la parole, I, Technique et langage* (Paris: Albin-Michel, 1964).

32. Jean Pierre Vernant, *Mythe et pensée chez les Grecs* (Paris: Maspero, 1965), especially sec. 4, 'Le travail et la pensée technique' [Eng. trans. Janet Lloyd, *Myth and Society in Ancient Greece* (Brighton, Eng.: Harvester Press, 1980)].

33. Jurgis Baltrusaitis, *Anamorphoses, ou magie artificielle des effets merveilleux* (Paris: O. Perrin, 1969) [Eng. trans. W. J. Strachan, *Anamorphic Art* (New York: Abrams, 1977)].

34. Lewis Mumford, *Technics and Civilization* (New York: Harcourt, Brace, 1963); Bertrand Gille, *Historie des Techniques* (Paris: Gallimard, Pléiade, 1978).

35. A striking example of this, the use of amateur radios to verify certain implications of the theory of relativity, is studied by M. J. Mulkay and D. O. Edge, 'Cognitive, Technical, and Social Factors in the Growth of Radio-Astronomy,' *Social Science Information* 12, no. 6 (1973), 25–61.

36. Mulkay elaborates a flexible model for the relative independence of technology and scientific knowledge in 'The Model of Branching,' *The Sociological Review* 33 (1976): 509–26. H. Brooks, president of the Science and Public Committee of the National Academy of Sciences, and coauthor of the 'Brooks Report' (OCDE, June 1971), criticizing the method of investment in research and development during the 1960s, declares: 'One of the effects of the race to the moon has been to increase the cost of technological innovation to the point where it becomes quite simply too expensive . . . Research is properly speaking a long-term activity: rapid acceleration or deceleration imply concealed expenditure and a great deal of incompetence. Intellectual production cannot go beyond a certain pace' ('Les Etats-Unis ont-ils une politique de la science?' *La Recherche* 14 [1971]: 611). In March 1972, E. E. David, Jr., scientific adviser to the White House, proposing the idea of a program of Research Applied to National Needs (RANN), came to similar conclusions: a broad and flexible strategy for research and more restrictive tactics for development (*La Recherche* 21 (1972): 211).

37. This was one of the Lazarsfeld's conditions for agreeing to found what was to become the Mass Communication Research Center at Princeton in 1937. This produced some tension: the radio industries refused to invest in the project; people said that Lazarsfeld started things going but finished nothing. Lazarsfeld himself said to Morrison, 'I usually put things together and hoped they worked.' Quoted by D. Morrison, 'The Beginning of Modern Mass Communication Research,' *Archives européeennes de sociologie* 19, no. 2 (1978): 347–59.

38. In the United States, the funds allocated to research and development by the federal government were, in 1956, equal to the funds coming from private capital; they have been higher since that time (OCDE, 1956).

39. Robert Nisbet, *Degradation*, ch. 5, provides a bitter description of the penetration of 'higher capitalism' into the university in the form of research centers independent of departments. The social relations in such centers disturb the academic tradition. See too in *(Auto) critique de la science*, the chapters 'Le prolétariat scientifique' 'Les chercheurs,' 'La Crise des mandarins.'

40. Niklas Luhmann, *Legitimation durch Verfahren* (Neuweid: Luchterhand, 1969).

41. Commenting on Luhmann, Mueller writes, 'In advanced industrial society, legal-rational legitimation is replaced by a technocratic legitimation that does not accord any significance to the beliefs of the citizen or to morality per se' (*Politics of Communication* [note 2], p. 135). There is a bibliography of German material on the technocratic question in Habermas, *Theory and Practice*.

42. Gilles Fauconnier gives a linguistic analysis of the control of truth in 'Comment contrôler la vérité? Remarques illustrées par des assertions dangereuses et pernicieuses en tout genre,' *Actes de la recherche en sciences sociales* 25 (1979): 1–22.

43. Thus in 1970 the British University Grants Committee was 'persuaded to take a much more positive role in productivity, specialization, concentration of subjects, and control of building through cost limits' [*The Politics of Education: Edward Boyle and Anthony Crosland in Conversation with Maurice Kogan* (Harmondsworth, Eng.: Penguin, 1971), p. 196]. This may appear to contradict declarations such as that of Brooks, quoted above (note 36). But (1) the 'strategy' may be liberal and the 'tactics' authoritarian, as Edwards says elsewhere; (2) responsibility within the hierarchy of public authorities is often taken in its narrowest sense, namely the capacity to answer for the calculable performance of a project; (3) public authorities are not always free from pressures from private groups whose performance criterion is immediately binding. If the chances of innovation in research cannot be calculated, then public interest seems to lie in aiding all research, under conditions other than that of efficiency assessment after a fixed period.

44. During the seminars run by Lazarsfeld at the Princeton Radio Research Center in 1939–40, Laswell defined the process of communication in the formula, 'Who says what to whom in what channel with what effect?' See D. Morrison, 'Beginning.'

45. This is what Parsons defines as 'instrumental activism' and glorifies to the point of confusing it with 'cognitive rationality': 'The orientation of cognitive rationality is implicit in the common culture of instrumental activism but it only becomes more or less explicit and is more highly appreciated among the educated classes and the intellectuals by whom it is more evidently applied in their occupational pursuits'

[Talcott Parsons and Gerald M. Platt, 'Considerations on the American Academic Systems,' *Minerva* 6 (Summer 1968): 507; cited by Alain Touraine, *Université et société*, p. 146].

46. What Mueller terms the *professional intelligentsia*, as opposed to the *technical intelligentsia*. Following John Kenneth Galbraith, he describes the alarm and resistance of the professional intelligentsia in the face of technocratic legitimation (*Politics of Communication* [note 2], pp. 172–7).

47. At the beginning of the academic year 1970–1, 30–40% of 19-year-olds were registered in higher education in Canada, the United States, the USSR, and Yugoslavia, and about 20% in Germany, France, Great Britain, Japan, and the Netherlands. In all of these countries, the number had doubled or tripled since 1959. According to the same source (M. Devèze, *Histoire contemporaine de l'université* (Paris: SEDES, 1976), pp. 439–40), the proportion of students in the total population had increased from about 4% to about 10% in Western Europe, from 6.1% to 21.3% in Canada, and from 15.1% to 32.5% for the United States.

48. In France, the total higher education budget (not counting the CNRS) increased from 3,075 million francs in 1968 to 5,454 million in 1975, representing a decrease from about 0.55% to 0.39% of the GNP. Increases in absolute figures came in the areas of salaries, operating expenses, and scholarships; the amount for research subsidies remained more or less the same (Devèze, *Histoire*, pp. 447–50). E. E. David states that the demand for Ph.D.s in the 1970s was scarcely higher than in the 1960s (p. 212 [see note 36]).

49. In Mueller's terminology, *Politics of Communication* (note 2).

50. This is what J. Dofny and M. Rioux discuss under the rubric 'cultural training.' See 'Inventaire et bilan de queiques expériences d'intervention de l'université,' in *L'Université dans son milieu: action et responsabilité* (AUPELF conference, Université de Montréal, 1971), pp. 155–62. The authors criticize what they call the two types of Northern American universities: the liberal arts colleges, in which teaching and research are entirely divorced from social demand, and the 'multiversity,' which is willing to dispense any teaching the community is prepared to pay for. On this last system, see Clark Kerr, *The Uses of the University: With a Postscript – 1972* (Cambridge, Mass.: Harvard University Press, 1972). Moving in a similar direction, but without the interventionism of the university in society recommended by Dofny and Rioux, see the description of the university of the future given by M. Alliot during the same conference: 'Structures optimales de l'institution universitaire,' ibid., pp. 141–54. M. Alliot concludes: 'We believe in structures, when there really ought to be as few structures as possible.' This was the goal of the Centre expérimental, subsequently Université de Paris VIII (Vincennes), as declared at its founding in 1968. See for this, the dossier *Vincennes ou le désir d'apprendre* (Paris: Alain-Moreau, 1979).

51. It is the author's personal experience that this was the case with a large number of departments at Vincennes.

52. The higher education reform law of 12 November 1968, numbers continuing education (conceived in a professionalistic sense) among the duties of higher education, which 'should be open to former students and to those who have not been

able to study, in order to allow them to increase their chances of promotion or change occupations, according to their abilities.'

53. In an interview with *Télé-sept-jours* 981 (17 March 1979), the French minister of Education, who had officially recommended the series *Holocaust* broadcast on Channel 2 to public school students (an unprecedented step), declared that the education sector's attempt to create for itself an autonomous audiovisual tool has failed and that 'the first task of education is to teach children how to choose their programs' on television.

54. In Great Britain, where the State's contribution to the capital outlays and operating expenses of the universities increased from 30% to 80% between 1920 and 1960, it is the University Grants Committee, attached to the Ministry of State for Science and Universities, which distributes the annual subsidy after studying the needs and development plans presented by the universities. In the United States the trustees are all-powerful.

55. In France, that means distributing among the departments the funds earmarked for operating expenses and equipment. Instructors only have power over salaries in the case of temporary personnel. Financing for projects and administrative reorganization, etc., is taken from the overall teaching budget allocated to the university.

56. Marshall McLuhan, *Essays* (Montreal: Hartubise Ltd., 1977); P. Antoine, 'Comments' informer?' *Projet* 124 (1978), 395–413.

57. It is well known that the use of intelligent terminals is taught to school children in Japan. In Canada they are used regularly by isolated university and college departments.

58. This policy has been pursued by American research centers since before the Second World War.

59. Nora and Minc (*L'Informatisation de la société*, p. 16) write: 'The major challenge for the advanced poles of humanity in the coming decades is no longer that of mastering matter – such mastery is already assured. The challenge is rather that of constructing a network of links allowing information and organization to move forward together.'

60. Anatol Rapoport, *Fights, Games, and Debates* (Ann Arbor: University of Michigan Press, 1960).

61. This is Mulkay's Branching Model (see note 36). Gilles Deleuze has analyzed events in terms of the intersection of series in *Logique du sens* (Paris: Editions de Minuit, 1969) and *Différence et répétition* (Paris: Presses Universitaires de France, 1968).

62. Time is a variable in the determination of the power factor in dynamics. See also Paul Virilio, *Vitesse et politique* (Paris: Galilee, 1976) [Eng. trans. *Speed and Politics* (New York: Semiotexte, forthcoming)].

63. Jacob L. Moreno, *Who shall survive?*, rev. edn (Beacon, N.Y.: Beacon House, 1953).

64. Among the best known are: the Mass Communication Research Center (Princeton); the Mental Research Institute (Palo Alto); the Massachusetts Institute of Technology (Boston); Institut für Sozialforschung (Frankfurt). Part of Clark Kerr's argument in favor of what he calls the Ideapolis is based on the principle that collective research increases inventiveness (*Uses of the University*, pp. 91ff.).

65. Solla Price, *Little Science, Big Science* (note 11), attempts to found a science of

science. He establishes the (statistical) laws of science as a social object. I have already referred to the law of undemocratic division in note 11. Another law, that of 'invisible colleges' describes the effect of the increasing number of publications and the saturation of information channels in scientific institutions: the 'aristocrats' of knowledge are tending to react to this by setting up stable networks of inter-personal contact involving at most about a hundred selected members. Diana Crane has provided a sociometric analysis of these colleges in *Invisible Colleges* (Chicago and London: University of Chicago Press, 1972). See Lécuyer, 'Bilan et perspectives'.

Chapter 5

The Affect-phrase (from a Supplement to The Differend*)*

1. Is feeling a phrase? And if it is, to what sort or family of phrases does it belong? In §22 of *The Differend* we read: 'The differend is the unstable state and instance of language wherein something which must be able to be put into phrases cannot yet be. This state includes silence, which is a negative phrase, but it also calls upon phrases which are in principle possible. This state is signalled by what one ordinarily calls a feeling. "One cannot find the words", etc.'[1] And in §105: 'The absence of a phrase (a silence, etc.) or the absence of a linkage (the beginning, the end, disorder, nothingness, etc.) are also phrases. What distinguishes these particular phrases from others? Equivocality, feeling, "wishes" (exclamation) etc.' It is not clear whether the feeling is a non-phrase, a negative phrase or a particular sort of phrase. Nor is it clear whether the feeling results from an impossibility of phrasing an event or, on the contrary, it is the cause of this deficiency. Do we remain silent because we are greatly moved, or find ourselves moved because the words are lacking and we are obliged to remain silent? – The question is badly formulated. It presupposes a relation of causality. It might be thought that this category is, in this instance, inapplicable.

2. Feeling is a phrase. I call it the affect-phrase. It is distinct in that it is *unarticulated.* – We read in *The Differend* that a phrase presents a universe (§§18, 25, etc.). A phrase universe is in principle (i.e. transcendentally) polarised according to two axes: the poles of addressor and addressee on the axis of address, the poles of meaning and referent on the semantico-referential axis (which Aristotle designates apophantic). According to the latter axis, something (a meaning) is phrased about the subject of something (a referent). According to the former axis, that of the address, this something (the meaning) is phrased by or in the name of something (the addressor) towards something (the addressee). We can say, in order to be brief, that the former connotes the semantic axis, the latter the pragmatic. A phrase universe is in principle arranged according to this double polarisation. A phrase is articulated to the extent that it presents a universe.

3. It is necessary to say that this double polarisation is a transcendental condition of the articulation of a phrase, rather than an empirical fact. Many given phrases neglect to mark this or that instance or such and such a relation between instances. They presuppose them or imply them. Such omissions are not, in general, obstacles to linking. On the contrary, it is the foreseeability of

linking (the rule of the genre) which makes them acceptable. The demand for an articulation that is as complete as possible characterises certain genres of discourse. The questions which actualise this demand are: What exactly are you talking about? How do you know what you have said; who told you? What exactly do you mean by . . . ? etc. One argues in response. In the cognitive genre, one seeks to establish not only *what* the referent, the addressor, the addressee and the meaning are, but also the *reality* of the first three, as well as the legitimacy of the linkages. Establishing these realities demands procedures which are specific to the cognitive genre and which link together groups of phrases bearing upon the meaning, upon the designation and upon the nomination.

4. In the 'Preface' to *The Differend* we read: 'A damage [*un dommage*] results from an injury done to the rules of a genre of discourse, but which is reparable according to those rules. A wrong [*un tort*] results from the fact that the rules of the genre of discourse according to which one judges are not those of the judged genre or genres of discourse'.[2] And further on, in §7: 'This is what a wrong would be: a damage accompanied by loss of the means to prove the damage'.

5. Many noteworthy characteristics follow from the fact that the affect-phrase is unarticulated. Here are three: (1) The affect-phrase appears not to allow itself to be linked on to according to the rules of any genre of discourse; on the contrary, it appears only to be able to suspend or interrupt linkages, whatever they are; (2) The affect-phrase injures the rules of the genres of discourse; it creates a damage; (3) This damage in its turn gives rise to a wrong, because the damage suffered by discourse can be settled within the rules, but argumentation is in all cases inappropriate to the affect-phrase, if it is true that it does not give rise to a genre and cannot be argued. Consequently the damage that the affect-phrase makes the genres of discourse suffer is transformed into a wrong suffered by the affect-phrase. – The articulated phrase and the affect-phrase can 'meet' only in missing each other. From their differend, there results a wrong. If articulation and inarticulation are irreducible to one another, this wrong can be said to be radical.

6. A phrase can be more or less articulated, its polarisations more or less marked. But the affect-phrase does not admit of these gradations. *Unarticulated* would signify: this phrase does not present a phrase universe; it signals the meaning; this meaning is only of one kind, pleasure and/or pain ('it's alright, it's not alright' ['*ça va, ça ne va pas*']); this meaning is not related to any referent: the 'it's alright' and the 'it's not alright' are no more attributes of an object than are the beautiful or the ugly; ultimately, this meaning does not proceed from any addressor (I) and does not address itself to any addressee (you). The signal that the affect-phrase is, is tautegorical: *aisthèsis, Empfindung*. The affect-phrase is at once an affective state (pleasure or pain) and the sign of this state; this is

what Kant said about aesthetic feeling. Equally Freud separated affects from representations of a thing or a word: they are testimonies, but testimonies that represent nothing to anyone.

7. One or more articulated phrases can take the affect-phrase as their reference. They can endow pleasure or pain with a referent: 'the spectacle of this misery was intolerable'; and place them upon the axis of destination: 'your friend's little comment was enough to get me down'. Thus the affect is attributed and addressed in the same way as a cognitive signification. – It appears that this transcription is inevitable, if only because within the order of discourse the affect-phrase is inopportune, unseemly, and even disquieting. Your joy, your suffering, will be shown, despite everything, to have been legitimate all along; they would only have been distressing because their 'logic' was misunderstood. It could almost be said that the affect-phrase demands to be articulated in this way, and even argued – as if the scandal that it causes for discourse was intolerable. Discourse does not appear to be able to support for long an unarticulated and unargued remnant remaining outside of its grasp.

8. Would it not be simpler just not to deal with affect-phrases? This appears to be easy since they are silences, and silence implies consent. Let's simply leave feeling to its mutism; 'You were too emotional, you didn't know what you were saying (or: you didn't know what to say); pull yourself together.' – We can neglect a particular feeling to the point of forgetting it. To this strategy of forgetting it is often objected that the feeling will come back. But how can we know that it is the same affect-phrase which returns, given that it cannot, unarticulated as it is, furnish any signs allowing it to be recognised? Could it be claimed that we can recognise a certain quality of melancholy or jubilation that we have experienced previously and elsewhere? This can be said, certainly, but it is not attestable. A question of 'private language', but also of time.

And why would a forgotten (repressed) feeling necessarily have to come back? Is it necessary to admit the hypothesis, hazy even in the eyes of Freud, of a repetition compulsion? Of an eternal return of the same?

9. The time of feeling is *now*. An actual feeling – joyful, nostalgic, a mixture of both – could come to be associated with the articulated phrase which refers to a joyful past. How are we to establish that the joyful present, for example, is the same as that which was experienced before? The feeling cannot be identified with itself by itself. It can only be experienced, as we say: it signals itself, it is tautegoric in the moment that it occurs. In order to be recognised as identical to itself through time, it must be chronologically localised. Chronology is one of the nominal systems necessary for the recognition that establishes the reality of a referent. Dated, the feeling is fixed as a reference of cognitive phrases: 'Do you remember the emotion that we experienced, on that particular day, when we first found this shore'? We can recall this emotion. That is not to say that we experience it again. We can actually experience an emotion in evoking

a past emotion. We could say that a feeling appears and disappears as a whole in an instant; that it is ageless.

10. We read in the *Nichomachean Ethics*: 'Just as the act of sight appears to be perfect [perfect, finite, *teleia*] at any moment . . . this also appears to be the case with pleasure. It is, so to speak, entire [complete, *holon ti*] and in no moment of its duration can one find a pleasure whose proper being [*eidos*] could be rendered more perfect [more final] by a prolongation of time' (X, 4, 1).[3] And further on: 'It is the *eidos* of pleasure to be finished, perfect at any moment [. . .]. It comes under that which is entire [complete] and final [. . .]. In contrast to movement, which cannot be conceived outside of time, pleasure owes nothing to duration. Because what is in the now is, so to speak, entire [complete]' (X, 4, 4). An analogous observation drawn from the clinic: the hysterical attack (phobic phrasing, for example) is each time brand new. 'Brand new each time' means: at each time the *jouissance*, pleasure and pain, what it is and what it signals, is complete. It awaits nothing.

11. We have to be careful about the 'each' of 'each time'. It is not within the remit of that which belongs only to the *now*. The 'each' demands memory and counted time, thus articulation. Aristotle writes of the pleasure-phrase that it is 'in the now'. We ought to say that it is now. It is the same for the 'in' as it is for the 'each'. If there is an inside of the now, there is also an outside, i.e. the before and the after, the *hystèron* and *prostèron* of the *Physics*. I am not saying that there is not. There are clocks. But even the now framed by the *no longer* and the *not yet* of the temporalising consciousness must not be confounded with the now of pleasure: the former is relative, it is a differential measure; the latter is absolute, a 'one' without two. – Such is the difficulty: to think the affect-phrase not outside of time, but outside of diachrony. *Pathèmata* do not know anything of the *dia-*.

12. How can you say that the affect-phrase is a phrase, considering that it is not articulated and does not present a phrase universe? – The ancient grammarians, who reserved the 'articulated voice' (*phônè énarthros*) for humans, conceded to animals a 'mixed (or confused) voice' (*phônè sunkékhuménè*). This employment has its source in the *Politics* of Aristotle: 'Alone amongst the animals, only man has discourse (*logos*). Without doubt, the voice (*phônè*) is the sign of pain and of pleasure; thus it belongs to the other animals' (1253 a 10). All animals, man included, have the *aisthèsis* of pain and pleasure, and the *phônè* by which they signal this *aisthèsis* to one another (*sèmainein allèlois*). The *logos*, reserved to human animals, which Aristotle also names *dialektos*, appears heterogeneous to the *phônè*: to it belongs the capacity 'to render manifest the useful and the harmful, and as a result of this the just and the unjust, and other similar things' (1253 a 15). It notably follows that a properly political community, where what is at stake is not only the signalling of pleasure and pain but also deliberating and deciding upon the useful and the just, requires this *phônè énarthros*, this articulated phrase, that is the *logos*.

13. There is, nevertheless, a communicability of pleasure and pain, of the *pathèmata*, without the mediation of the *logos*, by the 'confused voice' alone. Animals 'signal their feelings to one another', says Aristotle. Certain ones, like birds, even divide the unarticulated voice into distinct sonorities, which make 'a sort of *dialektos*' (*History of Animals*, 5335 a 27–8; I follow here the argument of Jean-Louis Labarrière in '*Imagination humaine et imagination animale chez Aristote*', *Phronèsis* 29, 1, 1984). – We know what stakes will come to be attached, in Kant, to this sentimental communication. We can call it *mute* if we recall that the root *mu* connotes the closed lips indicating that one remains silent or emitting a mute sound. From this root come *murmur*, *moo*, *mystery* and the low Latin *muttum* which has given us the French word, *mot*. This mute communication is made up of non-discrete inspirations and expirations of air: growlings, pantings, sighs. It spreads over the face and it spreads through the whole body which thus 'signals' like a face. The essence of the face considered negatively (referred to by an actually articulated phrase) is that its lips are mute. Thus it will be necessary to extend the *phônè* as far as the *gesture*.

14. Yet, even with birds and dolphins a continuous transition between *phônè* and *logos* cannot be found. It is written at the beginning of *De Interpretatione*: 'Even when inarticulate sounds (*agrammatoi psophoi*), such as the noises of the beasts, manifest something (*dèlousi ti*), none of them constitutes a name (*onoma*)' (2, 16 a 27–9). The name belongs to the voice that is divided into elements devoid of entirely conventional signification. It is this arbitrary sign that Aristotle calls the symbol. In contrast to the *phônè*, it has lost all immediate affective value.

15. Leaving the theory of language, which is not our concern, we follow rather the destiny of phrases. What happens to the *phônè*, the unarticulated phrase, when the *logos*, the articulated phrase, is at work? It is banished from human language. Barbara Cassin shows that, from Aristotle to K. O. Apel, the *logos* excludes *a priori* (transcendentally) all phrases and all genres of discourse which are not argumentative or, at least, arguable.[4] The exclusion of the *phônè*, of the affect-phrase, is the threshold of this exclusion: the *phônè* is not only unarguable, it is unarticulated. – Classically the process of exclusion is that of the dilemma: if the *phônè* belongs to language, it is articulable; if it claims not to be articulable ('my feeling is unsayable'), it at least argues this claim (just about what we are doing here), and thus places itself under the rule of the *dialektos*.

16. I will illustrate this procedure. Take the example of articulation that I have named the axis of destination. The affect-phrase is said to be non-destined. What would it be to respect its mutism with regard to its address? At the very least it would be to lend it one's ear. This is, notably, the Freudian rule of 'free-floating attention', sometimes spoken of as that of the 'the third ear'. 'Why aren't you saying anything to me?' In asking why this mutism is addressed to the person questioning it, the question articulates the silence by presupposing that it is at least addressed to the present interlocutor, the questioner. We call this presupposition

of address a request. The questioner asks: 'Why are you addressing your affect to me, without saying a word to me?' The questioner's request requires the mutism of the question to be addressed. Here the affect-phrase is transcribed into the pragmatic scheme. This, however, demands that phrases be articulated.

17. This transcription appears to be inevitable. It is called transference. The affect can *present* itself only by *situating* itself in the universe presented by an actual phrase. If it is not to remain the unattestable referent of a solely cognitive discourse, it must be actualised in the addressing [*la mise en adresse*] of what phrases itself now. – But, it will be asked, how is it possible to know that this present, transferential, address is indeed that of the affect? Is it not imaginary? 'You claim to love me or hate me, but your feelings are addressed to someone else'. Following the direction thus indicated, one would attempt to go back as far as a reputedly *initial* phrase universe, where the affect is supposed to arise along with its genuine address. Hence Freud searched for the 'primal scene'. He will renounce this. It is not only that one never stops passing through screen-memories (of imaginary addresses and referents); it is rather that the presupposition itself is false: the affect-phrase is not originarily sent to somebody. The capacity to feel pleasure and pain, affectivity, *aisthèsis*, is independent of its possible articulation. It does not await it (it is the *logos* which declares that it awaits it), it has no need of it in order to perfect itself (this is what Aristotle says). It is perhaps indifferent to articulation. This is why the latter *wrongs* it.

18. The *phônè* and the *logos* can only meet each other, and not link onto each other. This meeting gives rise to a differend. For the human animal at least this differend cannot be treated by litigation. Certainly, the human being is born, like all animals, well endowed with *aisthèsis* and *phônè*. But in contrast to other animals, excepting the domestic kind, it is born right in the middle of thousands of discourses, into the world of articulated phrases, and in contrast to domestic animals, it is granted to him to phrase in an articulate manner, after a certain time. This time before the *logos* is called *infantia*. It is the time of a *phônè* that only signifies affections, *pathèmata*, the pleasures and the pains of the moment, without relating them to an object taken as referent, nor to the couple addressor-addressee. Pleasure and pain are signalled with vocalisations (and I would add: with gestures – *The Différend*, §110) provoked by objects that are not objects of thought, under the regime of a 'narcissism' prior to all *ego*. This is what Freud has described under the two headings of polymorphous perversity and primary narcissism. – But this description (here mine, often that of Freud) remains anthropological. One would have to elaborate the transcendental status of *infantia*.

19. There is a *body* only as the referent of one or several cognitive phrases, attested to by the procedures for the establishment of reality. There are many sorts of body, according to the nature of the knowledge sought. Bodies, like existence, suppose the *logos*. Only the logical animal *has* a body. – The *phônè* does not have

a body since it is not referential. The pleasures and the pains experienced in the adventure of the *infans* are only attributed to the excitation of this or that erogenous zone by the articulated discourse of adults, which takes the organism as its reference. – It is necessary to elaborate the status of the world or of the incorporeal chaos associated with the affect, the status of the Thing. And since it is not referential, the *phônè* is not addressed, from which point one might conclude that the concourse of voices, their sharing, does not make up a community properly speaking (which requires addressors and addressees) but a sort of communicability or transitivity of affects without expectation of a return. Freud might have persisted in wanting to name this infantile affectivity *sexuality*, yet it is certain that it is completely ignorant of the polarisation linked to sexual difference.

20. The infantile *phônè* is innocent not because it has not committed an error or been seduced, but because the question of what is just and unjust is unknown to it given that this question demands the *logos*. This question is only posed with phrases that can present referents, addressors and addressees – that is, every instance necessary to the thought of distribution, equality, and the communicability of proper names on the instances of destination, which permit debate and argumentation. Childhood, like Adam, does not know that it is naked. And inasmuch as the *logos* conceals the *phônè* (covers or dresses it) rather than either suppressing or even domesticating it, this shameless innocence can always arise in the course of articulated phrases, in an impromptu manner. – But then one would make it ashamed of its nakedness. The impudence of the affect would be culpable. Innocence and culpability arrive together, under the name of anxiety.

Notes

This is a lecture delivered in January 1990 in Brussels under the title 'The Inarticulate or the Differend Itself' during the colloquium 'Rhetoric and Argumentation', organised by the European Centre for the Study of Argumentation. A first version of this text was published in the same year in the imprint of the University of Brussels, in a collection entitled *Rhetorical Figures and Conflicts*, edited by Michel Meyer and Alain Lempereur. The title chosen here corresponds to the name which Lyotard most recently gave this text.

1. Translator's note (TN): we have used G. Van Den Abbeele's translation for all quotations from *The Differend*.
2. TN: ibid. p. xi.
3. TN: for all quotations from Aristotle we have consulted the translations given in the bilingual Loeb Classical Library. We have, however, modified the translations in accordance with Lyotard's French where appropriate.
4. Compare B. Cassin, 'Parle si tu es homme', Introduction to *La Décision du sens: Livre Gamma de la Métaphysique d'Aristote* (Paris: Vrin, 1989).

Part II

Literature

Introduction: Literature

In the first of the Wellek Library Lectures, delivered at the University of California in 1986 and published under the title *Peregrinations: Law, Form, Event*, Lyotard recalls his youthful ambition to be a writer. He tells us that at around the age of fifteen he began to write poems and short stories; somewhat later he began a novel (Lyotard is not explicit about when, but the indications he gives suggest it was whilst he was at university), which he abandoned. By opening this series of lectures in which he was asked by the organisers to define his ' "position" in the field of criticism and the path that led to that position'[1] with a declaration of his youthful desire to be a writer, Lyotard makes clear the early and significant claim literature made on him. He never ceased to respond to that claim. Not only did Lyotard write on literary authors, and not only did he go on to write literary works – publishing two narrative-fictional texts in the late 1970s (*Récits tremblants* and *Le Mur du Pacifique*) – but his philosophical and political works are informed by his concern with literature and literary writing.

That this is the case is not due to the fact that Lyotard had a particular 'taste' for, or inclination towards, literature. The claim that literature made on him is a claim which, he argues, it makes on all thought. Lyotard sometimes expresses this by saying that literature seizes hold of thought, exerting a fascinating threat over it. What he means is that literary writing exceeds every attempt to explain it or interpret it and in so doing, rather than being laid claim to by thought, it comes to make a claim on thought. There is, then, in any attempt to say what a particular piece of writing means, a certain violence done to the literary work. We give voice to this when we complain that analysing a poem or a piece of writing spoils it. We are registering the doubt that any literary criticism can finally account for the impact and meaning of its object. However, the violence that we feel that literary criticism or analysis does to its object only masks another violence, which is that of literary work itself, since through literature the mastery that the mind supposes itself to have over language is undone.

The literary authors that are most important for Lyotard are the ones whose works most insistently expose the power of language to unsettle the self-assurance of the mind, writers whose writing troubles or disrupts the conventional ways in which language is used, and thus our habitual forms of understanding. Most often these are 'modern' writers, that is, late nineteenth and twentieth-century writers, such as the poet Stéphane Mallarmé (1842–98), and the novelists James Joyce (1882–1941), Franz Kafka (1883–1924), Samuel Beckett (1906–89) and Michel Butor (1926–). However, since Lyotard's focus is on the particular capacity of works of literature to exceed our ability to grasp them conceptually, the range of authors he refers to and writes about extends beyond such canonical writers to include, for example, the popular science-fiction writer Philip K. Dick (1928–82). It also reaches further back than literary modernism to include such authors as Laurence Sterne (1713–68), Denis Diderot (1713–84) and François Rabelais (c. 1494–1553).

In the late 1970s Lyotard came to identify such writing with what he called 'the postmodern', and it is important to note that in making this identification, Lyotard is not, as is sometimes supposed, referring to an historical period. As the list of writers mentioned above shows, instead of being a period in literary or artistic history that comes after 'modernism', for Lyotard the 'postmodern' refers to writing, or indeed art, that, no matter when it was written, inflicts a distortion on the materials, forms and structures of thought.

It is because of its unsettling capacity that for Lyotard literary writing plays an essential role in relation to philosophy. For this reason his readings of literary texts are nothing like conventional literary criticism. Lyotard is not concerned to say what a text means; he does not seek to account for the motivations of characters; and he does not seek to evaluate the literary merit of a work. Rather, he shows how literature touches upon fundamental philosophical questions. Here we should note a possible criticism, namely that Lyotard does not respect the literary integrity or specificity of the texts on which he reflects. Such a criticism is fundamentally mistaken, since Lyotard is not concerned to subordinate literature to philosophy, but to let literature or literary works pose questions to philosophy and ask questions of philosophy. The reason why literature can do this is because, ultimately, it resists assimilation to philosophy.

In the following sections of this introduction we shall set out some of the principal issues that literary writing raises for Lyotard. We begin with Lyotard's important reflection on the space of the literary work in his first major work, *Discours, figure*; we then go on to look at the way in which literature informs Lyotard's most famous idea, the postmodern; we finally show how in his subsequent work literature becomes an important aspect of his reflection on politics.

The Space of Literature

In an essay from 1969, 'Principales tendances actuelles de l'étude psychanalytique des expressions artistique et littéraires', translated as 'The Psychoanalytic Approach to Artistic and Literary Expression', Lyotard claims that 'the question posed by literature . . . to criticism . . . concerns the space *in which* the works appear, in which they become possible.'[2] One of the most important examples of this, for Lyotard, is Mallarmé's poem *Un coup de dés jamais n'abolira le hasard* (*A Throw of the Dice Will Never Abolish Chance*, 1897), on which he reflects in *Discours, figure*.

As Lyotard argues in *Discours, figure*, language has always been understood to involve and put to work a certain negativity. *Un coup de dés* poses the question of its own space through its disruption of this negativity. In particular there are three distinct, but interconnected modalities of this negativity that are important here.

First, and as Mallarmé himself stressed, in its communicative function language negates the reality of its referent. For example, the word 'table' stands in for the actual object to which it refers, taking its place; but it does not just stand in for the particular object, since in so doing it destroys its particularity. The word 'table' can be used not just of this table that I am sitting at now, but of all tables. In this sense the word has a universal and ideal significance; it negates the actual, particular thing and replaces it with the concept. It is because the word works in this way that we are able to communicate by its means. To put this another way, language imposes truth on experience, because it imposes the unchanging and non-contingent identity of the concept upon it. In drawing attention to this capacity of language to negate the reality of things, Mallarmé is indebted to the work of the German philosopher G. W. F. Hegel (1770–1831).

Second, and as Mallarmé also emphasised, in communicative language the word negates its own 'presence'. In reading or writing, listening or speaking, we do not ordinarily think about the words themselves. Rather, the words turn interest away from themselves and direct us instead toward their sense; they efface themselves as things and manifest a meaning. The less effectively the word withdraws, the less effectively does it communicate: for example, take the words you are reading now – the more your attention is fixed on the actual words printed here on the page, the less do you have their meaning in hand.

Third, there is the negativity of what Lyotard calls 'linguistic space'. For Lyotard, this negativity is made most apparent in the structural study of language put forward in the work of the Swiss linguist Ferdinand de Saussure (1857–1913). Recognising that language negates its object, Saussure excluded from his study of language the referential function of words, and instead focused on the relation between the sound-image (the signifier) and the conceptual meaning (the signified) of the word. Saussure argued that the relation between signifier and signified could only be properly accounted for in terms of the totality of the system of *langue*. For Saussure the sense a word carries depends only on the structural relationship between linguistic terms: a word has a particular meaning because of its difference from the words that surround it, the signified being simply the summary of these differences. It follows from this that the space of a text, determined on the level of structure and in terms of its signification, comprises simply 'the intervals that separate its elements: letters, words, phrases, . . . are the projection on the sensible support – page, stone – of intervals which separate the distinctive and significant terms in the table of *langue*.'[3] In principle, such a space is barely spatial: the only space that matters is the more or less invariant spacing between the linguistic terms that assures them of their signification. From this point of view the aesthetic value of the printed signs and that of the gaps between them is irrelevant.

All three modalities of negation in one way or another negate the sensible: the word suppresses its actual referent; the sound/image of the word retreats in favour of its meaning; and the space of the text is reduced by the demands of signification. In general, Lyotard is interested in the capacity of literature to expose another power of language that upsets these negations. Since, however, every work of literature is singular, it is necessary to look at how works do this individually.

As Lyotard acknowledges, in one sense the Mallarméan aesthetic exacerbates the capacity of language to negate its referent, leading to the complete destruction of its referential function. The typographical arrangement of *Un Coup de dés*, in which its words are irregularly spaced across the pages in different type faces and sizes, undermines any representational content the language of the poem might be thought to have, taking away from the words their ability to refer to any discernible reality. The radicality of this aesthetic bears on Mallarmé's desire to realise what he called an 'absolute' work of art. Such a work of art would be one that pushed to the extreme what is sometimes called the 'autonomy' of the artwork, its independence of the sensible world, its author and its readers. Mallarmé seeks to create a work or poem that would speak only of itself, and which is thus outside of time and space, abolishing all contingency in its own linguistic self-sufficiency.

Yet, as Lyotard argues, *Un Coup de dés* also stages the disruption of this aesthetic. On the one hand, for Lyotard, this is simply stated: the title of the poem affirms that 'chance will never be abolished'; on the other, the disposition of the words on the page introduce the sensible – the very emblem of contingency – back into language: the poem speaks not only by its signification, but renders expressive the space of the text (a space normally forgotten in communication) through its 'blanks, its body, the fold of its pages.'[4] In so doing, the work does not renounce its bond to the sensible but makes itself part of it.

As Lyotard observes, the space of *Un Coup de dés* is complicated. It is complicated in the literal sense of the word, since it folds the sensible and the intelligible into one another. On the one hand, Lyotard says, the space of the poem is a logical space because words are written in it; but it is also a sensory space, because the gaps between the words are as important as the words themselves. Lyotard writes that this poem, or 'book object':

contains two objects: an ideal object of signification (made of signifieds linked together according to the rules of syntax), which says: 'there is no notion (signified) outside the sensible'. We *understand* this object. And then, an object of *signifiance*, made up of graphic and *plastic* signifiers (gaps, typographical variations, use of the double page, distribution of signs on this surface), in truth, made of writing disturbed by considerations of sensibility (of 'sensuality'). The first object allows the second to be understood, the second shows the first.[5]

The poem signifies and shows. Consequently, it cannot simply be *read*, its words cannot efface themselves before its meaning, but it must also be looked at: it solicits vision. It has made the sensible enter into language as the very condition of its sense.

In this way, *Un Coup de dés* undoes all three modalities of language's negativity, each of which bears upon the retreat of the sensible. First, the arrangement of the poem disrupts the regular spacing of the text. It thereby calls attention to the very space and spacing of the text which normally effaces itself in subordination to the demands of signification; it makes that space speak. Second, through typography, the plasticity of the words themselves is invested with meaning. Third, the very thing of which the poem speaks is not held at a distance, or negated by language, but introduced into what is said.

In one sense, then, the poem poses the question of the space of language, unsettling it from its conventional locus, by introducing into the heart of intelligibility, as its very condition, the sensible itself. However, as Lyotard notes, if the poem does this, it is not because its words imitate any-thing. Rather, they figure the space of the poem itself. Through them the poem simply imposes its own taking place. Or, as *Un coup de dés* itself says: 'nothing will have taken place but the place'. In posing the question of its space the poem is a true *poiesis* – it is the creation of its own space, the setting-up of its own possibility.

Narrative, Literature and Time

In 1979 Lyotard published a book with which his name has since become indelibly associated: *The Postmodern Condition: A Report on Knowledge*. As the subtitle indicates, the focus of that book was on the transformation in 'the status of knowledge . . . as our societies enter what is known as the postindustrial age and cultures enter what is known as the postmodern age.'[6] In *The Postmodern Condition* Lyotard was most immediately concerned with the role of science and technology. However, the impetus behind Lyotard's concept of 'the postmodern' derives as much from his concern with literature, art and philosophy as it does from his analysis of contemporary scientific practice.[7]

Something of the importance that literature plays for Lyotard in the development of the idea of the postmodern can be seen from the emphasis that he places in *The Postmodern Condition* on narrative, an emphasis that runs throughout his work from the early 1970s (see, for example, 'A Short Libidinal Economy of a Narrative Set-up', included here) until the early 1980s. It is important to be careful here: Lyotard does not identify narrative with literature, since not all narratives are literary. Nevertheless, because literary works are often narrative in form, literature has an important bearing on the idea of the postmodern.

Narrative, as Lyotard observes, is fundamental to all societies: every culture tells stories about itself, and these stories importantly are not merely diversions, but carry a whole range of knowledge. Typically, narratives – the stories parents tell their children, for example – contain and transmit a set of competences that bear on what we call 'know-how': 'knowing how to live', 'how to listen', 'how to talk', and so on. Lyotard says that such narratives determine a whole series of competences that come to define a culture, and distinguish those who know from those who do not.

In particular, Lyotard examines a characteristic of such traditional narrative forms that bears on time. Such narratives, Lyotard observes, have a very particular rhythmic property; in them there is a meter beating time in regular periods. Such a meter is most apparent when the narratives are sung as chants (the meaning of which is sometimes obscure) in initiation ceremonies. Lyotard appeals to the ceremonies of a South American tribe, the Cashinahua Indians, to make this point, but such a characteristic is apparent in all religious ceremonies and, as Lyotard remarks, in nursery rhymes and some children's stories. The importance of this property is, Lyotard says, that through it time ceases to be a support for memory and instead becomes an immemorial pulse. Because of this emphatic rhythmic quality, the act of recitation prevails over what is recited. Lyotard suggests that a society that makes such narratives key to its identity has no need to remember its past. It is not the material of the narrative, the tale it tells, that is important to the community's sense of self; the act of recitation alone secures the collective's identity.

Societies that accord centrality to such narrative forms are relatively static; they tend to remain in a stable state, and if left to themselves, they remain unchanged over many generations. In contrast, modern societies are unstable and dynamic. They do not simply reproduce themselves, but transform themselves, capitalising on past experience and acquisitions in order to do so. This distinction between modern and traditional societies is quite conventional. It is normally drawn by appealing to the invention of writing, as a result of which the experience of successive generations could accumulate and be put to work. (A good example of this explanation is to be found in the work of the anthropologist Claude Lévi-Strauss.) Lyotard does not link such societies to the invention of writing, but nevertheless connects them to the stockpiling of the past (and finds the origin of modern societies in the institution of philosophy; see, for example, his remarks on Plato in both *The Postmodern Condition* and *The Differend*). For Lyotard, modern societies – unlike traditional cultures – imply a diachronic temporality, a memory and a project.

In such modern societies the traditional types of narrative come to be classified as belonging to 'savage, primitive, underdeveloped, backward, alienated' mentalities; they are regarded as 'fables, myths, legends, fit only for women and children',[8] a view articulated in its most forceful form by Plato in *The Republic*. Nevertheless, narrative itself is not abolished. It is still necessary for people to tell stories and in such a way that is linked to our very identity: for example, we tell ourselves the story of the development of our civilisation, we narrate the discoveries that liberated us from our past: fire, the wheel, the cultivation of crops and the domestication of animals, the discovery of mathematics, of writing, the steam engine, and so on. What happens, then, is that narrative, in its function of securing our identity, takes a different form. Narrative becomes entwined with history, becomes diachronic, recording and recalling the past – whether that past be mythical, fictive or 'real'. That function becomes progressively more explicit, or more dominant, in modern societies. For example, the early Greek epics recount the past and the adventures of heroic figures such as Odysseus and Achilles, but these characters are essentially unchanged by their experiences. Increasingly, however, narrative becomes the recitation of a collective's or individual's development; this is perhaps best exemplified by the flourishing of the great novels of education (*Bildungsroman*) in the eighteenth and nineteenth centuries. Thus, as Lyotard succinctly puts it in the essay 'Return upon the Return', included here, 'we moderns, sons of Ulysses, cannot believe that an expedition, an exile, experience in general would not imply some sort of alteration or alienation.'[9] Identity profits from this alteration and alienation; consciousness comes to constitute itself and arrive at its truth, conquering its substance through its exposure to the risk of the adventure. Not only is this narrative organisation found in novels or epic poetry; it also informs the great philosophical and political discourses of modernity that legitimate the state and its culture, which in *The Postmodern Condition* Lyotard calls 'grand narratives'.

For Lyotard, postmodern literature disrupts this canonical modern form of narrative. This is nowhere better exemplified than in what Lyotard says about the relation between James Joyce's *Ulysses* and Homer's *Odyssey* (one of the founding texts of European literature) in 'Return upon the Return'. The name *Ulysses* is, as Lyotard observes, a Latinised derivative of the Greek *Odusseus*, and Joyce's novel is, according to Joyce himself, based on Homer's epic poem. But, for Lyotard, accepting that there is a relationship between *Ulysses* and the *Odyssey* does not provide a key to the former text: *Ulysses* is not merely simply modelled on the *Odyssey*; rather, in its relation to it, it puts that relation into question. It is not that *Ulysses* simply diverges from the *Odyssey* in certain respects, but through a whole series of displacements at the level of plot, character, and writing itself it unravels the very ideas of origin, identity and difference that structure the notion of tradition and history, and thus effects the decomposition of the lineage from the Greek epic to ourselves – the great adventure of narrative and language – that is supposed to constitute Europe's self-identity.

In particular, Joyce's writing undoes the pretension of the mind to self-mastery, exposing language's power to exceed consciousness. Lyotard makes this point in his book on Malraux, *Soundproof Room*. *Ulysses* prevents the voice 'from assembling its experience in some consummate remembering, from re-membering itself',[10] since through its puns, ambiguities, mispronunciations and innuendos it shows that language can never be mastered, that it is never at the disposal of an intention to speak. It is for this reason that Lyotard says the postmodern writer does not set out to write in order to realise a particular idea, to put his thoughts into words. Rather he or she writes and exposes him or herself to language. Lyotard puts this succinctly in 'Answering the Question: what is Postmodernism?':

> Work and text . . . always come too late for their author, or, what amounts to the same thing, their being put into work, their realisation (*mise en oeuvre*) always begin too soon. Post modern would have to be understood according to the paradox of the future (post) anterior (*modo*).[11]

This quote tells us precisely what Lyotard means by 'postmodern'. It is a particular modality of a work or an act – or better still, since what he is concerned with is not the product of a deliberate intention, it is an 'event', something that simply takes place – that we find exposed most insistently in literature and art. Such an 'event' takes place before consciousness can lay hold of it. In exposing this peculiar modality of the event, and in particular its capacity to disrupt diachronic narration, literature is central to Lyotard's thinking about the post-modern.

Literature and Politics

For Lyotard, literature – or what he later simply calls 'writing' (*l'écriture*) – has a profound bearing on politics. For example, in *Instructions païennes*, Lyotard pointed to the political potential of the stories, the little narratives, retold in Alexander Solzhenitsyn's *Gulag Archipelago*, refusing incorporation in the general narrative of Stalinism, eroding its power. The political aspect of these stories lies not merely in what they tell, not simply in the lie given to Stalinism by what they say, but also and perhaps more importantly, in their being told. Since political power is the power to command speech and to silence dissenting voices, the very existence of such narratives eats away at established political discourse. This swarm of narratives, competing, dissenting, constitutes the strength of the weak; it testifies to the power of speech to rise up against the pretension of any single narrative to hold a monopoly over language.

For Lyotard, then, it is no accident that the *Gulag Archipelago* exercised such a powerful political influence over its readers. Narrative or language is not merely contingently political. The political nature of narrative lies in the fundamental implication of language in communities. As the analysis of narratives in *The Postmodern Condition* showed, there is, in fact, no community without language. The very identity of a community and its members is given through narrative, and thus through language, since 'even before he is born, if only by virtue of the name he is given, the human child is already positioned as the referent of a story recounted by those around him, in relation to which he will inevitably chart his course.'[12]

We might say that the problem for Lyotard is that contemporary Western societies suppress the very fact of language's precedence over the individual. As he argued in *The Postmodern Condition*, and as he continued to argue in such works as *The Inhuman*, such societies are driven by the need to maximise performance, and to improve efficiency. Attached to this is the desire under capitalism to maximise profits – to increase the quantities of surplus-value by minimising labour-time. In such societies everything is reduced to utilities that can be put to work and products – books and food, for example – that can be rapidly consumed with the minimum disruption to our lives. Politics is reduced to what are basically economic considerations, not only or even primarily questions about the distribution or redistribution of wealth, but simply of predicting how people will react to certain events, and trying to manage these reactions to secure the greatest efficiency. Language comes to be regarded as simply another utility, a more or less effective vehicle for the transmission of information, at the service of the intentions of a speaker, and thus as subordinate to them; a means that the human uses for his or her own ends. This is a complete overturning of the actual precedence of language over the individual.

For Lyotard, the political significance of literature, of writing, lies not in its ideological significance, and he does not propose founding a politics on literature. Rather, its political significance lies in its resistance to the reduction of everything to a utility. In 'Time Today', Lyotard argues that this reduction is rooted in reason. Simply put, reason seeks reasons, and in so doing looks to govern and predict all events, rendering them calculable. Reason rationalises the given and neutralises the future, bringing everything under the control of knowledge. The literary work holds out against this since it does not seek to increase our knowledge of the world, but simply to expose us to language. In so doing it brings us before the claim of language on us. Certainly, through language we accede to adult consciousness and reason, yet what literature makes apparent is that language exceeds every intention and action of the individual and it cannot be entirely absorbed into the consciousness and reason it founds. Since language stands at the foundation of all community, literature bears witness to the possibility of a being together that cannot be absorbed by reason and thus subordinated to the demands of utility and economic efficiency.

Notes

1. Lyotard, *Peregrinations: Law, Form, Event*, p. 4.
2. Lyotard, *Towards the Postmodern*, p. 9.
3. Lyotard, *Discours, figure*, p. 61.
4. Ibid. p. 68.
5. Ibid. p. 71.
6. Lyotard, *The Postmodern Condition*, p. 3.
7. An important aspect of the relation between the postmodern and literature/art is developed in connection with the aesthetic category of 'the sublime'. Since we discuss the sublime in some detail in the introductions to the third and fourth sections of this book, we instead look here at the connection between the postmodern and literature in relation to narrative and time.
8. Lyotard, *The Postmodern Condition*, p. 27.
9. Lyotard, 'Return upon the Return', in *The Lyotard Reader and Guide*, p. 136.
10. Lyotard, 'Lost Voice', from *Soundproof Room* in *The Lyotard Reader and Guide*, p. 150.
11. Lyotard, 'Answering the Question: What is Postmodernism?', in *The Lyotard Reader and Guide*, p. 132.
12. Lyotard, *The Postmodern Condition*, p. 15.

Chapter 6

Answering the Question: What is Postmodernism?

A Demand

This is a period of slackening – I refer to the color of the times. From every direction we are being urged to put an end to experimentation, in the arts and elsewhere. I have read an art historian who extols realism and is militant for the advent of a new subjectivity. I have read an art critic who packages and sells 'Transavantgardism' in the marketplace of painting. I have read that under the name of postmodernism, architects are getting rid of the Bauhaus project, throwing out the baby of experimentation with the bathwater of functionalism. I have read that a new philosopher is discovering what he drolly calls Judaeo-Christianism, and intends by it to put an end to the impiety which we are supposed to have spread. I have read in a French weekly that some are displeased with *Mille Plateaux* [by Deleuze and Guattari] because they expect, especially when reading a work of philosophy, to be gratified with a little sense. I have read from the pen of a reputable historian that writers and thinkers of the 1960 and 1970 avant-gardes spread a reign of terror in the use of language, and that the conditions for a fruitful exchange must be restored by imposing on the intellectuals a common way of speaking, that of the historians. I have been reading a young philosopher of language who complains that Continental thinking, under the challenge of speaking machines, has surrendered to the machines the concern for reality, that it has substituted for the referential paradigm that of 'adlinguisticity' (one speaks about speech, writes about writing, intertextuality), and who thinks that the time has now come to restore a solid anchorage of language in the referent. I have read a talented theatrologist for whom postmodernism, with its games and fantasies, carries very little weight in front of political authority, especially when a worried public opinion encourages authority to a politics of totalitarian surveillance in the face of nuclear warfare threats.

I have read a thinker of repute who defends modernity against those he calls the neoconservatives. Under the banner of postmodernism, the latter would like, he believes, to get rid of the uncompleted project of modernism, that of the Enlightenment. Even the last advocates of *Aufklärung*, such as Popper or

Adorno, were only able, according to him, to defend the project in a few particular spheres of life – that of politics for the author of *The Open Society*, and that of art for the author of *Ästhetische Theorie*. Jürgen Habermas (everyone had recognized him) thinks that if modernity has failed, it is in allowing the totality of life to be splintered into independent specialties which are left to the narrow competence of experts, while the concrete individual experiences 'desublimated meaning' and 'destructured form,' not as a liberation but in the mode of that immense *ennui* which Baudelaire described over a century ago.

Following a prescription of Albrecht Wellmer, Habermas considers that the remedy for this splintering of culture and its separation from life can only come from 'changing the status of aesthetic experience when it is no longer primarily expressed in judgments of taste,' but when it is 'used to explore a living historical situation,' that is, when 'it is put in relation with problems of existence.' For this experience then 'becomes a part of a language game which is no longer that of aesthetic criticism'; it takes part 'in cognitive processes and normative expectations'; 'it alters the manner in which those different moments *refer* to one another.' What Habermas requires from the arts and the experiences they provide is, in short, to bridge the gap between cognitive, ethical, and political discourses, thus opening the way to a unity of experience.

My question is to determine what sort of unity Habermas has in mind. Is the aim of the project of modernity the constitution of sociocultural unity within which all the elements of daily life and of thought would take their places as in an organic whole? Or does the passage that has to be charted between heterogeneous language games – those of cognition, of ethics, of politics – belong to a different order from that? And if so, would it be capable of effecting a real synthesis between them?

The first hypothesis, of a Hegelian inspiration, does not challenge the notion of a dialectically totalizing *experience*; the second is closer to the spirit of Kant's *Critique of Judgment*, but must be submitted, like the *Critique*, to that severe reexamination which postmodernity imposes on the thought of the Enlightenment, on the idea of a unitary end of history and of a subject. It is this critique which not only Wittgenstein and Adorno have initiated, but also a few other thinkers (French or other) who do not have the honor to be read by Professor Habermas – which at least saves them from getting a poor grade for their neoconservatism.

Realism

The demands I began by citing are not all equivalent. They can even be contradictory. Some are made in the name of postmodernism, others in order to combat it. It is not necessarily the same thing to formulate a demand for some referent (and objective reality), for some sense (and credible transcendence), for an addressee (and audience), or an addressor (and subjective expressiveness) or for some communicational consensus (and a general code of exchanges, such as the genre of historical discourse). But in the diverse invitations to suspend artistic experimentation, there is an identical call for order, a desire for unity, for identity, for security, or popularity (in the sense of *Öffentlichkeit*, of 'finding a public'). Artists and writers must be brought back into the bosom of the community, or at least, if the latter is considered to be ill, they must be assigned the task of healing it.

There is an irrefutable sign of this common disposition: it is that for all those writers nothing is more urgent than to liquidate the heritage of the avant-gardes. Such is the case, in particular, of the so-called transavantgardism. The answers given by Achille Bonito Oliva to the questions asked by Bernard Lamarche-Vadel and Michel Enric leave no room for doubt about this. By putting the avant-gardes through a mixing process, the artist and critic feel more confident that they can suppress them than by launching a frontal attack. For they can pass off the most cynical eclecticism as a way of going beyond the fragmentary character of the preceding experiments; whereas if they openly turned their backs on them, they would run the risk of appearing ridiculously neo-academic. The *Salons* and the *Académies*, at the time when the bourgeoisie was establishing itself in history, were able to function as purgation and to grant awards for good plastic and literary conduct under the cover of realism. But capitalism inherently possesses the power to derealize familiar objects, social roles, and institutions to such a degree that the so-called realistic representations can no longer evoke reality except as nostalgia or mockery, as an occasion for suffering rather than for satisfaction. Classicism seems to be ruled out in a world in which reality is so destabilized that it offers no occasion for experience but one for ratings and experimentation.

This theme is familiar to all readers of Walter Benjamin. But it is necessary to assess its exact reach. Photography did not appear as a challenge to painting from the outside, any more than industrial cinema did to narrative literature. The former was only putting the final touch to the program of ordering the visible elaborated by the quattrocento; while the latter was the last step in rounding off diachronies as organic wholes, which had been the ideal of the great novels of education since the eighteenth century. That the mechanical and the industrial should appear as substitutes for hand or craft was not in itself a disaster – except if one believes that art is in its essence the expression of an individuality of genius assisted by an elite craftsmanship.

The challenge lay essentially in that photographic and cinematographic processes can accomplish better, faster, and with a circulation a hundred thousand times larger than narrative or pictorial realism, the task which academicism had assigned to realism: to preserve various consciousnesses from doubt. Industrial photography and cinema will be superior to painting and the novel whenever the objective is to stabilize the referent, to arrange it according to a point of view which endows it with a recognizable meaning, to reproduce the syntax and vocabulary which enable the addressee to decipher images and sequences quickly, and so to arrive easily at the consciousness of his own identity as well as the approval which he thereby receives from others – since such structures of images and sequences constitute a communication code among all of them. This is the way the effects of reality, or if one prefers, the fantasies of realism, multiply.

If they too do not wish to become supporters (of minor importance at that) of what exists, the painter and novelist must refuse to lend themselves to such therapeutic uses. They must question the rules of the art of painting or of narrative as they have learned and received them from their predecessors. Soon those rules must appear to them as a means to deceive, to seduce, and to reassure, which makes it impossible for them to be 'true.' Under the common name of painting and literature, an unprecedented split is taking place. Those who refuse to reexamine the rules of art pursue successful careers in mass conformism by communicating, by means of the 'correct rules,' the endemic desire for reality with objects and situations capable of gratifying it. Pornography is the use of photography and film to such an end. It is becoming a general model for the visual or narrative arts which have not met the challenge of the mass media.

As for the artists and writers who question the rules of plastic and narrative arts and possibly share their suspicions by circulating their work, they are destined to have little credibility in the eyes of those concerned with 'reality' and 'identity'; they have no guarantee of an audience. Thus it is possible to ascribe the dialectics of the avant-gardes to the challenge posed by the realisms of industry and mass communication to painting and the narrative arts. Duchamp's 'ready made' does nothing but actively and parodistically signify this constant process of dispossession of the craft of painting or even of being an artist. As Thierry de Duve penetratingly observes, the modern aesthetic question is not 'What is beautiful?' but 'What can be said to be art (and literature)?'

Realism, whose only definition is that it intends to avoid the question of reality implicated in that of art, always stands somewhere between academicism and kitsch. When power assumes the name of a party, realism and its neoclassical complement triumph over the experimental avant-garde by slandering and banning it – that is, provided the 'correct' images, the 'correct' narratives, the 'correct' forms which the party requests, selects, and propagates can find a public to desire them as the appropriate remedy for the anxiety and depression that public experiences. The demand for reality – that is, for unity, simplicity, communicability, etc. – did not have the same intensity nor the same continuity in German society between the two world wars and in Russian society after the Revolution: this provides a basis for a distinction between Nazi and Stalinist realism.

What is clear, however, is that when it is launched by the political apparatus, the attack on artistic experimentation is specifically reactionary: aesthetic judgment would only be required to decide whether such or such work is in conformity with the established rules of the beautiful. Instead of the work of art having to investigate what makes it an art object and whether it will be able to find an audience, political academicism possesses and imposes a priori criteria of the beautiful, which designate some works and a public at a stroke and forever. The use of categories in aesthetic judgment would thus be of the same nature as in cognitive judgment. To speak like Kant, both would be determining judgments: the expression is 'well formed' first in the understanding, then the only cases retained in experience are those which can be subsumed under this expression.

When power is that of capital and not that of a party, the 'transavantgardist' or 'postmodern' (in Jencks's sense) solution proves to be better adapted than the antimodern solution. Eclecticism is the degree zero of contemporary general culture: one listens to reggae, watches a western, eats McDonald's food for lunch and local cuisine for dinner, wears Paris perfume in Tokyo and 'retro' clothes in Hong Kong; knowledge is a matter for TV games. It is easy to find a public for eclectic works. By becoming kitsch, art panders to the confusion which reigns in the 'taste' of the patrons. Artists, gallery owners, critics, and public wallow together in the 'anything goes,' and the epoch is one of slackening. But this realism of the 'anything goes' is in fact that of money; in the absence of aesthetic criteria, it remains possible and useful to assess the value of works of art according to the profits they yield. Such realism accommodates all tendencies, just as capital accommodates all 'needs,' providing that the tendencies and needs have purchasing power. As for taste, there is no need to be delicate when one speculates or entertains oneself.

Artistic and literary research is doubly threatened, once by the 'cultural policy' and once by the art and book market. What is advised, sometimes through one channel, sometimes through the other, is to offer works which, first, are relative to subjects which exist in the eyes of the public they address, and second, works so made ('well made') that the public will recognize what they are about, will understand what is signified, will be able to give or refuse its approval knowlingly, and if possible, even to derive from such work a certain amount of comfort.

The interpretation which has just been given of the contact between the industrial and mechanical arts, and literature and the fine arts is correct in its outline, but it remains narrowly sociologizing and historicizing – in other words, one-sided. Stepping over Benjamin's and Adorno's reticences, it must be recalled that science and industry are no more free of the suspicion which concerns reality than are art and writing. To believe otherwise would be to entertain an excessively humanistic notion of the mephistophelian functionalism of sciences and technologies. There is no denying the dominant existence today of techno-science, that is, the massive subordination of cognitive statements to the finality of the best possible performance, which is the technological criterion. But the mechanical and the industrial, especially when they enter fields traditionally reserved for artists, are carrying with them much more than power effects. The objects and the thoughts which originate in scientific knowledge and the capitalist economy convey with them one of the rules which supports their possibility: the rule that there is no reality unless testified by a consensus between partners over a certain knowledge and certain commitments.

This rule is of no little consequence. It is the imprint left on the politics of the scientist and the trustee of capital by a kind of flight of reality out of the metaphysical, religious, and political certainties that the mind believed it held. This withdrawal is absolutely necessary to the emergence of science and cap-italism. No industry is possible without a suspicion of the Aristotelian theory of motion, no industry without a refutation of corporatism, of mercantilism, and of physiocracy. Modernity, in whatever age it appears, cannot exist without a shattering of belief and without discovery of the 'lack of reality' of reality, together with the invention of other realities.

What does this 'lack of reality' signify if one tries to free it from a narrowly historicized interpretation? The phrase is of course akin to what Nietzsche calls nihilism. But I see a much earlier modulation of Nietzschean perspectivism in the Kantian theme of the sublime. I think in particular that it is in the aesthetic of the sublime that modern art (including literature) finds its impetus and the logic of avant-gardes finds its axioms.

The sublime sentiment, which is also the sentiment of the sublime, is, according to Kant, a strong and equivocal emotion: it carries with it both pleas-ure and pain. Better still, in it pleasure derives from pain. Within the tradition of the subject, which comes from Augustine and Descartes and which Kant does not radically challenge, this contradiction, which some would call neur-osis or masochism, develops as a conflict between the faculties of a subject, the faculty to conceive of something and the faculty to 'present' something. Knowledge exists if, first, the statement is intelligible, and second, if 'cases' can be derived from the experience which 'corresponds' to it. Beauty exists if a certain 'case' (the work of art), given first by the sensibility without any conceptual determination, the sentiment of pleasure independent of any inter-est the work may elicit, appeals to the principle of a universal consensus (which may never be attained).

Taste, therefore, testifies that between the capacity to conceive and the cap-acity to present an object corresponding to the concept, an undetermined agreement, without rules, giving rise to a judgment which Kant calls reflective, may be experienced as pleasure. The sublime is a different sentiment. It takes place, on the contrary, when the imagination fails to present an object which might, if only in principle, come to match a concept. We have the Idea of the world (the totality of what is), but we do not have the capacity to show an example of it. We have the Idea of the simple (that which cannot be broken down, decomposed), but we cannot illustrate it with a sensible object which would be a 'case' of it. We can conceive the infinitely great, the infinitely powerful, but every presentation of an object destined to 'make visible' this absolute greatness or power appears to us painfully inadequate. Those are Ideas of which no presentation is possible. Therefore, they impart no knowledge about reality (experience); they also prevent the free union of the faculties which gives rise to the sentiment of the beautiful; and they prevent the formation and the stabilization of taste. They can be said to be unpresentable.

I shall call modern the art which devotes its 'little technical expertise' (*son 'petit technique'*), as Diderot used to say, to present the fact that the unpresentable exists. To make visible that there is something which can be conceived and which can neither be seen nor made visible: this is what is at stake in modern painting. But how to make visible that there is something which cannot be seen? Kant himself shows the way when he names 'formlessness, the absence of form,' as a possible index to the unpresentable. He also says of the empty 'abstraction' which the imagination experiences when in search for a presentation of the infinite (another unpresentable): this abstraction itself is like a presentation of the infinite, its 'negative presentation.' He cites the commandment, 'Thou shalt not make graven images' (*Exodus*), as the most sublime passage in the Bible in that it forbids all presentation of the Absolute. Little needs to be added to those observations to outline an aesthetic of sublime paintings. As painting, it will of course 'present' something though negatively; it will therefore avoid figuration or representation. It will be 'white' like one of Malevitch's squares; it will enable us to see only by making it impossible to see; it will please only by causing pain. One recognizes in those instructions the axioms of avant-gardes in painting, inasmuch as they devote themselves to making an allusion to the unpresentable by means of visible presentations. The systems in the name of which, or with which, this task has been able to support or to justify itself deserve the greatest attention; but they can originate only in the vocation of the sublime in order to legitimize it, that is, to conceal it. They remain inexplicable without the incommensurability of reality to concept which is implied in the Kantian philosophy of the sublime.

It is not my intention to analyze here in detail the manner in which the various avant-gardes have, so to speak, humbled and disqualified reality by examining the pictorial techniques which are so many devices to make us believe in it. Local tone, drawing, the mixing of colors, linear perspective, the nature of the support and that of the instrument, the treatment, the display, the museum: the avant-gardes are perpetually flushing out artifices of presentation which make it possible to subordinate thought to the gaze and to turn it away from the unpresentable. If Habermas, like Marcuse, understands this task of derealization as an aspect of the (repressive) 'desublimation' which characterizes the avant-garde, it is because he confuses the Kantian sublime with Freudian sublimation, and because aesthetics has remained for him that of the beautiful.

The Postmodern

What, then, is the postmodern? What place does it or does it not occupy in the vertiginous work of the questions hurled at the rules of image and narration? It is undoubtedly a part of the modern. All that has been received, if only yesterday (*modo, modo.* Petronius used to say), must be suspected. What space does Cézanne challenge? The Impressionists'. What object do Picasso and Braque attack? Cézanne's. What presupposition does Duchamp break with in 1912? That which says one must make a painting, be it cubist. And Buren questions that other presupposition which he believes had survived untouched by the work of Duchamp: the place of presentation of the work. In an amazing acceleration, the generations precipitate themselves. A work can become modern only if it is first postmodern. Postmodernism thus understood is not modernism at its end but in the nascent state, and this state is constant.

Yet I would like not to remain with this slightly mechanistic meaning of the word. If it is true that modernity takes place in the withdrawal of the real and according to the sublime relation between the presentable and the conceivable, it is possible, within this relation, to distinguish two modes (to use the musician's language). The emphasis can be placed on the powerlessness of the faculty of presentation, on the nostalgia for presence felt by the human subject, on the obscure and futile will which inhabits him in spite of everything. The emphasis can be placed, rather, on the power of the faculty to conceive, on its 'inhumanity' so to speak (it was the quality Apollinaire demanded of modern artists), since it is not the business of our understanding whether or not human sensibility or imagination can match what it conceives. The emphasis can also be placed on the increase of being and the jubilation which result from the invention of new rules of the game, be it pictorial, artistic, or any other. What I have in mind will become clear if we dispose very schematically a few names on the chessboard of the history of avant-gardes: on the side of melancholia, the German Expressionists, and on the side of *novatio*, Braque and Picasso, on the former Malevitch and on the latter Lissitsky, on the one Chirico and on the other Duchamp. The nuance which distinguishes these two modes may be infinitesimal; they often coexist in the same piece, are almost indistinguishable;

and yet they testify to a difference (*un différend*) on which the fate of thought depends and will depend for a long time, between regret and assay.

The work of Proust and that of Joyce both allude to something which does not allow itself to be made present. Allusion, to which Paulo Fabbri recently called my attention, is perhaps a form of expression indispensable to the works which belong to an aesthetic of the sublime. In Proust, what is being eluded as the price to pay for this allusion is the identity of consciousness, a victim to the excess of time (*au trop de temps*). But in Joyce, it is the identity of writing which is the victim of an excess of the book (*au trop de livre*) or of literature.

Proust calls forth the unpresentable by means of a language unaltered in its syntax and vocabulary and of a writing which in many of its operators still belongs to the genre of novelistic narration. The literary institution, as Proust inherits it from Balzac and Flaubert, is admittedly subverted in that the hero is no longer a character but the inner consciousness of time, and in that the diegetic diachrony, already damaged by Flaubert, is here put in question because of the narrative voice. Nevertheless, the unity of the book, the odyssey of that consciousness, even if it is deferred from chapter to chapter, is not seriously challenged: the identity of the writing with itself throughout the labyrinth of the interminable narration is enough to connote such unity, which has been compared to that of *The Phenomenology of Mind*.

Joyce allows the unpresentable to become perceptible in his writing itself, in the signifier. The whole range of available narrative and even stylistic operators is put into play without concern for the unity of the whole, and new operators are tried. The grammar and vocabulary of literary language are no longer accepted as given; rather, they appear as academic forms, as rituals originating in piety (as Nietzsche said) which prevent the unpresentable from being put forward.

Here, then, lies the difference: modern aesthetics is an aesthetic of the sublime, though a nostalgic one. It allows the unpresentable to be put forward only as the missing contents; but the form, because of its recognizable consistency, continues to offer to the reader or viewer matter for solace and pleasure. Yet these sentiments do not constitute the real sublime sentiment, which is in an intrinsic combination of pleasure and pain: the pleasure that reason should exceed all presentation, the pain that imagination or sensibility should not be equal to the concept.

The postmodern would be that which, in the modern, puts forward the unpresentable in presentation itself; that which denies itself the solace of good forms, the consensus of a taste which would make it possible to share collectively the nostalgia for the unattainable; that which searches for new presentations, not in order to enjoy them but in order to impart a stronger sense of the unpresentable. A postmodern artist or writer is in the position of a philosopher: the text he writes, the work he produces are not in principle governed by preestablished rules, and they cannot be judged according to a determining judgment, by applying familiar categories to the text or to the work. Those rules and categories are what the work of art itself is looking for. The artist and the writer, then, are working without rules in order to formulate the rules of what *will have been done*. Hence the fact that work and text have the characters of an *event*, hence also, they always come too late for their author, or, what amounts to the same thing, their being put into work, their realization (*mise en oeuvre*) always begin too soon. *Post modern* would have to be understood according to the paradox of the future (*post*) anterior (*modo*).

It seems to me that the essay (Montaigne) is postmodern, while the fragment (*The Athaeneum*) is modern.

Finally, it must be clear that it is our business not to supply reality but to invent allusions to the conceivable which cannot be presented. And it is not to be expected that this task will effect the last reconciliation between language games (which, under the name of faculties, Kant knew to be separated by a chasm), and that only the transcendental illusion (that of Hegel) can hope to totalize them into a real unity. But Kant also knew that the price to pay for such an illusion is terror. The nineteenth and twentieth centuries have given us as much terror as we can take. We have paid a high enough price for the nostalgia of the whole and the one, for the reconciliation of the concept and the sensible, of the transparent and the communicable experience. Under the general demand for slackening and for appeasement, we can hear the mutterings of the desire for a return of terror, for the realization of the fantasy to seize reality. The answer is: Let us wage a war on totality; let us be witnesses to the unpresentable; let us activate the differences and save the honor of the name.

Chapter 7

Return upon the Return

And then coming back was the worst thing you ever did.

1

How can one be sure that what returns is precisely what had disappeared? Or that what returns not only appears, but is reappearing? Our first gesture would be to challenge reality. What is past is not here, what is here is present. We require a sign – some proof that we are not dreaming – in order to be convinced.

As in a dream, Athena disguises Odysseus as a wandering and miserable old man to make him unrecognizable before he returns to his home in Ithaca. Argos, the dog who has been waiting for him for twenty years, identifies his master (by his smell, I suppose), while the faithful old nurse, Euryclea, identifies him by the scar on his thigh. As for Penelope, expert at deluding suitors, she only decides to trust him when he shows that he knows the secret of the conjugal bed's construction.

Indicators – smell, scar, sexuality – are proofs by the flesh. Only Telemachus takes his father at his word when he says that he is Odysseus. The nominative voice is a sufficient indicator. A son recognizes his father not by his body but by his name.

Several millennia later, here we are, the offspring of the *Odyssey*. We have to believe in the word. Joyce entitled a book *Ulysses*: we are in Ithaca; our father has returned home. From there, Joyce proceeds with his little travel narrative. Confidentially, he will reveal that each of the eighteen sequences of the narrative in fact bears the name of a sequence in the Homeric voyage. An entitled itinerary, the *Odyssey* returns to us in the form of *Ulysses* – or so the work's master assures us.

But how? Some god or goddess has metamorphosed the work to make it unrecognizable. The body of the text bears few indicators that would prove the event of return: no *Odyssey* is perceptible in the *Ulysses* narratives.

As to the name, we sons of Homer cannot trust it. The Greek father's name was *Odusseus*. *Ulysses* is a mere derivative: first from the dialectical Latin,

Olusseus, and then to the English. The name of the book was deformed by crossing through two cultures, two worlds of names: the Romance world and then classical modern Northern Europe.

Moreover, Joyce's title designates no literary genre, as does the *Odyssey* or the *Aeneid*; these titles designate epic or romanesque cycles. His title indicates nothing of the book's mode of exposition. Some say that this type of title, using the name of the hero, is an old custom (from theater or the novel). But, technically speaking, *Ulysses* is not the name of the book's hero. Rather, it is Bloom, Leopold.

We could say that this is no great transformation: no one is fooled by it. But there is something shifty about it. The title shifts. It does not unravel. It is not a declension of the identity of the *Odyssey*. It evokes it, but in a blurred manner. It makes it equivocal.

Could we say that the journey that Homer traces has served as a model for Joyce and that, at the very least, the *Odyssey* accomplishes a return to *Ulysses* by lending it its compositional structure? We readers, true sons that we are, once in possession of a concordance between Joyce's work and the songs of the Homeric poem, will find it easier to spot the logic of return. But I fear that this ease might also be a trap.

Were we to follow the principle of correspondences, we would never finish counting all the displacements indicating *Ulysses'* divergence from the *Odyssey*. Some of these displacements affect the diegetic universe: namely, reference. Others modify the very story that Homer narrates. And still other displacements (and not the fewest) completely upset the narrative operators lending the *Odyssey* its epic status. I will leave for narratologists the task of counting up these displacements. Their number is such that we would have to wonder how *Ulysses* could ever be recognized as the offspring of the *Odyssey*, especially because the correspondences that we use to designate the episodes in *Ulysses* are only implicit in the text.

Further, the facility that correspondences offer us is an illusory one, for it only reveals to the viewer of classical painting the grid organizing that painting. In the painting, we rediscover the clarity of a *costruzione legittima*, the transparent logic of an ordered spatial and temporal placement. We know, of course, that Joyce employed this ordering not only to make it invisible, but also to unravel it in detail, episode after episode. I am reminded here of something of which we are all aware: his proliferation of the most diverse modes of writing, the heterogeneity of genres and styles, something like a quasi-desperate effort to escape the logic of the artwork in order to render the book inoperative, to prevent it from closing itself into a beautiful totality. The work's construction only serves as a spur for deconstruction. It is not the logic of space-time that is at stake in *Ulysses*, but its paralogisms – paratopisms, parachronisms. While the beautiful classical form closes in upon itself, concludes, and thus makes its return, and while it *is* in itself the return, it is essential that Joycean writing place the cyclical motif under the rule of its disordering and its inconsistency.

Everything is familiar: times of day, places, people encountered, the most insignificant passerby, animals. The adventure is in the language, its proliferation, its dispersion, the transgression of its horizons. *Ulysses* is not the story of a return: the hero has never left. He finds himself at once in the position of an immigrant or a ghost or even a wanderer [*métèque*]. Dubliner though he may be, he does not quite qualify for being *from* Dublin, nor does he manage *to be there*. He does not return: he errs; he is a *flâneur*. He suffers from a breakdown of presence. Each now evokes a once upon a time or another time; each here evokes a there. It is an intermediate state – half awake, half asleep – which can be likened to the revery of a solitary walker. Everything that is perceived, well-known, too well-known, gives rise to an evocation, to an attentiveness, to a call from elsewhere. Thus Dublin becomes a mere reserve, a depository of day's residues of which the *flâneur*'s daydreaming constitutes itself in order to free him from that city. T. S. Eliot said of Bloom that he 'says nothing.' In such a *'silent monologue'* all the inner voices call out with no regard for how they might be orchestrated – an orchestration that will become the artwork or the subject.

If the *Odyssey* returns in *Ulysses*, it is in its absence. Ulysses wanders around Ithaca, a place inhabited by its people but deserted – peopled with phantoms. At home, he is not at home. Of King Hamlet, the father's ghost, Dedalus says (in the library episode), that his 'speech (his lean unlovely English) is always turned elsewhere, backward'. His house is no longer his *oikos*. Thus Hamlet shifts and thus *Ulysses* shifts its gaze toward the *Odyssey*. Hamlet only alluded to the beautiful protective abode and concludes his cycle only in order to direct his speech 'elsewhere, backward,' according to a space that is not there and a time that is not present.

2

The fact that Ulysses is called *Bloom* is a serious claim to paratopia and to parachronia, to the spatio-temporal breakdown that afflicts the ghost. It is a flagrant trace of the displacement that *Ulysses* imposes upon the *Odyssey* in order to recall it. Bloom the wanderer [*métèque*] par excellence, the converted Jew. A tradition of life and of thought evades the Greek *epos* by a type of being-toward-being that comes from 'elsewhere' and from behind, and that is itself largely denied. This is a Ulysses who would shift, through today's Ithaca, toward the land of Canaan and toward a protohistory, without, for all that, returning. The interpolation of the Jewish theme into the Homeric motif, of which there are many occurrences in the Joycean text, should be examined under the title of the return. I will outline some of the characteristics of such an examination.

First, we should recall the parallel suggested by Erich Auerbach, in the first chapter of *Mimesis*,[1] between the Homeric and the Biblical scenes.

At each instant and in every place, the Greek hero *embodies* entirely and expressly his role – the one with which legend enjoins him. His saturation of his own presence to the situation is such that he fulfills his destiny, fills it to completion. He is devoid of sentimentality, by which I mean he has none of the depth, the individual historicity, the unexpected, the 'backward,' the 'elsewhere' that we moderns attach to affectivity, to the capacity to be affected.

The bard leaves no emotions, situations, or motifs in the shadows, none in reserve. Prosody, the recurrence of stereotypes, and ornamental description render states of the soul and states of fact equally visible. This clarity makes it possible to readily identify voices, references, intentions, and dramatic relations. On the stage thus overexposed, the protagonists are like pure *actants* by which Homeric poetics renders semiotics transparent.

'Homeric stylé knows only a foreground,' writes Auerbach, where the recounting of events unravels a 'uniformly illuminated, uniformly objective present,' generating a world that 'contains nothing but itself.' Auerbach points out that 'Homeric poems conceal nothing, they contain no teaching and no secret second meaning.'[2] They leave no room for interpretation.

To himself as to us, Odysseus is none other than the ever-exposed identity of his role, of his 'character.' Specifically, he never ages. Athena must disguise him, twenty years after his departure, in order that he be unrecognizable. 'Odysseus on his return,' notes Auerbach, 'is exactly the same as he was when he left Ithaca two decades earlier.'[3] His return would provide an example of perfectly identical recurrence, except for the entirely circumstantial modification that the goddess imposes on him.

We moderns, sons of Ulysses, cannot believe that an expedition, an exile, experience in general would not imply some sort of alteration or alienation. Travel stories, *Bildungsromane*, Hegel's *Phenomenology* – all odysseys of consciousness – accustom us to thinking that the spirit only conquers its substance and its final identity, its self-knowledge, by exposing itself to the risky adventure of all its possibilities. We think of the return not as recovered identity of the same with the same, but as the self-identification of the same with the 'surveying' [*relève*] of its alterity. At the end of the voyage, Ulysses's truth, for us, is not the same as it was at the moment of departure: the voyage *is* that truth. The truth is in the method, as Hegel said, and the method – the passage through mediations and changes – is in no way extrinsic to self-knowledge (as Athena's metamorphosis of Odysseus is): it *is* self-knowledge.

This amounts to saying that with modernity, what is true ceases to be a place, a dwelling – *domus* or *oikos* – from which some unessential circumstance (external war, the Trojan War) dislodges the master from the house: a place that one would merely need to clean, whose floor need only be washed (by massacring suitors or hanging unfaithful servants) in order to restore intact its cleanliness – a cleanliness that includes the nuptial bed, still resting on its olive stump, the token of an ineradicable self-reference.

In this regard, modernity owes the interiorization of war to Christianity. The return to peace in the house is prevented by an initial exile that drove us out and keeps us from returning. This exile is caused by an altogether internal transgression for which only expiation, the accepted suffering of exile – that is, sacrifice – can bring reparation and allow the return to innocence. The theme of self-sacrifice, of which Christ is the paradigm, subtends the speculative motif of an experience conceived as death and resurrection of the spirit.

Helen's beauty assuredly spreads disorder in Greek houses. Yet that beauty only gives rise to a distant war. Under the name of Eve, woman incarnates the primal figure of sin, the eternal source of the secret war that prohibits the spirit from returning to the house of the father. Yet, in the Christian *geste*,[4] the power of the 'surveying' is such that Mary Magdalene, the evil Eve, attends the son in this agony. And thus the prostitute is redeemed. When that pagan-Christian and very Catholic Claudel reads the Homeric *nostos*, he makes sure that Penelope is the symbol of this inner war's conclusion. In his eyes, the olive tree of the conjugal bed, what he calls the 'mediator between substance and heaven,' is the figuration of the flesh's redemption and the true return.

I am amazed that occasionally some commentator places Molly Bloom and her final 'Yes yes' under this pagan-Christian motif of the Virtuous Mother and of shelter regained. Claudel, who was more clear-sighted, returned to Joyce his signed copy of *Ulysses*, labeling it 'diabolical.' It doesn't matter that Bloom was baptized three times (the same number of times that Peter renounced Jesus), the sacrificial and redemptive dialectic celebrated in the cemetery and the church that he visits remains foreign to him. And we well know that, for Joyce, Rome, every bit as much as London, was the name of Ireland's oppressor.

If there is return in *Ulysses*, that return is no more Christian than it is Greek. I return to Auerbach's parallel. He notes that the text of the Old Testament is a juxtaposition of little stories. Their conjunction requires no more than the *and* that lends order to paratactical time, without distinction between main stories and subordinate ones. These stories touch upon the most ordinary aspects of life. Far from being heroes, the protagonists are petty tribal chiefs or heads of families, shepherds threatened by scarcity, displaced here and there by migrations and by wars in the vast Orient. These brief narrations pass over anything having to do with the decor where the scene unfolds: no descriptions, not even ornamental ones, of persons or sites – just names. Hardly a word is exchanged. The injunctions, the entreaties, the decisions all appear briefly, leaving motives and arguments in obscurity. As in Beckett's theater, silence and a certain indefiniteness suggest that something is at stake that no one, actor or reader, identifies.

Homeric gods deliberate in council and then go out in person to support their protégés while they carry out the plan of strategy imparted to them. Unique and invisible, Yahweh (like Godot) forces, prohibits, promises, makes himself heard without explaining his goals – all this to a people that he holds hostage. 'In the Old Testament stories the peace of daily life in the house, in the fields, and among the flocks, is undermined by jealousy over election and the promise of a blessing . . .'[5]

Auerbach concludes two things concerning this altogether different scenography:

1. On the one hand, it opens onto a demand for realism, a concern for the concrete fact, an exactness stripped of all epic amplification in which he believes the rules of historiography have their source.
2. On the other hand, the enigma surrounding the logic of episodes requires a ceaseless, perhaps interminable effort at interpretation on the part of the reader or the member of the audience – an effort that will engender hermeneutics.

I recall these few observations from Auerbach not because I subscribe to them, nor to discuss them, but because they explain the extent to which the interpolation of the Jewish motif into the return of the Homeric *epos* displaces it. The details of the demonstration need not be reviewed: impenetrability of motifs; attention to the most everyday detail, examined as if under the microscope; the solitude of characters; the difficulty of attributing to individuals the voices as they gossip, discuss, or 'monologue'; ruptures in narrative rhythm; propagation of discursive genres and tones . . . while all of this does not derive from Biblical writing alone, none of it belongs to the epic tradition.

Even though polymorphous or metamorphous prose, for example, must be attributed to the modern decomposition of literary languages, and therefore derives only indirectly from Biblical writing, it must nonetheless be linked to it. For this labor of writing inscribes itself in an aesthetic or a counteraesthetic (an an-aesthetic) of the sublime, which, since Longinus, through the Ancient-Modern quarrel and Romanticism, has relentlessly assaulted signifying syntheses. This an-aesthetic not only assaults the rules that establish classical framing (notably spatio-temporal framing) and genres, it assaults the deeper cultural, ideological, and perhaps even ontological syntheses that fix the signifier (scriptural or pictural) into syntactic and semantic groups ranging from the local trope or figure to the broadest finalities on manners of writing or painting. These are the very syntheses that, again and again in ages past, lent their signifying value to the signifier as well as foundation and authority first to poetics and later to the aesthetics of the beautiful.

Now, this anti-synthetic work I have in mind, this work that strives to match the default of representation to which the feeling of the sublime attests, has distant sources in the Biblical text. Longinus, in his *Treatise*, points to this, but still confusedly. It comes to light, however, following Boileau (and notably in the French debate) on the subject of religious eloquence. Recourse to the *'je ne sais quoi'* creates at least the effect of intervention in order to confound 'grand style,' the 'foreground' style, the Greek ideal of beauty and the Roman ideal of eloquence. It opens a breach in the classical wholeness constituted of gods, men, and nature. Through this breach, one begins to perceive a non-world, a desert where a voice calls out in peremptory fashion, saying nothing more than, 'Listen.'

By the time Joyce wrote *Ulysses*, artists and writers knew (in divergent ways, to be sure) that in a very broad sense the stakes of writing are (as they have always been, but now explicitly) not to create beauty, but rather to bear witness to a liability to that voice that, within man, exceeds man, nature, and their classical concordance.

The aesthetics of a Baudelaire or a Flaubert already prove this. Everything, down to the motif of the city so predominant in *Ulysses*, belongs to the new stakes of writing. It is not enough to consider Bloom as a historian or a sociologist, as the literary counterpart of urbanization in progress. He is also and especially, I believe (with Benjamin), the return of solitude, of the desert, and of inoperativity at the heart of the community. The modern city is the operativity [*œuvre*] in the bosom of which the community and the individual are deprived of their artwork [*œuvre*] by the hegemony of market value. Far from being a free city, Joyce's Dublin is, to use Jean-Luc Nancy's words, an inoperative community.[6] Bloom, the ad salesman, is witness to this painful futility. But his witnessing should not constitute a work in the academic sense; that witnessing is only the muffled mumbling of phrases free-associating 'inside' when no one is speaking to you, when you're in the desert. Nor, further, must Joyce be allowed to constitute a work out of Bloom's witnessing. He can only bear witness to the fact that witnessing does not constitute a work – that witnessing is not Greek. *Ulysses* is one of the greatest works devoted to, consecrated to inoperativity. The *Odyssey*'s framework returns in it only to be deconstructed and to leave room for the void of interpellation.

Witness the 'Aeolus' episode: 'We were always loyal to lost causes, professor [MacHugh] said [in the offices of the *Evening Telegraph*]. Success for us is the death of the intellect and of the imagination' (110). The name of this death is England: under its domination, Ireland is doomed not only to palpable misery, but also to the same radical inoperativity as Israel in Egypt. At the college historical society, where assimilation has just been advocated, John F. Taylor explains that it is, on the contrary, by preserving and observing the tables of the law 'graven,' he says, 'In the language of the outlaw,' by refusing the law of the empire, that the Irish people will, as the Jewish people had done before, succeed in escaping 'their house of bondage' (117).

I do not claim that *Ulysses* is the book of the law and the exodus. It is simply written in the writing of the outlaws that were Joseph's sons in Egypt and Parnell's sons in Ireland. In a bastardized [*météquisée*] Ireland situated beyond the pale of Europe, Bloom, the wanderer [*métèque*], is more Irish than the Irish. Being suspicious of his people, Moses looked askance at a people subservient to the idolatry of the false Roman god and to the interests of British power. But Parnell failed to deliver this people. And Bloom, a bad Jew and an ordinary Irishman, is incapable of holy anger. The only thing left in him of Moses' call to rise and leave is a disavowal of what is here, indignity at ordinary life, a cowardly concession of the soul to derisive reality.

'And yet [Moses] died without having entered the land of promise,' says J. J. O'Molloy in the same episode. To which Lenehan adds, 'And with a great future behind him' (118). The exodus is perhaps a return. It is at least the promise of a return. But this promise remains, and must remain, held as a promise: never realized. Moses, Parnell: dying before fulfillment. The return's future remains hidden in the promise made long ago. The paradox of all ages is what structures the work of an anamnesis: what was announced in the past was that there would be a future to attest to it. Writing is this work of bearing witness to a presence that is not the 'foreground' present. Once and for all, presence will have been promised; writing is devoted to not forgetting it.

Speaking to himself in the 'Lestrygonians' episode, Bloom says: 'Can't bring back time. Like holding water in your hand. Would you go back to then? Just beginning then. Would you? Are you not happy in your home you poor little naughty boy?' (137). The enticing, vulgar interpellation comes from a woman's voice: the quote from a letter Bloom found at the *poste restante* from a correspondant, Martha, answering an obscene solicitation he had sent under the pseudonym, Henry Fleury.

Thus, two things find expression in the lowest of languages and feelings: the sorrow of captivity in Egypt and the misery of a false flight that would be no more than a repetition of the flight Bloom carried out in Molly's company and upon her person. Martha, Molly, the sirens, Bella, Zoe, Flora, Kitty, the girls on the beach – women never assist in the flight from Egypt: they *are* Egypt. Being unhappy at home means being unhappy at *their* home. One must not want or even hope to 'repossess' this home of one's own, that is, to return to it. *Home* is not what was promised. Bloom will never again find Penelope. He will lay down, head to feet (the Beckettian position). And he is not the one to whom she will say 'yes yes.'

Pell-mell, and merely hinted at, these are some indicators for following the cleft or the crack that Jewishness (the Irish condition) creates in the beautiful amphora representing the Homeric voyage.

3

I should address the question of fatherhood insofar as it affects the motif of the return in *Ulysses*. The question of fatherhood or lineage is also that of authority, or of the author, or, as we say, of creation. Under the title of lineage, Joyce lays out his poetics.

I will restrict myself to three observations, all of which concern the motif of return.

To begin with, lineage conforms to the general principle of reversibility. The father is also son of his son, as the son is father of his father. They engender one another. We could say that they are the same individual, self-engendered.

This does not seem to be the case for the *Odyssey*. We do, however, find a trace of this principle in a fact well known to scholars. 'Telemachus' is, in addition to Odysseus's voyage, placed prior to it in the narrative order. To complete this collage, Telemachus, who leaves for Ithaca in Song 4, only arrives there in Song 15, just shortly before his father. The son's adventures are like a pre-image of his father's.

Joyce respects this disposition in the composition of *Ulysses*. When Dedalus first meets Bloom at the brothel, only in the fifteenth episode, the question to be posed is whether, when this return of the son to the father and of the father to the son occurs, the father recognizes himself in the son, as if he were himself the son, and vice-versa. This is apparently the case in the *Odyssey*.

In *Ulysses*, the encounter, as we know, concludes with a separation. I would even venture to say that it begins with this separation. In the end, Bloom settles back into his home, while Dedalus leaves it. The lineage appears shattered, impossible. The son does not re-create his father. But it is precisely by this failure of identification that the true principle of generation is made clear. The authentic lineage requires the rupture, the interruption of the link between father and son.

Let me address the *mise-en-scène* of this rupture. In the Ithaca episode, Dedalus has just refused Bloom's hospitality, and they leave together, saying goodbye. Bloom heads off first with his candle, followed by Dedalus, diaconal hat on his head and rod of ash in hand (two props of the exodus introduced in the third episode, 'Proteus') (40). Question: 'With what intonation *secreto* of what commemorative psalm?' Answer: 'The 113th, *modus peregrinus: In exitu Israel de Egypto: domus Jacob de populo barbaro*' (573). Commemoration, secret, peregrination or pilgrimage, exodus — this text is that of the Vulgate Bible. In the Torah, the rabbinical translation of Psalm 114 reads: 'When Israel came out of Egypt,/ the House of Jacob from a foreign nation.'

Note, obviously, the resurgence of the wandering Jew at the precise moment of non-return. If the son rejects the father, the father also persists in returning toward the flesh of his house, toward his wife and carnal generation, that is, toward the Egypt of representations.

I refer to only two indicators of this movement in the second part of Bloom's journey: to the fact that his meeting with Dedalus alters the figure of the father and that it renders it alien to the son.

At the moment that Dedalus finds Bloom, in the brothel, Bloom is in the process of reclaiming the potato (Irish misery, once more) from Zoe. He carries this potato in his pocket and had given it to her upon entering, like a fetish. He reclaims it in these terms: 'It is nothing, but still, a relic of poor mamma. There is a memory attached to it. I should like to have it.' To which Stephen replies: 'To have or not to have that is the question' (453).

To possess the memory of the wife and the house, to have it back. The son comes upon the father engaged in the imaginary dimension of this return – that of nostalgia. The scene of domestic *jouissance* and its appropriation, where this movement is completed, unfolds sumptuously in the Ithacan episode. The lady daydreams upstairs in the tepidness of intimate flesh and underwear. Downstairs, in the kitchen, her husband totes up all the petty modern (or postmodern) interests of a semi-skilled worker: puttering, minor patents, astronomy-made-easy, subway eroticism, playing the horses, moonlighting to supplement the budget, gardening, obtaining credit, seeking petty distinction. Already in the 'Eumaeus' episode, we are reminded that Parnell has failed to free Ireland because of a woman. As soon as they offer themselves, flesh and incarnation, by their furor, cause writing and exodus to fail. Once one is satisfied, exaltation fails also, because it requires accounting. These are two meanings of the French word *jouissance*. We also learn that Bloom has been thrice baptized: Protestant, English, and Egyptian.

A complementary indicator of the necessary separation between father and son can be found in the son's story. From the beginning of 'Telemachus,' Dedalus is en route for, or rather, is rehashing, an irremissible inner exodus. I only mention one example (out of thousands) of distancing within apparent presence. Dedalus has sent Mulligan a telegram. Mulligan reads it aloud joyfully in front of the library debating club, which Dedalus himself has just met up with ('Scylla and Charybdis'): '*The sentimentalist is he who would enjoy without incurring the immense debtorship for a thing done*. Signed: Dedalus' (164).

This inscription from afar, this telegraphy (Does 'Telemachus' mean 'the end of battle' or 'battle at a distance'?) recalls the indignity of all sentimentality: getting something for nothing. To assume that one is free from debt because one has paid the 'returned' object through *jouissance*. But the debt is enormous, prohibiting the completion of this return that is *jouissance*. Through this, the flow of 'sentimentality' that inundates Bloom, having returned from Ithaca, finds itself distanced.

A second observation. The thesis of fatherhood or true lineage is expounded, in this same library and primarily through Stephen's words, regarding the case of Shakespeare's identification with Hamlet. Elsinore is a failed Ithaca. The suitor has conquered Penelope, and Ulysses (the king) has been murdered. Penelope has been unfaithful like Helen. The father can only return to the son in absence, through his voice, which recalls the debt. You must revenge me, reestablish me, that is, engender me anew. Dedalus holds (without sustaining it) the thesis that Shakespeare was this absent, humiliated, cuckolded father, that he always played the dead king at the Globe, and that his wife, Anne, was, like the queen, a whore, a Molly.

In the end, there is no consubstantial fatherhood, except in the mystical sense that is also the highest degree of uncertainty concerning lineage. 'Fatherhood, in the sense of conscious begetting, is unknown to man' (170). And further, 'In the economy of heaven, foretold by Hamlet, there are no more marriages, glorified man, an androgynous angel, being a wife unto himself' (175). In the domestic economy, incest rages along all lines of kinship, except the father-son lineage. 'They are sundered by a bodily shame . . . What links them in nature? An instant of blind rut' (170–1). What links them separates them: the complusion to copulate, woman, the 'agenbite of inwit.'

> Fatherhood . . . is a mystical estate, an apostolic succession, from only begetter to only begotten. On that mystery and not on the madonna which the cunning Italian intellect flung to the mob of Europe the church is founded and founded irremovably because founded, like the world, macro and microcosm, upon the void. Upon incertitude, upon unlikelihood . . . Paternity may be a legal fiction. (170)

Lineage, or more precisely, true paternization, is only the transmission of what I have termed *calling*. There is no carnal lineage between males: the feminine house is useless, even harmful to it. At Shakespeare's birth, '[a] star, a daystar, a firedrake, rose' (172). It is the star William follows upon leaving Stratford and the 'arms' of his future. 'A star by night, Stephen said. A pillar of the cloud by day' (173). Once again the theme of the wandering Jew. Shakespeare answers the call that comes to him from the desert. In fleeing from the incestuous and lascivious mother, Egypt, he also flees from the pretenders to carnal fatherhood. One leaves *here*, one goes over there, backward, elsewhere, toward the true past that is still to come.

A final remark on the question of fatherhood as unfulfilled return. What is said of the father and son must also be understood with regard to the writer and reader. The reader engenders the author, and the author is the reader of his reader. But there is also a flesh interposed between them that impedes a pure genealogy: language, the whore that language is. It can represent, say, and make love to everything. It is the Egypt of writing.

Language is like water, a kind of great profligate carnal sea that offers itself to everything, infiltrates everywhere, redoubles and represents everything. Joyce's writing, plunged in this water, tries to defer the effect of representation and ductility, to hold back the insidious tide. In the catechism recited at Ithaca, Bloom's elegy to water takes on the dimension of an inundation. Bloom surrenders himself to the immersion. But he is careful not to inform Stephen of his adoration and his drowning. The reason: 'The incompatibility of aquacity with the erratic originality of genius' (550).

One must necessarily give in to language when one writes, but one cannot give in to it either. The defeat, which consists in the trust one puts into language, must necessarily be continuously defeated in its turn; the trust must remain suspended. 'I believe, O Lord, help my unbelief. That is, help me to believe or help me to unbelieve? Who helps to believe? *Egomen*. Who to unbelieve? Other chap' (176). What says yes to the permanent yes of woman-language is the Ego. As for the 'other chap' (who tells him no, no, that's not it, you haven't got it, arise and leave), I hear in him the shattering voice that calls. ('To chap' is also 'to split,' 'to cleave.' And a 'chap' is a 'peddler,' the traveling salesman.)

Literary genealogy responds to the same demand and runs into the same aporia as lineage. How, if one writes, is it possible not to say yes to the sea of language? Genius consists in inscribing within it what it cannot espouse. One thing that cannot be done with water is to part it. Joyce-Dedalus lacerates language. It closes up again immediately under his flamboyant style.

I return to the catechism of the Ithaca episode. Question: 'For what creature was the door of egress a door of ingress?' Answer: 'For a cat' (573).

This is thus a final return, accompanied by this she-cat [*chatte*], a return upon and of sexual difference. An argumentative genre.

On the one hand, since the father is son of the son and the son father of the father, *male* is what engenders itself without sexual intercourse. Or, rather, only engenders itself, in truth, according to the voice, which is male. From oneself, through the sole obeyance to the injunction, issues nothing (fire and storm cloud) to hear, that is, nothing to write. With regard to carnal fatherhood, the Lord, blessed be His name, can very well pull some Isaac from the withered belly of an old woman and make of him a gift to his old man. But there will nonetheless come a day when the voice will come to reclaim him, if not by sacrifice, at least by *ageda*, by binding or alliance. This is a warning that males, the Ulysses's and the Abrahams, would be mistaken to expect any revenue from what their wives claim to offer them. Bloom has lost his son Rudy. And Stephen has rebuffed the final wishes of his dying mother. The sexual generation is only the occasion for sin, for forgetting memory's debt. This memory is that nothing returns, that everything is an advent. This is what anamnesis means: a thinking, a struggle backwards, of which the work of writing consists. And this is endless. A peregrination without return.

But, on the other hand, there is the she-cat [*chatte*] (it is, as we know, a term of endearment the French give to the female sexual organ), which is the passage through which the father enters and out of which emerges his son. The pussy objects that it is, in the male-to-male lineage, the obligatory threshold, the inevitable path for the transmission of the seed. It argues that if the Lord has created us sexed, sectioned and separated, and if he holds the power to reunite us according to the fire in our loins, it is not only to test us, but to expose the mystery of his ways. In particular, that the self-engenderment, of which sexuality is the sole heavenly guardian, resides (oh so palpably!) *ad portas mulieris*.

We see the argument. It is that of the Virgin Mother and the prostituted saint.

Now, what relation can this *disputatio* on sex have with the return and the return upon the return? That relation in which the things are not properly ordered: first, the adequation of the father-son, of voice and writing; second, the passage through the woman, the feminine passage, the concession and *jouissance*. No, it is the contrary, or, rather, not even the contrary: it is not even the same order returned on the same time line, it is the initial definitive disorganization of that so-called time line, which is only time consciousness.

The question *Ulysses* poses in return is not even whether one can step twice in the same stream, which is a pardonable uneasiness of consciousness faced with chronological succession (that succession forcing consciousness to forever defer its actualization, so that it must always catch up with itself, so that it must hold back at every step of its advance along the time line). *Ulysses* poses another question altogether: Is not sexual difference the same as ontological difference? Is it not from sexual difference that the temporalizing separation of consciousness with itself is engendered? And from it that the unconscious as extra-memorial past is formed? – a past that does not last as past and that one cannot have back, that is, an inappropriable past. Is it not this immemorial that calls out? And is it not writing that attempts, desperately, to formulate an answer to this remainder to which the soul is held hostage?

Objection: Why would sexual difference occupy this eminent position in engendering when it has been established that, according to Joyce-Dedalus, true generation, fecundity, and propagation owe nothing to it and that it is carried out in the father-son identity?

Answer: It is readily demonstrable that the idea of male self-engendering – autochthony of warriors in the Greek version, the voice's injunction ('call') in the Hebrew version – only betrays (translates and disguises) the irreparable preeminence of sexual difference.

Argument: Homeric males go off to war to seek an unfaithful woman and Odysseus would simply have no need to return had he not taken part in this expedition. By this consecution, and also because the whore lies dormant in the matron, Helen takes precedence over Penelope. As for the Jews, their book recounts the fact that original sin (the offense of claiming to equal and substitute for divine transcendence: the voice) is the doing of a woman. By this consecution, and here because the she-devil lies awake in the wife, Eve takes precedence over Sarah. As proof, the laughter that overcomes the old woman when her belated pregnancy is announced: this is the same offense that Eve committed against the Lord. Another name for Israel is 'it will laugh.'

Concession: To be sure, this return that the *Odyssey* is attempts to form the scar of difference, and this exodus that the Pentateuch recounts attempts to free itself from it.

Conclusion: Both attempts bear within them the admission of an initial and recurrent servitude. This is why an originary position, before any mediation, as perennial source, must be granted to sexual difference. It is not because Joyce is overly obsessed, obeying some realist scruple or bent on shocking us, that there is so much sex in *Ulysses*. Rather, it is because the writing of Homeric return – even returned via the Biblical exodus – cannot fail to come up against that difference, that more ancient, intimate obstacle that is opposed to return, to crash into it and ceaselessly return to it.

In returning upon and against the event of sexual difference (a difference that has no site, no representation, one that engenders uncontrollable anxiety, but whose ductile force ceaselessly immerses this anxiety and impotence), and in reinscribing this event in language, Joyce's writing announces the irreparability of the offense and the impossibility of return. The writer can only bear witness to his magnetic attraction at the level of language. For it is not enough to take this anxiety linked to the irremissible hidden separation as the object of a discourse (as I myself am doing here). To truly bear witness to it, one must make language anxious.

There is an eternal undoing of the spirit. We cannot avenge it. By avenging it, we repeat it, as Hamlet does. It is not situated in a temporality of successions. This anxiety, this obsession for pleasure, this horror, always begins again. This is what supports parataxis, the return of the *and*; this is what interferes with any return.

I shall end. Dedalus presents Shakespeare's initial undoing in these terms:

> Belief in himself has been untimely killed. He was overborne in a cornfield first (a ryefield, I should say) and he will never be a victor in his own eyes after nor play victoriously the game of laugh and lie down. Assumed dongiovannism will not save him. No later undoing will undo the first undoing. The tusk of the boar has wounded him there where love lies ableeding. If the shrew is worsted yet there remains to her woman's invisible weapon. There is, I feel in the words, some goad of the flesh driving him into a new passion, a darker shadow of the first, darkening even his own understanding of himself. A like fate awaits him and the two rages commingle in a whirlpool . . . The soul has been before stricken mortally, a poison poured in the porch of a sleeping ear (161).

Stephen slips this message to King Hamlet: 'The poisoning and the beast with two backs that urged it King Hamlet's ghost could not know of were he not endowed with knowledge by his creator' (162).

Suppose that the creator reveals nothing to us of this poisoning. And suppose that, because the creator does not exist or, at least, does not speak, the voice having silenced itself, we take an entire lifetime to learn that we were not murdered but engendered by this poisoning of the flesh.

It is then that Dedalus adds these words that will have served to return me upon the return, to return it and to attempt (with Joyce) to turn myself away from it: 'That is why the speech [Hamlet's, Shakespeare's, Joyce's] is always turned elsewhere, backward' (162). Words that Dedalus comments upon as follows: 'Ravisher and ravished, what he would but would not' (162); in other words, the very designation of the work of inoperativity. With this one last joke: 'He goes back, weary of the creation he has piled up to hide him from himself, an old dog licking an old sore. But, because loss is his gain, he passes on towards eternity in undiminished personality' (162). *Dog* is the re-turned truth of *God*, yet no writing can prevent *Dog* from returning, in its turn, into *God*. Return, nonetheless, of inoperativity. Amen.

Notes

Lecture delivered at the Eleventh International James Joyce Symposium in Venice, June 1988. *Ulysses* page references are to the 'corrected' edition: James Joyce, *Ulysses*, ed. H. W. Gabler with W. Steppe and C. Melchior (New York: Random House, 1986).

1. E. Auerbach, *Mimesis: The Representation of Reality in Western Literature*, trans. W. R. Trask (Princeton, NJ: Princeton University Press, 1953). The chapter on the *Odyssey* is entitled 'Odysseus' scar' (pp. 3–23).
2. Ibid. pp. 7, 13.
3. Ibid. p. 17.
4. TN: Lyotard uses this word to designate *chansons de geste*, medieval Biblical chronicles in verse. The genre is akin to the passion play.
5. Auerbach, *Mimesis*, p. 22. [TN: to alleviate any ambiguity between Lyotard's use of this quote and Auerbach's meaning, we have decided to furnish more of the sentence than appeared in the original French.]
6. Cf. Jean-Luc Nancy, *The Inoperative Community*, trans. P. Connor, L. Garbus, M. Holland and S. Sawhney (Minneapolis: University of Minnesota Press, 1990).

Chapter 8

Soundproof Room, chapters 4–6

Lost Voice

Is it time to despair? Incarnated in the course of events, living and recounting the promise, reckoning on emancipation, will the 'first person' have only been an episode of the return, an inconsequential levy doomed, like all the others, to decline? a dawn soon gone dark? Called on to bury modern subjectivity, to take note of the bankruptcy of eschatological narrative, the option for hope – be it religious or rationalist – raises the objection that if one supposes one modernity finished, another one is always taking shape. A different one, to be sure, but one bearing a significance to assign to history: the postmodern is still modern. Argument without consequence, however: there is no need for any 'new' initiatory decision to come along and conclude or even interrupt the death throes of old hopes. Further, even if this were the case, far from refuting the universality of redundancy, such a 'renewal' would confirm it and encourage hopelessness.

Instead of repeating the disappointment by denying it, the lesson of an altogether different way of thinking and of living the presence of the promise within history may be learned. Having from the outset woven disappointment together with the strand of its promise, the Jewish narrative seems invulnerable to cyclical despair. No identifiable subject – not even 'the people' – is its author. It recounts that the community never fully heard the voice in vivo and that the community may only consult a written summary – one that is consonantal, mute, risky to decipher and vocalize. As for its interpretation, the immense corpus of readings and commentaries thereupon – a millennial accumulation – offers its precious and cumbersome services. The first written letter, the aleph, can barely be heard: a breath before the breath, the throat about to open as it prepares to give voice. I do not make the decision to begin; I do not proclaim that decision; a voice that is not mine readies me for entering into the covenant. Symmetrical prudence as to the notion of an end. A Hasidic story says that if you forget a prayer's exact form, what it asks, the circumstance in which it should be said, you can at least evoke the series of things forgotten, invoke the pardon, and 'that's enough.' By recounting the forgotten voice, one does not make it heard as is – vain hope, illusion – : one safeguards the covenant. Narrating its loss is still to honor its unpresented presence. In order to acquire a precarious renown, Kafka's Josephine has only to whistle weakly, almost inaudibly, the tunes that the mouse people once knew how to sing but no longer remember.[1]

The West of modernities was duty bound to persecute quite plainly this melancholic and peculiar prudence. So much care applied to listening to the evanescent meanings entailed by the least event or the worst catastrophe or some obviously good fortune: on principle all this constituted an annoyance to the proclaimed and reiterated project of concretely achieving full possession of meaning, of freedom. Furthermore, it is no coincidence if the failure of that project – a failure resulting mechanically in its opposite: the mad deduction of mastery under the fraudulent auspices of a race self-proclaimed as always already, by nature, in full possession of itself and of the world, a race thus meant to actualize the completion of history in its own beginning – it is no coincidence, then, if the Nazi frenzy to totalize meaning without remainder culminates with the Final Solution. The *Endlösung* aimed to cause the definitive forgetting of witnesses of a voice forgotten from the outset and whose forgetting can never and must never be forgotten. As to the extermination program and its implementation in the souls and on the bodies of the wretched, the order was given under threat of death to the yes-men to silence them. The crime was to be perfect, the annihilation annihilated, the end deprived of itself. 'The disappearance of death,' wrote Adorno.[2]

Not only is no trace of anti-Semitism detectable either in the writings or in the conduct of Malraux – rarest of exceptions for his time – it is legitimate to think that there is a correspondence between, on the one hand, the kind of validity that the psychology of art bestows on artworks,[3] a validity that his own poetics aims at – the only validity capable, possibly, of resisting the debacle of values – and, on the other, this unforgetting of forgetting and listening to the inaudible whose paradox is sustained in the Jewish tradition.

Moreover, Malraux comes to learn of or to recognize the precariousness by which the subjective voice is stricken in spite of its claim to speak and realize the truth in the great works born of the modern tradition itself. Cervantes's *Quixote* recounts an epic whose conclusion is doomed to failure from the outset. By the same stroke, Cervantes strips the voice that recounts the epic of its authority over the sense of the story. If the story fails to lead to the glory of its fulfillment, to *fama*, then the voice that recounts this misunderstanding must confess to his own *infamy*. It is on the grounds of this infamy that Borges deploys the paradoxical implications for the various narrative polarities. Determining distinct positions for hero, narrator, author, and reader gives rise to suspicion and confusion. Diegetic reality proves almost indiscernible from the 'reality effect' produced by the narration. The moderns think they can close the gap between the plane of the reality told and that of the narrative voice by making the latter flesh right in the story. The substance is subject; the drama that I recount is mine . . . Modern revelation consists of the self-affirmation of this self-affectation.

Yet if such is the case (and how is one to know?), then object and meaning begin to circulate freely, to switch positions at each of the sentence's posts. How is the original to be distinguished from the imitation? A character in a novel is no less real than the author or the reader. And the latter are no less fictional than the former. Universal history exists solely through the books that contain it, and no single one of these holds the privilege of pronouncing the beginning or the end, let alone the privilege of being one or the other. Again, establishing a *terminus a quo, ad quem* requires that one pass beyond: the position of the sentence announcing that the preceding one was the last or that the following one will be the first bars it from taking its place within the segment of duration that it closes or inaugurates.

From Malraux's standpoint *Remembrance of Things Past* was the last great modern novel. The voice, whose position throughout the narrative is immanent to the story that it recounts, finally manages to reach the revelation of its initial decision to speak (or write). These plots were impressed on the register of speech. Proust notes that they make up the spontaneous archive of 'impressions' deposited by the diegesis in the discourse of the narrative. Through its authority as instance that knows and wishes what it says, the voice must then say what was initially said through it. *The Past Recaptured* concludes with the promise of this beginning that is conscious of itself and of its end: thus the modern gesture par excellence – Hegel's speculative sentence – hitches the truth-to-come together with the coming-to-itself of completed experience. Recall without remainder is presumed. Against this recall Malraux writes *Anti-Memoirs*.

Joyce's *Ulysses* explodes the lie of the chronicles. The great return through narration is an illusion concocted by desire: an ideology. Now, what prohibits the putative voice from assembling its experience in some consummate *remembering*, from re-membering itself in some subject of an Odyssey, is the 'means' of narrative itself: language. The narrator can very well believe and delude others into believing that he commands the use of language: it is not at his disposal; it doesn't *return* to him.[4] Undisciplined vocables laden with myriad meanings that are sometimes contradictory or unknown, placed in syntaxes replete with innuendos, mispronunciations, ambiguities: everything in linguistic material leads honest intention to signify astray and betrays loyalty to meaning. The voice can never be done with trying to master rebellious language. Writing becomes enamored of the wild one, weds her, seeking to honor the powers of this maid of all work who is infinitely more opulent than her supposed employer.

Role reversal, inversion. What 'I' would still dare to introduce itself as master of narrative when the promise of final freedom that it proffers instantly runs aground on the inextricable and restrictive perversity of the language in which it is formulated? 'Perversion' since, additionally, the slippage of roles and meanings on the discourse of experience can be such as to render the voices of God and Satan indistinct. Evil is no longer the rebellious angel, a dark prince who wages direct war with sovereign good: it is the executioner ordained into the priesthood, the paranoiac beatified, the people freely electing its tyrants, the exploiter clothed as the civilizer, the radiant future deporting and assassinating its supporters.

'Having another round,' as the popular saying goes, doesn't mean beginning: one can only pretend to begin. Already present, the end is deferred, made to forget. Cynical imposters, false prophets proliferate. Before abjection furiously spouting its gospel, even the most tenacious faith retracts. Bernanos wrote *The Imposter* and *The Star of Satan* and confided to Malraux that to be Christian in that day was to believe in the devil.[5] Thomas Mann radicalized this diagnostic in *Doktor Faustus*: Satan inspired the Third Reich and the worldwide carnage. But the New Music was also his handiwork.[6] The act of writing or the act of art is authorized by no voice, aims at no end. Sovereign, with no regard for the law or for others, the art work *is*. Literature in collusion with evil: Bataille stakes claims to their complicity.[7] The practice of insubordination to the voice, to the project is the only way to measure up to the nothingness left by the death of God and Man. For an instant, in the ecstasy of the blackened void, 'inner experience' abolishes the subject.[8]

Moribund Ego

In the midst of the ruins the sincerity that religious denominations claim as an excuse is as futile as the faithfulness demanded of a biographer: both believe they can regulate their narration on a suppositum[9] – a sort of egotic identity more or less in control of itself yet an identity that the narrative itself would be responsible for founding in order to unify its attributes and successive trials. To some Malraux's entire œuvre appears autobiographical. And doubly so insofar as that life itself – one that the œuvre draws on abundantly – appears to have been 'written' for it. But what might the term *autobiography* mean when the ego's autonomy is packed away along with the other illusions? when its existence is overrun by every subordination, then deserted? when the *bios*, stripped of all finality, is cosmic? nothing more, that is, than the illusory moment of a death more total than death? 'With death, lying in wait up there among its stellar plains, which caused the network of the veins of the living earth to appear to me like the lines on my dead mother's hand' (*AM*, 69).

The spider's nest is within the ego; a sinister mother, she devours it: 'we can see it disappear before our very eyes,' unmasked, overcome. 'The Ego, a deserted palace that each of us enters alone, contains each of the jewels of our temporary madness jumbled together with those of our lucidity; and consciousness of ourselves is woven mainly of vain desires, hopes, and dreams' (*JE*, 142). Woven into a spider's web, texture of temporary and vain madness: all that gets caught there is fit for liming and delitescence. Except for a few stones whose nature is lucid, instead of lunar, but that are difficult to distinguish from the imitations. The stones from the temple at Benteaï-Srey? If it had simply been a question of inventing a biography, Malraux had instantly revealed the major theme when he set off in search of that art treasure lost in the Khmer cloaca. Phobia of unspeakable creatures, obsession for inscribing on the swarm his name as inventor of the site: if the idea was to compose the picture of a firmly entrenched destiny compulsion, nothing was missing.

Total misinterpretation, however, with regard to the stakes of writing. *Compulsion, destiny, phobia, obsession*: these are all terms borrowed from the clinic, all words – like *biography*, even – that belong to the redundant one.[10] You will have been what you were meant to be, what you couldn't help but be. The pen is not applied directly to the repugnant pulp in order to sign and extract an artwork because it is spurred by neurosis, some maniacally egoistic heroism or delirium for sovereign will – so many cases of submission to this itself: the abject repetition from which one thinks one can be exempt. 'However forcefully I wish to become conscious of myself, I feel subjected to a random series of sensations that escape my grasp altogether.'

The artwork rises precisely from the invalidation of the ego decomposed into ordinary impressionistic stirrings at the very instant that it proves incapable (except if it cheats) of hearing its own voice or of having it heard. The very inconsistency revealed by the dissipation of the subjective screen then lends support to an absolute writing. For immortal is the underground of dead life and of living death. Such is the seatless, shifting foundation, the nothingness in whose proximity Malraux's poetics seeks the fulmination of truth. After the fashion of Bataille's blinding night, immortality does not mean perpetuity. The cycle of the same may be so for speculation, but experience only affords this feeling in flashes, in instants beyond doubt.

Something resists, one reads in 'D'une jeunesse européenne': 'the feeling of our distinct existence at this instant. Consciousness of being *one* is one of the irreducible givens of human existence' (*JE*, 143–4). The feeling that one exists – not self-consciousness; instantaneous existence – not life lending itself to biography: the immediate and intensely obvious fact of a 'There, now!' that is oblivious to history slices the interminable ebb and flow with the thinnest of wires. In no manner does this feeling transcend lunar redundancy: its relation to it is *instant*, unpredictable at its advent, irrefutable like a convulsion.

Some forty-five years later, in the Salpêtrière Hospital, Malraux is teetering between life and death, stricken by repeated comas, staggered by dizzy spells. One night he finds himself roaming about on all fours, confusing walls with the floor in a room that seems to tip. 'Amputated from the earth,' he writes as soon as he can pick up a pen again, 'the promixity of the death throes of others drowns the question "What am I?," makes it otiose . . . This tourist trip through the archipelago of death disregards any sequence of events, lays bare only the most inchoate and most intense consciousness, the convulsive "I am"' (*Laz*., 79). What 'I'? – 'an "I" without a self' (*Laz*., 84). And, as if to complete the diagnostic sketched in 'D'une jeunesse européenne': 'It has thus been proclaimed that man consists of his phantasms, his drives, his hidden desires. I feel like writing that he is what gets constructed upon this vehement consciousness of existing, only existing.' The work is written in the ink of the Scourge: man is only that which exceeds the inhuman of artwork.

To Perken's question, 'No one ever makes anything of his life . . . What do you expect from yours?' this is how Claude, in *The Royal Way*, responds: 'I think I know best what I do *not* expect of it.' Perken insists: 'Whenever you've had to choose between alternatives, surely . . .'; Claude interrupts: 'It's not I who choose; it's something in me that resists.' 'Resists what?' the other asks. 'Being conscious of death' (*RW*, 52–3). One understands: to the lucid dread of redundancy.

The minuscule, intense position of this resistance is called '"I" without a self.' Existence toiling like a beast on all fours against the dissolution of personal identity: Is this where true life lies? inscribed in syncopated dotted lines? in the hiccoughs of the mortally wounded? in the flaccid movement of dead life? 'I suddenly discovered,' writes Lazarus, 'something other than a life–other. I did not take it for death; but *it speaks of death*' (*Laz*., 92). This something other speaks of death as close as is possible while continuing to resist in the fetid nothingness where the ego decomposes.

'Belatedly,' comments a recovered Lazarus, 'I encountered the god of dread. Dread independent of fear, like sexuality independent of any object (except ourselves)' (*Laz*., 92). Dread, as has been said, is the name Malraux gives to the fascination excited by the vile mire where that which is something dissolves and prepares its renewal. Fear has an object; not dread. 'Far beyond fear,' he writes, 'deep inside me, as much a part of me as the beating of my heart. A sacred horror inhabits us, awaits us, as the mystics tell us that God awaits them . . . The inner forces which drive us to self-destruction, to shame, provoke despair rather than terror; this force does not drive us to anything' (*Laz*., 92).

Devoid of any project, subject or rejection other than obstinate existence, the entity that crawls around in the corners of the Salpêtrière Hospital room like Kafka's Gregor and whose memory strikes dread in the ego, this presence that resists the death of presences and whose only test of itself consists of surviving it – this entity is an instant in necrophagous life, a hole in the hideous cycle of reproduction through consumption. Malraux attempts to name this anonymous one: 'I encountered it in the way that a psychiatrist discovers within himself the spiders and octopuses of his patient's nightmares. The monster occupied my ruins' (*Laz.*, 92). On all fours within his own tomb, a man deprived of his human life gropes at the floor as if it were a wall, coils himself up on the night stand that he confuses with his bed. This exists, obstinately: it's a larva.

Here is the truth when God is dead and the Ego moribund: there remains the bestiality of an 'I am' of which the ego knew nothing and that will presently terrify it. Strange polar conversion: life for the ego – its life – is doomed to putrescence and, as it lies dying, the vermin within it resists, struggling furiously to be. Stranger still: it says 'I' as from a voice that no one is left to hear.

An autobiography of the spider is inconceivable. She says 'I' yet has no identity. 'One has no biography except for others,' writes Lazarus (*Laz.*, 74). The monster has no interlocutors. Indeed it endures without being durable, being revealed only in extremis to the 'me-that-dies,' as Bataille called it.[11] Monster of simplicity or, rather, of the absolute. Without dimension, timeless, connectionless: 'incomparable monster' is Kyo's term in *Man's Fate* (*MF*, 50).

I, the Fact[12]

'I' is that which writes? Yes and no. Belatedly, after the fact. Monstrous and irrelative, experience has it that the 'I' does not write. It is nothing. Writing creates links. Whence the aporia: to write as *this* would write. So, it's 'I.' Not ego. Ego has a proper name, can be situated within dated time and locales, participates in activities and the commerce of phrases, in the human community, in all that perishes and is born again, all that repeats itself. Ego lends its name to the written that *this* does not write, that 'I' quasi-writes. Whereas ego countersigns liminal existence, 'I,' the anonymous, the spider's lieutenant, signs it. With an X, a mandibular mark. Signs or, rather, signals existence: the gash signals that I *was* here, within the experience of crude and null existence. Inevitable deferral of writing with respect to experience of the monster. Dread is voiceless, deaf. That's why it cannot lie.

A piece of writing – text, painting, sculpture, music, dance step – freed as much as is possible from linkages, meanings, transferences, separated, without message, devoid of ins and outs: an artifact capable of evoking absolute presence should be such. A piece of writing as absolute as writing (which is relative, by definition) can make it.

To the constitutive oxymoron of art, art's *technè* – poetics – the art of art asks how to determine the thought and willed means for making the mute experience of '"I" without a self' audible without violating its silence. This question must remain without response. The least one can say is that the ego inflicts on itself the discipline of listening before-beyond the audible, of sensitizing itself to that which is insensitive to it. 'Supreme beauty in a refined civilization,' writes the Chinese character in *The Temptation of the West*, 'consists of an attentive inculture of the ego.'[13] The fruit of this asceticism is called *lucidity* – the term Malraux adopted from Valéry. It befalls consciousness to assemble and unify diversity while lucidity mercilessly trains a *flash* of light on the worst of it all: Lucifer's eyes yield not. Ego takes care of discourse while 'I' sees to asserting that *this* is nothing, that this *is*: unqualifiable. The perfect poem proffers: 'There, now!' Such a poetics professes *the fact* as ideal. Trenchant and equivocal term: the fact is simultaneously factual and phony, as if born of a technique under protest. To express the wonderfully impossible cross between a manner of writing and the absolute, the agnostic Malraux steals the theologians' term for that which is unsolvable: creation. A term whispered by Satan.

In his first published article, 'Des origines de la poésie cubiste' (1920), Malraux indicates the masters: Apollinaire, Max Jacob, Reverdy, and Cendrars. He adopts cubist poetics in accordance with the way Max Jacob set it down in his preface to *The Dice Cup*.[14] The artwork is tantamount to dice thrown haphazardly into the night. Far from abolishing the nothingness that is history, it takes its chances with an improbable *deal* – one that blind chance has not yet composed in living form. The artwork 'means nothing.' It is a singular, unexpected arrangement of its constituent elements: words in literature; shapes and colors in painting. It relates to no reference, history, event, or perceptual reality that might have come before it. It in no way expresses the subjectivity of its 'author.' No representation, no expression. And, because it signifies no preexisting 'ideas,' no symbolism either. No meaning or celebration. Max Jacob christens it 'prose poem': something that Baudelaire perhaps sought but didn't find. Prosaic because the writing draws its elements from ordinary language just as cubist painting draws its elements from the prose of the visible. Poetics and poematics because words unset from contexts and usages and grouped into a little dense and hard mass like a 'jewel,' says Max Jacob, such words compose a writing equivalent to *fact: poiein* means to make.

Such an art is openly opposed to the surrealist (or supposed so) belief that the unconscious is the foreman and that automatic writing or the chance of collages should release it. 'I hold what we call the unconscious,' declares Malraux, 'to be confusion itself.'[15] The account of a psychoanalytic cure is more violent than any confession, and certainly it doesn't constitute an artwork. The prose poem is indeed a toss of the dice but one worked, according to Max Jacob, by 'style': 'The style or will creates, that's to say separates' (7). Style is not the man, as Buffon thinks, but his elimination. 'Artists, today,' writes Apollinaire, 'must become inhuman.'[16] To the demand of style, Max Jacob adds the requirement that the artwork be 'situated'. 'The situation distances, that is, it excites the artistic feeling' (7). Thus he summarizes the effect of this twin demand: 'One recognizes that a work has style if it gives the sensation of being self-enclosed; one recognizes that it's situated by the little shock that one gets from it or again from the margin which surrounds it, from the special atmosphere where it moves' (7).

'The use of materials and . . . the composition of the whole' (ibid. 6): in the final analysis, this is a classic definition of style. The following, which is less so, may cause confusion: 'the will to exteriorize oneself by one's chosen means' (ibid. 5). The exteriority obtained by extracting linguistic ore from its gangue and polishing it owes nothing to the expression of some inner ego. Malraux reminds us that one doesn't create in order to express oneself.[17] And Jacob: poetic 'will can only be exercised on the choice of means, because the work of art is only a collection of means' (6). A formulation, once again, that can cause misunderstanding – the kind to which Malraux sometimes falls victim when it happens that his search for a process absorbs his entire art of writing and reading.

As to the 'situation,' this shields the work from the impatience of the reader eager for appropriation by setting up a 'spiritual margin' (ibid. 7). What can the poet expect from this distanciation? – That the amateur's desire will only be exacerbated as when spurned by a coquette? Without doubt. But, in addition, that the halo of oddity will convert the massive transferential motion into artistic emotion. Intensely, severely, writing *distracts* the ego, shields it from the misery of plots. So much so that the ego is converted from an absentee of realities into a very real visionary of Absence: Jesus appears before Jacob on the wall of his room.

The least one can say is that this epiphany is unnecessary for nihilist poetics, which aspires to the scarcely more modest ambition of having the artwork be here – present to 'real' presence, as truly 'poetic fact,' as Reverdy wrote just when Braque was jotting down in his *Notebooks* that a painting derives all of its value from being a 'pictural fact.'[18] Yet, given that it constitutes a hole in perceptual space-time and discursive reason, what does the artwork have to do with a fact? – Everything, precisely, by the naked fact of existing that the '"I" without a self' experiences while the ego lies dying in the Salpêtrière Hospital: 'the convulsive "I am"' (*Laz.*, 79). That which resists: 'There, now!' The haiku, a wash whose substance is liminal: their silence defies reading, absolutely. *The Voices of Silence*: 'The great work of art is not wholly identical with truth, as the artist often believes. It *is*. It has issued forth. Not something completed but a birth – life confronting life on its own ground' (*VS*, 461). It has neither nature nor property.

The artwork breaks with convention, with the commonplace, with the flow. It is obtained through a conscious and conscientious labor that relentlessly endeavors to lay bare the ego. Through art the human bends its will to strive toward this inhuman that sometimes forces it wide open.

Notes

1. Franz Kafka, 'Josephine, die Sängerin' (1924); translated as 'Josephine the Singer, or, The Mouse People', trans. Clement Greenberg, *Partisan Review* 110 (May–June 1942): 213–28.
2. Theodor W. Adorno, *Jargon der Eigentlichkeit: Zur deutschen Ideologie* (Frankfurt am Main: Suhrkamp, 1964); translated as *The Jargon of Authenticity*, trans. Knut Tarnowski and Frederic Will (Evanston, Ill.: Northwestern University Press, 1973), p. 157.
3. The 'psychology of art' refers to four essays that Malraux published originally in the journal *Verve* between 1937 and 1940, then fused together, expanded, and reshuffled into three volumes under the general title *La Psychologie de l'art* published by Skira following the war.
4. Where 'elle' refers to *language* and 'lui' to *the narrator*, 'elle ne lui reviet pas' translates idiomatically as 'He doesn't like the look of it.'
5. Georges Bernanos, *L'Imposture* (Paris: Plon, 1927); translated as *The Impostor*, trans. J. S. Whitehouse (Lincoln: University of Nebraska Press, 1999). George Bernanos, *Sous le soleil de Satan* (Paris: Plon, 1926); translated as *The Star of Satan*, trans. Pamela Morris (New York: Macmillan, 1940).
6. Thomas Mann, *Die Entstehung des Doktor Faustus* (Frankfurt am Main: S Fischer, 1976); translated as *Doktor Faustus: The Life of the Great Composer, Adrian Leverkuhn, As Told by a Friend*, trans. H. T. Lowe-Porter (New York: A. A. Knopf, 1948), then as *Doktor Faustus*, trans. John F. Woods (New York: Knopf, 1997).
7. Cf. Georges Bataille, *La Littérature et la Mal* (Paris: Gallimard, 1957); translated as *Literature and Evil*, trans. Alastair Hamilton (London: Marion Boyars, 1973).
8. Cf. Georges Bataille, *L'expérience intérieure* (Paris: Gallimard, 1943; 2nd edn 1954) translated as *Inner Experience*, trans. Lesley Anne Boldt (Albany: State University of New York Press, 1988).
9. English translations of *suppôt*, a term found frequently in the works of Pierre Klossowski, and, later, used by Lyotard in such works as *Économie libidinale*, are characteristically inconsistent. The Latin, *suppositum*, meaning an individual that is substance or subject, best conserves the link to ancient and medieval philosophy.
10. In my translation of Lyotard's *Signed, Malraux*, I suggested 'the redundant one' for *la redite* with the following explanation: 'the feminine noun, *redite*, derives from the past participle *dire* (to say) to literally mean that which is said again. This repetition specific to voiced language provides Lyotard with an incisive allegory to represent Malraux's peculiar way of feeling the recurrence of death in his personal experience of life. *Redite* connotes not only some word, some phrase or thought that is reiterated or "rerun", but also palpable uselessness or superfluity in repetition': Jean-François Lyotard, *Signed, Malraux*, p. 307, n. 2.

11. Cf., for example, Georges Bataille, 'Sacrifices', in *Œuvres complètes* (Paris: Gallimard, 1970), 1: 92.

12. Lyotard includes this comma. Without it, the title would translate better as 'I does it', where 'I' is thought in scare quotes. With the comma, even, this alternate title still resonates.

13. A variant of the quote Lyotard has here is the following epigraph to 'D'une Jeunesse europeénne': 'Le plus haut objet d'une civilisation affinée, c'est une attentive inculture du Moi' [The highest purpose of a refined civilisation consists of an attentive inculture of the ego] (*JE*, 131).

14. Max Jacob, *Le Cornet à dés* [1917] (Paris: Stock, 1923); translated as *The Dice Cup*, trans. John Ashberry, David Ball, Michael Brownstein, Ron Padgett, Zack Rogow, and Bill Zavatsky (New York: SUN, 1979). All quotes attributed to Jacob in the text are from Ashberry et al.

15. Gaëtan Picon, *Malraux par lui-même, avec des annotations d'André Malraux* (Paris: Seuil, 1953), p. 60.

16. Guillaume Apollinaire, *Le Peintre cubiste*, 1913.

17. This is a paraphrase of the following remark: 'If, as it has been affirmed, the novelist created in order to express himself, things would be simpler. But you know I believe that, like all artists, he expresses himself in order to create' (Picon, 58).

18. See Georges Braque, *Cahier de Georges Braque* (Paris: Maeght [Carnets de voyage], 1994).

Chapter 9

Sendings

Work [*Oeuvre*]

Of whom are the *Confessions* the work, the *opus?* To put it differently, what are they working at, what are they setting into work, and what are they opening up, to what do they open the work?

The opening gives the tone. This tone is a leitmotif, a guiding thread that relentlessly rivets my tone to the order of your omniscience. The introit of the work opens to your presence. This *invocatio*, the voice through which I call upon your voice to come and speak within mine, is repeated throughout the thirteen books, my voice recalls itself to your voice, appeals to it, like a refrain.

My work of confession, of narration and meditation, is only my work because it is yours. The life that it recounts, the conversion and the meditation that it relates are the work of your force, your *virtus*. It is your *sapientia*, your knowledge and wisdom, that grants me what I know thereof, as well of what I am ignorant.

Of me, you know everything, having made me in an instant, having established in an instant the plan of my terrestrial journey and my peregrination (my pilgrimage) through the *peripeteia* of events, acts, and passions.

The tone of *invocation* is that of *laudatio*, of praise that the work addresses to its authentic author. The tone is given by a rhythm, which is that of the *Psalms*, the book being quoted profusely in the recurring stream of invocations. The psalm constitutes a song of praise, sung with the harp. The harp is the instrument of the guiding chord, and Augustine is something like the psalmist working the strings, the vibration of which calls forth the voice of the Lord. The psalm rises up, it takes the work out of its immanence, it gathers up its interior transcendence, concealed more deeply than the work can show. The invocation is an act of praise, and this praise is a melody.

The work, before being narration and meditation, is *mélos*, a poem in which the chord of disquiet and that of rest, the chord of death and that of true life, of question and response send out their assonant and dissonant vibrations to the address of the Absolute. Between the narrative moments, between the meditative moments, where the work visibly proceeds according to the

canons of rhetoric (the *narratio* constitutes an element of the lawyer's discourse) and the moments of philosophy (the meditation, for example, on
matter as formlessness, *informitas*, owes a lot to Plotinus) – between these
moments, the confession punctuates and suspends its procedure with invocation, it recalls that this procedure is *your* procedure, it praises it according to
the (Mideastern) *poetics* of the psalm. The argumentative 'disorder', the
sequential dissonance of the questions, to which other questions 'respond' are
to be understood foremost as music that the soul strives to *tune* to the harmony
of the involuntary divine will, and with which the soul strives to pay it
homage.

'Strives' since this praise is itself placed under the overall question of the
work: who sings your praise when I sing it? How could the derisory I that
I am, weakest of creatures, even muster within it the ability to praise you?
How could your incommensurability be put into work, even with regard
to a poem, into my finitude, how could your atemporality be put into duration, into the *passage* of melody? The very desire to praise you is already
your work, and my disquiet (*inquies*) issues from the fact that what is relative is agitated by the absolute. Besides, how could the *invocatio* operate, be
satisfied, while it calls you, you the infinite, to come and inhabit me, I who
am finite? How could I contain you, how could my work lodge you in the
minuscule *place* (*locus*) that I am? In truth, it is the space of my work, a space-
time that inhabits the atemporality and aspatiality that you are, this sky that is
not of the skies of the earth, but the 'sky of the skies, the heaven of the
heavens.'

To inhabit is still to say too much since the sky of skies is a non–place and
a non-time. What my work and my life inhabit, my *bios* and my *graphè* at once,
are the mystery of your creation. It is not you, but your *work*, this originary
mystery through which, from nowhere and from time immemorial to time
immemorial, time and space have been generated. Through the enigma of your
appearance and withdrawal, through this 'skin' that you have stretched and
drawn like a veil between yourself and the world of creatures, you nevertheless
diffuse your power and your knowledge. You effuse (*effunderis*) over us; your
'presence' in your work, and so in mine, in my life and my book, has neither
place nor moment, it is the presence of an *effusion*. You do not disseminate yourself in your creation, you gather it (*collectio*). My *confession* is not only the recital
of the gathering of my life under the law of your work, it *is* this recollection
that is due to you.

And if, after all, I wonder, as philosophers are wont, how I can know that
it is *you* that I invoke, and not some idol, then I can respond that I do not
invoke you because I know you, but *so as* to know you. The invocation is
a quest and search for you, you who have already found me. After all, if
I believe that it is you who are in fact looking for yourself in my confession,

it is because you have been preached, and because I believe this *preaching.* *Praedicatus* through the ministry of your son, the preacher who has announced you, speaks in advance. You have wrought through him the *advance* of your presence. My work confesses this advance, strains to be acquitted of it. Its inquest disquiets, its restlessness holds in its advance its *rest*, it rests upon your announced but still concealed presence, it has as its end the quiet of your direct presence, in the sky of skies, the heaven of heavens. It has as its end its own end, the end of works, the vision of the glory: as its end its becoming an angel.

1992

Umbilical of Time

The *Confessions* are written under the temporal sign of waiting. Waiting is the name of the consciousness of the future. But here, because it is a question not only of confessing faith in an end that awaits, that lies in sufferance, but of confessing the self, of displaying the sufferance of what has been done, waiting must go back through the past, climb back to its source, the upstream of this faith, toward the life that has been unhappy, toward the work that it once was.

That which had been promised and which turns waiting into hope is that the work would return to being an *epigraph.* The reversion of writing into the past is demanded by the conversion of what I believed I wrote in your writing. The temporal being that I am can only lend itself to your reappropriation through the reappropriation of my temporality.

Our body with its weight strives toward its own place. Weight makes not downward only, but to its own place also. The fire mounts upward, a stone sinks downward . . . My weight is my love; by that am I carried, whithersoever I be carried. We are inflamed by thy gift and are carried upward: we wax hot within, and we go on. (XIII, IX)

The past is akin to the below, and love lifts me up toward the above of the future, which is pure quiet. As long as I am not in my place, which is you, restlessness and the impatience of desire are my lot. They are the effects of my own weight. Rememoration makes me run backward, but to do so in order to attain the future that you promise in the very movement of my weight. Things a little out of their place become unquiet, but when they have been put in order again, they are quieted. (IBID)

So takes shape the temporal intrigue, the story of my life. It gives to the succession of events the place that is their due, as facts of my history, in their literal sense. But chronology reduced to itself is pure nothing, appearance and disappearance, passing-away. The past is what is no longer, the future is what is not yet, and the now has no other being than the becoming past of the future. The chase after the future through the past that drives and troubles the *Confessions* is only *possible* if, in the evanescence of these times, something withholds, is maintained, immutable.

The trance of life is this transitivity of finite being. Its literal meaning is non-time, for the 'letter' is in itself nonbeing. The plot of confessive narrative is only possible if the event doubles up with another meaning, called 'allegorical' by exegesis, if the *opera*, things as they are given, also constitute *signa*. It is conversion, then – since it gives us the ability to read signs in works, to read a little of divine writing in the writing of the *bios* – that justifies confession as a journey that goes backward so as to move forward. The narrative plot, which ties together times in themselves of no import, rises up from a point of time that is not in time, from a point from which time deploys its threefold move to nothingness, but which is itself never destroyed.

It is the exploration of this uncanny anchoring of what happens in what does not pass by that is the concern of the entire end of the *Confessions*. The narrative itself draws to a close at the end of book IX, with the death of Monica, his mother, at Ostia. Nothing on the return to Africa, on the community at Thagaste; then at Hippo, nothing on his hard episcopal life. Hardly a mention of him renouncing the life of a hermit.

The 'chase after your voice' comes to an end in book X. Or rather, the chase is pursued in the direction not of the narrative of the past, but of the point from which this narrative is made possible. No longer in the narration of external events, but in the epiphany of the consciousness of time. The agitated movement of things is succeeded by the dizziness of the soul meditating on the peaceful umbilic of this movement, the motif of which will be resumed by Descartes with the *Cogito*. The prose of the world gives place to the poem of memory, or more exactly the phenomenology of internal time. The whole of modern, existential thought on temporality ensues from this meditation: Husserl, Heidegger, Sartre.

The past is no longer, the future is not yet, the present passes by, but as things (*opera*). And yet, I am aware of their nothingness, since I can think them in their absence. There is therefore a present of the past, and this present, as long as I think it, does not pass. It is this present that Husserl will call the *Living Present*, oddly. In Augustine, this present, immanent to internal consciousness, this umbilic, from which signs become readable to me, this present, then, is like the echo in temporality of the divine Present, of his eternal today.

So autobiography (if it is one) changes into cryptography: the last books of the *Confessions* devour this encrypting of the atemporal in the temporal, eat the Word become flesh and single out within the three temporal ecstasies in which it has been sacrificed and, as it were, dispersed, the kernel of permanence in which they are recollected.

1992

You [*Toi*]

To guard himself against the endemic pride kindled by the confessive exercise, the confessant has one recourse: to summon you.

A second person indeed hangs over, surveys the *Confessions*, magnetizes them, filters through them. A you, nameless patronym of the catholic community. You is the addressee of the avowal that I write. And yet you is not an interlocutor; you never begins to speak, you never calls me you in turn. I only hear of you from bits of phrases that are reported about your son, about your curses. I invoke you and call you as witness to the purity of my humility: you will never give me quiet, will never acquit me, your jealous love dogs me. My petition leaves you silent. Does it not merit some response? I am only of worth, I exist only through this entreaty, this supplication that is turned toward you, suspended before you. Your silence turns it into a form of torture. But be careful not to take pride in my endurance! May I say that you test me, that you yoke me to the trial of writing this confession in your silence so as to be assured that, wavering on the thread run out between yourself and myself, I do not fall back into the arrogance of being me without you, in my nothingness? If so, you would not only be the addressee of my writing, that to which it is addressed, but also that which gives rise to it, its author.

The suspicion dawns, approaching closer and closer, but very rapidly, that the you, you the silent one, pulls all the strings of the confessive sentence, 'carries' all its valences, occupies all the strategic positions, holds them and defends them against any invading conquest. The two poles of the address – addressee and addresser – are both yours, as well as the two poles of meaning – referent and signification. You who remain silent, not me, are the sole concern of the confession, constituting also the content of what is written about it, if to contain and to constitute are permitted terms when what you might signify, under the *stylus* of Augustine, eminently escapes the circumscription of the concept – I was about to say, its inaneness.

You the sole object of the writing and its sole content. If it is true that you thus saturate the entries and exits of the confession, you who confess and you to whom I confess and about which I confess, then I am reduced to receiving nothing but the smallest share. This means little, reduced to nothing, to this nothing which seemed someone, this lure of someone who is no one. I, the apparent subject of the confessive phrase, finds himself, rather loses himself, undone at all ends. And while he confesses his submission to lures, the desire for which continues to rage, while he disavows abject worldliness, he passes under an even more despotic authority, he must accept and savor a quite different radical heteronomy under the law of an unknown master of whom he obstinately delights in making himself the subject.

1997

Part III

Politics

Introduction: Politics and the Political

Political Activism

Lyotard's work is political throughout – from beginning to end, and within nearly all his books and articles. But this political activism does not take place within structures of established politics and in line with the economic systems that sustain them. Instead, his work speaks for those who have been excluded from these structures and systems. It also extends political activity to work to change a wide variety of subjects and practices (how we write, how we create, how to commemorate, how we behave with respect to ideas of gender and sexuality, how we treat outsiders).

This exclusion does not have to be seen as deliberate. In his studies, Lyotard shows that certain forms of exclusion are necessary aspects of politics, in the strong sense of being impossible to eliminate even when they are noticed. Structures and systems involve exploitation and identification. They have an incapacity to recognise that they have excluded something in a way that cannot be repaired. So exclusion is extreme. It does not even involve an acceptance that there has been an illegitimate move or an irreparable wrong.

It is therefore important to draw a distinction between established political management – party politics – and political activism on the margins of that structure – the political. Politics is relatively narrow and well defined in terms of its form (the different ways in which political leadership is selected, governs and comes to decisions). The political is extremely broad. It can touch on all aspects of life, since all can involve exclusion or misrepresentation. For Lyotard, all aspects of life have local political struggles.

However, politics and the political are not separate; they interact and overlap. An established politics is built on a series of political moves, for example, in the way a democratic structure comes out of a political struggle against tyranny. Those political roots can be forgotten. Each new politics can give rise to new political struggles on its margins. For instance, Lyotard is concerned that, for all their benefits, the great narratives of enlightenment and emancipation can lead to new injustices based on the exclusive and local nature of the narrative (for example, that universal reason is primarily a creation of the West).

The reverse is also true. The political is not completely separate from politics, as if it had no role to play in bringing about change in structures and systems. Instead, Lyotard works on two particularly difficult and sensitive problems. How can political activism bring about change, but without having to work completely within a structure that implicitly or explicitly denies a wrong or an exclusion? How can political activism express a wrong within a structure without transforming the wrong in a destructive manner?

Lyotard's political work has often been defined as an opposition to meta-narratives, such as accounts of scientific and technological progress allied to liberal democracy. There is some truth in this, but only if we realise that he is not claiming that we would have been better off with no meta-narratives or that there is a clear alternative to them (in a 'superior' narrative – Marxist possibly). Instead, he is claiming that narratives require a special form of opposition that works for what they necessarily exclude.

The problem of speaking for something, but with a deep awareness of the distorting dangers of representation, explains the fluidity, inventiveness, depth and difficulty of Lyotard's political writings. He is attempting to give voice to a claim, but without fixing it as something that can be managed and handled by systems that continue to exclude it whilst claiming to hear its case. The very idea of a legitimate case is already one such structure of exclusion.

For example, in 1983, when the French politician Max Gallo called for French intellectuals to renew their supporting role within party politics on the left, in line with the advent of a socialist government, Lyotard argued that this was not the role of intellectuals. This was because the ideas expected of such intellectuals by the parties were no longer true ideas of resistance and political activism. For all their past and current values, they had themselves become structures of exclusion.

Ideas of liberal politics and enlightenment based on the concept of the universal subject and victim (*we are all united as subjects and as victims*) give rise to new totalisations, that is, to systems that claim to be able to handle all claims and forms of life. But, for Lyotard, many forms escape them and, once the universal subject has become a dominant form, the role of the 'intellectual' must be to think outside its restrictions:

> The decline, perhaps the ruin, of the universal idea can free thought and life from totalising obsessions. The multiplicity of responsibilities, and their independence (their incompatibility), oblige and will oblige those who take on those responsibilities, small or great, to be flexible, tolerant and svelte.[1]

Three key themes of Lyotard's political work, and three key objections to them, come out of this passage. His political activity is opposed to seamless unity and to systems that recognise no legitimate outside to them (universalism and totalisation, empire and global reach). It is therefore a politics of multiplicity in terms of claims (responsibilities) and in terms of styles (flexible). Finally, and perhaps most importantly, this political work is about the radical incompatibility of claims. We have different just political calls on us. They cannot be managed in a way that is just for all.

The objections to Lyotard's political work draw out possible contradictions and weaknesses in these positions. First objection: it is retrograde and immoral to oppose universal values and ideas. They have brought us out of ignorance and misunderstanding. They allow us to struggle against each new wrong on the grounds of shared human rights. Second: multiplicity is fine, but only within a system that does not fall into relativism. Not all claims are equally valid and we need a moral and political structure capable of judging between them.

Third objection to Lyotard: there is no such thing as radical incompatibility, because, for there to be a claim at all, it has to be represented and recognised as such. This structure of representation (language) and of recognition (judgement) provides a minimal starting point of relating claims. They are therefore not radically different, since they take place within a shared framework – and hence a starting point for the just resolution of conflicts.

Lyotard's political work can be read as an engagement with these objections. He attempts to define political activity, but without having to include it in overall structures and systems. Instead, his political philosophy works on events that resist this incorporation. Such events are signs that some claims and conflicts cannot be resolved justly, instead, they must be testified to in their resistance to resolution. Lyotard's work then becomes a reminder of the limitations and necessary injustice in any established politics.

When brought together, the objections to Lyotard's politics move from accusations regarding the logical consistency of his position (that it is self-contradictory) to claims about its quietism (that it lacks effectiveness because it has abandoned the right way of making claims). His answer is that there is a place for the political as a troublesome reminder of the limits of this logical treatment and these right ways:

> Intelligences do not fall silent, they do not withdraw into their beloved work, they try to live up to this new responsibility, which renders the 'intellectuals' troublesome, impossible: the responsibility to distinguish intelligence from the paranoia that gave rise to 'modernity'.[2]

In the following sections, we shall trace his different attempts to define this political intelligence and its productive role on the margins of politics through each of the main periods of his political work. This will start with his early essays on Algeria, since these can seem to relate his work to earlier politics and universal structures. It will be shown, against this first impression, that these early revolutionary essays contain the seeds of his later positions.

Algeria and Nihilism

Lyotard taught in Algeria in a Lycée in Constantine from 1950 to 1952: 'I owe Constantine a picture of what it was for me then, when I arrived from the Sorbonne to teach in its high school. But with what colours should I paint what astonished me, that is, the immensity of the injustice? An entire people, from a great civilisation, wronged, humiliated, denied their identity.'[3]

To create the conditions for a spontaneous revolution against this injustice, he wrote a series of articles for the French revolutionary Marxist group *Socialisme ou Barbarie*. The Marxism of the group was of a late kind, post-Trotskyite, that is, it did not believe in a revolution led by a cadre of leaders, or a series of cells, or fostered by the Soviet Union, or based on international leftist movements. Instead, Marxist analyses and readings would lead the reality of capitalist terror to become clear. This would lead to spontaneous creative forms of resistance and revolution at local levels. Instead of organised revolution, there would be spontaneous and creative uprisings galvanised by accounts of the real state of oppression.

Lyotard's essays in the group's eponymous journal (1956–63) reflect this desire to inform readers of political and economic reality. They are carefully-researched arguments on the connections between political repression and terror, capitalist economics, and colonialism. Ruling classes maintain power through economic exploitation (threats of unemployment, poverty) and social repression (denigration of local cultures, destruction of social organisations and historical cultures).

The repression takes place in Algeria, but it depends on a similar repression in France. The French population is depoliticised and loses its capacity to rise up in solidarity with Algerian workers and with their demands for independence and revolution. This process depends on hiding the reality of class exploitation and social and cultural impoverishment: 'The very idea of a global political project is immediately neutralised in the workers' own heads. Incredulity, lassitude, and irony keep an exploited class in step much more effectively than open violence.'[4]

Four important points from the articles on Algeria should be retained, in order to understand Lyotard's later political work. First, the revolution in Algeria failed. Though independence was achieved, there was no successful revolutionary uprising and, instead, the old economic and social order remained, though relatively freer of French influence.

Second, since the *Socialisme ou Barbarie* analysis was already a limit extension of Marxism, arriving after successive refinements, there was little room for manoeuvre in terms of claiming that the failure was due to a rectifiable error in revolutionary theory. Any disillusionment with the politics of the group would have to lead to a radically new way of thinking about the political.

Third, the basic study through classes was shown to be lacking, not through any fault of the proletarian class or revolutionary movement, but through the lack of such homogeneous classes. Yet, this did not mean that wrongs disappeared with the large groupings that were meant to stand for victims. On the contrary, the complex multiplicity of desires and wrongs hidden within classes was still produced by political and economic repression.

So, fourth, since society can be seen as a multiplicity of shifting wrongs and claims, the political had to be flexible enough to respond to this variation, rather than hide it under larger groupings better suited to party politics and to revolutionary movements allied to new parties and forms of government. The complex and changing variety of wrongs can never be rectified simply through revolution, yet they still place a responsibility on us. What are we to do?

The possible despair brought on by this question leads Lyotard into a confrontation with nihilism. From the end of the essays on Algeria, through all of his major books, right up to his last work on Augustine, nihilism became one of the main influences on Lyotard's political thought. Nihilism is a combination of negation of life, loss of values and loss of will. With the failure of just revolutions, did we have to give up on the value of justice and of ethical political action?

But Lyotard is not a nihilist. Rather, he believes that nihilism is a constant threat for political thought due to the latter's necessary failures. Each political act tries to do justice to a wrong, but it only succeeds partially (Algeria liberated, but without revolution). Worse, each success sows the seeds for new injustices (thinking in terms of classes masks the multiple new arrangements within each class and across many). If political action focuses on eliminating wrongs once and for all, and to the satisfaction of all legitimate claims, then it must fail. If political action focuses on structures of just resolution, then it will become disenchanted as those structures breed rottenness of their own.

Libidinal Economy and the Figural

Lyotard never abandons his early belief in the importance of presenting reality as a key tool for political action. However, as his work develops, his understanding of reality becomes much more original and distant from orthodox political and economic models. In addition, his sense of the nature and scope of political action changed – in tune with the change in accounts of reality.

This dual focus has often been underestimated due to the impact of Lyotard's philosophy of the event. His political work, after Algeria, can be seen as based on questions of how to do justice to unpredictable events that force us to act to testify to them. This testimony is itself twofold. We have to do justice to the individual event, but we also have to testify to the openness to events in apparently closed structures.

However, this politics of the event must be paired with a careful critique of political, economic, philosophical, cultural and social structures. Put simply, in his 'libidinal' work (from *Discours, figure* in 1971 to *Libidinal Economy* in 1974), Lyotard reflects the multiplicity of social structures and the repression inflicted by political and economic systems. This is explained by drawing distinctions between desire, structure and system.

For Lyotard, desire is a double flow of intensity. It is inspired by Freud, but then taken out of any Freudian orthodoxy. The duality indicates the creative and destructive power of intense events. Feelings occur as unpredictable events; they feed new libidinal energy into structures. This is creative. But this new energy also draws out the weaknesses and insufficiencies of structures – forcing them to change and to clash with others. This is the destructive side of desire. The two sides cannot be treated independently of one another.

Structures impose an identity on desire and on reality by setting things into relations of negations (A is not B), groups and hierarchies (As are more valuable than Bs). In contrast, systems allow desire and energy to flow through structures in a manageable and productive manner. There is therefore an alliance of structure and system in the organisation of desire, but there is also a disruption of both by desire as it unleashes new intense events that challenge the fixity of structures and the managed flow of systems.

Lyotard deploys this metaphysics, or theory about the nature of reality, in a political context in three ways. First, he gives detailed studies of these 'libidinal dispositions' to show how structures and systems exploit and control libidinal events. For example, in *Discours, figure* myths and narratives are unpicked to show the illegitimate hierarchies and exclusions at work in the way they control desire (around gender, for instance).

Second, Lyotard describes the political activity of resistance as the good conduction of intensities, that is, as the search for the release of creative and destructive desires into structures and systems. The key will be to find the weak points and points of repression in structures, often where they overlap or involve internal contradictions. It will also be to accelerate and shift the energies that systems depend upon, but cannot control fully.

Third, this conduction cannot lead to a new fixed politics, since this would become a new structure and system, thereby requiring a further study and creative destruction and leading to an infinite regress. Instead, Lyotard defines his libidinal politics as a politics of flight, that is, as a continued movement that constantly undoes fixed positions – including its own.

This combination of movement and political intensity appears in Lyotard's continued commitment to Marxist intensities, that is, the drives behind revolutionary movements. This can be found in his later work on his former ally, Pierre Souyri, included here. It is also an important aspect of *Libidinal Economy*: 'It would make us happy to be able to retranscribe, into a libidinal discourse, those intensities which haunt Marx's thought and which, in general, are dissimulated in the brass-tacks solemnity of the discourses of economy and politics.'[5]

A surprising aspect of this libidinal political thought is worth pointing out. Since desire and intensity lie outside structures, including structures of linguistic representation, they cannot be approached directly and inserted predictably into a political strategy. Instead, the political good conduction of intensities must involve an active passivity. That is, the critique of structures and systems, and an opening-up to the possibility of libidinal events, prepare for events that must be welcomed when they occur, but that cannot be set beforehand. Indeed, if they were, they would not be events in Lyotard's sense.

This powerful combination of the careful study of narratives, of a philosophy of the event, and of the effort to open the way to new and revolutionary feelings and short-lived movements comes out strongly in Lyotard's newly translated account of Pierre Overney's murder outside the Renault factory at Billancourt. Lyotard reveals the hidden political and economic motivations and effects in Renault's statements after the murder.

Lyotard shows how the death is an event to which no statement, no narrative can do justice. Yet he also shows how the event demands a critique of the Renault statement and its situation within much wider forms of control and repression in politics and exploitation in economics. The event is a challenge to this alliance of narrative and repression. Its power comes from the variety of libidinal intensities that surround it and from the incapacity of the narratives to control their number and variety.

The libidinal political study prompts further creations and destructions. It destabilises the obviousness and apparent transparency of narratives. They are replaced by a profusion of accounts that do not make claims to a final politics. Instead, many different desires and the structures they flow into return and do justice to the intensity of the original event – protecting it from the base reduction of the Renault narrative.

This kind of destructive and sceptical analysis of narratives still has a crucial function to play today, when the management of news and events has grown and become more skilled and brutal. It is not a struggle for the Truth, but rather a resistance against the ways in which events are betrayed and managed. This resistance is for the initial open intensity of events: not so much a claim for a given line, as a claim to oppose restricted ones by working with the resistance of events to any single narrative.

The Politics of the Sublime

Lyotard's interest in the libidinal shifts toward the end of the 1970s. This change is strongly influenced by a reading of Kant and by a concern with the relation between judgement, feelings, political ideas and narratives. Put simply, instead of the metaphysics of structures and intensities, Lyotard emphasises the feeling of the sublime and its role in events that thwart linguistic accounts, such as narratives, or claims to knowledge, or claims to just forms of judgement.

The main questions from his work in this period are 'What kind of events show the limits of knowledge and of our capacity to judge?' and 'How can there be a just way of following on from such events?' The reference to Kant is all-important here because Lyotard sees an answer to the first question in Kant's theory of the sublime, but he differs from Kant in the scope and role of the sublime feeling in philosophy. Lyotard is searching for a philosophy that is just, but without imposing a single form of judgement with its single narrative and set of guiding ideas.

Lyotard's later political philosophy is based on the feeling of the sublime and on its capacity to reveal a presence, but without allowing for knowledge or for judgement. The key to understanding this apparent paradox of a presence that cannot be known lies in a dual quality of the sublime, as defined by Lyotard. The sublime feeling combines a pleasure or attraction towards an event – rather than an object, since this would imply knowledge – with a pain at the impossibility of going beyond that first attraction.

Unlike the beautiful, the sublime cannot stand as the basis for shared knowledge, judgements or morality. This is the point made in the section from *Lessons on the Analytic of the Sublime* given here. Instead, in opposition to any emergent consensus about matters of taste, the sublime is cause for a 'dissensus' that allows it to drive opposition to hegemonic claims.

This break with consensus and with judgements that bridge between different viewpoints connects the work on the sublime to Lyotard's work in *The Differend*, where he argues that we should testify to radical differences called 'differends'. This testimony should resist bridging the difference. One of the main problems in the book is therefore how to register differends without starting to resolve the differences within them, since any form of understanding or judgement appear to begin to reconcile supposedly incommensurable positions. The feeling of the sublime solves this problem since a difference is indicated by the feeling, but also shown to be unknowable and beyond satisfactory judgement.

In terms of the political, the feeling of the sublime is important because it is a focus for opposition to dominant narratives and ideas. This is the reversal operated by Lyotard on Kant. Instead of providing a confirmation of an idea of reason, such as the human race is progressing towards the good (as in Kant's study of the enthusiasm of spectators to the French revolution), the feeling of the sublime breaks with such ideas. Thereby, it provides one of the key political strategies in Lyotard's essays after *The Differend* – collected in *The Inhuman* and *Postmodern Fables*.

For example, in the essay 'Time Today', Lyotard shows how a series of familiar and dominant ideas and narratives fall foul of the sublime feeling that accompanies the occurrence of events 'today'. In the essay, irony is used to trigger a sublime feeling through an attraction to familiar ideas and narratives accompanied by a repulsion or shock at their implications. Having given an account of our reliance on hope based on a technological future that saves the human race from a precarious and contingent position, he then dashes that hope by showing the cost of the idea (for example, in what it implies in terms of the violence of technological advances and the exusive values they imply).

There is an important lesson for the reception of Lyotard's work in this use of irony. It is possible to read him unilaterally, for example, as if he were pro-technology or simply anti-technology. This is a mistake similar to the one of reading him as a postmodernist, when in fact he wishes to raise questions about postmodernity based on ideas about postmodern events and how they function. Instead, by conveying our dependence on an idea or a narrative, as well as drawing our attention to their limitations, he wants to defend political action for those who are excluded by both, but without making promises for new and better forms.

It is easy to see this ironic and paradoxical form of the political as contradictory and ineffective, but that is to misunderstand its role. Politics, ideas and narratives exist and require traditional forms of refinement and opposition. Lyotard want to remind us that, whatever forms this work of improvement takes, it is always in danger of hiding that which it cannot handle or recognise. The task of philosophy is to bear witness to this concealment. As such, his political work 'preserves and reserves the coming of the future in its unexpectedness'.

Notes

1. Lyotard, 'Tomb of the Intellectual', in *Political Writings*, p. 7.
2. Ibid. p. 7.
3. Lyotard, 'The Name of Algeria', in *Political Writings*, p. 170.
4. Lyotard, 'The State and Politics in the France of 1960', in *The Lyotard Reader and Guide*, p. 198.
5. Lyotard, *Libidinal Economy*, p. 104.

Chapter 10

The State and Politics in the France of 1960

Barricades in Algiers from January 24 to February 1. Proclamation of a state of siege. On February 2, special powers are passed by the government for a year. The Jeanson network is dismantled on February 24, and its members are judged and sentenced in September and October.[1] On September 6, the Manifesto of 121[2] proclaims the right to insubordination.

M. de Sérigny[3] nibbling Ben Bella's crusts in the Santé prison, M. Thorez calling on the people to defend the general's republic against the 'fascist agitators of disorder', the employers and Matignon encouraging the workers to take an hour of strike holiday without loss of productivity bonuses: in the face of this apparent inversion of all political indicators, a traveler who had left France in May 1959 would believe he was dreaming. Only one constant factor would allow him to feel at home: the attitude of the immense majority of this country, as always spectatorial.

What was called 'political life' not so long ago was the fact that a significant fraction of the population took initiatives relative to the problems of society, participated in political meetings and spoke at them, displayed solutions it believed just, and in this way challenged the establishment and, if it couldn't overthrow it, at least shook up its plans. Yet, with the exception of Algeria (where such a political life, even if it is in decline, appeared in January among the Europeans, and where it manifests itself every day without fail in the shape of the armed activity of the Algerians themselves), France is politically dead.

It is in relation to this fact that the phraseology of the 'left' appeared, during the January crisis, as completely anachronistic; it is this fact of which the revolutionaries (no less isolated than the organizations, though for other reasons) ought to become aware, on which they ought to reflect, from which they ought to draw new ways of thinking, new ways of acting, if they intend to become the thought that human reality is in search of, as Marx put it.

Gaullism and Modern Capitalism

The Algerian crisis had been the immediate occasion for de Gaulle's accession to power in May 1958, but the new republic in reality had to untie the inextricable complex of problems that the Fourth Republic had allowed to knot together over thirteen years. All these problems could be formulated in one sole question: was the French bourgeoisie capable of initiating the changes necessitated by the modern capitalist world, in France and beyond?[4] By its very existence, this world constituted an ensemble of challenges to the structure and functioning of French society, whether it was conceived as an economic totality or as a state or as the metropole of a colonial empire.

The Fourth Republic had manifestly failed to make the necessary changes. An incoherent economic policy alternated between modern investment decisions and laws supporting the most backward productive sectors. The restoration of prewar parliamentarianism allowed different sectors of the bourgeoisie and petite bourgeoisie to make their particular interests prevail one after another and reduced the executive to nothing more than the stake in a struggle between various pressure groups. Finally, the situation created in the old empire by the immense liberation movement that stirred up colonial peoples throughout the world did not evoke any collective response in Paris. But the reflexes of colonialist repression, which led in the long run to disastrous surrenders, alternated with sporadic attempts to find more flexible forms of imperialist domination than the old colonial link . . .[5]

The May 1958 crisis was therefore the result of a conspiracy. It was the whole crisis of French capitalism that erupted in it, and it was immediately clear that it could not be resolved like the 'crises' of the Fourth Republic. This time, the question Who governs in France? was posed explicitly and in such a way as to interest not only professional politicians, but in fact all social classes, beginning with the proletariat. This was not a cabinet crisis; it was at least a crisis of the regime, at most a crisis of society as a whole.

It was at least a crisis of the regime in that, in any case, the Fourth Republic's mode of government, or of nongovernment, appeared inevitably doomed. At most a crisis of society, if capitalism could not manage to both develop and gain acceptance from the whole of society for a new regime, a regime capable of putting things in order, that is, strong enough to solve the most pressing problems (public finances, the franc, foreign trade, Algeria), a regime stable enough to begin to free the economy from the most serious obstacles to its development.

It is true that the political disorganization of the proletariat, resulting from several decades of compromises made by the Communist party and SFIO [the French International] with the bourgeois parties, gave rise to the 'hope' that a serious crisis could be avoided. On the other hand, the adversary that big capital had to defeat immediately was not the working class, but the bloc of the colonels and the extreme right. But domination by this bloc, even temporary, risked leading the whole of society into a much more profound crisis than a simple crisis of regime.

The forces that openly attacked the Fourth Republic obviously only sought to impose a state in France that would serve the interests of the European colonial class of Algeria. These interests were completely incompatible with those of French imperialism as a whole. It is evident, for example, that major French capitalism could not envisage for a second the economic integration of Algeria into the metropole: that would amount to giving up ten or twenty years of normal expansion in order to end up a half century later with the whole country from Dunkirk to Tamanrasset at a still greater distance from the modern capitalist countries – not to mention what integration would have implied in the realm of domestic and international politics.

But what big capitalism could do, and what it did, was make use of the dynamism of the May 1958 insurrection in order to rid itself of the regime blocking its development in France and, once the new power had been consolidated, to rid itself of the very forces that had allowed the first phase of the operation. It thus remained master of the terrain without a serious crisis that might have called the domination of capitalism over French society into question having occurred. On the other hand, it brought about the 'strong state' demanded by the army and the extreme right, while at the same time confiscating that state for itself.

In reality, the two phases were telescoped into each other, both because the project of big capitalism was not as immediately explicit as it seems in hindsight and because even had it been absolutely premeditated it would have been necessary to espouse the cause of its provisional accomplices for a short while. The current of May 13 thus swept up contradictory elements, defenders of *Algérie française* along with more or less innocent tools of modern capitalism. But, above all, this internal contradiction continues in the Gaullist state itself and explains both the essential ambiguity of its political (and oratorical) style and the permanent crisis that inhabits it. On the one hand, it cannot be denied that the diverse measures taken by this state with regard to the most urgent problems inherited from the Fourth Republic converge into one sole and identical meaning: to make the interests of big capital predominate in the domestic economy and in foreign trade as well as in relations with the colonies and Algeria. On the other hand, however, this significance could only be revealed very slowly. Each of these measures is matched or is followed by a concession to the adversary that it aims to suppress; the power of big capital can only consolidate itself little by little in maneuvering its accomplices, just as the Gaullists of May 14 manipulated the men of May 13 in Algiers. In large part, the aborted crises that ended in the resignation of the ministers representing the French bourgeoisie of Algeria or the most backward sectors of the metropole expressed nothing other than the carrying out of a settlement of accounts between the partners of May 13.

That is to say, in this respect the Fifth Republic already shares certain essential features of the Fourth. Of course, the subordination of the particular interests of this or that sector of the dominant classes to those of big capital is much more explicitly pursued than in the preceding regimes; but the resistance of these sectors has not disappeared, and de Gaulle's power has not ceased to employ trickery to put an end to it.

We will return to the precarious character of this power. First, it is advisable to emphasize the fact that dominates all the others: the whole operation could only succeed provided that a massive intervention of the workers, proposing a revolutionary solution to the problems of society as a whole, did not cause the 'response' to the crisis planned by the ruling circles to fail, and did not enlarge the crisis to its real dimensions. Now, this intervention did not occur. By an apparent paradox, while the crisis openly expressed the incapacity of French capitalism to manage society, the proletariat left capitalism at leisure to resolve the crisis in its best interests. What is more, the proletariat helped in the process, first by its abstention, then by its vote in the referendum.

De Gaulle was only possible because he was available to the French bourgeoisie to contain the crisis within the limits of its legality, that is, to turn it into a simple crisis internal to the ruling sphere, and not a crisis *of* the ruling sphere as such. The power of the Fifth Republic was constituted and the power of the bourgeoisie was reconstituted because the workers did not attempt, during those few days when the decayed state ended up in the streets, to take it over, to destroy it and to impose their solution. They did not even dream, as a class, of such a solution and setting it into motion, and finally did not seriously contest – that is, through their actions – capitalism's capacity to settle this crisis.

This *depoliticization* of the exploited classes (and of this exploited class, the industrial proletariat, whose working and living conditions always created the avant-garde of the worker movement) was thus the foundation of de Gaulle's regime, but it is also its permanent atmosphere, and this is what the January crisis showed anew. This is the fundamental fact of this period, and on two accounts: first because (as we just said) an analysis of the Fifth Republic that omitted the depoliticization out of which it arose and in which it maintains itself could not understand either its genesis or its present life; second because for revolutionary critique and organization such a depoliticization constitutes a kind of challenge, almost a refutation: how, in effect, is one to persevere in the socialist project if it appears that this project no longer exists among the proletariat, at least in its *political* form? That is the question that de Gaulle's France puts to us, and it would be contrary to the task of the revolutionaries to avoid it by imposing outdated political categories on this world, by applying a political practice to it that does not correspond to reality.

We have always affirmed,[6] that in the absence of a massive intervention of the workers, French capitalism is capable of carrying out a transition to the structure required by the modern world; it is moreover a kind of tautology, if one admits that the only obstacle that makes a ruling class absolutely incapable of continuing to manage the ensemble of the society on its own account consists precisely in the revolutionary initiative of the masses.[7]

Of course, this adaptation of French capitalism does not happen smoothly; it encounters obstacles within the propertied classes themselves that come from the very structure of French society, these same obstacles that delayed as much as possible the necessary collective reorganization. But one can propose this idea by way of an overall assessment: however violent the resistance opposed by one section or another of the petite or middle bourgeoisie to the reorganization of the state, of the economy, of relations with the colonies, none had the power to make it fail irreversibly. This reorganization is not, in effect, a merely formal operation, like the arranging of a closet or the putting in order of a dossier; it has a social and political content; it means that big capital intends from now on to make *its* interests predominate over those of the petite and middle bourgeoisie.

Now, one does not risk much in prophesying that big capital will emerge victorious from this test of strength, within the limits imposed on it by its own interests, of course. It suffices to take stock of the means possessed by its adversaries and to analyze the problems that French society must resolve in the coming decade if it wants to continue to exist as a capitalist society that matters, in order to predict the final success of the 'recovery' set in motion by big capital, that is to say, a still greater centralization of capital, the ever more complete domination of 'organizers,' the proletarianization of the former middle classes, and so forth.

In this sense, the present system, even if it is precarious in its political form, has an irreversible importance as the instrument of a deep transformation in French society. Even if de Gaulle were to disappear tomorrow, even if a 'military power' established itself in France, the profound change that is taking place in this society would not be stopped. The disorder of the Fourth Republic did not hinder it, and the offensive of the Algerian colonial class, the most retrograde class in the country, which objectively sought the preservation at all costs not only of Algeria, but also of 'daddy's' France, only succeeded finally in drawing big capital closer to direct political power. If it is true, as we will see, that de Gaulle's regime is extremely precarious, it is also true that the transformation of the very bases of French society, of which it is the instrument, is durable and decisive.

The first precondition for the recovery of French capitalism was political, and paradoxically it is perhaps still the least satisfied. In effect, the bourgeoisie had first to endow itself with the statist political instrument that would allow it to impose on all classes the appropriate measures for freeing society from the impasse of the Fourth Republic. This instrument had to fulfill two functions and, consequently, to take on two forms: on the one hand, to free the government from the control that the parties and the pressure groups had previously exercised over it, and therefore to incarnate itself in a 'strong' power; on the other hand, to create a political organization, a mass party, capable of maintaining the contact between the ruling power and the whole of the population, capable of controlling it, and of obtaining from it finally the indispensable simulacrum of its support for government policy. We shall see later on why neither one of these forms could be achieved by Gaullism, and consequently why its political situation remains precarious.

But in the absence of this perfect instrument of domination, the Fifth Republic nonetheless profits from the political crisis in which it originated. Parliamentarianism and the parties have come out of that crisis completely discredited. De Gaulle can therefore find a pretext in the profound distaste felt by the whole of the population, including the working class, for the regime of the parties, in order to assign a purely figurative role to Parliament and to leave the parties to pursue their henceforth harmless games there with complete irresponsibility. The referendum shows that de Gaulle was not wrong in betting on general contempt for the political forms and forces of the Fourth Republic. Constitutionally at least, he has a free hand. The new Constitution in effect endows the state apparatus with a 'strong' structure, that is, sufficiently centralized and hierarchical for its organs to become in principle relatively inaccessible to impulses other than those that come from the top.

In fact, this structure is really strong only insofar as the pressure groups do not continue to divert certain branches of the state apparatus in their own interests. Otherwise, it is evident that directives from the top cannot have repercussions at the executive level, and one is presented with (which is the case) the paradox of a power whose form is strong and whose effectiveness is very weak. The pressure that interest groups, and particularly *Algérie française*, exercised through Parliament has apparently been eliminated, but in reality it is only displaced; from now on it works directly in certain departments of the administration and in the most important executive branches (army, police, information). This contradictory situation results, as has been noted, from the very conditions in which de Gaulle came to power: the ultra faction, which carried him to leadership, had all the leisure, during the summer of 1958, to place its people in certain essential posts, and thus it acquired the ability to delay the implementation of measures decided at the top, or to neutralize them on the ground. If one adds to this that the branches so colonized are principally the army and the police, that the ground is Algeria, that the confusion of the state instrument and Algerian society is almost total there and has lasted for years, one can understand that the Algerian lobby found things made singularly easy.

Consequently, the present regime can only satisfy the requirement of a strong state formally, so to speak. In a sense, that is the defect it inherits from the preceding regime: the habits of unpunished disobedience in the army, the police, the administration (of Algeria above all), added to the pressures that come from the most backward sectors of society, are not easy to overcome, above all when one came to power thanks to them. But, more deeply, this precariousness of the state, so visible at the time of the January 1960 crisis, expresses more than a political heritage: it carries the real heterogeneity of the dominant class into the very structure of the administrative apparatus. It is because there are considerable inequalities of development in French capitalism – and, consequently, in sections of the bourgeoisie whose interests are radically at odds – that the instrument of bourgeois domination in this case continues to be the object of attempts at permanent seizure. A stable state presupposes at least a homogeneous dominant class. At present, the French bourgeoisie could deliberately sacrifice its particular interests to its interests as dominant class only if the working masses exercised a really threatening pressure on the political institutions that it imposes on them. But as long as the proletariat as a whole will not intervene, and as long as big capital has not, in the long term, destroyed the fundamental bases of the most retrograde strata of the bourgeoisie, the problem of the state will remain at issue. This problem is a kind of circle: the bourgeois state in France will never be 'strong' while the bourgeoisie remains divided among profoundly contrary interests on most of the problems that it faces. But overcoming this division and leading the ensemble of this country's structures to modern forms coinciding with the interests of big capital requires a strong state.

This objective difficulty was only shifted by de Gaulle's accession to power, not removed. The Constitution was completely tailored to the size of the president, not worked out with a view to a durable stabilization of political institutions so as to make them relatively independent of the person of the head of state. In pushing de Gaulle to power, in giving him practically total power, big capital evidently resolved the most urgent problem posed to it by the insurrection of May; but it did not respond and could not respond to the fundamental problem of the form that its interests should give the state apparatus in the long term. Because of this, the question of de Gaulle's longevity remains a troubling question for the ruling class.

Should one say that the same is true in Germany, in the United States? This would be at once accurate and inaccurate. It is true that in all the countries of modern capitalism, the subordination of all economic and social activities to an apparatus of political administration endows it with considerable powers and that centralization within the state apparatus itself makes its leader into the symbol of the stability of the society as a whole: that is why he always appears irreplaceable, that is why the leader's cardiac arrest or senility troubles the ruling classes. But, at the same time, these regimes are equipped to avoid an excessive interregnum: they have the parties. After a fairly long gestation, to judge by the average age of their offspring, these enormous machines end by vomiting from their entrails the fully prepared successors of the great man in power. The 'competence' of these successors is beyond doubt, because it has been tried over long years of purgatory within the party bureaucracy. The transmission of power thus takes place smoothly after the disappearance of the head of state or government.

But the parties have another, still more important, function in these regimes, and we discover here the second failure encountered by Gaullism with regard to the political problem.

On the political terrain, the ruling class confronts the same contradiction as in production: on the one hand, it monopolizes the functions of administration and decision, it completely excludes the worker from them; but, on the other hand, it needs the participation of the same people that it manages, even if only in order to know what they are, what they do and can do, what they want and do not want to do. Without a minimum of information, the bourgeoisie (or the bureaucracy) completely loses control of real society, its decisions remain a dead letter. In the political domain, this contradiction finds its expression and its 'solution' at the same time in the functioning of the parties, such as it exists in Great Britain, in the United States, in West Germany, and so forth. These parties fill exactly the same double function as the unions in the firm. On the one hand, they have their roots in real society thanks to their base, and they express this society's opinions despite all the deformations imposed by their bureaucratic structure. But, on the other hand, and above all, the party represents an irreplaceable instrument of control over the population. Thanks to its propaganda organs and its militants, it can orient opinion in a direction that is appropriate to the conjuncture; thanks to its structure, it can capture and channel dissatisfactions. Finally, when the party is in power, its hierarchy incorporates itself from top to bottom into the state hierarchy, which assures the latter the effectiveness that ideological discipline or, more simply, careerism, gives.

The competition of two large parties allows the dominant class, in safeguarding the trappings of democracy, always to have a 'spare state' in reserve; furthermore, the party of the 'left' obliges the bourgeoisie in power to preserve its class discipline, while, inversely, the opposition party's structuring as a quasi state (shadow cabinet) extracts all revolutionary content from the left. The parties are thus a kind of double of the state and at the same time probes that it pushes into the population in order to overcome its isolation in relation to society.

Now, the Gaullist authority does not possess these instruments. The very conditions in which big capital seized power in France required the pushing aside of all the parties, too compromised in the decay of the preceding regime, too numerous to produce uncontested candidates for the presidency. Big capital took power against the parties or at least despite them, and it appears condemned to govern for a long time without them. Despite the shared wishes of Mollet and Duchet, the evolution of the political spectrum toward a bipartisan structure appears highly improbable, at least in the foreseeable future.

For its part, the UNR [Gaullist party of the Fifth Republic] is not a party in the sense just mentioned but a movement whose internal institutions do not make of it a quasi state, and whose ideological and social composition forbids it from even playing the role of an intermediary between the authorities and the country: from this last point of view, the UNR is a heterogenous pack of local notables, where the men of big capital are placed side by side with the small reactionary owners. It would not know how to free Gaullism from its ambiguity; it incarnates it.

One has difficulty seeing, in these conditions, how the state will be able to put up with this lamentable political situation. In the short term, the split between the parties and power continues to deteriorate; technicians, high functionaries, and other 'organization men' have come, one after the other, to replace the fallen 'political' ministers. But such a solution, if it does not hamper the functioning of the state in the present period, in no way resolves the problem of the relations between power and society.

The contradiction that weighs on the political 'solution' that big capital has tried to give to the crisis of May 1958 necessarily recurs in other domains. But not everywhere equally: where the bourgeois adversaries of big capital cannot oppose a serious resistance to it, the general line of the latter's policy affirms itself clearly: when, on the contrary, the terrain in dispute is already occupied by these adversaries, this line bends, beats around the bush; power comes to terms, at least momentarily.

In December 1958, having obtained the double acquiescence the nation gave him in the referendum and in the elections, de Gaulle sets out 'his' economic program. Essentially, this program consists in taking a cut from the purchasing power of wage earners on the order of 15 to 18 percent, directly by restrictive measures (freezing salaries, slowing down of consumption), indirectly by devaluation. The reduction of domestic consumption that follows, added to the reduction in the exchange value of the franc, allows a much more important part of the national product to be devoted to export, that is, to the acquisition of strong currencies. In a few months, the balance of foreign trade is reestablished and the currency stock reconstituted; from spring 1959, the normal rhythm of expansion begins again, and, at the beginning of 1960, the employers can envisage, if social tension becomes a little too high here or there, the possibility of proportionally loosening their stranglehold on the wage earners.

These measures are welcomed by the ensemble of the bourgeoisie, and for good reason: in making the workers pay for their carelessness, they resolve the problem of financial stabilization in the most 'elegant' way. But the tidy equilibrium thus obtained is not sufficient. It is not enough to clean up the finances of the state or of foreign trade by aggravating exploitation; in the long run, one must undertake the rationalization of the most backward sectors of the French economy. Now, as we have just seen, attempts to put pressure on agricultural prices – even very limited ones – immediately provoke violent reactions from the peasant mass, for whom there is more at issue there than a haggling over its level of revenue. In the problem of the production cost of agricultural products, nothing less than the problem of the small rural property is posed: in relation to an 'American' kind of economy, the French system of land owner-ship and its methods of cultivation are completely outdated. The peasant malaise can only get worse. The same holds for distribution.

Of course the middle classes who find themselves doomed over the long term do not have sufficient strength to block this process; but they at least have enough inertia to jam, slow down, or ride out its unfolding. It is clear that big business capital will for some time have to make concessions to this section of the active population if it does not want to alienate it; and it cannot afford to alienate it because of its enormous relative volume, the heritage of a century of conserva-tive social policy. The extinction of shopkeepers, of artisans, of the peasants of the Midi and the West is thus not going to happen tomorrow, and French capi-talism, however modern it may become in the wage-earning sector, will keep for some time yet the specific feature that a third of the active population works in financial and technical conditions identical to those of 1860. Therein lies the source of considerable difficulties, be they only those resulting from the non-competitive character in foreign markets of the products manufactured under these conditions. The relaxation of trade restrictions by the most advanced sector of production will for some time have to accept import quotas on many prod-ucts that are in competition with those of French agriculture and small industry.

De Gaulle and Algeria

As for the problem of the relationship with the colonies, the Constitution already indicated that big business capital was going to try to resolve it through loosening the colonial link, that is, was going to break as much as possible with the exclusive tradition of violent and pointless repression. Further political development in Africa soon showed the effectiveness of this solution; the grant-ing of a large measure of autonomy (that is, of independence) allowed a privi-leged local class, whose essential interests coincide with those of imperialism and that takes on the task of channeling or repressing the forces unleashed among the African masses by political emancipation, to consolidate itself on the spot.

On this point, the Gaullist enterprise did not come up against any really orga-nized adversary. But the litmus test, the problem where 'one had hopes of de Gaulle', the problem from which Gaullism had arisen, remained the Algerian problem. No group inside the French bourgeoisie had known how to provide itself with propaganda organs capable of intoxicating public opinion, none had directly seized possession of a large proportion of the civil administration and almost the entirety of the military apparatus, none had defied the central authority, as had the colonial class of Algeria.

For these reasons, it proved extremely difficult to enforce a policy in conformity with the interests of big business capital. Throughout the summer of 1958, de Gaulle beats around the bush, maneuvers, does not come out either in favor of or against *Algérie française*. After the September constitutional referendum and the November elections, the first measures appear that tend to give Paris back its domination over the Algerian sector. The order given to the officers to resign from the Committees for Public Safety and the recall or reassignment of several superior officers manifest an intention to return the army to its executive function. Then de Gaulle's declarations seek to set in motion little by little a kind of third way, which would be neither that of the extreme right nor that of the GPRA [provisional Algerian government], but rather that of big business capital, of an association that would at the same time safeguard the essential elements of French imperialism's interests in Algeria and allow the nationalist leaders to win their case regarding participation in the affairs of the country.[8] In doing this, de Gaulle went much further than any president of the Council of the Fourth Republic; through him, large metropolitan capital tried for the first time to define a policy in line with its fundamental interests.

Meanwhile, the insurrection of January 24, 1960, should have shown that de Gaulle's adversaries had not given up. Beforehand, it was already evident that the directives emanating from the Elysée continued to be translated into the language of *Algérie française* on the other side of the Mediterranean: the superior officers, the generals, and other marshals continued to make clear their own opinions on the declarations of the president; the instructions Delouvrier had received when taking up his post almost remained a dead letter; the legate-general himself appeared to give way in his turn to the irresistible Algiers atmosphere; the 'patriotic organizations' and the extreme right wing groups openly declared their hostility to the policy outlined by Paris and threatened to oppose its application with arms.

All the difficulties of the regime seemed incarnate in the January crisis as those of the Fourth Republic were in May 1958. Pinay's departure (orchestrated in the Algerian manner by the extreme right wing of the independents) and the peasant agitation more or less dictated by the corporatists lent consistency to the hypothesis of an offensive by certain sections of the bourgeoisie against de Gaulle's policy. The uprising of the Europeans of Algiers threw out an explicit challenge from the Algerian lobby. The hesitation of the military command and the civil authority over several days finally seemed to affect the very texture of the Gaullist state. The whole ensemble allowed one to imagine a repetition of May 13.

However, notable differences soon appeared between May 1958 and January 1960 in the very style of the insurrection and in its development, differences that are explained finally by the new political situation constituted by this regime.

First, the Europeans who intervened effectively in the street were much less numerous and much less active than on May 13. In 1958, there were 100,000 persons in the Forum; in 1960, there were 15,000 in the center of Algiers during business hours, and not more than 1,000 permanent insurgents in total. In 1958, the movement had spread like wildfire through all the cities (thanks to the complicity of the army and the administration); in 1960, it affects the center of Algiers for eight hours, the center of Oran for three days, the war memorials of four or five cities for several hours. In 1958, the entirety of the administrative structure of Algeria entered into insurrection; in 1960, the insurgents manage to control no vital organ of Algerian society, they *retrench*.

Is this to say that the January insurrection is the creation of a few conspirators? If it had been so, it would not have lasted two hours, above all after the shooting. In fact, the men who made the insurrection possible were not Lagaillarde, Ortiz, and so on but the European blue- and white-collar workers, postal workers, railwaymen who really *rose up* against what they believe to be the destiny that the solution of an 'association' that de Gaulle wants to impose holds for them. They believe, in effect (and they are no doubt correct; the example of Tunisia and Morocco proves it), that such an association will oblige them to share their jobs with the Algerians, and that thus many of them will be obliged to expatriate themselves, to come to France to find work. Transposed on Algerian soil, that is, with the whole colonialist content inherent in their situation, the problem the 'poor whites' encounter in Gaullist policy is, when all is said and done, the same problem as that of the peasants, the artisans, the shopkeepers of the metropole. To change Algeria into a 'modern country' is to put an end to the 'privileges' of race (not, of course, to the privileges of money), just as to change France is to put an end to the 'privileges' of tradition. The rationalization of the capitalist world aims at the disappearance, not of the Bourgeauds, but the overseers of Bab-il-Oued, not of the Boussacs, but the farmers of the Moriban. The fear of these classes who feel themselves condemned and who know themselves to be defenseless is perfectly justified, even if the political reactions in which it is released are perfectly aberrant.

It is still the case that these reactions, we said, did not have in January 1960 the intensity they possessed in May 1958. There was an appreciable drop in tension in the Europeans' combativeness. It certainly must be linked to the reinforcement of power in France, which made an effective popular pressure on the orientation of the affairs more problematic and improbable for the *Français d'Algérie* as for the *Français de France*. Concretely, in Algiers, that meant that the rallying of the army to the insurrection appeared much less easy than a year and a half previously.

It cannot be disputed that in effect the army as a whole was run in an appreciably more 'loyal' way with respect to Paris than on May 13. No doubt, the troops that were placed in contact with the insurgents, when the gendarmes and the mobile guards had been withdrawn, treated them indulgently; but this fraternization became impossible when the paratroop division that had belonged to Massu had in its turn been replaced by domestic units. Over the period of more than two years that this division was stationed in Algiers, many Algiers men had joined its ranks, and many men and officers had married Algiers women. The interpenetration of the army and the European community was exemplified in this case in an extreme and unique fashion.

But the most decisive sign of the rediscovered 'loyalism' of the forces is the abstention of the Algerians throughout the entire insurrection, for this abstention was in reality that of the SAU and SAS officers [who commanded Algerians in the French army] of Algiers and its suburbs; these same officers had, in 1958, mobilized 'their Muslims' in the Forum to put on a show for both Paris and the extreme right, demonstrating to Paris that all of Algeria was against it, demonstrating to the extreme right that they could not hope for the return to the colonial status quo, and indicating finally a Gaullist solution to the insurrection at the time.

In opposing the attempts of the 1960 insurgents who sought to recommence the 'Franco-Muslim fraternizations,' the group of captains clearly decided in favor of supporting de Gaulle's policy, and it is not excessive to see in their attitude the most significant fact of the crisis. As for the situation in Algeria, it indicates in effect that these officers, each of whom, as one knows, is 'worth' the strength of thousands of Arabs voices, seem ready, in the event of a referendum, to exert pressure in the direction desired by de Gaulle, that is, for association. Thence proceeds the talk of a 'Muslim thaw,' thence the hurry to unleash a third force in favor of speedy regional elections. No doubt this orientation remains embryonic for the time being and can only come to fulfillment if the problem of relations with the GPRA, notably in the preelectoral phase, is positively resolved. But it nevertheless indicates an essential modification in the attitude of the section of the army that is finally the most important, the one that is occupied in the administration of Algerian society.

It is an error (which we never made here, even if we somewhat overestimated the retaking in hand of the army by Paris) to conceive of the army of Algeria, that is, the cadres in active service, as being endowed with a stable ideology, essentially fascist, and resolved only to enforce orders compatible with this ideology – not to mention those elements of the military, above all the oldest, who are officials mainly concerned with returning to a 'normal' home life. The spirit of the officers most actively engaged in the colonial war cannot be reduced to a fascism or a 'Francoism' of any kind. It is certain that they constitute perhaps the most politicized part of the country, in that they experience in the most immediate (in their everyday lives), most intense (their lives are at risk), and most persistent (since 1946) way the crisis of the regime that they obeyed for twelve years before bringing it down, the crisis of a society that they do not see as preferable to that of their adversaries, the crisis finally of the Western values taught to them by tradition and whose fragility they feel in the face of the enormous momentum of the colonial masses against the West. It is in this army that has for fourteen years defended an empire that it knows to be lost as such, defended a 'civilization' whose real significance it could judge from its exported form through contacts with the colonists of Madagascar, of Indochina, of Morocco and Tunisia, and lastly of Algeria. Finally, it is in this army that the contradictions of modern capitalist society are lived, if not thought, more intensely than in any other section of the bourgeoisie.

It would be surprising if the army, having carried out essentially political tasks for years, were not politicized, that is, it would be surprising if it continued to 'do its duty' blindly, without ever asking where it is. For even if 'do your duty' means something in the traditional exercise of the military métier, on a battle-field faced with persons who on their side obey the same imperative, it loses all meaning when the lieutenant and his forty men, left in the center of a Moi or Kabyle village, receive the order to 'pacify' it. The problem is then no longer to hold or die, but to find a way to give some content to the 'pacification.' Now, if this task is taken seriously, it inevitably means the reconstruction of a social community, integrating the soldiers and the peasants in relations that are as har-monious as possible. If therefore the military cadres as a whole harbor an ideo-logy, it is neither fascist nor 'Francoist', but 'administrative': the officer imagines his task as a task of putting all social activities back on track, and he knows that this is not possible without the participation of the peasant community, nor, furthermore, without *his* participation in the peasant community.

These aspects became more pronounced in the Algerian war because, more than any other, it is a social war. De Gaulle had to try to restore to the army a minimum of confidence in his actions by exorcising the specter of a depar-ture with arms and baggage that would have wiped out at a stroke years devoted to the reconstitution of an Algerian society. Hence the appeasements contained in his January 29 declaration and reinforced at the time of his trip at the begin-ning of March.

But no amount of appeasement can overcome the essential absurdity in which this administrative activity is steeped. As managers, it is true that officers tend to assimilate into the communities for which they are responsible. But this assimilation is of course impossible: first, administrative regulations concerning assignments, changes, promotions, and so forth, do not leave them in their vil-lages for very long, which already shows that merely belonging to the military apparatus is incompatible with the task of administration. Second, and above all, their administrative ideology remains a *class* ideology. For them it is not a matter of participating equally in the reconstruction of society by following the project that the Algerians develop for themselves, but finally of imposing, under fraternal or paternal guise, a model of society as much in conformity with the interests of French capitalism as possible. And they must themselves be conscious of this fact, because they know and observe daily that the most active elements (the very force that obliged Algerian society to pose the problem of its organization anew) are not in the villages, but in the mountains, bearing arms against the village; they also know, however, that no social reconstruction is possible without these elements. The absurdity of the military task in Algeria is that it wants at the same time to manage Algeria *with* the Algerians and *without* them (not to say *against* them). There is not an SAS or SAU officer who is not aware of this, and there is no 'taking in hand,' even with an iron fist, that can prevent it.

For this absurdity is nothing other than the very absurdity of capitalist society transposed onto the terrain of Algeria, where violence brings it fully to light: in the factory, as well, the employers try to make the workers participate in the organization of their work but only within the framework of methods and objectives defined by the employers themselves, that is, without ever letting the workers actually manage. In this respect, the Algerian war is exemplary because it crystallizes and strips bare *the* most fundamental contradiction of the capitalist world, the only one that is truly insoluble *within* the system itself. French society, even if it were to be endowed with a state still 'stronger' than de Gaulle's, would not know how to fill the gaping void hollowed out in military ideology by the crisis in that society over the past fifteen years (what pious souls call the 'malaise of the army' and the phraseologues of the left its 'fascism').

Therein lies an objective limit to the success of de Gaulle's policy in Algeria. That is not to say that the Algerian war will last forever, but only that de Gaulle must find a solution to the impasse in which the army is caught if he wants to be able to put an end to the war without his state being seriously shaken. The modification that we said earlier could be detected in the spirits of the SAS and SAU officers will perhaps give him the means of getting out of this impasse, if they will henceforth accept working within the perspective of self-determination. That is not to say that the intrinsic absurdity of their task will be done away with, because all in all they will be asked to manage until the time when it will be preferable not to manage any longer, but for de Gaulle as for the employers, the problem is not that of knowing whether the absurdity will really disappear, it is that of knowing whether one can act as if it did not exist.

Finally, and if one does not take the fundamental contradictions inherent in the class structure of society into account, the immediate result of the Algiers insurrection appears to be the defeat of the European bourgeoisie of Algeria in the face of French capitalism. The relative isolation of the activists in relation to the demoralized population at large, along with the resigned obedience of the military cadres, allowed those in authority in Paris to decapitate the organizations of the extreme right and to displace the most compromised officers, thus at the same time consolidating its hold on the military and administrative apparatus of Algeria and breaking down, or at least seriously splitting up, a major obstacle to its policy.

The Transformation of Everyday Life

The barricades of Algiers were, like Lagaillarde's beard, anachronistic. But the appeals to antifascist vigilance that resounded in France at the end of January were hardly less so. If it is correct that an endemic fascism raged in Algeria because of the particular structure of this society, it is no less so that there is no fascism imaginable in France today, nor in any other modern capitalist country.

In order for fascism to arise and spread, it is first necessary that a profound crisis call into question the capacity of capitalism to govern society as a whole, and particularly its economy, as was the case following the 1929 crisis. Next it is necessary that a significant segment of the proletariat that violently suffers this crisis no longer has the force to develop a revolutionary and socialist response and accepts the solution that big business capital offers it through the intervention of the fascist organizations. There is no fascism without a radical and open crisis of all the traditional institutions of capitalist society, nor indeed without the almost physical elimination of the political and union organizations the working class had previously provided itself.

Now the French economy is currently 'bursting with health.'[9] There is no need to be a cynical banker to understand this. It is enough to look at the unemployment figures,[10] the balance of exports and imports,[11] the speed of expansion in industrial production,[12] or any other indicator: it is impossible to imagine what aberration might lead so 'prosperous' a capitalism to offer itself the expensive and risky luxury of fascism. Furthermore, there is no question of eliminating the workers' organizations, but rather of their growing participation, over the past ten years, in economic responsibilities, at least at the company level. This is an inescapable necessity for modern capitalism. To diagnose fascism in these conditions is the effect of paranoia.

And it is true that, apart from their dated little plots, organizations (like the Communist party, the UGS, and the PSA) that have called for the formation of antifascist committees do suffer from an ideological archaism close to psychosis. No doubt the phantom of fascism served them as a pretext for soliciting common actions, that is to say, cartel formations, from one another (which in any case will remain on paper); perhaps they could dream of 'outflanking de Gaulle' in their defense of his republic. But whatever they may have dreamed or wished, they showed above all, on the occasion of the Algiers insurrection, their complete inability to rethink the political problem of the modern society or of the society on the way to modernization in which they find themselves. They do nothing but chew over the old slogan of the union of the left; they would almost be thankful if fascism existed because at least it is a situation with which they are *already* familiar, for which they already have tactics prepared. The fact that these tactics have always failed matters little: at bottom, they cried fascism in order to bring it to life and, at the same time, to give life to themselves. This is no longer politics; it is the hypermemory of the dying.

The total indifference of the population to its appeals revealed the confirmed decay of the ideology of the left as did the open hostility or disillusioned irony with which the workers greeted the 'strike' for which the unions and the bosses called with one voice.

If either the unions or the bosses hoped to politicize the workers in one direction or another, on the occasion of the Algiers insurrection, it must be agreed that they completely failed. The persistent repulsion that the proletariat as a whole feels when faced by 'politics' could not be overcome despite the ingredient of fascism. The proletariat no more stirred in January 1960 than in May 1958. To tell the truth, for what, to what ends, might it have stirred? There was no question of its defending de Gaulle: the workers had directly experienced the class meaning of power, through the reduction of their standard of living and through the acceleration of working practices in the firms. Yet what did the organizations propose to them? Safeguarding the Gaullist order, that is, their own exploitation. Evidently, no political perspective could be outlined by the organizations of the 'left,' which deserve no further critical attention.[13]

But this distaste for worn-out organizations is not enough to characterize the attitude of the proletariat toward politics. This distaste seems to extend to the political sphere itself. The working class, if it is still capable of fighting, and hard, at the company level, is not producing new stable organizations in which not only its protest program but its communist project might crystallize. The idea of a global and radical transformation of society seems absent from the present attitude of the workers, along with the idea that collective action can bring about this transformation. The spread of this depoliticization greatly exceeds implicit criticism of the parties and the unions.

We must search for the true reasons for this, decide to open our eyes, to identify the immense transformation in the everyday life of the working class (which has been going on in the bowels of our society for the past ten years) in which this depoliticization inscribes itself, to give it its full historic and social significance and to draw from it the political conclusions that must serve as a guide to our action. We can only hope to provide a sketch of this task in what follows.

The health with which the French economy is 'bursting' implies first of all a more rapid use of its labor force for workers, both blue and white collar. The present rhythm of expansion supposes in effect an increased productivity, even taking into account the entry of the younger generation into production. The 'rationalization' that the employers impose almost everywhere on the proletariat operates according to completely different processes from one location to another, sometimes employing brutal Taylorism, sometimes using the police methods borrowed from Ford, sometimes adopting the most modern techniques drawn from industrial psychology and sociology, but always with the machine itself as an objective constraint imposing rhythms and gestures. But all these processes converge into a single project, which is the increased alienation of the workers in their labor, the more and more subtle disruption of their traditional means of struggle against exploitation, their more radical expropriation from any initiative, their ever more visible degradation into the simple appendix of a management that is itself ever more invisible. The exteriority of workers in relation to what they do thus continues to deepen, and correlatively their activity appears more clearly than in the past as a simple moment in the circulation of capital: on the one hand, work has now become for the majority of wage earners time wasted in gestures stripped of all interest and all real meaning; on the other hand, the money received in exchange for this time does not seem to result from this time itself in any thinkable way. The relation that exists between the eight hours passed figuring on a cash register the price of the objects that the clients of a supermarket present when leaving the store and the 30,000 or 35,000 francs [$60 to $70 at 1960 rates] that are given the employee in exchange for these eight hours is felt as absolutely arbitrary. That means that even the pecuniary stimulant, this final reason behind the whole organization of capitalist society, has lost all effectiveness, not as a stimulant, of course, but as the expression of a real hierarchy in the value of different kinds of work.

There is thus at once a more complete incorporation of the workers into the working sphere (and this is what we mean by emphasizing that the workers feel themselves to be merely a phase in the capitalist process) and a more complete exteriority of labor in relation to the workers. The rhythms are more rapid, the working practices are more oppressive, the harassments of control are more petty – and at the same time the content of what one does is more indifferent. The tensions that result from this situation are thus different from those produced by work of a more technically simple nature. The new working practices require higher and poorly remunerated professional qualifications, and these tensions are released in strikes and demonstrations decided on the job, which tend to hold firm, to be directed as much at local working conditions as at wages, and which are usually rewarded with success. Even in France, where the breakup of the organizations of struggle has been significant, such workers' actions now appear frequently; they are common currency in countries like Great Britain and the United States where 'rationalization' is more advanced. But these strikes do not spread, given the lack of organizations with suitable structures and ideologies.

The 'compensation' for this alienation (but need it be said that this alienation does not allow, cannot allow any 'compensation,' and that the very idea of 'compensation' is a product of the capitalist philosophy of the permanent possibility of a cash equivalent?) is provided by modern capitalism, and is beginning to be provided in France, in the form of a more elevated standard of living. Part of the product is or can be given back to the workers, not because the employers become philanthropists, but because this payoff is finally indispensable for enlarging the capacities of the 'market' as production rises, and consequently for increasing the purchasing power of wage earners.[14]

Does this 'compensation,' which causes the foolish to claim that the working class is becoming middle class, mean more freedom of consumption? On the contrary. There would be no end to an enumeration of the techniques that capitalism employs in order to be able to regulate consumption in such a way as to preserve the harmony of its system: the destruction of products through consumption currently attracts almost as much attention (market surveys, motivational research, consumption inquiries, etc.) as does their manufacture. And these studies do not aim only to adjust production to needs, they aim no less at constantly refitting needs to production (from both a qualitative and a quantitative viewpoint). This is to say that capitalism tries to incorporate the dynamic of needs ever more strictly within its global economic dynamic: this incorporation operates both in the form of prediction, henceforth indispensable to the functioning of the system, and in the form of a control effectively adjusting needs to production possibilities.

Thus an increased alienation in needs is added to alienation in the labor process. The needs we feel are less and less our needs, more and more anonymous needs, and the infallible symptom of this alienation is that the satisfaction of these needs does not procure a real pleasure. Many activities of consumption, on the contrary, become chores.[15]

But this behavior coincides perfectly with the functioning of the modern capitalist economy: it assures the full use of the labor force without its being necessary to employ constraint – by means of the simple self-determination of that force – and at the same time, it guarantees the full use of purchasing power. Thus the labor force is more and more caught up in the exclusive use of its capacity by the employers, and so it is that variable capital from now on incarnates itself in almost the entirety of the labor force available in society.

In the same sense, one of the notable results of economic expansion lies in the fact that social categories previously untouched by 'modern life' are proletarianized. That is, they are not impoverished, but abstracted from their traditional mode of working and consuming and subjected to the increased alienation we just described: this is the case for the peasants, particularly the young; this is the case for the shopkeepers and artisans. This movement sooner or later implies a homogenization of ways of living in France, which would already be appreciable from a comparison of the pattern of consumption of a contemporary peasant family with what it was twenty years ago.

But modern capitalism does not only overthrow habits of working and consuming, it profoundly transforms all human relations, that is, everyday life itself. The remoteness of the home in relation to the workplace (it would take too long here to examine the origin of this phenomenon) brings about a considerable extension of the time taken in commuting, that is, in indirect relation to production. Correlatively, the time devoted to familial life or private life in general is appreciably reduced, and new tensions in the relations between men and women, between parents and children evidently follow. These relations are more and more abbreviated, it is more and more difficult to share experiences, the familial community as such tends to pulverize itself, and the old idea according to which it is proper to 'raise a family' loses all content when husband and wife see each other for two hours a day from 6:00 to 8:00 p.m. (if there is no television), when the children are taken care of by the school, the canteen, homework, holiday camp. One of the fundamental values of traditional society crumbles away; the effect is that workers no longer find a relatively stable human milieu outside their work in which they can escape from the obsession with production – that they grasp themselves instead as isolated, that is, abandoned *individuals* – and that they lose, with the family, a goal in the conduct of everyday life.

More generally, a kind of anonymous human relation, which corresponds to the pulverization of the communities of the previous period, tends to develop: for example, the old neighborhood community, so important in the proletarian life of the nineteenth century, is broken up in the new dormitory suburbs where the occupants of the same building no longer know one another. The destruction of the stable familial and perifamilial entourage affects fundamental emotional attitudes. In the past, it was in this milieu that the choice of partners (friends, sexual partners) was traditionally carried out; today, this choice functions with ever greater difficulty. On the other hand, the fact that mixed labor becomes the rule favors the multiplication of precarious sexual and affective experiences and stabilizes a form of behavior consisting of *trying out* the other and oneself. This precariousness, when it concerns sexual relations, no doubt explains the French woman's attitude of anxiety, taking into account the prohibition of birth control, as well as her reaction in the direction of security: for her, marriage offers above all the sense of a defense against anxiety, it takes place in conditions that make her sexual success problematic.

From all of this there results an increased relativization of human relations: individuals are immersed in a society that they endure rather than understand, not because it is unbounded, but because its overall meaning, the thing that guaranteed the tissue of values out of which everyday life was made, has disappeared, along with the feeling that it is possible to reconstitute this meaning. Whence proceeds cynicism in political matters, if politics is indeed the activity through which persons intend collectively to transform the meaning of their lives, whence proceeds the apparent indifference to and the real anxiety concerning the problems that overshadow the field of everyday life.

This overall attitude manifests itself particularly among the young (whose relative importance in France is considerable given the age pyramid). They are less inclined (and indeed less able) than anyone else to oppose the good conscience and the bad faith of political or sociological 'explanations' borrowed from the previous period to this general crisis; the fraction of working and student youth that is politically organized is extremely weak. Their nonpoliticization is simply the general form taken by their nonadhesion to social values. Society such as it exists is incapable of offering the young the least reason to live, and it is only on this basis that one can understand the style common to the kids in black leather and the 'hoodlums,' the aesthetic of violence.

One finds oneself faced with an overall situation for which it would be superficial to want to impute responsibility to a particular factor. In gestation in France, but already constituted in other countries, this society is in its fundamental features neither the effect of a simple internal transformation of capitalism nor the unique result of the degeneration of workers' organizations, nor is it the sign of the extinction of the communist project in the proletariat.

One must not lose sight of the fact that the transformation of capitalism that led it to modify profoundly the relations in which exploitation takes place itself results from the workers' struggle. Through its wars and its 'peaces,' its 'prosperities' and its recessions, the real history of capitalism is the history of a dominant class constrained by the proletariat constantly to revise the ensemble of its modes of domination. The workers have fought for a shorter working week, for security in production, for insurance, for wages, for vacations, for allocations, for administration; and the bourgeoisie, for a century, has not ceased to retreat, to make concessions. It has always tried to take them back, when the occasion has presented itself, when the working class was beaten down and divided. The workers had to begin the struggle again in order to regain what they had lost and in order to overcome the new forms that the employers had given to exploitation. In a sense, the whole history of mechanization (if one excepts the relatively autonomous development of science and technology), the whole history of the forms of constraint in the factory and the office from the twelve-hour day to 'human relations',[16] the whole history of political and juridical institutions, is only the succession of the results of the conflict between the communist project stirring up society and the exploitative function imposing its structure on it. These results are essentially unstable, they are never anything other than precarious compromises continually made between the two forces when they can no longer carry on the struggle further.

But this fundamental conflict, which animates all of capitalist society, contains a much more important significance if one places oneself within the workers' movement itself. In these everyday struggles as in its large-scale battles, the proletariat constantly encounters the opposition of institutions and organizations that it created, that it nourished, and that have become weapons in the hands of its adversary. The political or protest organizations with which it provided itself in order to put an end to exploitation, the institutions that were created out of its victories, are left in the sphere of the ruling class by the ebbing of the tide; they have been incorporated as so many organs of the functioning of class society, and in order to carry on its struggle, the proletariat has not only to undo the stranglehold of exploitation, it must furthermore unmask, denounce, and destroy its own works. Everything that is institutionalized in a class society becomes a class institution. All activity in the past tense becomes a passivity, not through some kind of curse, some kind of burden that weighs on mankind, but simply because the ruling class assimilates it, makes it into *its* institution, turns it against those same ones who have acted and weighs them down with it. That is its function as an exploiting and alienating class: to place humanity in the past tense, in the passive mood.

This process of ruling-class takeover of the organizations and institutions whose meaning was originally proletarian attains its height in contemporary capitalism. More than ever, the bosses assimilate the forms of struggle, of resistance, that belong to the humanity they exploit and use these forms as intermediaries between themselves and the workers. Wage increases become the means of enlarging the market and of avoiding the old crises, the 'frank' (face to face)[17] discussions between employers and wage earners allow the leadership to inform itself about worker opinion and to control it, employers' responsibility for vacations allows them to enforce even the modes of workers' leisure, the extension of schooling makes possible the diffusion of a completely mystifying culture, the ruling class's claim to resolve the problem of housing for the workers provides it with the means of controlling even the use of familial space. The unions are on the road to integration in the hierarchy of the factory and the office, the 'workers' parties are on the road to integration in the sphere of the bourgeois state. No doubt the process is less complete than in some countries of modern capitalism such as the United States, Sweden, or Germany; no doubt there are still specific obstacles in France (essentially the nature of the Communist party) opposed to the complete incorporation of the former workers' organizations into the institutions of the society of exploitation. But the phenomenon does not differ qualitatively between France and these countries.

It is in this political vacuum, older than Gaullism, that the Gaullist state has been able to institute itself. And it maintains this vacuum. The concrete conditions of everyday life that are given to the workers are not the causes of depoliticization, any more than depoliticization is *their* cause, but there is a social totality that is present and expresses itself in each of its parts: in the forms of the exploitation of labor and in the forms of consumption, in the cooperation of the 'workers' leaderships with the class state and in the indifference of the workers toward these leaderships, in the pulverization of individuals, and in the brief and resolute struggles they carry on sporadically in the firms.

The workers no longer give life to their organizations through their struggles (the organizations detach themselves from them – become bureaucracies – incorporate themselves into the structure of class society – the ruling class tries to use them as intermediaries – the proletariat withdraws itself from them even more – the bourgeoisie increases its exploitation) but through the organizations and the institutions that had produced the proletariat, in underhanded forms. One can read this sequence in either direction – there is no absolute beginning, there is totalization. Muffled totalitarianism is this control by the leaders of the whole wage-earning population in all its activities, which takes place thanks to the organizations that the proletariat had imposed through its former struggles.

It is thus proletarian political life itself that is alienated, that is displaced from its own class in hybrid organisms (in that their genesis is worker and their function bourgeois or bureaucratic), that is seized by the ruling class. The very idea of a global political project is immediately neutralized in the workers' own heads. Incredulity, lassitude, and irony keep an exploited class in step much more effectively than open violence.

Assuredly, the proletariat was always worked upon from the inside by the ideology of class society, and the essential element of this work was always to convince it that it was not itself *a class*, that it was not this communist project. It would be a pleasant simplification, and an enormous political error, to conceive of proletarian political life as a pure development toward socialism, as a project never contested in itself by the fact of its existence in class society. But in the preceding period an important section of the workers organized themselves against the assault of the dominant ideology, banded together, counterattacked, and through this very counterattack broke the 'spell' of the mystification for themselves and for everybody. Today, there are no signs of the birth and explicit organization of this activity of contestation of class society: the proletariat is no longer present in society as manifest political will. This is not to say that the communist project has been annihilated and that the dominant class has succeeded for all time in its task of reifying the workers. On the contrary, the inability of the ruling class to offer the society that it claims to govern a direction, a sense, values, reasons for doing and being what this society is and does has never been clearer, never has its incapacity to ground a really social life broken into the open as completely as today. This is what we tried to sketch out, very briefly, a while ago. More than a century ago, it is true that the proletariat was not the object of 'a particular tort, but of a tort in itself,'[18] But the problem posed by this profound erosion of activities and ideals is precisely that of how to know *how, by what means* the revolutionary project can henceforth express itself, organize itself, fight.

A certain idea of politics dies in this society. Certainly, neither the 'democratization of the regime,' called for by unemployed politicians, nor the creation of a 'large unified socialist party' (which will only regroup the refuse of 'left' can give life to this idea. Such notions lack perspective, are minuscule in relation to the real dimensions of the crisis. It is now time for revolutionaries to measure up to the revolution to be made.

Notes

1. Translator's note (TN): the Jeanson network was a French clandestine organisation – named after its leader – that sheltered deserters from the French army of Algeria and supported the independence movement.
2. TN: a declaration signed by 121 noncommunist French intellectuals affirming the right to refuse the draft.
3. TN: De Sérigny was a prominent right winger, editor of the newspaper *L'Echo d'Alger*, involved in the anti-independence insurrection of 1958.
4. See the collection of articles on 'La crise française et le gaullisme' in *Socialisme ou Barbarie* 25 (July–August 1958).
5. TN: a summary of economic statistics detailing the crisis of the Fourth Republic is omitted here.
6. See P. Chaulieu, 'Perspectives de la crise française'.
7. See P. Chaulieu, 'Sur la dynamique du capitalisme', *Socialisme ou Barbarie* 12 (August–September 1953).
8. See Lyotard, 'The Social Content of the Algerian Struggle', in *Political Writings*, pp. 221–51.
9. *L'Express*, 4 February, 1960.
10. At its height, in February 1959, registered unemployment was less than 1 percent of the labor force, and it has since declined.
11. In deficit by $1,020 million in 1956, by $1,080 million in 1957, and by $480 million in 1958, this balance showed in 1959 a surplus of exports over imports of $516 million.
12. In the fourth quarter of 1959, the index of industrial production was 11 percent higher than that of the fourth quarter of 1958.
13. See 'Bilan', *Socialisme ou Barbarie* (November–December 1958).
14. Which is not to say that it happens always or automatically.
15. See D. Mothé, 'Les ouvriers et la culture', *Socialisme ou Barbarie* 30 (April–May 1960).
16. TN: in English in the original.
17. TN: an ironic allusion to the language of Stalinist communiqués, which tend to speak of 'frank and comradely discussions' attendant upon the imposition of central policy.
18. TN: the analysis of this phrase of Karl Marx's is conducted at length by Lyotard in 'A memorial of Marxism'.

Chapter 11

A Short Libidinal Economy of a Narrative Set-up: the Renault Corporation Relates the Death of Pierre Overney[1]

I

It is pointless to look for the origin of the story in an original narrative. The narrative is in our evening newspaper. It is here that the story ceaselessly produces and reproduces itself.[2]

We are in the habit of positing the following sequence: there is the fact and then the testimony, that is to say a narrative activity transforming the fact into a narrative. Thus, first a story or diegesis, which would be the reference of the narrative insofar as it has organised itself diachronically, into a chain. For example: 26 February 1972, a group of militant Maoists distribute tracts at the Emile Zola entrance to the Renault factory at Billancourt (these tracts call for a demonstration against racism after the assassination of a young Arab at the *Goutte d'Or*). A fight with uniformed guards. A man in plain clothes draws a revolver, fires a warning shot, then a shot in the direction of the group, and Pierre Overney is dead.

Is the foregoing diegesis, the story itself? No, it is already a *narrative*, an organisation of discourse according to a certain number of operators, which criticism designates by the generic term *narration*. But habit is obstinate and prompts us: Overney is well and truly dead, it is a fact; here is the evidence and the reference, the unfortunate fact that can be attested. And, as habit continues, it is by taking possession of this fact and by making of it its own material that the narrative activity, the activity of the narrating subject, produces the narrative (the one just read, for example, or another). And, habit concludes, the work proper to historical science will be to undo what is done by narration, starting from the linguistic datum of the narrative in order to attain, by critical analysis (of the document, the text, the sources), the fact that is the raw material of this production.

This manner of posing the problem of history is a theatrical position: on the exterior, outside the theatrical space, is the fact; on the stage, the narrative unfolding its drama; hidden in the wings, in the flies, beneath the stage, in the auditorium, is the director, the narrator, with all his machinery, the *fabricca* of the narration. The historian is supposed to take apart all the machinery and machination, and having knocked down the walls of the theatre, restore what has been excluded.

Now, evidently, the historian is himself only another director, his narrative another product, his work another narration, even if all of this is assigned the prefix *meta* – meta-diegesis, meta-narration, meta-narrative. A story in which it is a matter of history, certainly, but whose pretension to obtain the reference to the thing itself, the fact, to establish it and restore it, is no less mad – it is madder, all things considered – than the power of fiction freely deployed in the thousands of discourses from which is born the immense legend that is, for example, the *Odyssey*.

Madder perhaps, if the storyteller 'knows' that he produces the story along with his narrative, whilst in a sense the historian *does not want to know anything about this*: his discourse is unaware of itself as productive, recognising itself only as critical. He hides what the storyteller, perhaps, exhibits: that, critical or otherwise (because in no way does a tale exclude its own criticism as narrative position; re-read the beginning of Moore's *Utopia*, or the meta-diegesis which takes up Books IX to XI of the *Odyssey*), every narrative is not only the effect of a metamorphosis of affects, but it produces something other, the story, the diegesis. The storyteller does not begin from the reference; he produces it by means of his narrative. This is not the same thing as lying. Lying is impossible without an attested reference: yet here we find ourselves 'prior to' this attestation, the narrative alone providing it. The theatrical volume opened up by narration distributes an interior (the narrative, the stage) and an exterior (story, reality), but the narrator or director or novelist or storyteller 'knows' that the production [*mise en scène*] cannot occur without a concomitant putting out of play [*mise hors scène*], which is a putting into reality [*mise en réalité*]. Thus he proceeds by way of an artistic inversion, in which the object that the reader or the auditor of the narrative receives as the story which has provoked the narration is, on the contrary, for he who recounts it, the story that his narration engenders. Not what makes him speak, but *what he* names. Naming the thing as producing it.

But this inversion remains, as usual, in the field determined by the two inverted poles: story-reference and narrative-pronouncement. It is an artistic inversion because it instantiates the whole business upon production; but if the narrative production is not itself inverted, it risks falling back into a new credulity. For, to speak of production is without doubt to point towards an *economics* of narration; only this economics, more often than not borrowed from Marxism, is received credulously and substituted without examination for that reference which the artistic narrative activity is supposedly lacking. This missing support is once again slid under the narrating instance, as its productive accomplice.[3] One would then describe the activity of the narrator as if it were productive in the sense that wire-extrusion, milling, mixing plaster or morticing are metamorphoses of the elements of production into products – namely, wire, gears, cement, mortice. Sweet repose in the bosom of the industrial paradigm, and of its machine.

We could indeed call narration a machinic set-up, but only on condition that we see nothing mechanical in it; and if there is production, it is most certainly libidinal '*before*' being industrial. Consequently, the subject of the narrating instance, if there was one, not only could not be equivalent, in the universe of discourse, to the turner in the process of milling, but could not even be equivalent to the whole of organised capital, dead and living, that permits the operation of milling. The set-up of capitalist production obliterates what is at stake in production as such (which is libidinal, even desire itself); and if one is so trusting as to begin with its apparent stability and seriousness, then one covers-up everything that this productive organisation rejects, which could be included in a single word: errancy, or, to speak like Freud, displacement, *Verschiebbarkeit*.

All in all, in being satisfied with the Marxist or Marxian model of production as the paradigm of narration, one immediately surrenders oneself to misconceiving the pulsional forces that are everywhere at play, as much in the industry of things as in that of words; one closes one's eyes to the pleasure function carried out by the arrangements of instrumentation, which are equally material and linguistic. In place of the libidinal body, an organic body, already shut in upon itself like a theatrical volume, is set up as the object of critical discourse, thus supporting the polarisation of the activity in question – here that of narration – upon the axis of exterior/interior.

Not only does the industry that we are familiar with, capitalist industry, produce industrial objects, not only does it produce the proletariat, as Marx said, and along with it CEOs, executives, and managers, ideas and affects, housewives, employment schemes and television reports, that is the whole of the organic body of capitalist society itself; above all it contains a power of *other* productions and products, of incredible and pointless arrangements providing a place for objects that are complex, monstrous or disordered. It contains frenzied techniques and technologies; it contains the conjunction of science and fiction, the power of simulacra. Likewise, the history that we know, the diachrony of a supposedly social subject, is certainly not what narration comes to transform, and possibly to pervert, betray, or, conversely, set to rights in its authenticity, for narration is indeed what produces it and never stops producing it; but here also it is necessary to open up production to its entire field. Narration is what can engender the body of the story, a certain type of 'totality' organised according to a certain sort of temporality; it *can* engender it, but it does not necessarily engender it. When it is Joyce or Sterne who recount a story we know that the so-called historical totality and temporality come off very badly. The narrative set-ups are here employed almost in the wrong way (but what is the right way?), like Dürer's perspectival grid in the creation of the anamorphoses. We could say as much, without further ado, of Proust or Mann. And it is not only a matter of the status attached to narration by modernity; it is enough to open Rabelais in order to be assured of the contrary, in order to note that it is always a possible function of narration that it produce, in place of the socio-historical body, a non-object not unlike what Freud imagined the id or the primary process to be: a single-sided entity with heterogeneous regions crossed by aleatory intensities. Thus the Proustian or Gogolian narrative undoes the well-formed body of its reader. It engenders it as an indeterminate and creased skin, where intensities are not bound, or at the very least not immediately bound, to an order, to an instance dominating the narrative and the reader who would bear responsibility for it, and who could thus give an account of it. Instead, they are brought back, bit by bit, in their singularity as non-unifiable events to the fragments that are themselves incommensurable with the supposed unity of the reading body. A science-fiction narrative, for example, Philip K. Dick's wonderful *Ubik*, also fulfils this function – and perhaps in a manner much better suited to clarifying our object, because his work does not only bear upon the *order* of narrative presentation of the parts of time, but also upon the diegetic course through the parts by a supposed subject (who thus always hides from himself) – it fulfils this same function by dieresis, by the freeing-up and the heteroplasty of certain regions of the libidinal temporal surface.

Conversely, the communiqué that the management of the state-owned Renault Corporation presented to the press after the assassination of Pierre Overney on the evening of 26 February 1972 is a narrative which operates in such a manner as to channel and regulate the movement of affects set in motion by this event. And it is one of the objectives of the analysis which follows to display the elements of the libidinal-rhetorical machinery which accomplishes this function.

We shall begin, therefore, without supposing a reference or a support for the narrating instance. The narrating instance produces itself by itself at a stroke, 'each time', and engenders along with itself the distribution of functions that following thousands of others, and above all following Gérard Genette,[4] we call narrative [*récit*] and story [*histoire*]. We are not going to analyse the text of the corporation according to the axes: real story → narration → narrative → referential story. It is rather necessary to imagine the synchrony or complete achrony of the story, narration and narrative. It is from out of the complex block that they form that the axes in question emerge, along with the possibilities of articulated diachronisation. But the *time in which* the storyteller tells the story is not and cannot be the time of the story that he recounts, if it is true that this is an effect of the narration, and it is no longer that of the narrative, which is more or less that of the reader or listener of the story, for the reason that there is no common measure between the time of making and the time of use, as any cook, baker, cobbler, or speaker knows. To produce a common temporal instantiation, a common measure of duration for these three orders – narration, narrative, story – is precisely a function of a regulative type of narrative, of which the Renault corporation's communiqué is an instance. By contrast, Sterne, or Diderot in *Jacques le Fataliste*, or Proust, undo this unity, attesting both joyously and painfully to its archaic character, and magnify the imcompossible temporal instances.

Hence it is not a *temporality*, that is, a vectoral system, which is required in order for us to establish the analysis of the narrative set-up; a tensivity, a tensoral entity, is sufficient. An event is the tensor that we require. Here, that event is Overney's death. This event does not have to be taken into account by virtue of being 'real', attestable outside of the theatrical volume engendered by the narration. Nor is it worthy of consideration because it is 'sensational', likely to engender many metamorphoses on the 'social body' through the diverse institutions (the press, opinion, political parties, trade unions, television) which criss-cross its surface: communiqués, telephone calls, demonstrations, press statements and conferences, strikes, broadcasts . . . These effects are clearly not without their importance, but they are legible only on the surface of the 'social body', and considering them uncritically will, without fail, plunge us back into the ('sociological') naivety of belief in the social body, and thus in its pre-existence, and thus in a reference assignable to Pierre Overney's death. If this death is an event, it is *above all* as a tensor or intense passage, and this tensor supposes not the three-dimensional Euclidean space of the theatrical volume and the organised social body, but the *n*-dimensional, neutral and unpredictable space of the libidinal film engendered by the tensor event itself in its amnesiac singularity.

To speak in a less obscure manner (but also with less precision), Overney's death is an event not by virtue of its 'ins' and 'outs'; on the contrary, it is an event inasmuch as it is libidinally linkable neither upstream to causes or precedents nor downstream to effects or consequences. It is a *vain* death. It is its inanity that makes of it an event. Deaths on the roads, the deaths in Indo-China are not vain; they inscribe themselves, or could easily be inscribed, in a ledger, a register of income and expenditure, credits and debits, the sum total of which is calculable, endowing them with meaning and direction. That the accountants might not be in agreement on the bottom-line is not of any interest here; they all agree on the principle that there is a bottom-line. And evidently, it is this same unique principle of the imputation to a general accountability, which makes of *all* the statements following Overney's murder – Renault's, the CGT's, and even that read by Geismar at the doors of the Père-Lachaise cemetery during the burial on 4 March – so many different but convergent modalities of the production of an organic body of history and society.

If Overney's death is an event, it is not one occurring *on this body* (on the contrary this body must be (re)produced from out of the death); rather it is an event as an instantaneous and unlocalisable tension in a libidinal, *n*-dimensional, space-time. If there is a *body* which corresponds to such a space-time, it is certainly not the organic body, whose parts, duly isolated by their respective functions, co-ordinate themselves for the greater good of the whole according to the rule of the *Gestalt*, a well-formed body in very good shape; no, it would be the body which faints at the sight of blood, vomits before a squashed cat, which cannot tolerate any intra-muscular injection, cannot eat mussels, ignores its anus and its shit, wholly contracted on the very limited ocular-cortical circuit in the pleasure of reading, that trembles before the vulva, trembles before the penis, that understands nothing of mathematics, that is able to learn Italian, but not English, that takes easily to a chisel but is useless with a brush, or *vice versa*. A body that can become stressed, and stressed to breaking point, in an unpredictable situation, but remains the mediocre or non-existent vehicle of affect in other situations; a body whose every region could in principle be invested by libidinal energy and orgasmic power, but only a few of which, in an irreducibly fortuitous manner, are actually so invested.

This body has no limits. It does not stop at a surface or frontier (the skin) which would divide an exterior from an interior. It extends well beyond this supposed frontier because words, books, food, images, looks, parts of the body, tools and machines, animals, sounds and gestures are able to be invested, and thus function as charged regions and as channels of circulation, in the same manner as an 'organ' such as the liver, or the stomach does in emotions, or psychosomatic illnesses.

This body does not have the dimensional status of the organic body. The latter is a volume occupying a three-dimensional Euclidean space with Cartesian co-ordinates, in which every point is locatable, every displacement measurable, etc. The libidinal thing is at one and the same time a sort of band with one infinite side (a Moebius strip) and also a sort of labyrinth – a surface covered in nooks and crannies – of undecidable junctions for the billions of pathways upon which potential intensities run.

This body is not unitary. Intensities can be invested here and there simultaneously, currents of an *opposing direction* going past in the same place. By contrast, the organic body is represented as a complex such that each of its parts is instantiated upon a functional unity or group of unities: it is this that permits the use of cybernetic models in genetics or in the study of metabolisms.

The organic body is a *body-politic*, in the sense of the term within political economy. It is endowed with limits which circumscribe the *propriety* of its own body; it is affected by a *regime* or a *ruling* [*régie*] which is its constitutional system. Every investment of a zone of this body that does not conform to this rule is registered as a rebellion, a sickness, as anarchy and threatens the death of the whole. The interest of the whole serves to authorise its repression. In fact, the organic body is the incessant product (a product which must be constantly produced) of operations, manipulations, excisions, separations and conflations, grafts, occlusions and derivations, running across the labyrinthine libidinal band. These operations instantiate all events – every charge and discharge of potential – upon a regulative unity, and thus submit the heterogeneous space-time of the libidinal band to the domination of an empty identity. As for the social-body, it is the organic body of all organic bodies, a meta–organic body. Its production is concurrent with that of individuals.

The principal function of the state-owned Renault Corporation's narrative being to reproduce the social-organic body, the pointless tension of Overney's murder thus had to be effaced. By inscribing it in the diachrony of a story, the narrative issued by the Corporation produces a social body which becomes a receptacle, the memory or the surface of inscription of this event, and by dint of this simple fact, equips it with precedents and consequents, putting it into circulation among the cycle of thinkable objects, rendering it reversible, finding equivalents for it, *exchanging* it for other events.

This transformation of the singular tensor into the moment of a process, effectuated here by the narrative set-up, does not suffice to distinguish it from any other linguistic set-up. Narration can accomplish a function of liaison and disintensification as is the case here; or, on the contrary, it can upset the organic body by making intensities pass through it that it has difficulty bearing. But in both cases it operates specifically *by producing temporality*. It is in this way that it is appropriately opposed to other modalities or 'genres' of language, such as the discourse of knowledge, prayers, orders, theatrical or philosophical dialogue, polemical articles . . . Doubtless, temporality is implicated – probably uniquely – in each of these language types. The important thing, however, is that none of them, taken as linguistic forms, has for their principal correlate, from the perspective of reference, the instantiation of intensities on a chrono-logical distribution. It is with time, but not by time, that they bind or unbind that of which they speak. Despite our credulous habits, we have to learn to posit this distribution as an effect, just as we can the determination or the impossi-bility of determining a notion at the end of a Platonic dialogue, or a sentence proposed by the prosecution or defence at the end of their speeches.

And for this reason it will be necessary to come back once again to Freud, and to those admirable texts scattered throughout his oeuvre: the text of *The Unconscious* (1915) on the properties of the primary process; the text of *Civilisation and its Discontents* (1930) on the three Romes inscribed in the same space; the short passage at the end of *The Wolf Man* (1918) where the Wolf Man's unconscious is said 'to produce an analogous impression to that made by the religion of Egypt' which 'displays, in a certain manner, on the surface what other types of evolution have conserved only in the depths'; the metaphor of the third *New Introductory Lectures* (1932) that makes of the id a 'chaos, a cauldron full of boiling emotions' where desires, inaccessible to any temporal modification, remain 'virtually imperishable'. It will be necessary to reclaim these sketches of another, atemporal time, to superimpose upon this scarcely adumbrated, opaque *chrony*, upon this rough-draft, the chronological process of the story that is recounted, to us readers, by the Renault Corporation's statement, and to determine thus the narrative work, the famous narrative 'production', no longer by the gaps that there are between a supposedly original Story and a subsequent Narrative, but by the displacements, ablations, condensations, the surgical operations of every sort that would come to substitute the theatrical volume of a social body for the tensorial skin. This group of transformations is a set-up. By calling it a structure, not only does one give it the status of having a consistency of operation and duration that it most certainly does not have, but one implies a theory of knowledge; that is to say, one eliminates its libidinal function. Nobody denies that the production of a narrative is not run of the mill; that it is not functional in the ethnological or linguistic sense of functionalism, is also evident, since far from being subordinated to the interests of a pre-existent social whole, it contributes to the production of the latter. But in its unforeseeability and transience, as in its insistence, it is the actuality of desire; that it accomplishes desire according to its belonging both to the licentiousness of Eros and to the silence of death, this is what the term 'set-up' says: a formation that is entirely positive, affirmative, that distributes libidinal intensities, but always unsettling them to the point of rendering them dysfunctional.

The narrative set-up does not operate, then, between Story and Narrative, but here between pulsional singularity and temporal distribution, between the tensoral skin and the well-formed social body, between event-like intensity and unitary regulation; there is a transmutation of one into the other at one pole, the opposite at the other pole, and between the two all the various distributions . . . This must be said as clearly as possible for the reader to be able to assess our debt to, at the same time as our betrayal of, the remarkable analyses offered by Gérard Genette in his *Narrative Discourse*.[5] The simultaneously meticulous and daring dismantling of the most accomplished elements of narrative activity in Proust bears the marks of the skill, endurance and capacity for discrimination, which make Genette the most masterful dissector of narrative, whom it is necessary to follow. We do not hope to equal him here; worse, we are well aware of 'misappropriating' him. To Genette's art we owe both the larger and the lesser pieces of the narrative set-up that we have brought to light in the narrative of Overney's death. But Genette uses them as a poetician, voluntarily limiting himself to defining them as grids placed on the great linguistic axes of reference, modality and aspect, remaining in the field of language, only rarely daring to gauge their libidinal *effects*, to point out the affects distributed by these grids. By contrast, beginning from these grids, we attempt to restore their economic libidinal-political functioning. For this intense eclecticism we bear the entire responsibility. Our excuse, if it is necessary to have one, is the pleasure that one could experience in starting up a car by means of rhetoric.

II

The Management of the Corporation: The Violence of a Group of Agitators

Reprinted here is the entire text of the statement of the Renault Corporation sent to the press early on the Friday evening:

> Several months ago elements external to the factory began, on the immediate out-skirts of the Billancourt site, a systematic campaign with the aim of arousing and maintaining a climate of violence. Initially this only consisted in distributions of insulting and vulgar tracts at the gates of the factory, disparaging the supervisory staff just as much as the trade unions.
>
> Executives, managers, supervisors and the whole of the personnel responded calmly to all these attempts at provocation. Upon the manifest failure of these actions, the external elements, organised into commando squads, proceeded to engage in acts of aggression, attacking certain members of the personnel in the streets around the factory.
>
> This did not have any repercussions within the firm, where work continued calmly. The public authorities were kept informed of the incidents which occurred outside the factory. We then came to witness an escalation in the violence. These comman-dos attempted to penetrate into the factory in order to distribute tracts calling for violence, for revolution, even for murder, against the management. Such was the case particularly on 11 and 14 February last.
>
> However, these acts remained isolated and at no time did any member of the Corporation either participate or respond to these provocations and incitements to violence.
>
> These diverse and multiple attempts having thus completely failed, the comman-dos engaged this afternoon in a concerted attack on the principal entrance to the factory from the *Avenue Emile-Zola*. At the time when the evening shift takes over from the morning shift, when large movements of employees occur in the avenue, a commando group of around eighty people, armed with truncheons and iron-bars, rushed the few guards present at the entrance. Six guards, who were not bearing any arms, were overcome, hit and wounded.
>
> It was then that an administrative employee of the surveillance service, in no respect responsible for security properly speaking and who had nonetheless been subject to death threats, came to the assistance of the endangered guards. Before the group of assailants and being unable to escape or to free the guards, this administra-tive employee, carrying a pistol, drew it and fired in the air. A second shot came to hit one of the members of the attacking commando squad who succumbed to this

wound. This employee presented himself spontaneously to the police. An investigation is underway.

The injured guards were evacuated to the central infirmary and subsequently taken to *Ambroise-Paré* hospital. However, on the shop-floor work continued normally. At the end of the afternoon, representatives of the unions were unanimous in condemning the violence.

The calmness of the workforce is testimony to its complete disapproval of the violence unleashed in the area around the factory by a group of agitators. The management, which did everything possible to protect the factory from these agitators, deplores all the more this chain of events for its having led to the death of a young man.

This is the statement published in *Le Monde* of 27–28 February 1972. It is clear that it consists almost entirely of a narrative. An analysis of this narrative yields the following sections, each of which corresponds to a distinct moment of action in the diegesis.

Table 11.1

Beginning of the Narrative Section	Designation of the Narrative Section	Action in the Story	Designation of the Action in the Story
Several months ago . . .	N0	Systematic campaign of violence	S0
Initially this only consisted of . . .	Na	Distribution of tracts at the factory gates	S1
Upon the manifest failure . . .	Nb	Aggression against the employees in the street	S2
We then came to witness . . .	Nc	Distribution of tracts inside the factory	S3
These diverse and multiple attempts . . .	Nd	Violence against employees at the entrance to the factory	S4
It was then that an administrative employee . . .	Ne	Overney's murder	S5
However, on the shop-floor . . .	Nf	Testimony, denunciation	S6

Order

The question of order must be understood in the following way:[6] are the sections constituting the series that comprises the story (S0, S1, S2 . . .) presented in the same order of succession in N (Na/S1, Nb/S2 . . .) or not?

Here the answer is easy enough to find. The narrative 'follows' the story, or the 'story' follows the narrative, and this means two things: there is a bi-univocal correspondence between the sections N and the sections S; the two series are identically oriented. There is no reason, however, to hold such a set-up to be more natural or truer than any other; this correspondence and identity are but one ordering operation among others. What is specific about this set-up is its effacement of the traces of the 'narrative activity'. Between the narrative and the story, there is no identifiable intervention on the part of any storyteller; narrative and story arise together as two examples of the same diachrony. An equivalent model, in Quattrocento painting, would be the effacement of the orthogonals leading to the vanishing point, and of the large diagonal ordered according to the distance point: here, analogously, it is the instance of 'painting' which effaces itself. This is, therefore, production as the concealment of the producer. In Renaissance painting, objects seem to give themselves to vision; in the naive narrative, the facts, as Benveniste says, recount themselves. There is nothing to add to these remarks that would not have already been understood by the reader in saying that the effect produced is that of *objectivity*, in the sense of the position of an object presenting itself 'in person', in a way that gives rise to evidence (which is an evisceration [*évidement*] of the act of seeing). The gamut of phenomenological inanity is to be found in the construction and extensive exploitation of such a set-up. Again, it would be necessary to examine what is libidinal in this objectivity. It is produced by a specific folding back of the tensoral skin, which at a stroke, by invagination, envelops a closed space, positioning the narrative on the inside and placing, under the aegis of the story, the event 'on the outside' of the volume thus delimited. At the same time, it orders the latter so that it is homogenous with the narrative, and in such a way that this 'outside' is inside and synchronous. This ordering will come to form the scene. What is of interest in this adventure of representation is to grasp not the reason for such a displacement on the libidinal surface, but its mode or modes. With regard to the narrative set-up, it becomes apparent that the effacement of the narrating instance in the production of a strictly co-ordinated narrative and story is one of these modes, at least at the linguistic level.

Another effect resulting from this same co-ordination is that of *consecution*. This is the linguistic equivalent of the Koulechov effect in cinema, or, if one prefers, it is a confirmation of the suspicions – fed by Hume – about the idea of causality. It suffices for two sections to be placed in a position of chronological succession in order to produce a reciprocal encroachment of one upon the other, such that they appear to be associated not only by their temporal position but by a categorial function: causality, finality, etc. If the narrating instance is abolished, it deprives the reader of the capacity to play with the sections of the series S as of those of the series N, to separate them from their immediate prox- imity and thus to undo the links of meaning in which they appear caught up. It can be seen clearly here that by refusing to efface this instance the works of Proust or Joyce, as different as they might be, provoke in even the most reticent readers a certain disquiet concerning what they could believe to be the spatio- temporal forms of their sensibility and the categories of their understanding: when the sections S are presented narratively in an order so disrupted that their 'impossibility' or incompossibility, with regard to the demands of 'realism', must be admitted by criticism, as Genette shows *à propos* of the Proustian narrative, it is then that emerge a different space-time and a different sort of linkage than those that even the critical use of pure theoretical reason can give us.

In the Renault statement the opposite effect is produced. With the disap- pearance of the narrating instance, a tight linkage is established, on the one hand, between the two series, and on the other, between the sections of each. This correlation is so taut that what happens in the narrative appears to faith- fully imitate, to reflect what happens in the story, whilst the succession of facts (S), which is in principal an exclusively temporal order, also takes on the value of their 'logical' serialisation [*enchaînement*] (this is the key word at the end of the statement):[7] 'logical' is to be understood here as a *zweck-rational* series, as Max Weber terms it; rational in relation to a goal, ordering the diversity of events through the unity of a final cause. In this chain, the vain singularity of Overney's murder henceforth appears as the end, in both sense of the word: its conclu- sion, its goal. Thus one completely turns away from the space-time of the unconscious. This effect, I repeat, always depends on the effacement of the narrating instance in the production of its order. But other methods come to reinforce it.

Duration

Following Genette, the question of duration can be understood in the follow- ing manner: is the (temporal) length of each section of the narrative propor- tionate to each corresponding section of the story, or not?[8] We need not enter into the debate concerning the commensurability of narrative and story;[9] from the point of view of libidinal economy, their commensurability is both clearly legitimate, because it places both things and words at the same level, and clearly absurd inasmuch as this level is their measure. Overney's death and a television broadcast or a speech (speaking of this death) could just as well give rise to libid- inal intensifications; but to submit them to a common measure is evidently to make them lose their incomparable singularity.

Nevertheless, as a guide, the following is produced by an evaluation conforming to the method of calculation used by Genette.[10]

Table 11.2

N Sections	Length of N Sections	S Sections	Length of S Sections
Na	11 Lines	S1	Indeterminate Duration 'many times $\rightarrow$ long time'
Nb	14 Lines	S2	Indeterminate Duration 'many times $\rightarrow$ long time'
Nc	15 Lines	S3	*Particularly on 11th and 14th last . . .* $\rightarrow$ 'several times some times'
Nd	18 Lines	S4	*This afternoon, at the time when . . .* $\rightarrow$ 'a few moments'
Ne	23 Lines	S5	*It was then . . .* $\rightarrow$ 'a moment'
Nf	17 Lines	S6	*End of the afternoon* $\rightarrow$ 'a few hours'

It can be seen that the duration of the N sections go from a single unit (Na) to twice the length (Ne), whereas the duration of the respective sections of S go from a single unit (S1: 'many times', therefore, a long time; let us say, for example, *two months*) to 1/87,000th (S5: the time in which the employee of the surveillance service 'assists' the guards who were being 'assailed', shoots in the air, and Pierre Overney dies, cannot exceed *a minute*). This gap is extreme; nevertheless the general arrangement of the proportionality of the durations is the following: the group of sections Nabc serve as a summary of the 'facts' that constitute S123, whilst on the contrary the group Ndef open up a *scene* on S456; we retain here Genette's definitions,[11] according to which a *scene* names a relationship of durations N/S in which the duration of the story (here the murder) is nearly equal to the time it takes to read the narrative, the perfect scene being a dialogue read at the speed at which it would be spoken by the interlocutors. *Summary*, on the other hand, names that relation where the duration of the narrative is much less than that of the story. Approximatively, then, the Renault Corporation's narrative causes the reader to pass from a summary to a scenic duration.

However, if we look at it a little more closely, we will observe *small* variations in the relations of duration which, whilst they do not leave any traces in the reader's consciousness, doubtless imprint all the more freely upon his unconscious the intensities they carry. For example, within section Nd, the fragment: '*At the time when the evening shift takes over from the morning shift, when large movements of employees occur in the avenue*', constitutes a veritable *descriptive pause* interrupting the diachronic development of the events, in order to open, if only for an instant, a view upon the *always present*, always regulated world, a world free from the anonymous and numerous discontinuities of the productive enterprise. The verbal tense employed to this effect, the present, evidently instantiates the statement not upon the present of the speaker (Renault's directors), as is the case with the perfect tense in the preceding phrase ([. . .] *engaged this afternoon* [. . .]), but upon itself, so to speak, by the auto-instantiation of the predicate which characterises definitions from the point of view of modality: *the evening shift takes over from the morning shift* as *water boils at 100°*.[12] It is pointless to describe the effect which follows from this.

Another small but effective variation of duration: in Ne, the relative clause *who succumbed to this wound* acts almost as an ellipsis if its duration is compared to that of its immediate context within the same section: *before the group of assailants and being unable to escape or to free the guards*, etc, which almost has the dimension of a descriptive pause. Here again the reader will be able to judge the affective result of this transformation.

These variations of detail (and importance) must be related to the operations bearing upon *mood*, and more particularly upon *perspective*, that we will examine further on. The descriptive pause concerns *the employees*, that is to say the body as productive, a moment in the circulation of capital; the ellipsis bears upon *the* attacking *commando*. These small variations of duration converge with the traits of *focalisation*, that we will encounter: to the slow, regular, autonomous, time of the factory there correspond those intensities that are neutralised in the unique intention attributed to the said personnel of being true to itself; the short, heteronymous and discontinuous time of the actions of the commando leads to the opposite impression of inconsistency in their intentions and pulsionnal aggression.[13]

Returning to the organisation of the duration in its entirety, that is, from the summary to the scene, or more precisely from the summary, via the scene, to the 'moral'; it is classical narrative which is ordered according to this succession of rhythmic stages. Even if the maximal variations of the relations of duration (Na/S1, Ne/S5) appear to be considerable, they are very much less so than in most literary narratives. The extreme relations – the lengthy descriptive pause in Balzac, the almost complete ellipsis in Flaubert or Borges – are here eliminated. The meshing-together of the durations of both the narrative and the story stabilises itself in an average relation of speeds. In the pause or the ellipsis, the infinitely great or the infinitely small intervenes; such a lack of proportion between the two products of narration prevents the reader from being mistaken about their identity. It is the contrary that suggests the elimination of these excesses.

But the latter does not only have this effect of misrecognition; it is also a regulator of intensities. The occasionally enormous lags between the duration of the narrative and that of the story are powerful intensifiers, and the implausibility that they carry, if they have not disgusted the reader, propel him into an increasingly uncertain, perilous and testing reading, which presents the very features of the orgasm in its inextricable melee of Eros and death. Here, on the contrary, the foreseeability, if not the constancy, of the relations of duration N/S, is like a chronological control of libidinal investments: the summary (Nabc) *primes* the scene (Ndef); it is its repeated 'rehearsal' [*répétition*] beforehand that is 'simply' abridged; in this way, it captures and disperses in diachrony a part of the energy frozen upon the instant of the murder, on the scene.

Freud has shown that this repetition is at the very least an operator of the binding of affects,[14] thanks to which the imbecilic violence of the libidinal event that directly inflames entire zones of the sensorial skin (as does the absence of the small boy's mother) comes to be suppressed and shut in upon itself in a sort of auto-instantiation that effaces the aleatory heterogeneity of its sudden emergence. Through the repetition of its sections – something that one always finds in myths and popular tales – classical narration operates according to the same energetic schema as the child tirelessly throwing and retrieving his bobbin attached to the end of a string: libido expended, and *lost* in the intensity of the loss; saved, instituted in *return* in the return of the symbol. All classical narration, taken in a libidinal economic sense, is sustained by this repetition. The summary prepares the scene, it lowers the intensity of the murder in its bestial inanity, and the scene, resting upon the anticipatory repetitions of the summary, no longer appears as an accident, but as an ultimate, curative, repetition. With this function of repetition, we perhaps encounter the impulsional articulation of narration and representation; Freud's grandson – to repeat ourselves – is in need of a theatre, of the volume of a room/scene. The theatrical invagination of the libidinal skin probably has its rationale in the repetition of an unbearable pathos. But it is not useless to add that one repeats neither necessarily nor solely in order to make something bearable; underlying all repetition, even the most sober narration, there is also a mortifying madness which works 'in silence'. We engage in theatre and narrative in order to survive, and we engage in it to die more quickly.

Frequency

The fact that this new piece of the narrative machine, frequency, has an exceptional importance here, confirms what we have just said: if, above all, the Corporation's narrative has the function of binding, what we could term de-tensive or extensive repetition occupies a large place within it, and, therefore, within the set-up of frequency. Posed in terms of Genette's problematic,[15] the question of frequency is: is there, for every occurrence of an event in S, a corresponding *pronouncement* in N? Can we find in both the same diachronic determination of the recurrent whole, the same rhythm of recurrence, the same diachronic breadth of each occurrence? Or, if not the same characteristics, then at least characteristics that are in a constant relation? Or, conversely, nothing at all like this?

At first glance the Corporation's narrative seems *singulative* since an item of N corresponds to each section of S:[16] section Na of the narrative corresponds to the distribution of tracts at the gates of the factory (S1); another perfectly isolatable narrative section, Nc, corresponds to the distribution of tracts in the factory (S3). If we look more closely, however, we discover two characteristics that prevent us from maintaining this.

First of all, each section of the group Nabc (the summary) is by itself *iterative*.[17] This is attested, with regard to number, by the use of plurals: *distributions of tracts*, *to all these attempts at provocation* (Na), *acts of aggression, incidents* (Nb), *such was the case in particular*, *these acts* (Nc); as for the tenses, it is attested by the predominance of the frequentative imperfects: *responded [répondait] calmly to all these attempts at provocation* (Na), *proceeded [procédaient] to act aggressively*, *this did not have [avait] any repercussions* (Nb); and as for the determiners, by the use of indefinite forms: *distributions [des distributions]* (Na), *acts of aggression [des aggressions]*, at least in the two sections cited. On the other hand, the section Nc presents certain divergences in relation to Na and Nb; concerning the tenses, the use of the prospective:[18] *we then came to witness [on allait alors assister]*, whose use here implies the imminence of a singular event that is reported as the past, and which therefore orients the reader toward the singulative. Similarly, in the *commandos attempted [tentèrent* rather than *tentaient]* an aoristic rather than a durational tense appears. The same goes for *these acts remained*. Concerning the determiners, an analogical divergence is to be found: Nc presents many determinate forms: *these commandos, these acts, these acts of provocation and incitements*. At the end, temporal localisations appear for the first time that are no longer only roughly situated in relation to the present of the speaker, as in *several months ago* (No), but equally in relation to the calendar, to Benveniste's chronic time,[19] in a punctual manner. Nc hence produces a quite different temporalising effect to that which results from Nab; it moves across to the singulative, the pure aorist which dominates in Ndef. The effect is a magnification of the durations: shorter and non-reiterated temporal intervals (in S) occupying in N quantities of narrative, measured in lines, equal to or even smaller than those which corresponded to S1 and S2.

Let us follow for a moment the increasing effect of singulation up to Ndef, before coming back to iteration. The magnification of the durations is taken over by a rhetorical magnification which is not essentially an effect of frequency, but rather of *voice* and *mood*. It suffices here to note the temporal adverbs: *this afternoon* (Nd), *at the end of the afternoon* (Nf); and the tenses: *engaged* [*se sont livrés*], *rushed* [*s'est rué*], *were overcome* [*ont été roué*] (Nd), *presented himself* [*s'est présenté*], *were evacuated* [*ont été évacués*] (Ne), *were received* [*ont été reçus*], *were unanimous* [*ont été unanimes*], *is testimony* [*a temoigné*] (Nf). The adverbs instantiate the *pronouncement* on the present of the enunciation, just as the perfect tenses, in French, mark the existence of a relation between the enunciated event and the speaker:[20] compare *se sont livrés* with the simple past *se livèrent*, and *this afternoon* with *the afternoon of 26 February*. It is a matter of 'discourse' markers in Benveniste's sense, and that is to say of some of the operators of *aspect* that bind more strongly the reported event to the time of the enunciation.

These same characteristics appear in a predominant way in N0: *began* [*ont entamé*], *several months ago*. N0 is written in the same aspect and mood as Ne or Nf, those of 'discourse' rather than narrative, in the position of a litigant rather than that of a raconteur, of a moralist rather than that of an artist. N0 belongs *already* to the disapproval expressed in the conclusion.

Once again these remarks cause us to leave behind questions of simple frequency; they more properly pertain to those of mood and voice in Genette's sense, and particularly to that of *distance*; but it is important to note how, in the narrative machinery, the movement of one piece comes to set in motion that of another; more specifically, how the increasing singulation or the defrequentation, in magnifying the time of the narrative, allows for the deployment or redeployment of another tone, an implicitly inter-subjective instantiation, and to introduce not the narrating instance itself – which will never appear, as we will see – but an *edifying* instance that itself envelops the whole narrative between the sombre initial recollection and the final disapproval.[21]

To come back to the question of iteration: in Nab, the *limits* of the iterative series of the reported events are never specified, and this even in Nc: *distributions* (Na) – is this several distributions all at the one time, one repeated distribution, or several simultaneous and repeated distributions? And how many times, and how many distributions? *Acts of aggression* (Nb) provokes the same questions. The *rhythm* of recurrence, which Genette terms *specification*,[22] is no more specified: is it a matter of one occurrence, of two, three . . . a week, a day, a month? The temporal extension of each event remains completely unknown: the act of aggression or the distribution lasted a minute, ten minutes, an hour.[23]

Within some excellent passages bearing on the imperfect in particular, Genette speaks of an *intoxication with iteration* in Proust.[24] Yet here it is necessary to note a diametrically opposed effect produced by iteration, an effect of *sedentarisation* or *substantiation*. To be sure, there is nothing surprising in the fact that the same piece of the set-up can produce inverse effects: the movement of a cog can be transmitted as it is, or it can be reversed and/or increased if other cogs are interposed between the driving cog and the idler. It is the same with pieces of the narrative set-up: iteration can produce an effect of delocalisation if the intensities that it distributes in diachrony, instead of being instantiated on a 'subject' of the repetition, remain suspended in a non-unified spatio-temporal field. Yet what determines the latter possibility are dispositions of mood and voice, in particular those of *perspective*, of *narrative tense*, and of the *person* of the verb. In the Corporation's text we will see that these latter dispositions are such that the narrating instance, the supposed 'subject of the enunciation', never emerges whilst a subject of the statement is solidly drawn.

Hence it is in anticipating slightly (inevitably, since the whole set-up is contemporaneous with itself, whilst the analysis is developed diachronically) that we will say, in order to have done with frequency, the following: the Corporation's text presents a use of markers of determination, specification and extension – to take up once again the terms of Genette – such that the denounced distributions and attacks, no limits being fixed to them, not only appear innumerable, but above all symptomatic: the addressee of the Corporation's message cannot but construct the image of a hidden identity, that of the aggressive group, to which the reiterated events must be attached like so many attributes. By the purely formal arrangements that we have seen, these events are presented as particular actualisations (*particularly* . . .) of a constant and general motivation, which is not, properly speaking, an *intention*, but rather a *pathos* that is markedly pulsional. Regardless of anything else, there is nothing original about this method, about attacking as a way of defending, about presenting the victim as the aggressor, about placing reason on one's side and blind passion on that of the adversary. What is interesting here is simply to see with what small pieces of a linguistic set-up such effects of the channelling of emotional influxes can be obtained: the intense singularity of the death is metamorphosed into the predictable 'result' of an aggressive 'motivation' that is led back to a subject. The production of a *subject of the iteration* (the aggressive group – but as we will see, things are slightly more complicated) constitutes a vast displacement of affects, a freeing-up of the tensorial ribbon in the invested region, and a redistribution of the affective charges on a *theatrical* [*théâtralisé*] social body, whose production it is necessary to examine more closely.

Mood, Distance

Still guided by Genette, we have to divide the question of mood into two subsets. The question of *narrative distance* would be the following: does the narrative hold the addressee close to or far from the story? Does it recount in the manner of *showing*, of making something seen, or in that of *telling*, of speaking, of making something heard?[25] Terms which are taken from the problematic of the novel, in particular the problematic of Henry James and his circle at the end of the nineteenth century, but which go back, much further, to the Platonic opposition of *mimesis* (which would be the smallest distance) and *diegesis* (the opposite).

We are unable – it will become clear why – to follow Genette here in his development of this problematic. If, like the poetician, the libidinal economist says that there is no *mimesis*, then this is not because discourse is unable to mimic that which is not discourse (let us say the event); on the contrary, he thinks that discourse can be an intense event, and that this intense event partakes in precisely the characteristic that rationalism generally reserves for discourse, namely self-sufficiency or irrelativity. But if he does not admit the category of *mimesis*, and nor, therefore, the classification of narrative distances according to the *showing/telling* polarity, then this is because he does not accept what is presupposed by Genette as much as by Plato, namely that there is a reality, here named (hi)story, in the light of which it would be possible to measure the deformation that the narrative forces it to undergo.

What could reality be from the point of view of libidinal economy? This is the question that we have already encountered: how are we to understand *reference* in such a problematic? It obviously cannot be taken as a given, for it belongs to a field of reflection where there is a subject, object and denotative distance. But for us this field is that of the theatre, that of Platonism and its puppets; it is produced by the invagination, the orientation and the ordination of a single-sided surface that is able to be instantiated anonymously and randomly. A reality in the libidinal sense would be this tension and this *turning-back* on itself that forms the referential space, *extended to the whole band*; or, if you will, it would be the *consensus of all the libidinal regions concerning an intensity*. It is solely on condition of such a consensus that it would become possible to decide if a particular narrative, and thus a particular new load on a new region of the tensorial ribbon, *conforms* or not (*mimesis*) to this intensity of reference.

Yet such a consensus is not a libidinal given. Far from submitting itself to it, a text such as that of the Renault Corporation attempts to produce it, in submitting the intensity of Overney's death to the demands of the supposed body politic, and that is to say, in staging it. But it is possible to form a consensus on an intensity only by *cleaving* it, just as Marx explains that the object that he calls (quite unfortunately) *use* (for here it would be disuse) can only become a commodity by doubling itself up into an exchange value. Recounted, Overney's death must become exchangeable; the consensus cannot admit its inanity, its 'absolute loss'. The narrative eliminates the loss, conserving all that is (re)producible from a place where the event is instantiated, from a temple or theatre, from an organic body politic. The terrible irrelativity of Overney's death neither allows us to forget it nor to remember and localise it, the unconscious libidinal band being – due to a lack of filters, and that is to say, stable set-ups – a receptacle for everything and a memory of nothing. A narrative like that of the Corporation, taken as a libidinal set-up, is a small grouping of such filters; it is the active memoration of the disintensified event.

We will not, therefore, overly concern ourselves with knowing if the narrative is a narrative of words or a narrative of events in order to gauge its levels of *mimesis*; we should merely note that the narration of the Renault Corporation does not allow any character to speak, not even the group of aggressors whose tracts only contain *insults, vulgarity, calls to revolt, to violence, to murder*, therefore cries and not discourse. At the end of Nb it is possible, however, to suppose that someone has proffered something like a discourse when *the public authorities were kept informed . . .*, and that there is therefore already somewhere a relating of the events recounted here, at least of the first events. The erasure of the 'subject' of this first enunciation repeats, in miniature, the general erasure of the narrating instance in the communiqué that we are studying: an anonymity concerning *who is speaking*.

It would be more important to dwell on the question of the scene, which appears to us to be at the centre of the problems of mood. We will have to be content with a few remarks, correcting the preceding ones.[26] It is necessary to understand the word in a broader sense than that which we accorded it in studying *duration*. This latter sense only applies to dramatic art wherein the dialogue received by the intermediary of the narrating instance constituted by the director and the author is of the same duration as the 'real' dialogue, as the 'story'. We are compelled to introduce the notion of a *diegetical* scene, and thus to go back beneath Platonic-Aristotelian categories (and those of *quattrocentro* picturality).[27] The scene opened by a mythic narrative is in no way mimetic, for the reason that it does not have the function of procuring an illusion of reality, but rather a moral lesson. What this narrative presents is that there is a wrongdoing, that someone will pay for this wrongdoing, and this solely by the *linkage* of the facts, by the force of things. The wrongdoing, the disturbance, the hubris, the test; we recognise libidinal intensity in this detonator of the narrative. The price of this intensity is punishment, which is the reconciliation *in* the cleavage of which we have just spoken. All mythical narratives obey this restitutory linkage, and in this sense all myths are edifying.

The Renault management's communiqué stages a mythical scene, rather than a *scene* in the strict sense of so-called occidental dramaturgy. The function of this scene is to make Overney's death appear as a (fair) *restitution* of things. The *linkage* presented is the following: *this death is the price that the aggressive group had to pay in order to heal the wounds inflicted on the body politic during repeated demonstrations that manifested aggressive impulses.* Yet this mythical scene does not at all possess the same properties as those of what, in the Platonic-Aristotelian tradition, we call the *scene*: it differs from the latter to the same degree that the theatre that Artaud desired is able to turn its back on the scenographical tradition of the classical European age. To speak rapidly, let us affirm that the mythical scene does not have *edges*, that it obviously opens a space at a distance, but that this distance is not the distance required, if not by the illusion (for it doubtful that the search for illusion has ever been the concern of European scenographers and painters), then at least by the seduction that the classical spectacle achieves; it is a distance without the framework that delimits an outside and an inside; a distance, therefore, without a reflective or even a critical function, as Brecht wished it to have. It is the distance that comes from the fact that speech is not to be taken onto this mythical scene, that it has already been captured, that 'the facts recount themselves',[28] that men are not shown there as possible locutors or interlocutors, but as aleatory fragments of the libidinal body struggling with the supposedly necessary or fatal rule of the organic body. The efficacy of this property cannot be grasped by means of being marked on the axis of *mimesis/diegesis*; it is due to the intersection of quite different operators.

Mood, Perspective

What we have just rapidly suggested on the subject of the mythical scene is going to find its initial confirmation in the study of *perspective*. The question to which perspective responds is, according to Genette,[29] one of knowing if the narrative is focalised or not; and if it is, whether it is focalised on one character or several in the story; and in this latter case, whether it is so simultaneously (from the interior of the same sections of the narration) or successively. The focalising itself would admit several modalities according to whether the narrator gives over more information than the character is supposed to know ('omniscience'), or just as much (confidence), or less (behaviourist perspective).

Let us begin with this latter question. In the Renault communiqué two perspectives are opposed in relation to the two 'characters': for the group of aggressors, the perspective is that of omniscience; for the *personnel* (which includes the management), the perspective is behaviourist. The group of aggressors has a programme of action (Na: *Initially this only . . .*), quasi-conscious motives (N0: *a systematic campaign with the aim of*), it obeys transparent and almost dialectical psychic causes (Nb: *upon the manifest failure*; Nd: *these diverse and multiple attempts having thus failed*). On the contrary, from the side of the factory there reigned a sort of opaque impersonality, that of the personnel: who *responded calmly* (Na), *where work continued calmly* (Nb); it is not even the personnel who mill around the workstations, but rather *large movements of employees* (that) *occur* (Nd); that the murderer, a member of the personnel, instead of hiding from the law, as is the norm, gives himself up to the authorities, as if it went without saying that *this employee presented himself spontaneously to the police* (Nd). With a sobriety worthy of the Camus of *The Outsider*, it is added that an *investigation is underway*.

The distribution of the two modalities of focalisation is roughly congruent with the distribution of the durations: an omniscient modality in N0abc, that is, during the 'summary'; a behaviourist modality in Ndef, during the 'scene'. But it in no way excludes finer disseminations that do not simply derive from the fact that the modalities attached respectively to each of the protagonists appear everywhere with them; thus, in the middle of the summary we find: *the public authorities were kept informed* (Nb), which is a completely behaviouristic pronouncement: the narrator cannot say by whom; doubtless by the ONE who has kept them informed.[30] Conversely, the pronouncement: *before the group of assailants*, etc. (Ne), which concerns a member of the personnel active at the heart of the 'scene', is explicitly omniscient.

One 'detail' merits our attention. This is the value of *came to* [*devait*] in: *a second shot came to hit one of the members of the attacking commando* . . . (Ne). For, in the end, on this value hangs that of the crime, and it *ought* [*devrait*] thus to be that of the punishment. First of all, *came to* is not *must* [*doit*]:[31] through the use of the imperfect (the form ending in –*ait*), the time of the enunciation t_0 is situated *after* the time of the event (T_0). But in using the modal *devoir* [*dev-*], the narrator comes simultaneously to place himself slightly before T_0, let us say in T_{-1}, from where he *anticipates* the event. This little machinery of temporalisation functions quite clearly when the subject of the pronouncement is a human being: *you were supposed* [*devais*] *to go to the cinema* can be broken down into: 'I am saying at the moment that I am speaking (t_0) that you said before (T_{-1}): I have to [*dois*] go to the cinema (at T_0)'. The clarity comes from the fact that it is possible to introduce an articulation of the two instantiations, enunciation (narrative) and pronouncement (diegesis), because one is placed in a relation between subjects, and that *you* can say *I*. But this clarity carries its own shadow within itself: 'I have to go the cinema (at T_0)' admits in fact four values: this could be a necessity (hardly likely in the event), an obligation, a probability, and finally a simple eventuality, and that is to say the localisation of T_{-1}, a moment where I can still say: 'I must', in relation to T_0 where I can no longer say it because it is done (or not done, but no longer remaining to be done). In the case that occupies us, the subject of the pronouncement does not speak; it is a gun–shot [*coup*]. The values of necessity, of obligation, of probability are not pertinent. There remains the simple localisation of T_{-1} in relation to T_0, that is to say the relation established after the fact [*après coup*] to the event that is to come without any intention or declaration: this is the pure encounter that Aristotle named the *future contingent*. Example: *an apple fell* (T_{-1}) *that was to* [*devait*] *hit Newton on the head* (in T_0). This shot is a beautiful example; an almost perfect example of behaviouristic modulation, where the narrator, with a modal verb, a tense and a grammatical subject (inanimate) extinguishes the most incandescent heart of the emotional zone, at the same time as he clears the murderer of responsibility for the murder. He is not a criminal, for this shot killed the victim by a chance encounter, and this is why the man *presented himself* (immediately?) *to the police*.

The Koulechov effect: *he presented himself*, without even having to 'give himself up', because he clearly did not want to kill.

We should look more closely at the divergence of the perspectives according to which the two protagonists are presented. This divergence is a rhetorical procedure that is used frequently in court: the client does *not have any intentions*; he modestly contents himself with being what he is; the adversary bears, if not intentions, then at least dangerous impulses. Ultimately, and this is the case here, there is only one character, the adversary, the group of aggressors, whose every act is instantiated, as we have said, on a compulsion to harm that suffices to constitute it as a wholly nasty subject; opposite him, there are only repetitive behavioural acts. In the narration, they are marked, as we have seen, by the iterative imperfects of Nabc; but the design towards the present of Nde (*at the time when the evening shift takes over . . .; when large movements of employees occur in the avenue . . .; six guards, who were not bearing any arms . . .; an administrative employee . . .* [who is] *in no respect responsible for security . . .*) lead also to the presentation of these diverse traits as the permanent attributes of a body or a neutral substance. The desire of the narrator to produce this body of behavioural habits goes as far as leading him to make a slip: *these acts remained isolated and at no time did any member of the Corporation either participate or respond . . .* This is a phrase that condenses two phrases: 'These actions occurred and at no time . . .', 'these actions remained isolated to the point that at no time. . .'. So important is it to the defence that it *is not said* that these exterior elements could have, in any way at all, been interiorised by the 'personnel'.

But let us not go on in this sense; let us not exchange the repressive surveillance of the workers by their boss for the surveillance of the symptoms of this boss by the 'psychoanalyst'. We should rather remark that the alteration of perspectives, an essential but simple element of *mood*, has a decisive importance for the production of the story. The neutralisation of one of the protagonists makes of him an empty entity, a hollow space, instantiated on itself (*I am He who is*, or even: *who am*), tautological and sufficient, without exteriority; an immense habit, and that is to say a *habitus*, a *finding* oneself being what one is, an *il y a* or *there is* (*habere*). This body, whether it is called God or Kapital, is by no means a given, in the sense that it could be encountered on the tensorial skin in the forms of a particular intensity. No more than 'one's own body' is the organic body encountered in such forms. Both are formations of pulsional set-ups, with either an intensive or de-tensive function, as we have said. Here the de-tensive function is evident. Like Spirit in Hegel's *Phenomenology*, this empty shell, the factory, the 'personnel', absorbs, has absorbed, will absorb any exteriority, and will pro-duce it as commodities; as cars, as it happens, and also, let it be repeated, as workers, line-managers and executives. These things will be admitted to memory, but not *the death of a young man*.

Much worse, we will end up saying that if this death was an event, this is because it *had to* [*devait*] encounter the large, empty body of Kapital. Yet this is not at all the case; the death encounters it, but its intensity is not discoverable on it; it is not inscribed on the drum of vast memory that is supposed to turn at Billancourt; rather it makes incandescent one end of the tensorial ribbon, beneath and beyond all memory, exceeding all temporalising ventilation: on the one-sided libidinal body, Pierre Overney died on 26 February 1972, but he died on 25 May 1871 on the Place du Château d'Eau by the bullets of Gallifet, but he never died, but he was not born, all these phrases are simultaneously *effected* in their incompossibility, and the intensity of the affect derives from this coalescence itself.

Voice, the Time of Narration

The question of the time of narration: is narration posterior or anterior to, or simultaneous with the story?[32] Here it appears easy to resolve, given the quasi-constant presence of the past. One problem nevertheless deserves our attention: that of the *beginning*. In the working hypothesis (?) adopted, this problem is that of a play between three beginnings, and the solution provided for this problem is part of the set-ups operative in the narrative. There is the beginning of *the story*: on such a date, from such a time, etc.; there is the beginning of the *narration*, which is always situated at the moment when an enunciator assumes the message that the communiqué is and 'actualises' it, so to speak. This is the omni-temporality or the Living Present of the phenomenologists. It is analogous to the time that Benveniste designates 'linguistic', the time of the enunciation. The beginning of the story is accounted for, on the contrary, in 'chronic' time. The problem is one of knowing in what temporal order the beginning of the narrative, the start of the text, is located: it can be located in chronic time just as much as in linguistic time, obviously; but depending on whether the text leans towards one instance rather than the other, it will function according to a different set-up and will effect different affects.

In the declaration of the Renault Corporation, the beginning of the narration is indicated, as it must be, by deictics: *this afternoon* (Nf). On the contrary, the beginning of the story does not refer to the chronic time '15 November 1971' or '14 January 1972', but, by a new deictic, to linguistic time: *several months ago* (N0). This is without chronic indication of any import; and even when the dates will be given, the calendar will remain instantiated on the present of the enunciation: *11 and 12 February last* (Nc). The expression *several months ago* is different to a phrase of the sort 'that day' in that it necessarily refers to the present of the narrating instance.

We have here, therefore, a montage of beginnings whose set-up, as we will see, is decisive for the determination of the voice. The beginning as narrating instance: *today* (when I speak) is confused with the beginning of the story: *today* (when Pierre Overney was killed); the beginning of the story: 'that day' (of the calendar) is itself subordinated to the beginning of the story and narration: 11 and 14 of February *last*. From this group of condensations, it is necessary to draw out two effects: first of all, the confusion of the beginning as narrating instance with the beginning of the narrative is a particular case of the *general occultation* of the narrating instance in this text. Genette signals somewhere this singularity: that, with the exception of a few stories such as *Tristram Shandy*, the narrative act itself is almost never supposed to take any time. Here the uncoupling of the time of the production of the narrative and the time of the narrative is no more possible than that of the time of the directing and the time of the performance in the classical spectacle. Consequently, the subordination of the historical beginning to the moment of the enunciation draws the whole text in the direction of a language of discourse, to speak like Benveniste, rather than of narrative: the narrative of Overney's death, if it is instantiated on a *zero* moment which is at once the moment of *his* death and the moment when *I* speak, finds itself clothed in a discourse (here, one of defence, but which, linguistically, could be as much one of indictment, like Geismar's) whose principal function is certainly not to recount a story, but to edify the reader. If it had been a question of informing the reader, this intertwining of the beginnings would have been undone. This is, for example, the first *task*, in the painful and libidinally intensive sense, that the historian who seeks to inform accomplishes: that of disassociating the present of the narrative, the chronic present of the story and the omni-present of its narration. Michelet, in affirming loudly and in claiming explicitly for his discourse condensations between these three orders, not only 'restores' to history its pathos; he operates as a meticulous informer who allows, perhaps *a contrario*, these breaks of order to be seen.[33]

Voice, Function

If the question of the function of the story is indeed, as Genette says,[34] one of knowing if the narrator aims principally to narrate, to recount one of the stories, to communicate with the narratee, or to bear witness to his own affects, then we can move to this question on the basis of the preceding remarks. These led us to think that the narrating instance never manifests itself as such, whilst by the unapparent condensation of the three tenses, it pushes the addressee to instantiate his reading on the story (its reference), which is in turn localised on the empty and neutral centre of the factory. It is not affects that are communicated, but disaffects: the disaffected world of Kapital. And beneath the apparent predominance (which is quite crude, if we are allowed to make a judgement of literary value) of the referential function, by which the reader is supposed to be informed of the 'facts', it is rather *contact* with the reader that is sought.

It would be necessary here to analyse a function, which we think has an end-lessly increasing importance in the modern world: the function that Jakobson names *conative*, which governs pronouncements of the sort: *Do you hear me? OK? Hello!*

In making the reader of the narrative slip towards the story, and in the story of the living death of Overney towards the tin body, the empty belly of the factory, the declaration of the management of this factory sets in motion, from the perspective of the addressee, a simple disposition to communicate. The only affair of any importance is that the scene at Billancourt is accepted; an empty place, instantiated on itself; an empty body where all the intensities are lost, in order to transform themselves. The coldness or estrangement of the tone, which results from, amongst other things, the eclipse of the narrator, is by itself a signal made towards the narratee: what is asked of him is the same *calm*, the same *habitus*, the same redoubled *denial* (*at no time . . . not*), leant to the 'personnel'; the same indifference; and what is offered to him is therefore the very place of this indifference, the body of supposedly productive capital where the inten-sities are in principle commuted into exchangeability. The importance taken on by the conative function results from the generalisation of this situation in modern society: the functions bearing on the contents, the references, the expressivities, the codes, the messages themselves, become less important if the real law is equivalence and the real value exchange; such is, indeed, the law that reigns (or attempts to reign) on the surface of the belly. It is then that the contact, in allowing for transportation and selling, becomes essential by itself. The narrator and the narratee enter into contact, without fusion or effusion, thanks to the voluminous absolute zero of the organic body.

Voice, Narrative Level, Relation or Person

This is what is confirmed by the simultaneous examination of two questions: that of the *person*: is the narrator recounting a story that is his story, in the sense that he is a character in it, the hero, a stooge, even a witness, or else a story in which he occupies no place? and that of the *narrative level*: is the narrator presented, or is he not, as the *narrator of the story that he recounts* in this story itself?[35] To take up the examples of Genette, in *A Thousand and One Nights* Scheherazade recounts stories that are completely foreign in their tenor to her own: the narrator is, therefore, quite present as such in the story that we read (a position that concerns the *narrative level*, which Genette names *intra-diegetical*), but this story is in no way the story *of* this narrator (a position said to be *hetero-diegetical*). Conversely, Marcel, in *À la Recherche du temps perdu*, is not at all presented as a narrating instance in the story recounted (extra-diegetical level), and yet he ceaselessly recounts situations in which he is always, in one way or another, present as a char-acter, actor or witness: a homo-diegetical position for the person.

In the Renault communiqué the narrator is in an evidently extra-diegetical position. This narrative level corresponds to the pure and simple erasure, which we already noted, of the narrating instance. Here it is necessary to underline, as the master-dissector invites us to do,[36] the difference between the narrating instance and the instance of writing, the 'author'. The name of the author of the communiqué is known from *another* text, a context printed in italics and placed at the head of the declaration; a text which itself does not disclose its literary authority (the newspaper *Le Monde* or a press agency?): this author is *The State-Owned Renault Corporation*. But the text of the declaration no more allows us to name the narrating instance than the text of the *Chaperon rouge* or of *Madame Bovary* allows us to decide who is speaking. When, in the last paragraph, we read: *the management* [. . .] *deplores all the more . . .* we are in no way dealing with an intra-diegetical connection, with which the narrating instance would emerge in the story itself: for nothing indicates that *the management* is the narrator of this story. On the contrary, everything is attempted, as we saw, so that it *is not* this narrator; so that there is no narrator at all. The disconnection of the two instances contributes to the effect of objectivity, of an empty stage, of anonymity. The Renault Corporation has a narrative circulated that is a story recounted by nobody, but rather in which things recount themselves. Yet the erasure of the narrating instance – already noted on other parts of the set-up – does not only produce the liquidation of the emotional intensities amassed on Overney's death in the direction of an interlocutor always given *in absentia*, so to speak; it also provokes a making-absent [*la mise en absence*], a dispersion of the intense reader in the void of the organic body.

Here we encounter the questions of *relation* or of *person*. With the narrating instance being in an extra-diegetical position, how are we to know if the story that it produces bears a relation or not to 'its own' history, whether in the guise of a hero or of a witness? The position in homo- or hetero-diegesis remains un-decidable, and thus so too does the investment of libidinal charges, the *imputation* of good and evil to a narrator who remains unreal and all-powerful because he does not have a place in the story that he recounts. A 'closed' [*bouclée*][37] relation corresponding to an utterance like *Once upon a time*; a relation that excludes all localising markers concerning places and times that would allow for the identification of the speaker, and that would give a good image of the *power* of the un-decidable extra-diegetical position of the person. Doubtless this is not exactly the case in this communiqué, not only because it is preceded by a note identifying its origin, the Renault Corporation, which it is difficult to ignore in reading it, but because indications of time and place that are just as identifiable by the reader are provided here and there in the course of the narrative, as we have seen. Nevertheless, with the position of the narrator remaining in suspense, the narratee (the reader or the listener) lacks a person opposite, an adversary or a friend, and a place situating his own relation to this story.

Genette remarks that an extra-diegetical narrator has a corresponding and similarly extra-diegetical narratee: with the narrator not addressing himself to anybody, the auditor, in order to hear him, must nullify himself.

Hence it is not only the narrating instance that is obscured, it is rather the whole function of address proper to the message, producing here at its two poles the same *de-tension*, the same *nullification*, that we isolated in other processes. Genette observes with perspicacity that the more the instance of the narrator is effaced, the more irresistible is the identification of each real reader with this virtual authority, or his or her substitution by this authority.[38] In libidinal economy, this substitution is not that of a concrete self by an abstract self, but the displacement and the release of emotional intensity, accumulated through the contact of the body of this reader with Overney's death, towards the organic social body, the receptacle of all pathos. In keeping the instance of the narrator empty, Renault's communiqué provokes movements of influx that are able to flow out through the ear that hears it or the eye that reads it, thus creating consensus when there was *sensus inane*. An operation of conversion suffered by the intensive skin. In the emptiness of the instance of the narrator marked on the small piece of the narrative machinery named *relation* or *person*, we should recognise the absolute zero of the organic social-individual body in its active principle.

Two remarks in order to conclude. The first might seem to be simply a standard qualification, but it is not: the study that we have just read runs the risk of remaining enigmatic without further clarification of, in particular, the libidinal 'effects' of linguistic set-ups, here narratives with a *detensive* function. The junction between formal analysis (*poetician*) – in the event entirely borrowed from Genette – and libidinal analysis (*economistic*) will appear insufficiently elaborated, almost wild or, and worse, sterile. The reason for this is that we are only just beginning to perceive what libidinal economy is, and that a long study, of a completely different tone and of a completely different import, will be necessary in order to intensify this one. Nevertheless, this study is a contribution to such a project. The second observation which remains for us to make is in one sense only an illustration of the first: the effect of an empty stage, of an anonymous body politic that is produced by the Renault communiqué, as we have noted several times in the course of the analysis, has been led back, as the reader will doubtless have noticed, both to the specific characters of the mythical scene, and also to those of capital. This hesitation was not very serious *here*. It is clear that it is pregnant with considerable difficulties, which concern the at-once economic and representative (theatrical) singularity of the libidinal set-ups proper both to the man of myth and of the man of capital. It thus also concerns the texture of the story which brings them into contact; a texture, if there is one, which is also libidinal. Assuming that it ever could be, this hesitation cannot be overcome here.

Notes

1. The analysis of the state-owned Renault Corporation's communiqué was begun with C. Coulomb, A. Lyotard-May and C. Malamoud. But none of them bears the least responsibility for the misfortune that it suffers here.

2. Translator's Note (TN): Throughout this essay Lyotard frequently uses the terms *récit* and *histoire*, which we have translated (with a few exceptions) as 'narrative' and 'story' respectively. In so doing, we follow J. E. Lewin's translation of these terms in Gérard Genette's *Narrative Discourse: An Essay in Method* (Oxford: Basil Blackwell, 1980). *Narrative Discourse* is a translation of 'Discours du récit', a part of Genette's *Figures III* (Paris: du Seuil, 1972), which Lyotard draws upon heavily – if critically – in this essay. For Genette the word *story* designates 'the signified or narrative content', whilst the word *narrative* refers to 'the signifier, statement, discourse or narrative text itself' (*Narrative Discourse*, p. 27). Following Genette, it can be said that a narrative tells a story. (Unless otherwise stated, all further references to this text are taken from *Narrative Discourse*).

3. TN: We have translated the French 'instance narrative' by 'narrating instance' in order to maintain continuity with the English translation of Genette's *Narrative Discourse*. For Genette, the narrating instance is the generating instance or agency of the narrative, i.e. 'the entire set of conditions . . . out of which the narrative statement is produced' (Genette, *Narrative Discourse*, p. 31)

4. See Genette, *Narrative Discourse*.

5. Ibid.

6. Ibid. p. 33ff.

7. TN: '*enchaînement*' is a term used by Lyotard throughout this essay. There is no single, straightforward English equivalent for this term. Depending on the context, we have translated it variously as 'chain', 'chain of events' and 'serialisation'. Here, Lyotard refers back to the use of the term '*enchaînement*' in the final paragraph of the Renault Corporation's statement (translated as 'chain of events').

8. Genette, *Narrative Discourse*, p. 86ff.

9. TN: in *Narrative Discourse* Genette had already claimed that it is impossible to establish a rigorous isochrony between a narrative and the story it tells for the very good reason that the time of reading cannot once and for all be established. For all that it comes closest to such isochrony, even the narration of a dialogue cannot exactly reproduce the time of the story, since even if it reports everything that was (supposedly) spoken, it does not restore (or indicate) the time it took to speak those words. Genette's suggestion, however – which Lyotard follows – is that one can calculate the relation between the duration of the story, measured in seconds, minutes, hours, days, etc, and the length of the narrative, measured in lines and pages. The reader should bear in mind that Lyotard's calculation of the length of the N sections corresponds to the original lay-out of the Renault Corporation's statement.

10. Genette, *Narrative Discourse*, p. 87f. We have accounted for N0 and S0 for reasons which appear, or will subsequently appear, obvious.

11. Ibid. pp. 93–5.
12. See the studies of A. Culioli on this subject. Doubtless, in the repetition *evening shift-morning shift*, it would be possible to find a trace of the meta-operator of localisation in its auto-, and that is to say reversed, usage. Culioli loves to give as an example: *glass breaks* (= is breakable by whoever breaks it). Similarly, here the shift is taken over by itself, that is to say, capital is capital.
13. Such is the production of the *nomad*, an invader worrying the frontiers of the empty social body, as Deleuze seeks to distinguish it. A production comparable to the problematic of J.-P. Faye, at the beginning of his *Théorie du récit*, where it is also this contact and passage which are supposed to give narration its matter.
14. See S. Freud, *Beyond the Pleasure Principle* (1920).
15. Genette, *Narrative Discourse*, p. 113ff.
16. TN: the French term '*singulatif*', here translated as 'singulative', is Genette's neologism for that form of narrative that narrates once what happened once. See *Narrative Discourse*, p. 113ff.
17. TN: Genette terms 'iterative' a narrative in which a single narrative statement relates several occurrences together of the same event, for example, 'every morning that week I ate cereal' (ibid. p. 116ff.).
18. E. Benveniste, *Problèmes de linguistique générale* (1966), p. 239.
19. E. Benveniste, 'Le language et l'expérience humaine', *Diogène* (1965), p. 5ff.
20. E. Benveniste, *Problèmes de linguistique générale*, p. 237ff.
21. These discourse markers are not to be confused with the 'perfect tense' at the end of Nb: The public authorities were kept informed of the incidents [*les pouvoirs publics ont été tenus au courant des incidents*] . . . The context would demand: *étaient tenus . . .* It is doubtless possible to suggest that the tense 'selected', in referring more energetically to the *enonciateur*, brings out even more its present responsibility. But it is possible that what motivated the decision is the greater facility created by the use of the passive form of the perfect tense with a singulative value for effacing the agent; a passive imperfect with a strong iterative value creates a demand for responsibility: cf. *the empire has been attacked* [*a été attaqué*] and *the empire was attacked* [*etait attaqué*], understood as complete statements.
22. Genette, *Narrative Discourse*, p. 128.
23. Genette names this dimension *extension* (ibid. p. 129).
24. Ibid. p. 123.
25. Ibid. pp. 161–4.
26. Cf., here, the section on *Duration* above.
27. Genette offers this comparison: ' "Distance" and "perspective", thus provisionally named and defined, are the two essential modalities of the *regulation of narrative information* that is mood, just as the vision that I have of a painting depends, for its precision, on the distance that separates me from it, and for its fullness, on my position in relation to whatever partial obstacle obscures my view' (*Narrative Discourse*, p. 162, translation modified).
28. As both Benveniste and Lubbock, cited by Genette (ibid. p. 163), say.
29. Ibid. pp. 161, 185ff.

30. As Maurice Gross would have liked to note.
31. To the extent that it is not false, this analysis proceeds entirely from the linguistics of modality elaborated by A. Culioli in his research seminar.
32. Genette, *Narrative Discourse*, p. 215ff.
33. We have already said above that this work must be taken in a libidinal sense and that it is not to be accorded a special merit, particularly the merit of knowledge.
34. Genette, *Narrative Discourse*, p. 255ff.
35. Ibid. p. 227ff.
36. Ibid. p. 212ff.
37. Culioli.
38. Genette, *Narrative Discourse*, p. 259ff.

Chapter 12

A Memorial of Marxism: For Pierre Souyri

The only testimony worthy of the author of *Révolution et contre-révolution en Chine*[1] is the one I cannot give him: it would be to write the history, in Marxist terms, of the radical Marxist current to which he belonged, and in particular the history of the group which published in France the journal *Socialisme ou Barbarie*, and subsequently the newspaper *Pouvoir Ouvrier*, from just after World War II until just before 1968. It would be to show by this history how his analysis of the class struggle in China is above all a contribution to the critique of bureaucracy which was developed by the group during that period. And it would thus be to minimize in my testimony or omit from it everything that did not contribute to the construction of a portrait of the class struggle apart from which, in his eyes, his work could have no meaning.

If I am not able to do this, it is not because I do not know that history or the theses of that radicalism. I participated in the former at the same time as Souyri, and the latter were for a long time part of both of our lives. The impossibility does not reside there. It derives first of all from the fact that I am not a historian. It is not a question of 'specialization', of academic disciplines. Obviously, I lack the expertise, the knowledge, the fine tuning of the mind to the methodology; but above all, I lack a certain way of interrogating and situating what is being spoken of in relation to what one is saying. To be brief, let us call this the postulate of realism. That which the historian recounts and explains had to be real; otherwise what he is doing is not history. As in legal rhetoric, everything is organized in order to explore the clues, produce proofs, and induce the belief that the object, the event, or the man now absent were indeed once there just as they are being depicted. The opposing party against whom the historian argues with all his force is not easy to beat; it is death, it is the forgetting which is the death of death itself. And if he expends so much energy to make us hear his heroes, it is in order to preserve, in the life of our memory, what has disappeared from the other life. Would I have written these pages if Souyri were alive?

This essay originally appeared in *Esprit* (January 1982), 61(1), as 'Pierre Souyri: Le Marxisme qui n'a pas fini.' It is included here to give a more detailed account of one aspect of the peregrinations described in the other essays, that of a *différend* with Marxism. EN: This note originally appeared in the quasi-autobiographcal *Peregrinations*.

However, I cannot manage to make this pious activity my own, to share the historian's confidence in its ends, to believe in the fidelity or the plausibility of that which is, in any case, only a representation. I cannot manage to forget that it is I, the historian, who makes my man speak, and speak to men he did not know and to whom he would not necessarily have chosen to speak. If I write: Souyri was both modest and inflexible, he hated to be put in the spotlight – which is true – then I immediately betray him, I put him in the spotlight, and I know that he must be objecting to this with the full force of his retort, which was cutting. The Greeks were right; there is a humiliation of the dead, they have much to reproach the living, who never stop misusing their memory. Souyri would not forgive me for botching the great fresco in which his work, beginning with his book on China, had its place; and he knew as I do that I am not able to paint it. It was precisely his work which should have succeeded in painting it. He would more readily forgive me for speaking of him on the condition that I do not hide the fact that it is done in my own way, and that I do not claim to decide whether my picture is or is not realistic.

Another reason which must be added to the previous one to prevent me from testifying properly is less personal and perhaps of greater scope. The history of this Marxist radicalism ought to be thought and written in its own language, which was that of Souyri. It was no longer mine fifteen years before his death, and to speak it today would add a useless political imposture to the inevitable betrayal by memory. So-called divergences which were in fact a profound *différend* had long before fractured the former solidarity of friendship and comradery. In 1966, I resigned from 'Pouvoir Ouvrier,' one of the two groups resulting from the schism of 'Socialisme ou Barbarie' in 1964. In September, I sent Souyri a copy of my letter of resignation, 'so that it cannot be said that the one with whom I entered the group was the last to know that I am leaving it.' Admitted together in 1954 to take part in the practical and theoretical activities of the group that published the journal *Socialisme ou Barbarie*, we had during those twelve years devoted our time and all our capacities for thinking and acting to the sole enterprise of 'revolutionary critique and orientation' which was that of the group and its journal. We had even kept up the habit, developed after our first meeting in late 1950, of getting together on our own, or writing to each other, in order to debate as much as necessary all the political questions which we happened to confront through experience or reading. Nothing else, with the exception of love, seemed to us worth a moment's attention during those years.

He answered me in October in a letter full of painful humor. He affirmed that our divergences dated from long before, divergences so deep that he considered it pointless to try to resolve them. He attributed to me the project of elaborating a new philosophy of history, one which he felt he had every reason to fear would be eclectic and idealistic, even though I might be unaware of it. He added: 'The problems we confront are, in my eyes, neither ill-posed nor insoluble within the framework of Marxist concepts . . .' There followed several lines in which he pastiched the grand political style. My future seemed to him, in sum, to be necessarily peaceful; a stage of my life was ending, I was leaving the service of the revolution, I would do something else, I had saved my skin. As for him, he knew himself to be bound to Marxist thought as though to his fate, without, however, being unaware that it was no longer, and perhaps had not for a long time been, 'the thought that reality seeks.' He prepared himself for the perhaps pointless solitude that the search for truth required of him.

We saw each other again, never as political men engaged in common or parallel undertakings, even in '68, but rather as long-lost friends. These encounters were the occasion for cheerful and bitter reminiscences, shared like a common good and scorned like a vain remedy for divorce. Sometimes brief and violent conflicts erupted: on terrorism, on the situation of capitalism, on the 'final solution,' on the scope of the opposition movement . . . Neither of us wanted to pretend, concede, or flatter – but neither wanted either to break off irrevocably. We did not confront head on what confronted us, but the conversation, as though carried by a constant wind, pushed every subject toward that reef, and it was necessary to tack in order to avoid it, while still signaling that one had seen it and had done nothing more than contain one's anger. I felt myself scorned for the direction I had taken, as I knew we had scorned the intellectuals and politicians who had retired from class combat or who were blind to its stakes. He knew that I felt this, and drew from it no advantage or guilt. On his side, he must have felt both impatience and weariness at sensing that I was irritated by his obstinacy in preserving intact the problem of history and society such as we had received it from Marx, Lenin, Luxembourg, Trotsky, and Pannekoek, and in wanting to resolve it exclusively within the theoretical and practical framework of Marxism.

I believe that our *différend* is of some importance for an understanding of the present. It was not only personal, and it was not only conceptual. What was at stake seemed to be knowing whether 'with' Marxism – and with which Marxism? – one could still understand and transform the new direction taken by the world after the end of the Second World War. This was open to debate, which was most definitely the case in our group, and between us. But in what language should it be debated, and in what language should it be decided? The debate had to do with content: class struggle in modern capitalism, the drop in the rate of profit, imperialism and the third world, the proletariat and the bureaucracy, etc.; but what was at stake was the way of expressing those contents. How could the means of expression known as Marxism put itself into play and debate about itself as though it were just one content among others? The problem was one of logic. A *différend* is not a simple divergence precisely to the extent that its object cannot enter into the debate without modifying the rules of that debate.

Our *différend* was without remedy from the moment that one of us contested or even suspected Marxism's ability to express the changes of the contemporary world. We no longer shared a common language in which we could explain ourselves or even express our disagreements. And yet each of us had in principle sufficient knowledge of the partner's idiom to be able to translate into his own idiom what the other was privately saying to himself about him, and sufficient experience and friendship to know that he was thereby betraying the other. Marxism had probably been for both of us a universal language, capable even of accepting within itself, under the name of dialectical logic, the rupture and opposition of universals which were abstractions, and the paradoxical and infinite movement by which they are concretely realized. We had known, by experience and reflection, and each of us differently, what it is to be enclosed within a particular life and point of view, within a particular language, and to be able to get out only through conflict and paradox. But now it was dialectical logic itself, with its still irrefutable operator, the anti-principle of contradiction, that was in the process of becoming a simple idiom. The machine for overcoming alterity by negating and conserving it, the machine for producing universality out of particularity, had for one of us – for me, as it happened – broken down. In the language of the dialectic since Hegel, this blockage was a portent of my imminent relapse into the thinking of the understanding, and into the logic of identity. I knew this, but the fact was that this risk, and the concomitant danger of political regression of which the Marxists warned, had ceased to frighten me. And what if, after all, the philosopher asked himself, there wasn't any Self at all in experience to synthesize contradictorily the moments and thus to achieve knowledge and realization of itself? What if history and thought did not need this synthesis; what if the paradoxes had to remain paradoxes, and if the equivocacy of these universals, which are also particulars, must not be sublated? What if Marxism itself were in its turn one of those particular universals which it was not even a question of going beyond – an assumption that is still too dialectical – but which it was at the very least a question of refuting in its claim to absolute universality, all the while according it a value in its own order? But then, in what order, and what is an order? These questions frightened me in themselves because of the formidable theoretical tasks they promised, and also because they seemed to condemn anyone who gave himself over to them to the abandonment of any militant practice for an indeterminate time.

For Souyri, that is, for me when I would try to speak of myself in Souyri's language, the cause for my 'relapse' seemed obvious: I again became that which I had tried in vain to stop being – a good petit-bourgeois intellectual reconstructing in his head for the thousandth time after others a vain palace of ideas, and who, believing he was freeing himself from dialectical logic, only fell all the more inevitably into eclecticism. That his judgment of it was as severe as this,

I had every reason to assume; I knew he thought that we have significance only through what we think and do in the immense war between exploiters and exploited, and that in these matters, the affection one has for someone must not be heeded. Certainly, his sympathies, indifferences, and hostilities were not based on his theoretical and political principles; he could keep a tenderness and fidelity for very old friends who had remained communists, or he could frankly dislike comrades from our group. In the domain of thought, however, a person was right or wrong, refutable or irrefutable. Not even the dearest friend was excepted from this rule; he had to hear without reserve what Souyri believed to be true, he had to argue his refutation with reasons and proofs. A general conversation, where ideas that were not yet tried were put to the test, soon took on the form of a dialectical joust, even an eristic exercise. He liked to provoke his interlocutor by confronting him with the arguments of an advocate of revolution. A sensitive and absentminded man in daily life, he could press on to the point of cruelty in discussion. Half in parody, half in sincere anguish, he thus reminded others and himself that there is no tolerance for the mind that forgets its only goal, the destruction of exploitation by thought and by acts. The dialectic was his way of thinking, a component part of the dialectic he tried to uncover in things. Theoretical experience proceeded for him like a practice of contradiction, just as contradiction formed for him the nervure of historical reality.

But on my side, this perserverance in thinking and acting according to the dialectic, as if for forty years the revolutionary movement had not suffered one failure after another – which Souyri moreover had no trouble admitting because that was the very thing he wanted to understand – seemed to me to be more and more alien to the exigencies of thought. Was one able to think, after these failures, without recognizing in them, first of all, the failure of a way of thinking? And in this latter case, did the 'failures' of the revolutionary movement really deserve to be called that? Capitalism had succeeded, after twenty-five years and a war without precedent, in coming out of the crisis of the thirties without the proletariat of the developed countries having seized the opportunity to take power. The revolution of 1917 had on the contrary given birth to new relations of exploitation. That was true and intolerable. But in thus characterizing this period of history, did not Souyri's Marxism hide from itself its own failure? Did it not project in the form of an accursed reality its own inability to understand the nature of what was at stake in the contemporary world? If in fact the stakes were not the suppression of relations of exploitation, the failure was only that of the thought that claimed the opposite. (And I knew what Souyri would say to that: if those are not the stakes, then all is vain, and it matters little to me.)

But how to know this? And even, how to discuss it, first of all? This suspicion, which made me drift imperceptibly and which separated me from Souyri, was no more arguable than a withdrawal of affective investment is explainable by reason, so that the essence of the *différend* could not be said. In what language would I have been able to dispute the legitimacy of the Marxist phrase and legitimize my suspicion? In Marxist language? That would have amounted to recognizing that that language was above suspicion, and that the Marxist phrase was legitimate by its very position, even though I might contest or refute it. The idiom was more important than the referent; it seemed to be the very stakes of the *différend*. Now, according to what rules can we debate the rules to adopt for the debate?

Some good souls think that this difficulty can be remedied by means of dialogue. But what are the rules of this dialogue? The same thing goes for the dialectic. The drift which separated me from Souyri made me measure the extent to which a *différend* is not a contradiction, even in the dialectical materialist sense. For our *différend* did not, in my eyes, affect mutually exclusive propositions which could each still be expressed by dialectical logic, and which that logic was supposed to synthesize. The alteration affected that logic itself. Perhaps reality did not obey one unique language, I told my self; or rather – and this was worse – the obstacle was not that there could exist several languages in reality, for after all, languages are translatable into one other, and their multiplicity so little hinders the universality of a meaning that the translatability of an expression is instead the touchstone of that universality. No, the multiplicity that constituted an obstacle to dialectical logic had to be analogous to the one that distinguishes the genres of discourse. One might well transcribe a tragedy into a soap opera, a news item, a Broadway comedy; the intelligible schema of the action might well remain identical to itself from one version to another (this can be ascertained, moreover, only if it is formulated in a theory, which is yet another genre of discourse), but in every case what is tragic in the original version is lost. It seemed to me that the discourse called historical materialism caused its referent, historical reality, to speak in the language of class struggle. Now, this latter was a genre of discourse, and it had its rules, of course, but its rules, prohibited me, precisely, from treating it as a genre, because it claimed to be able to transcribe all genres – or, what amounts to the same thing, to be able to say everything about its referent.

Our *différend* took on its full amplitude for me when it appeared to me that there was no symmetry between our respective situations. At least I supposed it to be so, and I can only suppose. Souyri must not be having too much trouble, I would say to myself, diagnosing what was happening to me. He did not have to overturn his way of thinking, he still had the ability to make the distinction, which was never fixed, of course – he was not a dogmatist – but which was always possible in principle, between what does and does not merit consideration in the struggle of ideas; between what continues to will the concrete emancipation of the exploited as its end, and what ceases to will it. With the critical

Marxism which was his own, he always had at his disposition an apparatus for reading facts as symptoms, and my miniscule adventure, which had no importance, did not in any case escape its jurisdiction.

Such was not the case for the one whom Marxism seemed to abandon. A sort of uneasiness or inhibition came over him at the same time as the reasons to argue began to escape him, and he began to lose the use of the dialectic. What was the point of refuting the other, the Marxist, if the logic of reality was not, as he had believed, governed by contradiction? How could an argument prove that one is more a 'realist' then he? And in the name of what could it be done, if it were not certain that a subject which is the victim of a radical wrong – the proletariat – awaited this refutation in the unconscious of history, like a reparation that was due it? And finally, according to what logic was one to argue, if it were true that between the Marxist phrase and others, the contradiction was not analyzable or dialectizable, like between the true and the false, but rather a difference or a *différend* to be noted, described, meditated, like that between genres which are equally possible and perhaps equally legitimate? What other name could I oppose to that of the proletariat, what other logic to that of the dialectic? I couldn't tell; or rather, I began to think that it was not in fact a question of opposition.

In this way, the *différend* took a paradoxical turn. It filled me with anger, but also left me stupefied. I found myself without words to speak, without words to tell myself what Souyri's attachment to the Marxist mode of thought could mean and be worth. And what is more, I could still, in his place and in his genre of discourse, demolish my own irresolution; but I did not see how, in what genre, in what place, which should have been my own, I could attack *his* certainties. It seemed to me, in an obscure and indistinct way, that I must not hasten to overcome this dissymmetry or to reestablish a parity of incomprehension. Only by my not mourning my powerlessness could another way of thinking be sketched out, I thought without justification, just as at sea a swimmer incapable of opposing the current relies on drifting to find another way out.

Thus I did not want or was not able to develop by means of a critique, and bring to a 'theoretical' conclusion, something which was at first only a faint and disagreeable insinuation: the suspicion that our radical Marxism was not the universal language. The page where Souyri's name was inscribed in this language had not been turned. It was not a question, for me, of refuting theses, of rejecting a doctrine, of promoting another more plausible one, but rather of leaving free and floating the relation of thought to that Marxism.

What took place as a result of this prudence was not, initially, what I expected, but rather at first glance the opposite. I did not immediately acquire a new way of thinking, but an occasion soon made me discover that there was in that vaguely outmoded discourse called Marxism – certain of whose expressions were even beginning to be unpronounceable for me, just as the flowers of a rhetoric can wilt – something, a distant assertion, which escaped not only refutation, but also decrepitude, and preserved all its authority over the will and over thought.

This occasion was provided me by the schism which in 1964 brought about the divorce between, on the one hand, a 'tendency' directed most notably by Castoriadis, who was to continue the publication of the journal *Socialisme ou Barbarie*, and on the other hand, a group of comrades, some resolutely 'Old-Marxists,' and others who were uncertain but who shared a common mistrust of the 'tendency.' This latter group intended to devote itself to building a proletarian organization and would continue to publish the monthly newspaper *Pouvoir Ouvrier*. The schism came at the end of a long collective reflection. In 1959, shortly after the discussion on revolutionary organization had ended in the withdrawal of the minority faction,[2] Castoriadis had submitted for discussion a group of theses which implied not only a profound reorientation of our politics, but also a questioning of the very language in which it was possible to describe and intervene in the contemporary world.[3] I felt myself to be close to these theses, open to their argumentation, because I could believe that they formulated in a clear manner the suspicions and misgivings of which I have spoken.

The theses were the following: that the revolutionary movement can expect nothing from struggles centered on claims of an economic nature, controlled by 'worker' bureaucracies; that the question of labor has ceased to be central when there is 'full employment' in all the developed countries; that the unions have become 'tools of the system'; that 'official political' life now arouses only the apathy of the 'people', that, apart from production, the proletariat has ceased to appear 'as a class having its own objectives'; that 'the dominant classes have succeeded in controlling the level of economic activity and in preventing major crises.'[4] Those were assertions that were easily verifiable, it seemed, in those periods of regular growth of capitalism in the most developed countries. And it seemed reasonable to conclude that under those conditions, if there were a revolutionary project, it would have to find its mainspring in a contradiction other than the one Marx described in *Capital*. Indeed, how could the elevation of the organic composition of capital, bringing about a drop in the rate of profit, have been able to continue providing the revolutionary perspective with an objective foundation if it was clear that the expected social and economic effects were neutralized by the functioning of modern capitalism?

From Lyon, Souyri communicated to me in December 1959 his 'perplexity' before the 'novelties' presented by Castoriadis. He pronounced himself profoundly hesitant from a theoretical point of view, 'never so hesitant in many years, since the break with Trotskyism.' He needed more time in order to make up his mind, along with additional information and explanations. He cautioned me: 'Are you fully aware of the meaning, in regard to the Marxist "tradition," of the concept that Castoriadis is developing on capitalism? He said enough to frighten me, but not enough to convince me. Those who already have a set opinion are very lucky.' And then suddenly he added: 'Is it necessary to resign? I have reflected, hesitated, debated many contradictory ideas. Finally, everything that opposes me to this group derives from the fact that it does not have a proletarian character.'

I had more reason to be surprised by this abrupt question than by the warning that preceded it: he was asking for a delay for theoretical reflection, and yet he was thinking about resigning then and there for reasons that were not theoretical but rather concerned the group's social composition and organizational functioning. In the course of the years 1960 and 1961, his perplexity gave way to the conviction that the description of modern capitalism presented by Castoriadis was erroneous. The temptation to leave was replaced by the resolve to prevent the group, as much as possible and from within, from hastily taking a stand by voting on the adoption of Castoriadis's theses: 'I find that by asking me to take a stand – and I must not be the only one – they are asking me to decide on a "scientific" problem of crucial importance about which, finally, I know very little. I find it deplorable in this situation to be exchanging epithets like paleo- and neo-Marxist. Polemics can only result in serious and useless disagreements within the group.' As for the content, he declared, in the same letter from January 1960, his 'fear that Castoriadis is taking as an accomplished fact a consolidation of capitalism which is only a tendency destined to confront new contradictions, and that he is confusing an economic *stage* with a durable and stable transformation.'

This conviction was to orient all his work in the years that followed: he reexamined in detail the analyses of the contradictions of capitalism made by the Austro-Marxist theoreticians Hilferding, Luxembourg, Lenin, and Boukharin; he began studying the enormous amount of social and economic literature on the functioning of contemporary monopolistic State capitalism; he set out to elaborate as fully as possible the contradictions that would not fail to result from this functioning. After 1967, he concluded the 'Remarques sur les contradictions du capitalisme,' which serve as the Introduction to *Impérialisme et bureaucratie face aux révolutions dans le tiers-monde*, with the following provisional diagnosis:

> Considering the system in its global functioning and concrete configuration, and from the point of view of its intrinsic dialectic, it remains legitimate to posit that the contradictions which are in the process of developing out of the growth of the present productive forces prepare – on the level of the relations of imperialist domination as well as on the level of the antagonisms of Capital and Labor and of the specific relations between the State and monopolizing capital – the disintegration of the relative equilibrium which capitalism has achieved in surmounting the crisis of 1930.[5]

In this text, his conviction shone through that the history in progress and to come was continuing and would continue to obey contradictions that neither the monopolizing groups nor the state bureaucracies could succeed in controlling. After the first great depression (1874–1896), overaccumulation had found its 'solution' in the remodeling of capitalism into imperialism; the second (1930–1950) had motivated its remodeling into monopoly State capitalism, thanks to the so-called mixed economy. But the new arrangement did not have the means to ward off the next crisis of overaccumulation that would be brought on by the very 'growth' it would have encouraged; this is what the premonitory text of this Introduction explained, fifteen years ago now. I admire today its somber perspicacity, when capitalism, now engaged in a new depression due in particular to overcapitalization, is indeed blindly searching for, at once, the expedients (perhaps war) and the new structures which will allow it to again put off the date of its ruin.

This was not what I was sensitive to at the time of the schism. For to that, I could object, and did in fact object, that the tableau was probably true, but what difference did it make if there were no revolutionary movement capable, ideologically and organizationally, of orienting the struggles, which would not fail to occur as a result of the new contradictions, toward the radical solution of those contradictions? The movement had never been as weak as at that time, in the early sixties; crushed by its own offspring, Stalinism, it had never so little realized what might have been, from then on, a radical solution to capitalist contradictions. Souyri asked himself the same question, but it was not for him a matter of objection. To Castoriadis who would say: there is no longer an objectivity leading to the ruin of capitalism, the problem of the revolution is that of critical subjectivity, Souyri would answer: indeed, that has always been the problem of the revolution, but it has also always been posed in objective conditions which are those of the contradictions of capitalism, and which are independent of that subjectivity. Even when this subjectivity does not become critical, the objective dynamics go their own way, blindly. If revolutionary consciousness is incapable of destroying the capitalistic relations of production, then those relations produce their necessary effects, at first euphoric when their consolidation has just taken place, but soon redoutable when the contradictions resulting from this very consolidation explode. It is not because we are powerless that capitalism is stabilized to such an extent. If we are unable to make socialism out of it, then it will make without us what it is in its logic to make: misery that is both uncultivated and 'developed' – barbarism.

I could not understand his obstinacy in wanting to understand how capitalism, and with it the entire world that it had attracted into the orbit of its movement, was to perish for lack of a conscious interruption of its course. At stake in this obstinacy was not, at any rate, the preservation of the security which the status quo of proven methods and received doctrines furnishes for the mind. It was suspiciously unjust to call Souyri a paleo-Marxist because he thought that there is a dialectical logic in capitalist objectivity. I suspected that the 'tendency' represented by Castoriadis wanted to bury something with objectivism, and this something is perhaps not matter for refutation or revision or something that can decline, what ever may be the transformations undergone by the reality of the fact of capitalist development. In the conflict between the innovators and Souyri, the concern to protect thought and life from anguish was surely not on the side of the latter.

I am trying today to understand why, in spite of the *différend* which opposed me to Souyri and the sympathy I had for the majority of the theses presented by Castoriadis, I found myself, at the time of the 1964 schism, with Souyri in the group which opposed Castoriadis. And also why, in May 1968, while I was working one morning with some comrades from the Movement of March 22 on the draft of a tract intitled 'Your Struggle Is Ours,' when one of the former comrades of 'Socialisme ou Barbarie' who had gone over to the 'tendency,' and whom I respected, came to get me from a nearby hall so that I could partici-pate in the elaboration of the Movement's platform, which the Movement had entrusted to the direction of 'Socialisme ou Barbarie' and ICO (*Informations et Correspondance Ouvrières*), I answered him stupidly: No, I don't have confidence in you. All in all, that was not an especially important event, and it was not an especially strong motive; I attach no particular importance to it. It was some-thing like a lapsus.

There was something that did not let itself be corrupted by the wealth of argumentation that the 'tendency,' and especially Castoriadis, expended in order to explain and justify the new orientation. Nothing was lacking from the argu-mentative panoply of these comrades, and yet this saturation revealed a lack, the same one that the philosopher senses on reading certain texts of Hegel: the disappointment coming from exhaustiveness. I am speaking of tone and method, for as to its content, it was rather existential. They were cleaning up Marxism, giving it new clothes. The old contradiction of Capital, judged to be economistic, was thrown out. A new contradiction – social, this time, and almost ethical – between directing and executing was designated as the right one. I certainly believed, along with the comrades of the 'tendency,' that the world was changing, but in the framework of capitalistic relations of produc-tion, and thus without the disappearance of the extraction of surplus value, exploitation, and necessity. They were disguised as something else, but it had to be that subjection, in respect to a non-dominated objectivity, persist for one part of society, and thus also for the whole. Ethics is born of natural suffering; the political is born from the supplement that history adds to this suffering. We had not left the realm of the political.

But those were platitudes. Who would not have agreed? The 'tendency' protested that it was not claiming the contrary. What, then, was lacking in its argumentation? No one among the opposition that we formed was able to say at that time.

Let us call it complexity, the *différend*, the point of view of class. That was perhaps the thing that my *différend* with Souyri, and paradoxically the retreat of Marxism for me, had revealed as more fundamentally political than any divergence, the thing within which divergences took form. If *Capital* had been the critique, or a critique, of political economy, it was because it had forced the *différend* to be heard where it lay, hidden beneath the harmony, or at least beneath the universal. Marx had shown that there were at least two idioms or two genres hidden in the universal language of capital: the MCM spoken by the capitalist, and the CMC spoken by the wage earner. The speaker of one idiom understood perfectly well the speaker of the other, and each idiom was translatable into the other; but there was between them a difference which operated in such a way that in the transcription of a certain situation, experience, or referent expressed by one in the idiom of the other, this referent became unrecognizable for the first one, and the result of the transcription became incommensurable with the initial expression. The 'same' thing, a day of work, said in the two genres, became two things, just as the 'same' affective situation which is tragic for one of the protagonists can be a melodrama for the other. And as I had discovered in my *différend* with Souyri, this incommensurability was not symmetrical, but rather imbalanced. One of the idioms proposed itself as able to say what the 'same' situation was, to explain how it was indeed a question of the 'same' referent on both sides. It thus presented itself not as one party in a suit, but as the judge, as the science in possession of objectivity, thereby placing the other in the position of stupor or stupidity in which I had found myself, confining the other within the subjective particularity of a point of view that remained incapable of making itself understood, unless it borrowed the dominant idiom – that is, unless it betrayed itself.

Inasmuch as there was in Marxism a discourse which claimed to be able to express without residue all opposing positions, which forgot that *différends* are embodied in incommensurable figures between which there is no logical solution, it became necessary to stop speaking this idiom at all, and I assented to the direction taken by the 'tendency' in this respect, despite Souyri's opposition. But he had known long before me that the question did not reside there. One could certainly make this critique, but all one had refuted by doing so was the dogmatism in Marxism, and not Marxism itself. Some speculative satisfaction was perhaps derived from this, but one surely lost that thing which, rightly or wrongly, remained in Souyri's eyes attached to the name of Marxism.

This thing that I call here the *différend* bears in the Marxist 'tradition' a 'well-known' name which gives rise to many misunderstandings; it is that of practice or 'praxis,' the name par excellence that theoretical thought misinterprets.

Souyri was not mistaken; he was not confusing Marx with Hegel. If there exists a class practice, and if at the same time the concept does not give rise to practice, it is because universality cannot be expressed in words, unless it be unilaterally. The roles of the protagonists of history are not played out in a single genre of discourse. Capital, which claims to be the universal language, is, by that very fact, that which reveals the multiplicity of untranslatable idioms. Between these latter and the law of value, the *différend* cannot be resolved by speculation or in ethics; it must be resolved in 'practice,' in what Marx called critical practice, in an uncertain struggle against the party which claims to be the judge.

If 'Socialisme ou Barbarie' had had a decisive importance for Souyri, it is because, coming out of the Second World War, after a period of class collaboration and at the outset of the cold war, its founders had dared to point the weapons of radical critique at what seemed necessarily to be most invulnerable to this critique, and even untouchable by it. As early as the second issue, Castoriadis had demonstrated that the relations of production in Russia implied the exploitation of the labor force by a new dominant class.[6] The society born of the first proletarian revolution was not more harmonious than bourgeois society. 'Marxism' played there the role of the dominant idiom; it had become, there, the genre of discourse of the bureaucracy. Souyri had had another notable sign that the group had a class point of view without blinders with the publication, in the earliest issues of the journal, of the French translation of Paul Romano's *The American Worker*. Written in the genre of testimony, it stressed the incommensurability of the 'same' experiences, depending on whether they are spoken in the idiom of the owner or the foreman or in that of the workers; and it did so without concern as to whether one side or the other spoke or did not speak 'Marxist.' In the height of Jdanovism, the affirmation seemed a provocation.

In this refound radicality there was a cry of deliverance: before the war, Trotsky had let it be suspected that the proletariat was perhaps not capable of carrying out the practical critique of the society of exploitation; it was first necessary, said 'Socialisme ou Barbarie,' to affirm Trotskyism's own inability to carry out its theoretical critique. Marxist analysis remained valid despite immense defeats undergone by the labor movement since the thirties and the domination of Stalinism. And that which, with Marxist analysis, escaped decrepitude, was not only the idea of reconstituting an international organization disencumbered of the hestitations of Trotskyism, not only the perspective of a new 'grand political line'; it was above all the emancipation of the critical capacity, the reaffirmation that the class point of view was to spare no object, and that the principal task of revolutionaries was to detect the *différend* everywhere, even where it was hiding under simple divergences.

Marxism had been for Souyri, as for many others, the only decisive way of responding to the challenge posed by capitalism to freedom and to the meaning of history; it did so by making conflict resurface there where it had been smothered. Why did the freedom to work mean the subjection of the wage earner, upon pain of death? Why did the development of the capacities of production here bring about their underdevelopment elsewhere? Why was the advance of technologies accompanied by the alienation of workers? Why did the increase in buying power not redistribute money? Why did the multiplication of the means of communication go hand in hand with the ruin of social networks and the solitude of the masses? Why peace and why war? Why did the progress of knowledge have as its counterpart the deculturation of the ordinary man? Not only were we able to understand all that thanks to Marxism, we were also able to hope to modify the course of capitalism, perhaps to put an end to it, by placing the force of radical critique at the disposition of the struggle of the oppressed, and on their side.

But to these paradoxes – as classic as capital itself – another scandal was added, and it was our generation's lot to have to recognize it and make it cease. It was, under the very trappings of the workers' movement, the general inversion of the meaning of the organs it had given itself: unions contributed to regulating the exploitation of the labor force; the party served to modulate the alienation of consciousnesses; socialism was a totalitarian regime; and Marxism was no longer anything but a screen of words thrown over real *différends*. More than one shrank before the formidable task of recognizing and denouncing these perversions and preferred to wait for history to take care of it in their place – which is exactly what those concerned did in the suburbs of Poznan or Warsaw, in the heart of Budapest, or deep in the Chinese countryside. It was a time of lightening revelations, it was a generation of irresolutes and laggards. But Souyri, who in 1942 was seventeen years old, became a member of the clandestine Communist Party of the department of Aveyron, had responsibilities in the FTP (*Francs-Tireurs et Partisans*) underground of the Aveyron and the Tarn, and then resigned from the Communist Party at the end of August 1944; he made contact with Trotskyites and ex-members of the POUM (*Parti Ouvrier d'unification marxiste*), joined the Fourth International in 1946, made inquiries into the RDR (*Rassemblement Démocratique et Révolutionaire*) in 1948, finished his history studies in Toulouse in 1949 and abandoned the Trotskyites and the Third Force, and took his first teaching position in Philippeville, Algeria, in September 1949. Some good souls might have said that he skipped steps; the fact is that the challenge presented by Stalinism to truth and freedom had struck him with full force, and he sought with all his strength a way out that would not be dishonorable. He hadn't a moment to lose. He loved Rimbaud, Mayakovski, Benjamin Péret.

There were many of us who came to teach in North Africa upon leaving the university. What each of us was looking for there is hardly important here; what is certain is that Souyri, when I met him at Constantine after a union meeting to which he had listened in silence, had over most of us – over me at any rate – the advantage of already knowing from experience and reflection what constitutes a class point of view, and of not being disposed to let himself be deluded by anything that would tend to make him forget that point of view. The argument that to criticize the left is to be on the right – so frequent in communist propaganda at that time and so favored by intellectuals, young and not so young, for whom the whole political stakes were to make themselves hated by their bourgeoisie – left him indifferent. He knew that 'left against right' is not a class point of view and that the true *différend* is much more subtle, requiring at once more intellectual scruples and more resolve. He brought the greatest possible meticulousness to everything that could be discussed in the area of tactics, strategy, analysis, or political philosophy, sometimes in the register of tragic anguish and sometimes in that of epic irony. Nor did he disdain resorting to the resources of farce. On occasion, we had together the very best uncontrollable laughs ever, both political and nonpolitical in nature. He was cheerful and satirical, like the truly anxious. His intellectual activity was always under affective tension, but this tension was protected by a usage, at once parodic and spontaneous, of the great genres of poetics and of classical rhetoric.

In short, he intimidated me. His Marxism was not academic, it was not one possible interpretation of the matter of history, nor was it a true doctrine; it was the form of sensibility, the schema of imagination, the rhetoric of affections, the analytic and dialectic of concepts, the law of the will. Far from offering to the mind the closed tranquility of an established knowledge or a pragmatic guide, it was the proper name of his anxiety; it provided him all the opportunities to put again into question what he believed he had imagined, felt, known, and identified. Those of our generation and those who followed us have only barely encountered the corpse or the ghost of Marxism, the ready-made thoughts of a party or a bureaucratic State put in the place of thought, securing it with its dogmatic, vulgar, and prudent phrases. I had the good fortune, while the great century of Marxism was already declining, to learn, by meeting Souyri, that the historical and materialist dialectic could not be just the title of a university chair or a responsibility in a political bureau, but rather the name of a form of resolve.

He taught me resolve at the moment when I was searching for it, after too many years of a work of mourning or in incubation. Like many French historians, and with the incredulous irony of a Lenin, he taunted the philosophers: you do no more than state problems. Well, there was one problem and he wanted to resolve it. The rest was futile. The presumption of intelligence to speak of everything to everyone must be abandoned; let it inquire instead into the tragic stupidity of that which has no words to make itself understood, nor any law to justify itself. It was necessary to descend into the substrata of necessity, to seek out there the meaning of the most irrational of historical effects. It was not enough to construct the comprehensible and complete tableau of reality; one had to listen to the obscure passions, the arrogance of leaders, the sadness of workers, the humiliation of peasants and of the colonized, the anger and bewilderment of revolt; the bewilderment, too, of thought. One had to find again the thread of class in the imbroglio of events, to reconstruct the dialectic of the needs, interests, and beliefs behind the declarations and acts of the powerful, to orient and reorient oneself endlessly in respect to one pole: the destruction of exploitation. And one had to critique everything that goes about this badly or not at all, in order to get to the bottom of it and understand why it is thus.

The tasks which awaited a radical Marxist critique just after the Second World War, and which 'Socialisme ou Barbarie' enumerated in its program since its beginnings did not take Souyri unawares. To critique the class structure of Russian society and of all bureaucratic societies; to analyze the dynamics of the struggles in underdeveloped countries; to understand the function of ideology, beginning with Marxism itself, and the role of the party, including the Bolshevik party, in the formation of a dominant class; to take up again the critique of the State on the basis of what had happened in Europe in the last thirty years (fascism, Nazism, Stalinism) – he was already devoting himself to all this. He was prepared to travel as far as necessary. I embarked with him on this journey, and, after three years of shared rumination where he taught me everything except what the Algerians themselves taught me, we found ourselves together on board 'Socialisme ou Barbarie.'

Then when it became evident that capitalism, once its production and market capacities were restored, had finally come out of the long depression begun in 1930 and had restarted the process of extended accumulation, new pitfalls appeared, new realities opposed their opacity to our Marxism: the reorganization of capitalism into bureaucratic or State monopolistic capitalism; the role of the modern State in the so-called mixed economy; the dynamics of the new ruling strata (bureaucratic or technocratic) within the bourgeoisie; the impact of new techniques on work conditions and on the mentality of workers and employees; the effects of economic growth on daily life and culture; the appearance of new demands by workers and the possibility of conflicts between the base and the apparatus in worker organizations – all the traits, in sum, whose analysis was to provide material, several years later, for the theses of the 'tendency' and for the schism of the group, while at the same time leading Souyri, in his stubborn search for an irrefutable refutation of those theses, to the most complete isolation.

But in the meantime, the fact is, as we now know, that many of these traits of Eastern and Western societies were analyzed and understood at that time, traits which others 'discovered' twenty or thirty years later without, however, being able to bear the revelation ideologically and even psychically. The accounting that was made gradually over the course of these fifteen years was implacable.[7] Once Stalinism was identified as the ideology of a dominant class, and totalitarianism as the political mode of domination proper to that class, a radical critique could no longer expect anything from labor organizations that obeyed, to the letter or loosely, the dictates of this class, or reproduced its traits. Nor was there anything to expect from intellectuals who believed themselves to be Marxists because they read Marx and disliked bosses. We were watching for the smallest signs of a *différend* between the proletariat and the bureaucracies which spoke in its name.

There were many of them, and they were conspicuous, as are all proletarian victories: the riots of East Berlin starting in June 1953; then, in the course of the year 1956, the Poznan insurrection in June, the Polish October, and the revolution of worker Counsels in Hungary in November; and from May to June 1957, the unrest in all of China which shook the party apparatus. By publishing, in 1958, Souyri's article entitled 'La Lutte des classes en Chine bureaucratique,' our group demonstrated once again that the *différend* between the 'communist' bureaucrats and those they exploited was no longer in doubt, at least for the interested parties themselves, and that the former no longer occupied the comfortable situation that had been theirs before the death of Stalin. But we also directly attacked the idolatry, with its disguised conservatism, of a displaced Stalinism which attempted to shelter the Chinese domain from a radical Marxist critique, and which was called Maoism. Rereading this study today, one recognizes there the effrontery and the mirth that Marx once claimed as the right of the true against the Prussian censure, except that the censure flouted here was that of the president of China exercised in the West thanks to the zeal he had encountered in some intellectuals (Sartre was backsliding), and except, too, that the *différend* to be revealed was hidden this time under the farcical figure of 'non-antagonistic contradictions.' At that time, 'Socialisme ou Barbarie' had only one voice, and it spoke the idiom of those whom oppression habitually reduces to silence and who were then making themselves heard. And Souyri's voice joined in.

His resolve, as I said, was turned against the 'tendency' when it became necessary to analyze the contradictions of bureaucratic capitalism, and when he thought he saw in its theses signs which for him announced the abandonment of the class struggle: that is, the loss of comprehension and will. For the thing that engendered history also sought to have itself forgotten, and the understanding had to muster all its forces in order to discern the thing's every effect in the infinite disorder of the givens; reason needed all its forces to elaborate the general process of the contradictions that the thing could not fail to produce; the will needed all its strength to focus itself without distraction on the destruction of that thing. That thing was the sole reality, the whole reality, but it never stopped disguising itself. It was the unconscious of humanity; the question was one of listening to it, of finding its expression, of suppressing it. Everything which, in the course of our thoughts, contributed to its omission, even tendentiously, was refutable, refuted, and scorned. Souyri lampooned all this with names like innovation, fantasies, reformism, Sorbonnish deviation. Each was always an accommodation of the thing: futile, illusory, and necessarily destined to abort. Even injustice was not the appropriate name with which to designate the thing. He said to me during a last dispute over terrorism: 'Justice, I don't like that word.' Because that thing was, in his eyes, such that one could not overcome it with just intentions or institutions. Irreparable in individual consciousnesses alone, and by individual wills alone, it was the intolerable source from which human history drew its non-sense and its sense. It was what made the course of things into a tragic necessity at the same time as it offered to the will the faculty for reversing this course, thanks to the memory of the experiences it had caused and the knowledge of the processes by which it had expressed itself; but thanks above all to the deepening of the *différend* it provoked.

Souyri had found in Marx words to name this irrefutable thing; exploitation was one of them. He could not turn his mind away from it. It alone was worth the limitless expenditure of all intelligence and all will. One could not be reconciled with oneself, be happy and discerning, enjoy life, as long as it was there. It was misfortune, malady, and the promise of death weighing on the species. And it was not the 'natural death' that saves the spirit, but rather the misery that exhausts it, condemns it to repetition, abuses it, and eliminates it.

Exploitation: that might appear to be a classic category of the critique of political economy, a dialectical necessity, an outmoded conception of the movement of history. In the eyes of certain readers or certain comrades, Souyri may have passed for the champion of an old-style Marxism, of economism, of necessitarianism, and also of centralism because of his suspicions in respect to spontaneism. To place confidence in the spontaneity of the masses was, in his eyes, a bit like counting on the unconscious alone for emancipation from neurosis. The evil done by exploitation went so deep that one could not hope to draw from the forces of human nature something with which to combat what oppressed it. Denaturation was at the origin of history; one would not get out of it by reestablishing a state of humanity anterior to the division into classes, a state which is moreover entirely imaginary. One would get out of it, rather, by organizing the supreme denaturation that was called socialism, of which capitalism bore within itself only the contradictory possibility. One had to listen to the unconscious of history, the experience of the struggles, just as one lends an ear to the patient; but one also had to defend that experience against whatever, within it, worked to distort it.

As for economism and necessitarianism, they could be imputed to Souyri only if one forgot that people do not do what they want and what they think, but something else that they do not want, that they conceive of with difficulty, and to which they are chained by a logic which exceeds them; and only if one forgot that this subjection cannot disappear as long as the thing motivating it is not suppressed. This is why, in Souyri's eyes, it was impossible that capitalism could in any way succeed in definitively controlling its own functioning and in freeing humanity from necessity.

In the so-called relations of production, it was not only the extraction of surplus value that entered into contradiction with its realization; it was the autocreation of humanity through work which reversed into its own destruction. Capital, because it was the name of an inexpiable crime against freedom and dignity, was by essence incompatible with any recognition of what it is, and with any effective mastery over what it does. Those who believed the bourgeoisie and the bureaucracy to be capable of effecting a definitive stabilization of the economic system by means of institutions expressly created for that end forgot that this thing, like the unconscious, thwarts any contractual rationality. Parliamentary democracy, social reformism, mixed economy, 'modern capitalism' according to Castoriadis: all certainly changed the conditions of the *différend*, displaced the class struggle, allowed certain hidden realities to appear, but at the cost of hiding other realities, and without suppressing the reasons for the blindness.

I think that Souyri conceived of the resistance of capital to revolutionary critique and intervention as similar to the resistance of the unconscious to analysis. Socialism was not an improvement of economic and social functioning, a more just redistribution of the fruits of labor; it was the alternative – the only one – to the barbarism immanent to the development of capitalism. Nothing could guarantee its coming. Only one thing was sure: that the alternative would not disappear with the development of capitalism. Just as the neurosis contains within itself – if we are to believe Freud – the clue to a therapy, but does not itself lead to its application, so socialism was not inside capitalism like a seed but like 'an opportunity to be seized.' Against the objectivism of a Kautsky, Souyri made his own the critique proposed by Rosa Luxembourg: 'If socialism is not, in due time,' he wrote, 'torn from the flanks of the old society by the decisive action of the masses, then the whole society will regress towards barbarism . . . Marxist theory is no longer only a science, delivering up objective knowledge of the laws of a historical process oriented toward economy, but also a critique of the real elaborated from a class point of view, with the purpose of awakening the masses to consciousness of their historical task and of opening the way to revolutionary practice.'[9]

All thought was threatened by the forgetting of this point of view. I even wonder if Souyri didn't think, deep down, that one thinks only in order to better forget it. He wanted to think in order to draw it out. If one concealed the immemorial thing, it would eventually catch up with the amnesiac –

whether it be called Empire, bourgeois republic, socialist State, party, or thinker – and destroy it. In the beginning, he had let me read, more for my guidance than for my opinion, the manuscript of a study written in the late forties or early fifties on the question of slavery in Rome and on decadence: the Empire being born from the stifling of the class struggle which had developed under the Republic, and succumbing because it had repressed it. A brief tableau, he said. This forceful sketch of ancient Bonapartism had nevertheless enlightened me. Decadence was the somber idea that hung over Souyri's intellectual and militant activity, like that of the group and perhaps like that of any revolutionary: the idea of a society where the *différend* was so well smothered that its manifestations could no longer be anything but wild, sporadic, inconsistent; a society where the thought and organization indispensable to 'seizing the opportunity' of socialism, upon the occasion of such a disorder engendered by the contradictions of the system of exploitation, abandoned their tasks because they met with no echo.

The 'fear' that he felt as early as 1960, when faced with the first formulation of the theses of the 'tendency,' was for him a signal of sorts that the end had come: the most radical thing in the world, in terms of a theoretical critique of contemporary capitalism, accepted, tranquilly and even flatteringly, the idea that this radical critique no longer had any roots in objectivity. The *différend* took place only between consciousnesses which were by definition equal and free; it was thus no longer a *différend*, but just a debate. The unconscious of history was thereby denied.

Now, he held it as certain that by means of such a denial, which was precisely what the system needed, history would come entirely under the regime of that unconscious, and that humanity would undergo the inevitable contradictions of a capitalism which had reached the stage of State monopoly or bureaucracy, having lost with the class point of view the means of assuming a critical consciousness of its fate, and of escaping it.

He immersed himself in the meticulous study of the mechanisms which would not fail to elicit the next worldwide depression. Death surprised him at the moment when he was identifying this event's premonitory symptoms in reality.[10] He would have felt only a bitter consolation if he had seen more, perceiving nowhere the signs of a critical, organized intelligence capable of confronting the crisis and the reactionary course that it would not fail to imprint upon the movement of history. Already in 1968 and later, he would have argued, the efforts made by the student and intellectual avant-garde to win the workers over to the opposition movement had had no result, while the objective conditions – those of a relative stability of the capitalist economies – had been favorable to that movement. Would it not be even worse in the case of a general crisis?

I shall not discuss here his reasons for thinking this or his perspectives on it.

His absence and our *différend* oblige me to remain silent. I have testified here to what I can evoke without betrayal, this *différend* itself, which betrayed each one of us to the other, and in which I experienced, to my surprise, what in Marxism cannot be objected to and what makes of any reconciliation, even in theory, a deception: that there are several incommensurable genres of discourse in play in society, none of which can transcribe all the others; and nonetheless one of them at least – capital, bureaucracy – imposes its rules on the others. This oppression is the only radical one, the one that forbids its victims to bear witness against it. It is not enough to understand it and be its philosopher; one must also destroy it.

Souyri thought, quite logically, that if it is not the victims of capital and bureaucracy – their 'others,' the exploited, the oppressed – who end their silence and begin to testify by themselves, then what we, the intellectuals, might think of it all has only the importance of a theoretical point of honor and the value of a utopia. It is thus that the last sentence of *Le Marxisme après Marx* must be understood: 'In fact, Marxism, which is in its essence a theory of class struggle, could be attacked at its core only if one succeeded in demonstrating that the world has gone beyond the divisiveness which inhabits it. Then, Marxists could no longer avoid recognizing that their doctrine was only the mask of a utopia.'[11]

In what logic could the end of the *différend* be demonstrated? In the logic of Marxism it is not demonstrable. But on the other hand, one can judge the *différend* to be insurmountable in the capitalist system without, however, await-ing its suppression – as Marxist doctrine at least would have it – through the seizure of power by a party/class which is the subject of history. Marxism is then the critical intelligence of the practice of the divisiveness, in both senses: it declares the divisiveness to be 'outside,' in historical reality; the divisiveness 'within' it, as a *différend*, prevents this declaration from being universally true once and for all. As such, it is not subject to refutation: it is the disposition of the field which makes refutation possible.[12]

Notes

1. The book (Paris: Editions Christian Bourgeois, 1980) has a history which Pierre-François Souyri recounts elsewhere. Its writing must have begun in the early fifties. Studies on the subject followed in the early sixties, and the last articles about China are from 1968. It is a question, in this work, of encompassing the history not only of modern China, but also of the People's Republic after 1949. In a letter of January 1960 addressed to me, Souyri wrote: 'I have all the same made some drastic deci-sions about China. Since one cannot be forever running after current events, I have decided to divide my work in two and publish a first volume which will stop at the

1949 revolution. I am putting the last touches on it now. I think that I will have finished it all by spring, and I will try to have it published at the beginning of summer.' He noted that the size of the text had made it impossible to realize his original intention to publish it in the journal *Socialisme ou Barbarie*. The manuscript was submitted to a Paris publisher. It came back with comments aimed for the most part at divesting it of its 'polemical' tone and even of its terminology. Souyri was asked in particular to rewrite, in this direction, the appendix to the first chapter. He forced himself to do this, but the rest remained unchanged, and the whole thing was put away and forgotten. I often reproached him later for this neglect, accusing him of being responsible for having allowed Maoism to develop among French students, something his book would have prevented. He laughed at this childish idea. After one of our last meetings, he nevertheless declared that he would take up the text again and publish it. Of the three appendixes on revolutionary China, the first two were published in *Socialisme ou Barbarie*, in numbers 24 (May–June 1958) and 30 (April–May 1960), respectively; the last is taken from articles written between 1965 and 1967 and collected in the booklet *Impérialisme et bureaucratie . . .* (see further on). They give an idea of what the second volume envisioned by Souyri would have been.

The other published texts are: *Impérialisme et bureaucratie face aux révolutions dans le tiers monde*, with a collection of nine articles written for the mimeographed monthly newsletter *Pouvoir Ouvrier* between 1965 and 1967, with a previously unpublished introduction and conclusion. This collection was published in booklet form as a mimeographed supplement to the January 1968 issue of *Pouvoir Ouvrier: Le Marxisme après Marx* (Paris: Flammarion, 'Questions d'histoire', 1970). Among the articles and notes he contributed regularly to the *Annales ESC,* some are more than clarifications: 'La Crise de mai' (January–February 1970); 'Quelques aspects du marxisme aujourd'hui' (September–October 1970); 'Marxismes et marxistes' (on books by Lerner, Haithcox, Harris and Palmer, and Paillet); and 'Variations dans le marxisme' (November–December 1972); 'Révolutions russes et totalitarisme' (on books by Liebman, Avrich, Medvedev, David Rousset, Solzhenitsyn, and Martchenko) (March–April 1976); 'Histoire et théorie economiques' (on books by Boukharine, Varga, and Mandel) (February–March 1979).

2. Claude Lefort and the comrades who maintained after 1958 the publication of the bulletin *Informations et liaisons ouvrières*, which subsequently became *Informations et correspondance ouvrières*. Lefort's positions had been stated in a text entitled 'Organisation et parti,' published under his name in *Socialisme ou Barbarie*, no. 26 (November–December 1958); those of the majority were published in a text signed by Paul Cardan, entitled 'Prolétariat et organisation,' and published in numbers 27 and 28 of the same journal (April–May and July–August 1959).

3. This 'platform' was published in *Socialisme ou Barbarie*, nos 31 and 32 (December 1960–February 1961) under the title 'Le Mouvement révolutionnaire sous le capitalisme moderne.'

4. The expressions in quotation marks are taken from the introductory resumé of the text mentioned in the preceding note, *Socialisme ou Barbarie*, no. 31, pp. 51 sq.

5. Souyri, *Impérialisme et bureaucratie*, p. xviii.

 6. Pierre Chaulieu, 'Les Rapports de production en Russie,' *Socialisme ou Barbarie*, no. 2 (May–June 1949), pp. 1–66.

 7. The study published by Claude Lefort in *Socialisme ou barbarie*, no. 19 (July–September 1956), entitled 'Le Totalitarisme sans Staline – l'URSS dans une nouvelle phase,' is now a classic model of what was formulated at that time on bureaucracy.

 8. *Socialisme ou Barbarie*, no. 24 (May–June 1958), pp. 35–103.

 9. Souyri, *Le Marxisme après Marx*, p. 22.

10. See, for example, the report on the book by Ernest Mandel, 'Le Troisième Ăge du capitalisme,' *Annales ESC*, no. 2 (February–March 1979), pp. 379–81.

11. Souyri, *Le Marxisme après Marx*, pp. 113–114.

12. Algeria scarcely appears in this testimony. It had for me the importance of something that initiates one directly into the political; such was not the case for Souyri. I have preferred not to run the risk of interposing my experience between the reader and Souyri's Algeria.

Chapter 13

The Communication of Sublime Feeling

A Mediatized Communication

One must ask oneself whether sublime feeling also demands to be universally communicated, like taste, and whether it is justified in doing so according to the same principle of *sensus communis* with its supreme finality in the supersensible. This question is raised in paragraph 39, which examines the communicability of a sensation *(der Mitteilbarkeit einer Empfindung*: 148–50; *142–44).*[1] The examination of the communicability of the sublime takes up very little space.

The text distinguishes four kinds of sensation, according to whether the sensation is due to the senses, to morality, to the sublime, or to the beautiful. This repeats the division made at the beginning of the 'Analytic of the Beautiful' in the name of the quality of taste (42–50; *40–48)*. The pleasure in the beautiful, 'favor' *(Gunst)*, is the only delight 'free' of all interest. The pleasure in the senses is 'conditioned' by the interest the senses take in the existence of the object, in its 'material' presence. As for the delight taken in doing or judging what is good, what is 'esteemed, approved' (49; *47*), it is determined by the interest that results from the obligation of the empirical will to realize moral law. Moral obligation, the *Gebot*, the commandment, does not result from an interest, and in this it is altogether different from the necessity experienced by the senses; however moral obligation creates an interest in the realization of the good (54–57, 112, 159–60; *46–48, 118, 152)*.

In the 'First Moment' of the 'Analytic of the Beautiful,' the critique distinguishes three kinds of delight (see Chapter 7, pp. 159–63). In paragraph 39, a fourth delight is added, the delight provided by 'the sublime in nature' *(die Lust am Erhabenen der Natur*. 149; *142)*. Furthermore, the category or the reflective space overseeing the examination is no longer the quality of the delight, but its possible communication, its *Mitteilbarkeit*, which has a modal character. Thus the entire elaboration of communicability in taste is to be reconsidered here in relation to the sublime. By this I mean that the quality of sublime feeling, disinterested like the feeling of the beautiful (they please 'on their own account': 90; *87*), but in which pleasure and displeasure combine 'dynamically' (see Chapter 5), is not enough to determine its communicability. As with the beautiful, one must proceed with the examination of sublime judgment accord-ing to its quantity and modality. The question is to know whether a singular sublime judgment immediately requires one to obtain, as taste does, a univer-sal and necessary agreement, and whether a sublime judgment requires this immediately, that is, whether its very occurrence carries with it this demand, prior to all concepts, as the simple sign of the subjective universality necessary in all thought.

To this question, the text clearly says 'no.' We must remember, however, that the feelings of the beautiful and the sublime were easily assimilated to one another with regard to their universalization: 'The judgments: "That man is beautiful" and "He is tall" do not purport to speak only for the judging subject, but, like theoretical judgments, they demand the assent of everyone' (95; *92*). Our text, on the contrary, asserts that sublime feeling 'lays claim also to universal participation' *(macht zwar auch auf allgemeine Teilnehmung Anspruch*: 149; *143)*, but this *call* cannot be immediate in the same way as it is in taste. The demand for universality that is proper to the sublime passes 'through [*vermittelst*] the moral law [*des moralischen Gesetzes*]' (ibid.). The pleasure in the sublime is said to be a pleasure 'of rationalizing contemplation' *(als Lust der vernünftelnden Kontemplation)*, the pleasure that we have in contemplating while reasoning (149; *142–43*).

We have seen (see Chapter 4, pp. 115–22) that, as pleasure, the contradictory feeling of the sublime holds exclusively to the 'soul-stirring delight' provided by the Idea of the absolute (as whole and as cause) and that only rationalizing thought, reason, can represent this unpresentable object, which is, properly speaking, an Idea. This pleasure is the 'attractive' component of the sublime emotion (or 'shock'). This component corresponds to the observation of an object that is a being of reason. The 'repulsion' that takes hold of thought and prevents it from pursuing the contemplation of the object comes from its powerlessness to present it through a synthesis of the imagination.

Thus the communicability of sublime feeling as delight would only belong to reason as a universal capacity, and its universality would in fact be that of moral law. The text suggests this so strongly that it almost breaks the precarious unity of the paradoxical feeling and almost destroys the dynamical synthesis that constitutes it. However, the very notion of a pleasure tied to the exercise of rational thought, even if only contemplative (and not directly ethical), is not a simple one. For if the demand for universal communication is mediatized in sublime feeling by the representation of 'moral law,' we also know that the concept of this law translates or is experienced subjectively as a feeling, respect, whose specific quality is that it is neither pleasure nor pain (KPV, 78–92; *89–104*). Yet the text we are discussing seems to escape this objection. It suggests that pleasure as a component of sublime feeling only claims to be communicated because 'it already [*schon*] indeed [*doch*] presupposes another feeling [*ein anderes Gefühl*], that, namely, of its supersensible sphere' (149, t.m.; *143*). (I emphasize the *doch*; the *seiner* of 'its . . . sphere' relates the sphere to thought.) Yet this 'other feeling,' however 'obscure' (*dunkel*) it may indeed also (*auch*) be, still has 'a moral foundation' (*ein moralische Grundlage*: ibid.).

The Other Feeling

This 'other feeling' is not named in the passage. Yet what is mentioned about it suffices to identify it. It is a very obscure feeling; it has a moral foundation; it signals the supersensible sphere of thought. We recognize respect, the *Achtung* or regard that the second *Critique* carefully isolates as the only moral feeling. 'And the capacity [*Fähigkeit*] of taking such an interest in the law (or of having respect for the moral law itself) is really moral feeling' (KPV, 83; *94*). The 'interest' in question is free of all motive. Respect does not satisfy the need thinking has to obey the law. On the contrary, as we have seen, listening to the law may simply produce in thought an interest in doing good (ibid.). This reversal is the central motif of the second *Critique* and a recurrent one in the third *Critique*. The regard thought feels for the law is not interested (in the sense of motivation). However the categorical imperative, without content (without 'matter'), that is, the commandment issued from the mere form of the moral law, determines the interest thought has in certain objects – good actions that have been done and remain to do (49, 122–24, 159; *47, 118–19, 152*).

The law must not prescribe what is good, for then the will would be affected 'pathologically' (KPV, 83; *94*) and could not claim to be freely determined. Because it is not 'pathological,' because respectful thought is not subject to any heteronomy, respect is 'singular' (*sonderbar*) and unlike any other feeling. Its manner is not like any other but is, rather, of a 'peculiar kind' (*eigentümlicher Art*: ibid., 79; *89*). It is obscure because it is 'blank' in relation to pleasure and pain. It is not a pleasure. One only 'reluctantly gives way to it as regards a man.' One even makes an effort to defend oneself against the respect due the law. Nor, however, is respect a displeasure (ibid., 80–81; *90–91*). One cannot 'ever satisfy oneself [*nicht sattsehen*] in contemplating the majesty of the law' (ibid., 81, t.m.; *91*).

These strange properties converge in the following property: respect is 'the only case wherein we can determine from *a priori* concepts the relation of a cognition (here a cognition of pure practical reason) to the feeling of a pleasure or a displeasure' (ibid., 75; *85*). Respect is produced 'by an intellectual cause,' which is the law, and as such it is the only feeling 'that we can know completely *a priori*' (ibid., 76; *86*). To say that it is produced by the law is going too far. It 'is not the incentive to morality', it is the 'presence' of the law regarded subjectively, its 'sign,' 'morality itself regarded subjectively as an incentive' (ibid., 78; *89*). Because of its *a priori* status it does not wait for the occasion with which an object might provide it in order to appear; respect is 'there' as the signal in thought of its disposition to desire the Good. It is the subjective *a priori* of moral thought. In this sense respect does not belong to the faculty of pleasure and displeasure. Respect is indeed the disposition and the sign of the disposition of thought, but only insofar as it wants or 'desires,' and not insofar as it suffers.

Thus it is 'another feeling' altogether from the sublime feeling. The sublime feeling is an emotion, a violent emotion, close to unreason, which forces thought to the extremes of pleasure and displeasure, from joyous exaltation to terror; the sublime feeling is as tightly strung between ultraviolet and infrared as respect is white. This does not prevent sublime pathos from 'presupposing' an 'apathetic' respect. For if thought did not have the power of concepts in the form of an Idea, if it did not have the absolute (free) causality that founds the law for which and from which it feels respect, it would have no chance of feeling the magnitude and force of 'raw' nature so intensely as signs negatively indicative of the 'presence' of this Idea. Sublime feeling is not moral feeling, but it requires the 'capacity' of taking a pure interest in the law. On the basis of this presupposition it is argued that sublime feeling cannot be recognized as having a 'communicability' analogous to that of taste. There is no sublime *sensus communis* because the sublime needs the mediation of moral feeling, and the latter is a concept of reason (freedom as absolute causality) that is felt subjectively *a priori*. Because it is felt subjectively by thought, this concept does indeed translate as a feeling (although an altogether different one). But as a concept that is felt, this feeling proceeds *a priori* from a faculty of knowing, i.e., reason in its practical usage.

This is the movement invoked by the text of the Deduction to explain why sublime feeling has no need for a deduction in the critical sense. The affinity (or finality) of the form of an object with the faculty of feeling pleasure or displeasure, or taste, even as it is expounded in detail according to the four 'headings' of reflective judgment, still requires a 'deduction.' The critique must reveal what is presupposed as an *a priori* condition for such an affinity (which is real, for taste exists) to be possible. This condition is the *sensus communis*, and beyond it the supersensible substrate. Such is not the case with the sublime. Its critical 'exposition' is 'at the same time' (*zugleich*) its deduction (134; *129*). Through the simple analysis of sublime feeling, this exposition discovers in it directly 'a final relation of the cognitive faculties,' a paradoxical relation: final for pure practical reason, 'contra-final' for the imagination. But this paradoxical relation attests by this very fact that it is *a priori* 'at the basis of the faculty of ends (the will)' (*dem Vermögen der Zwecke [dem Willen]* a priori *zum Grunde gelegt werden muß:* ibid.). This is because the sublime contains the concept of absolute causality, or free will, or practical reason which is the concept of a causality of the end. This end is the universalization of practical freedom. This is why sublime feeling is legitimate in demanding its universalization, without needing its own deduction (ibid.). It owes this privilege to its close cousinship with moral feeling: free will is a universal Idea, and respect, which is this Idea felt subjectively, is also universal.

This must be explained further still. The concept of freedom as absolute causality is not determinant. Its object, freedom, remains indeterminate (in the sense demanded by understanding), 'incomprehensible' (*unbegreiflich* for the understanding), '*inscrutable*' (*unerforschlich*: KPV, 7, 48, 49; *8, 56, 57*). But as such this object of the pure Idea of reason is indispensable (KPV, 7; *8*) to the realm of morality; it is its foundation, its condition of possibility. For this indetermination makes the determination of what freedom is impossible and keeps the law from having a content. It prescribes that one must judge the good and the bad, when thought so desires. But the decision about what is good and bad belongs to the thought that desires. Thus the thought that desires can desire freely, that is, morally. The law only provides it a guiding thread with which to help it in this decision.

Furthermore, this thread or regulative Idea is precisely that of the possible universal communication of the 'maxim' supporting thought in its decision. 'So act that' (*Handle so, daß*; KPV, 30; *36*), 'Act as if' (*Handle als, ob*: *Foundation of the Metaphysics of Morals, Akad., 4, 421*): these clauses modalize the rule of universalization (that is, the quantity of the imperative) in order to allow this rule its merely regulative character. But the content of the rule, thus modalized, is clearly the demand for a universal communication: 'that the maxim of your will will always hold at the same time as a principle establishing universal law' (KPV, 30; *36*). Thus we see how the communication required by morality is mediatized. It is mediatized by the law. More precisely still, it is required by the very form of the law. In fact it is the whole of the form. This form is borrowed from the form of a conceptual, cognitive rule and transposed analogically into the practical realm. The law is not a rule, but is formulated according to the 'type' of a rule of knowledge, retaining from this rule only the principle of its universal validity. This is what the typic of the second *Critique* explains (KPV, 70–74; *79–84*).

Universality, which is thus transposed from knowledge to the practical, loses through the analogy its determined character and assumes its function as 'guiding thread' – as indicated by the *als ob* and the *so, daß*. Meanwhile the concept of understanding is transformed into an Idea of reason, and the phenomenon, on the side of the object, is henceforth grasped as a sign. All voluntary action given in experience gives way to knowledge according to the series of conditions of which it is the conditioned. But the same action, subjected cognitively to the syntheses of intuition, of the imagination and understanding, can also be judged morally, as the effect (the sign) of a free causality. Thus the criterion for evaluating the action resides in the clause of a possible universalization. However, in spite of the profound transformation of the nature of universality as it passes from knowledge to morality, universality retains its conceptual foundation. The concept belongs henceforth to reason and no longer to understanding, yet as Idea it remains what legitimates the demand for universalization made of the moral maxim. Moreover, because this demand is the only demand heard in sublime feeling (and suffices to authorize or 'deduce' it in its claim for possible communication), one must say that the latter is in fact 'mediatized' by the concept of reason.

In conclusion we see that the demand to be communicated is of an altogether different nature in the sublime than it was in the beautiful. Twice different. First, the demand in sublime feeling does not properly belong to sublime feeling. The demand comes to sublime feeling from the demand to be communicated inscribed in the form of the moral law, and this latter demand is authorized by the simple fact that the law rests on the the Idea of freedom. The demand is authorized by the faculty of concepts and the faculty of desire. Far from being 'immediate' like the demand of taste, far from being a universality 'apart from a concept' (60; *58*), the universality in question in sublime feeling passes through the concept of practical reason. If one does not have the Idea of freedom and of its law, one cannot experience sublime feeling. Furthermore, the sublime differs from taste in the quality of the feeling. Violent, divided against itself, it is simultaneously fascination, horror, and elevation. This splitting can also be expressed in terms of a possible communication. For what authorizes sublime feeling to demand its communication is that part of itself, that component, which is the aesthetic analogue of respect. This alone, consequently, lays claim to the concept. The communication of the beautiful does not refer to any concept; this is why the critique must deduce it. Taste is immediately a thought that feels itself, the thought that does not think the object but feels itself on the occasion of the form of an object. The sublime is a thought that is felt on the occasion of an absence of the object's form. But this absence is only due to the thought of another object by means of a concept, the Idea of absolute causality and magnitude. Sublime thought is a 'rationalizing' contemplation. It is in this name that sublime thought demands to be communicated. Thus it only makes its demand under the direction of a concept. This is what gives the sublime its violence. It is an aesthetic feeling, and not merely any delight, because it demands to be universally communicated. But what demands this communication in this aesthetic feeling is not the aesthetic, but, rather, reason itself.

The Other Object

I will briefly point out a remarkable effect of the status given to the communicability of the sublime by the critique. The analytic of this feeling insists at various points that the sublime is only in thought (91–92, 92–93, 114, 134; *88–89, 89–90, 110, 129*), and that there is no sublime object strictly speaking. The critique also insists on calling the sublime a *Geistesgefühl* (see Chapter 7, pp. 181–87) in order to show the extent to which nature, which in the beautiful addresses itself to thought through the 'cipher' of its forms, is discredited in sublime feeling. As if thought were turning away from any given object only to be exalted by its power to think an 'object' that it gives itself.

Things are not quite so simple. For if it were only a question of thinking the absolute, one would be faced with a case of speculative reason, which would not belong to the aesthetic at all. Whereas here we do indeed have an aesthetic delight, and this implies the presentation of an object or at least the presentation of the form of an object by the imagination, even if the presentation is negative and the object formless. Thus there is an object that gives rise to the sublime, if not a sublime object. Paragraph 39 refers to 'the pleasure in the sublime in nature' (149; *142*). Moreover, the argument that refuses sublime feeling its universal communication also invokes the formless character of the object that may give rise to sublime feeling. 'There is simply [*schlechthin*] no authority for my presupposing that other men will pay attention to this object and take delight in contemplating the uncouth dimensions of nature [*in Betrachtung der rauhen Größe*]' (149, t.m.; *143*).

This argument against the hypothesis of a sublime *sensus communis*, which proceeds by way of the strangeness of the 'sublime object,' no doubt supports the argument we have just analyzed that appeals to the 'other feeling' hidden in sublime feeling. But instead of exploring the subjective state of thought seized by the sublime, the argument contents itself with remarking the uncertain status of the object that occasions this state. The object is indeed a phenomenon (pyramid of ice, ocean, volcano, etc.) and as such falls under the general rule of knowledge, the schematism. The 'Savoyard peasant' perceives and conceives the phenomenon, whereas Herr von Saussure, who finds in the same object occasion for a sublime emotion, seems unquestionably foolish (115; *111*). The first has good sense, understanding; he is *verständig*. The second feels in the object the 'presence' of something that transcends the object. The mountain peak is a phenomenon that indicates that it is also something more than a phenomenon. It indicates this precisely in that it 'almost' exceeds the capacity of the imagination's comprehension and forces the latter to beat a retreat. Space and time, which it must give up synthesizing (which are thus no longer space and time as forms of intuition), signal the unpresentable 'presence' of an object of thought that is not an object of experience, but which cannot be sentimentally deciphered anywhere except upon the object of experience. The analogy with morality imposes itself once again by way of this phenomenist or para-phenomenist means of access. For the virtuous act, if it exists, is a phenomenon, but if it is virtuous it points to the Other of phenomenality, absolute causality and its law.

One could say that the object's Other is not an object and that the sign is what de-objectifies the object. This is only true if one identifies the object with the phenomenon. However, in the vocabulary of the critique, this should not be done. An object is what offers itself to thought. The Ideas of reason have objects, those limits of understanding constituted by the absolute whole, the absolute cause, and the like. Although one cannot find a corresponding intuition for them, one can still think them, and thus take them as objects. These are the objects that Kant calls 'intelligible' (KRV, 467, 483–84; *527, 547*). When thought grasps a phenomenon as a sign, it thinks it in two different ways at once: as a given and conditioned object of experience, and as the effect of a transcendent causality. These two manners of thinking are transcendentally 'localized' in two different facultary realms. They are heterogeneous and characterize the same object in a heterogeneous way. The object that is presented to reason in the phenomenon is never 'big' enough with respect to the object of its Idea, and for the imagination the latter is always too 'big' to be presentable. The differend cannot be resolved. But it can be felt as such, as different. This is the sublime feeling. This feeling makes the raw magnitude of nature a sign of reason while remaining a phenomenon of experience. The sublime feeling does this with the help of the dynamical synthesis. Still one must have the 'sense,' the *Fähigkeit* of the heterogeneous and of the necessity that forces the heterogeneous ways of thinking to meet, without, however, reducing their differend in the least.

The Aesthetic Feeling Inspired by Moral Judgment

The following point remains to be examined: the 'soul-stirring delight' felt by 'rationalizing' (*vernünftelnd*: 149; *143*) thought in the sublime is not respect for the moral law itself. Rather, this delight is an echo of respect in the order of the aesthetic, that is, in the order of contemplation and not of practice. Should one therefore see this exaltation as the sensation that must subjectively accompany moral judgment or the 'maxim' of moral will in general?

Kant examines this sensation at the end of the 'Methodology of Pure Practical Reason' (KPV, 163–65; *182–85*). The question of method in morality concerns the learning of moral correctness. There are two dispositions to acquire. One must first learn 'to make judging according to moral laws' into something of a 'habit', that is, to acquire and/or have acquired a competence that allows one to distinguish between 'essential duties' and 'non-essential duties' (ibid., 163; *182*). The next step is to learn and/or teach how to judge whether an act is done not only in accordance with the moral law but 'for the sake of the moral law' (ibid., 163; *183*). For in the first case, the action or, rather, its maxim offers only a rightness of deed; it has a moral value only in the second case.

What is of interest to our discussion here is that this exercise of moral discernment in which reflection is formed in the practical realm – the reflection whose responsibility it is to 'decide' what is good – must 'gradually produce a certain interest even in its [reason's] own law [*selbst am Gesetze derselben*]' (ibid., 164; *183*). This interest is signaled by a feeling that should be the sensation we are trying to isolate: the state in which thought, discovering the purity of a maxim, finds itself and recognizes the 'sign' of the moral law's 'presence' in the maxim. This 'sign' signifies not only that the will obeys an interested motivation, including the one that may push it to accord itself with moral law, but that pure practical reason, the free (absolutely first) causality, is implicated in the determination of the will. This sensation is a kind of liking: 'We ultimately take a liking [*wir gewinnen endlich . . . lieb*] to that the observation of which makes us feel that our powers of knowledge are extended' (ibid.). Our powers of knowledge are 'extended' (*erweiterte*), because pure practical reason enters into the picture in the maxim of an empirical desire. It is this feeling of 'liking' that thought feels when it discerns (recognizes) true morality, beyond mere factual rectitude.

Thus there is a kind of subjective happiness in the observation of a pure practical judgment or of a strictly moral maxim – a happiness projected as a liking for the latter. This happiness can be critically analyzed as the harmonious accord of the 'faculties of knowledge,' i.e., the powers of thought insofar as they are directed at the object. This happy sensation stems from the way 'reason, with its faculty of determining according to *a priori* principles what ought to occur [*was geschehen soll*], can find satisfaction [*allein gut finden kann*]' (ibid., t.m.). Rational thought can thus 'find satisfaction' because its power of determining *a priori* 'the ends of freedom' is in 'accord' (*Übereinstimmung*) with freedom 'in the moral sphere' (*im Sittlichen*: 215; *205*). This is the definition given in the third *Critique* of the third supersensible Idea, the one which precisely authorizes the accord, the *Übereinstimmung*, of the *a priori* law of freedom and the maxim of moral desire. The 'extension' of the faculties of knowledge is thus considerable; it is even maximal, for it requires that the supersensible principle guarantee pure *a priori* desire its actualization in a concrete maxim (but always and only as a sign).

Moreover, with this accord, this harmony, and this happiness one cannot help thinking, by analogy, of the state that characterizes the thought judging the beautiful. Accord, harmony, and happiness are guaranteed to thought by the second Idea of the supersensible, according to which, I will remind the reader, there is a 'subjective finality of nature for our cognitive faculties' (ibid.). The analogy is inevitable because the text concerns practical methodology and the (subjective) feeling with which a moral judgment provides thought, and not the practical actualization of the law by the maxim. Kant does in fact make the analogy. This exercise of moral judgment 'only enables one to entertain himself with such judging and gives virtue or a turn of mind based on moral laws a form of beauty [*eine Form der Schönheit*] which is admired [*bewundert*] but not yet sought' (KPV, 164; *183*). *Bewundert, noch nicht gesucht*: one admires virtue. It is an aesthetic feeling, but one does not yet seek it; it is not an ethical obligation. Thinking entertains itself, is entertained by its accord on the occasion of virtue taken as an object. It does not, however, engage itself to practice virtue. The good ratio in which the faculties of knowing find themselves with each other, the power to prescribe absolutely and the power to realize the prescription, is so pleasant that thinking 'dwells' in its subjective state, 'lingers,' marks a pause, a *Verweilung* (64; *61*), and thus defers the putting into action of virtue.

The subjective state occasioned by the observation of moral rectitude should be compared to the feeling of the beautiful. 'The existence of the object remains indifferent to us, as it is seen only as the occasion [*die Veranlassung*] for our becoming aware of the store of talents [*Talente*] within us [*in uns inne zu werden*] that elevate us [*erhabenen*] above the mere animal level' (KPV, 164, t.m.; *183*). 'Talent' belongs to the terminology of the beautiful, their elevation, *erhabenen*, to that of the sublime. It is less important for the moral maxim (the 'object') to 'manifest' a transcendence of free will in relation to all other motivation ('animal,' 'pathological'); it is more important for the object to be grasped as the occasion of a pleasure, which is the case with taste. We have the proof in what follows: 'It is the same with everything whose contemplation produces subjectively a consciousness of the harmony of our powers of representation by which we feel our entire cognitive faculty (understanding and imagination) strengthened [*gestärkt*]' (ibid.). The formulation leads directly to the Analytic of the Beautiful, in particular to what goes by the name of animation (see Chapter 2, pp. 60–67).

One must not forget the determination of the 'satisfaction' thus described in the relative clause attached to it and with which the German sentence ends: 'produces a satisfaction that can be communicated to others [*das sich auch anderen mitteilen läßt*]' (KPV, 164; *183*). This specification returns us to the question of communication. The aesthetic feeling provided by moral judgment demands, 'it too,' to be communicated. We recognize the obligation to be communicated, the *Sollen*, inherent in taste. But let there be no mistake: that my taste should be communicable does not entail that duty should be. Taste is subjective, and duty is objective. In the Methodology of Practical Reason the first 'you must' is 'still' in a relation of analogy with the second, and the aesthetic feeling produced by virtue is only a means of instilling the habit of recognizing and practicing virtue. As the means to something other than itself, this feeling cannot be identified with pure taste. Furthermore, as something aesthetic, taste cannot be confused with moral feeling – strictly speaking, respect – nor can it be confused with the obligation of putting the law into action. There is even some danger in this kind of learning: the pleasure in admiring virtue may deter thought from the desire to practice it.

Thus the term to compare, in the order of the aesthetic, with the feeling provided by the ethical maxim is not sublime feeling but the feeling of the beautiful. Sublime feeling is in no way a happy disposition of thought. The powers of thought in sublime feeling in no way relate to one another according to a good proportion; they 'disproportion' themselves violently. The object that occasions the sublime is assuredly a 'sign,' the sign of a supersensible sphere, but it disarms the presentation and goes so far as to discredit the phenomenality of the phenomenon. The analogy (that one might suppose possible) between the 'raw' magnitude or force of nature and virtue, insofar as they both inspire a sublime feeling, finds its limit here. To judge a maxim to be morally estimable leads thought to feel it as beautiful. To judge the ocean 'too big' for presentation leads one to experience it as sublime. Duty can and must be called sublime: 'Duty! Thou sublime and mighty name that dost embrace nothing charming [*nichts Beliebtes*]' (KPV, 89; *101*). However, duty differs from the sublime in the strict sense in that it does not move thought 'by threatening aught that would arouse natural aversion and terror' (ibid.), and that the law it prescribes 'itself finds entrance into the mind' (*ein Gesetzt . . . welches von selbst im Gemüte Eingang findet*: ibid.). Thus in the description of the sublimity of duty one finds characteristics that make the *feeling* of duty, respect, *not* in fact a sublime feeling. If virtue were itself sublime, the sign of the law of freedom in it would not be graspable by subjective thought except by 'submerging' the phenomenality of the virtuous act, which would be too big or too strong to be presentable. This act would not be an act: the pure and free desire of which it would be a sign would prevent empirical will from actualizing it, just as the absolute of reason prevents the presentation of the phenomenon by the imagination.

All that can be conceded to sublime feeling in the consideration of morality is resistance (see Chapter 6, pp. 147–50), the resistance of virtue to passions, to 'fear,' 'superstition,' 'the frailty of human nature', and its 'shortcomings' (112–14; *108–10*). The courage of a soldier, or of a people at war, the submission of one who believes to God can be experienced by thought as something sublime, on condition that the maxim orientating the will of the soldier, of the people, of the one who believes, be virtuous. But even then it is not morality itself that is felt to be sublime, it is its resistance to temptations, its triumph over them, reducing them to naught. The sublime and aesthetic effect results from the disproportion of pure will to empirical desire. However, virtue consists in the simple 'presence' of the former in the latter according to their 'natural' accord, without resistance, and this is why virtue evokes beauty.

Morality thus intrinsically demands to be universally communicated, and it is analogous in this respect to the feeling of the beautiful. But it is analogous only, for this demand is legitimated by an Idea immediately or unconditionally present, always present, and present *a priori* to the thought that desires: the concept of freedom. Whereas the demand to be immediately communicated in taste must be deduced from a principle of *sensus communis*, that, in turn, is legitimated by a 'supersensible' Idea that is hidden and according to which the forms in nature are in affinity with the states of thought. As for the sublime, it escapes both demands for universal communication. In the face of the raw magnitudes and forces of nature (or the resistance of virtue) 'there is simply no authority for my presupposing that other men will pay attention to it [*darauf Rücksicht nehmen*]' (149, t.m.; *143*). The Idea of the absolute is not present to thought here in the necessary form of respect. The Idea of the finality without concept of a form of pure pleasure cannot be suggested by the violent contra-finality of the object. The sublime feeling is neither moral universality nor aesthetic universalization, but is, rather, the destruction of one by the other in the violence of their differend. This differend cannot demand, even subjectively, to be communicated to all thought.

Notes

1. The following abbreviations are used in this essay:

KPV   *Critique of Practical Reason*, trans. Lewis White Beck (New York: Macmillan, 1956). *Kritik der praktischen Vernunft* (Hamburg: Meiner, 1974).

KRV   *Critique of Pure Reason* (A: 1781; B: 1787), trans. N. Kemp Smith (New York: St Martin's Press, 1929); *Kritik der reinen Vernunft* (Hamburg: Meiner, 1956).

Numbers in brackets that are not prefaced by an abbreviation refer to *Kant's Critique of Judgement* (1790), trans. J. C. Meredith (Oxford: Clarendon Press, 1952); *Kritik der Urteilskraft* (Hamburg: Meiner, 1974).

References in brackets that take the form (see Chapter 7) are to other chapters in *Lessons on the Analytic of the Sublime*, trans. E. Rottenberg (Stanford: Stanford University Press, 1994).

The following note is given in *Lessons on the Analytic of the Sublime* from which this essay is taken: 'N.B.: For the three Critiques, reference is made first to the English translation and then to the German edition (in italics) [. . .] The abbreviation 't.m.' following a reference to the English translation indicates that the French translation has been modified in Lyotard's text.'

Chapter 14

Time Today

I

The title *Time Today* is not without paradox. *Today* is a time designator, a deictic indexing time in the same way as 'now', 'yesterday', etc. Like all temporal deictics, it operates by referring what it designates to the sole present of the sentence itself, or to the sentence only in so far as it is present. It temporalizes the referent of the present sentence by situating it exclusively with respect to the time in which this sentence is taking place, which is the present. And without at all having recourse to the time *in which* the sentence could in its turn be located, for example by means of a clock or a calendar. In this latter case, sentence 1 could itself be taken as referent of another sentence 2, which would say, for example, 'Sentence 1 took place on the 24 June.' Calendar and clock constitute networks of 'objective' time which allow the moment of sentence 2 to be located without reference to the time 'of' sentence 1. Even supposing that a new sentence (3) makes no use of dates and hours to refer to sentence 1 (for example (sentence 3): 'sentence 1 was uttered yesterday', in which the event of sentence 1 is indeed located by reference to the present of sentence 3 alone), the fact remains that sentence 1 is put in the position of being designated by the deictic 'yesterday'. Sentence 1 is no longer the presenting present, it becomes that present 'then presenting and now presented', in other words the past.

As an occurrence, each sentence is a 'now'. It presents, now, a meaning, a referent, a sender and an addressee. With respect to presentation, we must imagine the time of an occurrence as — and only as — present. This present cannot be grasped as such, it is absolute. It cannot be synthesized *directly* with other presents. The other presents with which it can be placed in relation are necessarily and immediately changed into presented presents, i.e. past.

When the time of presentation is glossed and we reach the conclusion that 'each' sentence appears at each time, we omit the inevitable transformation of present into past, and we place all the moments together on a single diachronic line.

We thus let ourselves slip from the presenting time implied in 'each' occurrence, to the presented time it has become or, better, from time as 'now' [*nun*] to time considered as 'this time' [*dieses Mal*], an expression which presupposes that 'one time' [*einmal*] is equivalent to 'that time' [*das andere Mal*]. What is forgotten in this objectifying synthesis is that *it* takes place *now*, in the presenting occurrence that effects the synthesis, and that this 'now' is not *yet* one of the 'times' it presents along the diachronic line.

Because it is absolute, the presenting present cannot be grasped: it is *not yet* or *no longer* present. It is always too soon or too late to grasp presentation itself and present it. Such is the specific and paradoxical constitution of the event. That something happens, the occurrence, means that the mind is disappropriated. The expression 'it happens that . . .' is the formula of non-mastery of self over self. The event makes the self incapable of taking possession and control of what it is. It testifies that the self is essentially passible to a recurrent alterity.

With its title *Time Today*, my discourse is clearly placed under the aegis of this passibility. It has not at all the object of exercising a complete control over the referent it designates, time – not even in theory. My intention is only that of trying to bring out some of the ways in which modernity deals with the temporal condition.

II

This brief reminder of the question of time, from the point of view of presentation, is conceptually marked by the privilege it accords to discontinuity, to 'discreteness' and to difference. It is clear that this description presupposes, as its opposite and complement, the ability to gather and retain, at least potentially, in a single 'presence', a certain number of distinct moments. As the word suggests, consciousness implies memory, in the Husserlian sense of an elementary *Retention*. By opposing discontinuity with synthesis, consciousness seems to be the very thing that throws down a challenge to alterity. In this conflict, what is at stake is to determine the limits within which consciousness is capable of embracing a diversity of moments (of 'information', as we say these days) and of actualizing them 'each time' they are needed.

There is good reason to assume two extreme limits to the capacity to synthesize a multiplicity of information, the one minimal, the other maximal. Such is the major intuition which guides Leibniz's work, and in particular the *Monadology*. God is the absolute monad to the extent that he conserves in complete retention the totality of information constituting the world. And if divine retention is to be complete, it must also include those pieces of information not yet presented to the incomplete monads, such as our minds, and which remain to come in what we call the future. In this perspective, the 'not yet' is due only to the limit on the faculty of synthesis available to the intermediary monads.

For the absolute memory of God, the future is always already given. We can thus conceive, for the temporal condition, an upper limit determined by a perfect recording or archival capacity. As consummate archivist, God is outside time, and this is one of the grounds of modern Western metaphysics.

Modern Western physics, for its part, finds its ground on the side of the other limit. One can imagine a being incapable of recording and using past information by inserting it between the event and its effect: a being, then, which could only convey or transmit the 'bits' of information as they are received. In these conditions, in the absence of any interfacing filter between input and output, such a being would be situated at the degree zero of consciousness or memory. This is the being Leibniz calls a 'material point'. It represents the simplest unit required by the science of movement, mechanics. In contemporary physics and astrophysics, the family of elementary particles is constituted of entities about as 'naked' (the word is Leibniz's) as the material point.

The fact remains that each subset of particles included in this family presents properties allowing the elements to enter into relation with others according to specific regularities. This specificity means that a particle has a sort of elementary memory and consequently a temporal filter. This is why contemporary physicists tend to think that time emanates from matter itself, and that it is not an entity outside or inside the universe whose function it would be to gather all different times into universal history. It is only in certain regions that such – partial – syntheses could be detected. There would on this view be areas of determinism where complexity is growing.

On this approach, the human brain and language are the sign that humanity is a complex of this sort, temporary and highly improbable. And it then becomes tempting to think that what is called research and development in contemporary society and the results of which constantly disturb our environment are much more the result of such a process of 'cosmolocal' complexification than the work of human genius attached to the discovery of truth and the realization of good.

III

I should like to develop a little that aspect of the hypothesis which is most particularly relative to our theme, 'time today'. It seems to me that the anxiety prevalent today in the philosophical and political domain about 'communication', *kommunikative Handeln*, 'pragmatics', transparency in the expression of opinions, etc., has practically no relation with the 'classical' philosophical and politocological problems relative to the foundation of *Gemeinschaft* [community], *Mitsein* [being together], and even of *Offentlichkeit* [public space] as thought by the Enlightenment.

If we are to interrogate properly this compulsion to communicate and to secure the communicability of anything at all (objects, services, values, ideas, languages, tastes) which is expressed in particular in the context of the new technologies, we must, I think, give up the philosophy of the emancipation of humanity implied by 'classical' modern metaphysics. All technology, beginning with writing considered as a *techne*, is an artefact allowing its users to stock more information, to improve their competence and optimize their performances.

The importance of the technologies constructed around electronics and data processing resides in the fact that they make the programming and control of memorizing, i.e. the synthesis of different times in one time, less dependent on the conditions of life on earth. It is very probable that among the material complexes we know, the human brain is the most capable of producing complexity in its turn, as the production of the new technologies proves. And as such, it also remains the supreme agency for controlling these technologies.

And yet its own survival requires that it be fed by a body, which in turn can survive only in the conditions of life on earth, or in a simulacrum of those conditions. I think that one of the essential objectives of research today is to overcome the obstacle that the body places in the way of the development of communicational technologies, i.e. the new extended memory. In particular, this could be the real stake of research bearing on fertility, gestation, birth, illness, death, sex, sport, etc. All seem to converge on the same aim, that of making the body adaptable to non-terrestrial conditions of life, or of substituting another 'body' for it.

Having said this, if we consider the considerable change to which our culture is subjected today, we will observe to what extent, analogically, the new technologies are unblocking the obstacle constituted by human life on earth. Ethnocultures were for a long time the apparatuses for memorizing information such that peoples were able to organize their space and their time. They were, notably, the way in which multiplicities of different times could be gathered and conserved in a single memory (Bernard Stiegler). Themselves considered as *technai*, they allowed collections of individuals and generations to have real stocks of information at their disposal through time and space. In particular they produced the specific organization of temporality that we call historical narratives. There are many ways of telling a story, but the narrative as such can be considered to be a technical apparatus giving a people the means to store, order and retrieve units of information, i.e. events. More precisely, narratives are like temporal filters whose function is to transform the emotive charge linked to the event into sequences of units of information capable of giving rise to something like meaning. I shall return to this.

Now it is clear that these cultural apparatuses which constitute relatively extensive forms of memory remain tightly bound to the historical and geographical context in which they operate. This context furnishes that memory with most of the events which it must seize, stock, neutralize and make available. Traditional culture thus remains profoundly marked by its local situation on the surface of the earth so that it cannot easily be transplanted or communicated. As is well known, this inertia constitutes a major aspect of the problems linked today to the general phenomenon of immigration and emigration.

The new technologies, on the other hand, in as much as they furnish cultural models which are not initially rooted in the local context but are immediately formed in view of the broadest diffusion across the surface of the globe, provide a remarkable means of overcoming the obstacle traditional culture opposes to the recording, transfer and communication of information.

It scarcely seems that this generalized accessibility offered by the new cultural goods is strictly speaking a progress. The penetration of techno-scientific apparatus into the cultural field in no way signifies an increase of knowledge, sensibility, tolerance and liberty. Reinforcing this apparatus does not liberate the spirit, as the *Aufklärung* thought. Experience shows rather the reverse: a new barbarism, illiteracy and impoverishment of language, new poverty, merciless remodelling of opinion by the media, immiseration of the mind, obsolescence of the soul, as Walter Benjamin and Theodor Adorno repeatedly stressed.

Which is not to say that one can be content, with the Frankfurt School, to criticize the subordination of the mind to the rules and values of the culture-industry. Be it positive or negative, this diagnosis still belongs to a humanist point of view. The facts are ambiguous. 'Postmodern' culture is in fact on the way to spreading to all humanity. But to this same extent it is tending to abolish local and singular experience, it hammers the mind with gross stereotypes, apparently leaving no place for reflection and education.

If the new culture can produce such divergent effects, of generalization *and* destruction, this is because it seems to belong to the human domain neither by its aims nor its origins. As is clearly shown by the development of the techno-scientific system, technology and the culture associated with it are under a necessity to pursue their rise, and this necessity must be referred to the process of complexification (of neg-entropy) which takes place in the area of the cosmos inhabited by humanity. The human race is, so to speak, 'pulled forward' by this process without possessing the slightest capacity for mastering it. It has to adapt to the new conditions. It is even probable that this has always been the case throughout human history. And if we can become aware of that fact today, this is because of the exponential growth affecting sciences and technology.

The electronic and information network spread over the earth gives rise to a global capacity for memorizing which must be estimated at the cosmic scale, without common measure with that of traditional cultures. The paradox implied by this memory resides in the fact that in the last analysis it is nobody's memory. But 'nobody' here means that the body supporting that memory is no longer an earth-bound body. Computers never stop being able to synthesize more and more 'times', so that Leibniz could have said of this process that it is on the way to producing a monad much more 'complete' than humanity itself has ever able to be.

The human race is already in the grip of the necessity of having to evacuate the solar system in 4.5 billion years. It will have been the transitory vehicle for an extremely improbable process of complexification. The exodus is already on the agenda. The only chance of success lies in the species' adapting itself to the complexity that challenges it. And if the exodus succeeds, what it will have preserved is not the species itself but the 'most complete monad' with which it was pregnant.

IV

You will smile at how much the picture I have drawn owes to fiction. I should like to sketch out a few 'realistic' implications it has by returning to the opening question: how is time synthesized in our thought and practice today?

I return to the 'Leibnizian' hypothesis. The more complete a monad, the more numerous the data it memorizes, thus becoming capable of mediating what happens before reacting, and thus becoming less directly dependent on the event. So the more complete the monad, the more the incoming event is neutralized. For a monad supposed to be perfect, like God, there are in the end no bits of information at all. God has nothing to learn. In the mind of God, the universe is instantaneous.

The growth of techno-scientific systems appears to be drawn by this ideal of *Mathesis Universalis* or, to use Borges's metaphor, the library of Babel. Complete information means neutralizing more events. What is already known cannot, in principle, be experienced as an event. Consequently, if one wants to control a process, the best way of so doing is to subordinate the present to what is (still) called the 'future', since in these conditions the 'future' will be completely predetermined and the present itself will cease opening onto an uncertain and contingent 'afterwards'.

Better: what comes 'after' the 'now' will have to come 'before' it. In as much as a monad in thus saturating its memory is stocking the future, the present loses its privilege of being an ungraspable point from which, however, time should always distribute itself between the 'not yet' of the future and the 'no longer' of the past.

Now there is a model of such a temporal situation. It is offered by the daily practice of exchange. Someone (X) gives someone (Y) an object a at time t. This giving has as its condition that Y will give X an object b at time t'. I leave to one side here the classical question of knowing how a and b can be made equivalent. What is not irrelevant for us here is the fact that the first phase of the exchange takes place if and only if the second is perfectly guaranteed, to the point that it can be considered to have already happened.

There are many 'language games' – I prefer to say 'genres of discourse' – in which a later defined occurrence is expected, promised, etc., at the time the first takes place. But in the case of exchange, the 'second' occurrence, the payment, is not expected at the time of the first, it is presupposed as the condition of the 'first'. In this manner, the future conditions the present. Exchange requires that what is future be as if it were present. Guarantees, insurance policies, security are means of neutralizing the case as occasional, or, as we say, to forestall eventualities [*prévenir l'ad-venir*]. According to this way of treating time, suc-cess depends on the informational pro-cess, which consists in making sure that, at time t', nothing can happen other than the occurrence programmed at time t.

As for the lapse of time between t' and t, we can say that it is irrelevant to the essential principle of exchange we have just recalled. But it is none the less interesting, it must be said, in that it commands interest. The more the temporal gap increases, the more the chance increases of something unexpected happening – the greater the risk. The growth of risk can itself be calculated in terms of probability and in turn translated into monetary terms. Money here appears as what it really is, time stocked in view of forestalling what comes about. I shall not develop this idea further here.

Let us say merely that what is called capital is grounded in the principle that money is nothing other than time placed in reserve, available. It matters little whether this be after the event or in advance of what is called 'real time'. 'Real time' is only the moment at which the time conserved in the form of money is realized. What is important for capital is not the time already invested in goods and services, but the time still stored in stocks of 'free' or 'fresh' money, given that this represents the only time which can be used with a view to organizing the future and neutralizing the event.

We can say, then, that there is a tight and relevant correlation of what I have called the monad in expansion, produced by the techno-scientific apparatus, with the predominance of capitalism in the most 'developed' societies and, in particular, with the use of money in them. Capital must be seen not only as a major figure of human history, but also as the effect, observable on the earth, of a cosmic process of complexification. What is at stake with capitalism is certainly to make exchange and communication between human beings more flexible, as can be seen with the abandoning of the gold-standard in the evaluation of currency and the adoption of electronic methods of accountancy, by the institution of multinationals, etc. So many signs of the necessity of complexifying relations between human beings. Where can this come from if it is true that these results are not always profitable to humanity in general, nor even to the fraction of humanity supposed to benefit directly from them? Why do we have to save money and time to the point where this imperative seems like the law of our lives? Because saving (at the level of the system as a whole) allows the system to increase the quantity of money given over to anticipating the future. This is particularly the case with the capital invested in research and development. The enjoyment of humanity must, it is clear, be sacrificed to the interests of the monad in expansion.

Among the many effects of this undeniable hegemony, I shall mention only one. From its origins, mankind has set-up a specific means of controlling time – the narrative of myth. Myth allows a sequence of events to be placed in a constant framework in which the beginning and the end of a story form a sort of rhythm or rhyme, as Hölderlin put it. The idea of destiny long prevalent in human communities – and even today in the unconscious, if we are to believe Freud – presupposes the existence of a timeless agency which 'knows' in its totality the succession of moments constituting a life, be it individual or collective. What will happen is predetermined in the divine oracle, and human beings have as their only task that of unfolding identities already constituted in synchrony or achrony. Although given out at the time of Oedipus's birth, Apollo's oracle none the less prescribes in advance the destiny of the hero up until his death. This initial and summary attempt to neutralize the unexpected occurrence was abandoned as the techno-scientific spirit and the figure of capitalism came to maturity, both of them much more efficient in controlling time.

Very different, and yet very close, is the way modernity treats the problem. Modernity is not, I think, a historical period, but a way of shaping a sequence of moments in such a way that it accepts a high rate of contingency. It is not without significance that this formulation can be verified in works as diverse as those of Augustine, Kant and Husserl. The description of the temporal synthesis that I sketched out to begin with also belongs to modernity thus understood.

But what merits attention is that modern metaphysics none the less gave birth to the reconstitution of great narratives – Christianity, Enlightenment, romanticism, German speculative idealism, Marxism – which are not entirely foreign to mythical narratives. They do, certainly, imply that the future remains open as the ultimate aim of human history, under the name of emancipation. But they retain from myth the principle according to which the general course of history is conceivable.

The modern narrative, to be sure, induces a more political than ritual attitude. The fact remains that the ideal situated at the end of the narrative of emancipation is supposedly conceivable, even if it comprises, under the name of freedom, a sort of void or 'blank', a lack of definition, to be safeguarded. In other terms, destination [*Bestimmung*] is not destiny. But both designate a diachronic series of events whose 'reason' at least is judged to be explicable, on the one hand as destiny, by tradition, on the other as task, by political philosophy.

Unlike myth, the modern project certainly does not ground its legitimacy in the past, but in the future. And it is thus that it offers a better hold for the process of complexification. Having said this, it is one thing to project human emancipation, and another to programme the future as such. Liberty is not security. What some people have called the postmodern perhaps merely designates a break, or at least a splitting, between one pro- and the other – between project and programme. The latter seems today much better able than the former to meet the challenge thrown down to humanity by the process of complexification. But among the events which the programme attempts to neutralize as much as it can one must, alas, also count the unforeseeable effects engendered by the contingency and freedom proper to the human project.

V

As is only fitting, I shall not have the time to 'conclude' the argument. Let it suffice to say how foreign to my own way of thinking is the Leibnizian hypothesis I have just presented. A few 'theses' will show this briefly in conclusion.

(1) The techno-scientific apparatus which Heidegger calls the *Gestell* does indeed 'accomplish' metaphysics, as he writes. The principle of reason, the *Satz vom Grund*, locates reason in the field of 'physics' by virtue of the – metaphysical – postulate that every event in the world is to be explained as the effect of a cause and that reason consists in determining that cause (or that 'reason'), i.e. rationalizing the given and neutralizing the future. What are called the human sciences, for example, have become largely a branch of physics. Mind and even soul are studied as though they were interfaces in physical processes, and this is how computers are starting to be able to deliver simulacra of certain mental operations.

(2) Capital is not an economic and social phenomenon. It is the shadow cast by the principle of reason on human relations. Prescriptions such as: communicate, save time and money, control and forestall the event, increase exchanges, are all likely to extend and reinforce the 'great monad'. That 'cognitive' discourse has conquered hegemony over other genres, that in ordinary language, the pragmatic and interrelational aspect comes to the fore, whilst 'the poetic' appears to deserve less and less attention – all these features of the contemporary language-condition cannot be understood as effects of a simple modality of exchange, i.e. the one called 'capitalism' by economic and historical science. They are the signs that a new use of language is taking place, the stake of which is that of knowing objects as precisely as possible and of realizing

among ordinary speakers a consensus as broad as that supposed to reign in the scientific community.

As for knowledge, any object will do, but on a double condition: first that one can refer to this object in a logically and mathematically consistent vocabulary and syntax, the rules and terms of which can be communicated with minimal ambiguity; and, next, that some proof can be administered of the reality of the objects referred to by the propositions thus formed, by exhibiting sensory data judged relevant with respect to these objects.

The first condition has not only given birth to the remarkable rise of logical and mathematical formalism seen since the middle of the last century. It has also allowed the accreditation of new objects or new idealities (let's say new sentences) in mathematical and logical culture, and thus brought out new problems. The fact that it is now possible to formulate a good number of paradoxes that left the tradition in perplexity is the indubitable sign that the complexification of symbolic languages is progressing, and that the sciences are now appropriating objects which previously they ignored. It will be noted that many paradoxes belong more or less closely to the problematic of time. It suffices to mention questions such as that of recurrence (the use of the enigmatic expression 'and so on . . .'), in particular in the argumentation of the liar paradox (which Russell eliminates with his theory of types), the development of logics and linguistics of time which allow the difficult problems of modality to be solved or better posed, the mathematics of catastrophes (René Thom), the theory of relativity . . .

As for the second condition required by 'cognitive' language, which is the necessity of administering the proof of the assertion, it carries the implication that the technologies be continually developed. For if the propositions to be verified (or falsified) are to be more and more sophisticated, then the apparatus given the task of providing relevant sensory data must be indefinitely refined and complexified. Particle physics, electronics and data processing are today indispensable for conceiving (and realizing) most 'machines for proving'. I observe that capitalism is powerfully interested in this question of the proof. For the technologies required by the scientific process open the way for the production and distribution of new commodities, either directly committed to scientific research, or modified with a view to popular use. To this extent at least, means of knowledge become means of production, and capital appears as the most powerful, if it is not the only, apparatus for realizing the complexity attained in the field of cognitive languages. Capital does not govern the knowledge of reality, but it gives reality to knowledge.

It is often thought that if the economic system is led to behave in this way, it is because it is guided by the thirst for profit. And indeed, the use of scientific technologies in industrial production allows an increase in the quantities of surplus-value by saving on labour-time. Yet it seems that the 'ultimate' motor of this movement is not essentially of the order of human desire: it consists rather in the process of negentropy which appears to 'work' the cosmic area inhabited by the human race. One could go so far as to say that the desire for profit and wealth is no doubt no other than this process itself, working upon the nervous centres of the human brain and experienced directly by the human body.

(3) Thought today appears to be required to take part in the process of rationalization. Any other manner of thinking is condemned, isolated and rejected as irrational. Since the Renaissance and the classical age, let's say Galileo and Descartes, a latent conflict has opposed rationality to other ways of thinking and writing, and notably to metaphysics and literature. With the Vienna Circle, war is openly declared. In the name of the same motif, that of 'overcoming metaphysics', Carnap on the one hand and Heidegger on the other cut Western philosophy in two, logical positivism and poetic 'ontologie'. This break essentially affects the nature of language. Is language an instrument destined *par excellence* to provide the mind with the most exact knowledge of reality and to control as far as possible its transformation? In that case the true task of philosophy consists in helping science to free itself from the inconsistencies of natural languages by constructing a pure and univocal symbolic language. Or ought language to be thought after the fashion of a field of perception, capable of 'making sense' by itself independently of any intention to signify? Sentences, in that case, far from being under the responsibility of the speakers, should rather be thought of as discontinuous and spasmodic concretions of a continuous 'speaking medium', like Heidegger's *Sage*, that same medium called on by Malraux and Merleau-Ponty under the name of 'voices of silence', a medium that in French we would call *langagier* rather than *linguistique*.

We can say that the first option fits up to a point with the type of 'rationality' demanded by the monad in expansion. But what limits its perfect merging with complexity is the remains of humanist philosophy which is paradoxically written into the principle that language is an instrument used by the human mind. For it is possible, and has been the case, that a good number of propositions, even though well formed and well established according to the criteria of the new sciences, are at first sight neither useful nor obvious to the human mind. Now this very difficulty can precisely be seen as a sign that the real 'user' of language is not the human mind *qua* human, but complexity in movement, of which mind is only a transitory support. It does not follow from communicating in general and from making every assertion communicable that a greater transparency of the human community to itself is favoured; it follows simply that a greater number of pieces of information can be combined with others so that their totality comes to form an operational, flexible and efficient system – the monad.

As for the second option, which I called ontological, it is by its nature turned towards those modes of language which do not aim solely to describe exhaustively the objects to which they refer. Among these language modes, one can mention, for various reasons, free conversation, reflexive judgement and meditation, free association (in the psychoanalytical sense), the poetic and literature, music, the visual arts, everyday language. What matters in these modes is clearly the fact that all should generate occurrences before knowing the rules of this generativity, and that some of them even have no concern for determining those rules. This is the fact that Kant and the Romantics, especially, thematized under the rubric of genius, of a nature acting in the mind itself. One can also refer the discursive genres I'm talking about to the principle of a productive imagination. But it will be noted that such an imagination plays no less a role in science itself, the role of the heuristic moment it needs if it is to progress. What these diverse or even heterogeneous forms have in common is the freedom and the lack of preparation with which language shows itself capable of receiving what can happen in the 'speaking medium', and of being accessible to the event. To the point at which one can wonder whether the true complexity does not consist in this passibility rather than in the activity of 'reducing and constructing' language, as Carnap proposed to do.

Finally, a rationality does not deserve its name if it denies its part in the open passibility and uncontrolled creativity there is in most languages, including the cognitive. To the extent that it really does comprise such a denial, technical, scientific and economic rationality would deserve the name of 'ideology', if that term did not in turn carry too many metaphysical presuppositions. Anyway, it is certain that the model of consensus which, it is claimed, is borrowed from the argumentative community of the sciences and is proposed as an ideal for human sciences shows to what extent that 'rationality' exercises its hegemony over the diversity of discursive genres which language has in potential. This rationality can only be said to be rational if one has accepted as sole value the performativity which commands the logic of the great monad faced with the cosmological challenge.

(4) It will come as no surprise that the hypothesis I adopt is the second. Being prepared to receive what thought is not prepared to think is what deserves the name of thinking. As I have said, this attitude is to be found in reputedly rational language as much as in the poetic, in art, ordinary language, if, that is, it is essential to the cognitive discourse to progress.

One cannot, consequently, admit the crude separation of sciences and arts prescribed by modern Western culture. As we know, it has as its corollary the relegation of the arts and literature to the miserable function of distracting human beings from what hounds and harrasses them all the time, i.e. the obsession of controlling time. I know that the resistance one can oppose to the process of formation and expansion of the great monad will do nothing to change this. But it must never be forgotten that if thinking indeed consists in receiving the event, it follows that no-one can claim to think without being *ipso facto* in a position of resistance to the procedures for controlling time.

To think is to question everything, including thought, and question, and the process. To question requires that something happen that reason has not yet known. In thinking, one accepts the occurrence for what it is: 'not yet' determined. One does not prejudge it, and there is no security. Peregrination in the desert. One cannot write without bearing witness to the abyss of time in its coming.

In this respect, we must distinguish two ways of assuming the questioning, according as the stress is or is not placed on the urgency of the reply. The principle of reason is the way of questioning which rushes to its goal, the reply. It involves a sort of impatience in the single presupposition that in any case one can always find a 'reason' or a cause for every question. Non–Western traditions of thought have a quite different attitude. What counts in their manner of questioning is not at all to determine the reply as soon as possible, to seize and exhibit some object which will count as the cause of the phenomenon in question. But to be and remain questioned by it, to stay through meditation responsive to it, without neutralizing by explanation its power of disquiet. In the very heart of Western culture, such an attitude has, or had, its analogue in the manner of being and thinking which issued from the Judaic tradition. What this tradition calls 'study' and 'reading' requires that any reality be treated as an obscure message addressed by an unknowable or even unnameable agency. As to a verse of the Torah, one must listen to the phenomenon, decipher and interpret it, of course, but with humour, without forgetting that this interpretation will itself be interpreted as a message no less enigmatic, Levinas would say no less marvellous, than the initial event. Derrida's problematic of deconstruction and *différance*, Deleuze's principle of nomadism belong, however different they may be, to this approach to time. In it, time remains uncontrolled, does not give rise to work, or at least not in the customary sense of the word 'work'.

A last remark on what has been called passibility. It would be presumptuous, not to say criminal, for a thinker or a writer to claim to be the witness or guarantor of the event. It must be understood that what testifies is not at all the entity, whatever it be, which claims to be in charge of this passibility to the event, but the event 'itself'. What memorizes or retains is not a capacity of the mind, not even accessibility to what occurs, but, in the event, the ungraspable and undeniable 'presence' of a something which is other than mind and which, 'from time to time', occurs . . .

(5) Heidegger tried to ground the resistance I am talking about on the Greek model of art understood as *techne*. However, since Plato, art or *Dichtung* has been

conceived of as a remodelling, a *plattein*, and it has been the principal mode in which politics has sought to fashion the community according to this or that metaphysical ideal. Following Lacoue-Labarthe in this, I think that there exists a narrow and essential correlation between the art of politics and the fine arts. An outstanding case of this combination is to be found in Plato's *Republic*: the problem of politics consists only in observing the correct model, which is the model of the Good, in fashioning the human community. *Mutatis mutandis*, the same principle is to be found in the political philosophies of the Middle Ages, the Renaissance and modernity.

Nazism in a sense reversed the relation: here it is 'art' which explicitly stands in for politics. As is well known, the Nazis made a widespread and systematic use of myth, of the media, of mass culture and the new technologies with a view to bringing about the total mobilization of energy in all its forms. In this way they inscribe in facts the Wagnerian dream of 'the total work of art'. Syberberg has shown that the *Gesamtkunstwerk* is realized in the cinema, in *tele-techne* in general, much more than in opera. Politics today, with different justifications, sometimes with opposite arguments, is of the same nature. In what is called modern democracy, there persists the hegemony of the principle according to which the opinion of the masses must be seduced and led by what I would call 'tele-graphic' procedures, by the various types of 'inscription-at-a-distance' descriptions and prescriptions. And in this sense, one Nazism has won: as total mobilization.

(6) In so far as they do not allow themselves to be subordinated to 'tele-graphy', thought and writing are isolated and placed in the ghetto, in the sense in which the work of Kafka deploys that theme. But this term 'ghetto' is not here simply a metaphor. The Jews of Warsaw were not only doomed to death, they also had to pay for the 'protection measures' taken against them, starting with the wall that the Nazis decided to erect against the supposed threat of a typhoid epidemic. The same goes for writers and thinkers: if they resist the predominant use of time today, they are not only predestined to disappear, but they must also contribute to the making of a 'sanitary cordon' isolating themselves. In the shelter of this cordon, their destruction is supposed to be able to be put off for a while. But they 'buy' this brief and vain delay by modifying their way of thinking and writing in such a way that their works become more or less communicable, exchangeable; in a word, commercializable. But the exchange, the buying and selling of ideas and words, does not fail to contribute, contradictorily to the 'final solution' of the problem: how to write, how to think? I mean that they contribute to making even more hegemonic the great rule of controlled time. It follows that public space, *Öffentlichkeit*, in these conditions, stops being the space for experiencing, testing and affirming the state of a mind open to the event, and in which the mind seeks to elaborate an idea of that state itself,

especially under the sign of the 'new'. Public space today is transformed into a market of cultural commodities, in which 'the new' has become an additional source of surplus-value.

(7) When the point is to extend the capacities of the monad, it seems reasonable to abandon, or even actively to destroy, those parts of the human race which appear superfluous, useless for that goal. For example, the populations of the Third World. A more specific meaning attaches to the choice Nazism made of the European Jews for extermination. I said that this part of the ancient European heritage – Judaic thought – represents a way of thinking entirely turned towards the incessant, interminable listening to and interpretation of a voice. This is what Heidegger's thought, fascinated by the Greek model, completely missed and completely lacked.

(8) As for the voice which prescribes 'You must resist (to the extent that you must think or write)', it of course implies that the problem of the present time is in no way to communicate. What holds the attention and is a question is much rather what this prescription presupposes: what or who is the author (the sender) of this commandment? What is its legitimacy? It is to be thought that this order orders that the question be left open, if it is true that this 'you must' preserves and reserves the coming of the future in its unexpectedness.

Part IV

Art

Introduction: Art-events

Thinking With Painting

Lyotard is much more than an art theorist, philosopher of art or art critic. His philosophy is written in conjunction with art, in particular painting, to the point where it is more accurate to speak of a 'co-creation', rather than a 'theorising-about'. He was an exhibition curator (for example, for 'Les immatériaux' at the Pompidou Centre, Paris, 1985). He wrote exhibition catalogues – for large shows, but also for smaller galleries. His many books and articles on individual artists and groups are an – as yet – under-estimated and relatively little known aspect of his work (see, for example, his works on Barruchello, Monory, Buren, Adami, Arakawa, Francken, Maccheroni, Duchamp, Newman). These books are among his most beautiful; they serve alongside and add to the better-known philosophical works.

Lyotard's knowledge and works on painting are extremely wide-ranging and innovative. They stretch from cave painting, through the middle ages, the renaissance, the enlightenment, the nineteenth and twentieth centuries, up to the most avant-garde works of his day. In covering all of these areas, his *Discours, figure* is one of the most important essays on art written in the twentieth century. Its thesis is that works of art are figural events where desire, matter and structures meet and are transformed in a way that always goes beyond any given discourse or narrative.

Art always exceeds what can be said about it. It does so in such a way as to transform intellectual and narrative contexts. To do this, art depends upon and releases matter understood in a strongly sensual and libidinal way. Through art, the productive power of desire is released in creative and troubling ways. This take on art can be seen as a radical version of the thesis on the interpretative openness of artworks, but allied to a sense that this openness is owed to the materiality and sensuousness of art, rather than to any property of interpretation.

The range of Lyotard's work can therefore be explained by the fact that he does not limit art-events to any given epoch, style or medium. Instead, works are events in the way they bring ways of sensing and ways of describing together with transformative desires. In any epoch, the art-event is a challenge to commentaries on art and much wider forms of thought (social, political, scientific, technical and philosophical). It is also a conduit for desires and the locus for sensations (in a strong sense of shocks, rather than well-managed perceptions).

This means that when Lyotard defends the figural in art, or the art of the avant-garde, or postmodern art, he is not limiting it to particular artists or times. Rather, he is making the surprising claim that works are not avant-garde through their artistic innovations, but as material events that erupt within many different forms of discursive and sensual contexts. This explains why his writing on art does not limit itself to any one of the work, the artist, the reception of the work, the feelings that it causes, or the discourse around it. Instead, all of them must come together in a description that attempts to convey the event.

We chose Campbell Sandilands' work for the cover of this book because his 'Luminescence' has the figural quality described by Lyotard; it is a strongly physical and material work that keeps us on the edge of sense and of a comprehensible sign (traceable back to Sandilands' long training in Japanese calligraphy and woodblock prints). It is a work that is neither representational nor fully abstract, but an event somewhere between the two, that invites us to interpret, whilst also thwarting any final interpretation, remaining between feeling and understanding thanks to what Lyotard calls matter:

> It has been represented without continuity, without memory, and without mind (neither images nor ideas) in order to get the closest possible fix on the mystery of sensation: a given sensible material (a sound, a scent, etc., to which we join, provisionally and with reservations, the word and the sentence, if it is true that literature deals with them as the matter of language), a given sensible material awakening an affect.[1]

There are two basic, but common, mistakes to be made about Lyotard's work on art. First, he is not a philosopher of postmodern art in the sense of an art that comes after a modern epoch and that has certain fixed characteristics, such as lack of cohesion, multiple heterogeneous styles or messages, and a simulated, fake quality. He often criticises this form of art for its lack of emotional power and inner movement.

So art from all epochs can be postmodern for Lyotard, but, ironically, what is commonly known as postmodern is the least likely to satisfy his special definition. There is indeed a connection to heterogeneity, but this is not in terms of content; rather, it is in terms of resistance to any given discourse and set of values, and in terms of its openness to multiple effects through its relation to desire. Art conveys difference and heterogeneity by bringing different accounts together in a way that resists merging or synthesising them.

The second common mistake is that avant-garde art does not necessarily mean modernist works that go beyond emerging traditions through boundary-breaking innovation. For Lyotard, the avant-garde does not imply a relation to an artistic tradition, or a particular capacity to scandalise, or very marked novelty. Instead, it means works that challenge a very open set of discourses, rather than a specific artistic tradition. It also means shock, not only on the grand scale, but also as a disturbance of a well-ordered relation between perceptions, tastes, values, economic exchanges and forms of knowledge. The avant-garde creates a disturbance through new desires and sensations, rather than merely through 'new' artistic forms.

For example, one of the key moments of *Discours, figure* involves an intricate and highly original account of the use of illustration in medieval religious texts. Lyotard is interested in the way the fine artwork on letters and illustrations adds to the meaning of the texts (for example, in bibles illustrated by hand). He observes this in terms of the complicated processes that link pictures, figures, words and meaning. Religious sense, desire and representation are articulated but also given new intensity through the use of illustrations. These are the figural moments of the texts and they make them events, just as much as the more familiar sense of the twentieth-century avant-garde that Lyotard writes about in his book on Duchamp (*Duchamp's TRANS/formers*), for example.

In *Discours, figure*, Lyotard expands on the function of the figural by explaining it in terms of the creative functions of displacement, condensation and deformation. These functions bring together given structures of discourse and their accompanying phenomena (forms of bodies, for example) with novel affects or feelings that are themselves the expressions of as-yet uncharted desire. The artwork displaces the many different ideas and accounts that surround it. It condenses them by bringing different and apparently heterogeneous ones together. But it also deforms them through the introduction of new feelings and desires within them.

For example, again, here is Lyotard's explanation of the deconstructive power of a Picasso drawing:

> The coexistence of many contours induces a simultaneity of many points of view. The scene where this woman sleeps does not belong to the 'real' space, since it tolerates many positions for a body in a same time and space. Erotic indifference to time and to reality in favour of postures.[2]

Picasso shows us how figures work in a different form of time and space than the one we ordinarily associate with reality. Desire is a relation to many postures in one space.

According to Lyotard, we literally experience a multiplicity in Picasso's drawing and in other relations to desired flesh and postures. The drawing is an event that undermines the notion that all things have clearly-defined spatial and temporal limits. Traces, in the sense of boundaries, do not reveal the proper limits of an object. They can be made to reveal many incommensurable limits in one place. For Lyotard, desire and sensations are driven by such events. In art-events, reality is opened up and shown to be much more than what is defined by a given discourse and understanding of reference.

This meshing of desire, of the political and of creativity, leads to Lyotard's commitment to the avant-garde as an artistic form that goes way beyond the artistic realm. Art is political because it challenges and transforms a wide range of social and political structures. This transformation can be found, in *Discours, figure*, in the study of the introduction of perspective in the quattrocento:

> The window traced by Masaccio on the wall does not give on to the discovery of a world, but of its loss, one could say that it is its discovery as lost. The window is not open and, in allowing us to see, the pane of representation separates. It makes that space oscillate over there, not here (as in a *trompe l'oeil*), nor elsewhere, as in Duccio.[3]

As avant-garde, perspective does not negate a world and confirm another. It challenges both of them by showing their relation and by introducing desires and feelings that mark the limits of all narratives in all worlds.

In short, Lyotard does not give a definition of art according to a fixed set of properties, functions or values. He defines art as an event that disturbs and transforms any such set. This explains the variety and sensitivity of his work on art and artists. He does not so much write on the artwork or artist, but with them. He does not seek to judge or categorise works. Instead, the work is revealed in its individual power to transform what art is taken to be and how it is taken to work. His leading question is always 'How can this combination work as an event?'

Art, Dispositions and Desires

In *Des dispositifs pulsionnels* (1973), Lyotard develops his work from *Discours, figure* towards the work on desire and structures from *Libidinal Economy*. *Des dispositifs pulsionnels* includes two of Lyotard's most important essays on art: 'Freud selon Cézanne' and 'Painting as a Libidinal Set-up' (translated here). Cézanne greatly influenced Lyotard's writing. References to him recur through his career. The essay on Cézanne is Lyotard's longest engagement with his paintings, whereas the latter essay is his strongest defence of the variety and openness of painting. He calls this the 'polymorphous' quality of painting.

The essay on Cézanne is important through the distance it takes from phenomenology and from Merleau-Ponty's famous discussion of Cézanne in 'Le doute de Cézanne' in *Sens et non-sens*. The difference between the two thinkers lies in Lyotard's uncompromising appeal to Freud and to desire, in contrast to Merleau-Ponty's appeal to a psychoanalysis tempered by human freedom. The former account is strongly materialist in describing the event of art as a function that does not depend on free human creativity or reception, or to any priority of the human body, flesh, unconscious and sensations. Instead, a much wider set of discursive structures, machine-like functions, and intense desires explains the power and revolutionary aspect of Cézanne's works. These structures and functions include human ones, but do not presuppose them.

Lyotard describes Cézanne's painting as a search for powerlessness, that is, as the search for a way of painting that allows desire, in its relation to matter, to flow through both the work and the artist, rather than be controlled or channelled through judgements and conscious selections. In order to do this, the artist must resist the dominance of established ways of feeling, painting, seeing, valuing and judging. The conscious acts and selections of painters are some of the strongest of these forms, This is why Lyotard advocates a search for passivity in art and in politics.

However, it is not that Lyotard thinks that art can just be about matter and desire. These are necessarily channelled through structures, for example through the ways we represent them, give form to them, exploit them in economic systems, set them into narratives, and associate them with objects, colours and valuations (hard/soft, good/bad). Against this necessity, though, the challenge for an artist is to release matter anew in order for it, in turn, to release transforming desires into the structures that entrap matter. Painting is revolutionary because it must experiment with the destruction of familiar ways of feeling and knowing, in order to reveal the open potential and power of matter – it can take hold of us and take us outside fixed ways of thinking and sensing.

It could be thought that this means that the effect of art wears off as an artwork becomes less relevant to structures, narratives and values. Art would then necessarily become out-of-date. A more traditional sense of the need for avant-garde could then be attributed mistakenly to Lyotard: there is a need for a constant renewal of art, as earlier forms lose their power. This is not his view since, for art-works to have released desires into structures, they must have had an original independence from them and a capacity to connect desire and matter that stands outside the process of historical erasure of discourses. Once a good conductor of intensities, always a good conductor of intensities.

This shows up well in Lyotard's discussion of Cézanne's paintings through his treatment of them as pure or absolute objects, that is, as things that stand outside any given reception and perception of them. However, this does not mean that Lyotard sees works as fixed – as if they were still and abstract, or as if they had an essence that could be defined in terms of identifiable properties. On the contrary, the pure object is a movement and it is as such that it connects to desire and captures matter (in the equally pure sense of something that varies and vibrates, rather than remains constricted in a representation or container).

This explains why Lyotard describes paintings as turning, vibrating, trans-forming. He seeks to express the movement within them and how that move-ment connects to desires as they themselves are set to work in undermining and overcoming structures. For example, in Cézanne's paintings, colour is liberated from encircling and containing lines, as well as from recognisable figures. The colours work together, free of the mediation of containers, and thereby help us to understand how sensation is not dependent on representation and spatial limits. Any given idea and concept, for example of the Montagne Sainte Victoire painted many times by Cézanne, falls short when we sense the role of colours in our desires and sensations prior to any conceptualisation.

Art's power to move is timeless, but it is also political. For Lyotard, art has a revolutionary social and political role, because it transforms the structures that surround it, by infusing them with new and unmanageable desires. This does not mean that art must participate in traditional political debate or support and depict forms of government. Rather, it means that works of art remind us of the limits of the political structures and economic systems that channel our energies and desires. They can do this on a grand scale, for example, in con-necting desires and corruption. But they can also do it on a micro-scale, for example, in releasing unexpected desires into apparently well-ordered patterns of life.

On the large scale, Lyotard has always seen art as capable of challenging capitalism by working new desires and immeasurable values into society. This resistance to monetary value can only ever be fleeting, in the sense that new art is eventually given its exchange value. It is also timeless, because monetary value is only one of the forms of exchange and desire that art carries. It always brings in many others and these cannot be reduced to monetary measures.

On a smaller scale, the polymorphous quality of art allows it to range over many different sensual and material experiences and events. In so doing, it draws together heterogeneous structures and desires, forcing them into new arrangements and calling for new structures as well as for the recognition of new desires (though this recognition must always be a form of betrayal, due to the impossibility of representing a desire independent of a structure that reduces its openness).

This is political because systems and structures depend on the definition of limits, of inclusions and exclusions, and on the definition of hierarchies, of good and bad, high and low. That dependence is broken by art and shown to be contingent rather than necessary. Political and social values are always secondary to art and imposed from the outside. Thanks to its capacity to change in line with the open and creative relation of matter and desire, art always exceeds the social determinations and political narratives that we try to impose upon it.

The painter, the work and the viewer are all potential targets of this artistic-political activity. Traditional views of the subject as producer of art (genius or high-technician), or of the work as well-located precious object, or of the viewer as educated judge are challenged in Lyotard's studies. At times, it seems that his works are an invention of art, rather than a commentary upon it.

> The destruction of composition is that of the painter-subject. Guiffrey never signs his work, never gives them titles, does not keep catalogues. He therefore abolishes himself as their owner. But all his force is dedicated to leaving the space alone . . . Painting is not the painter's expression. There is no painter. Only lines, surfaces, brilliance, that must be produced as ungraspable.[4]

The Sublime

Around the publication of *The Differend* in 1983 and thereafter, much of Lyotard's writing was dominated by work on the Kantian sublime. This is reflected very strongly in the collection *The Inhuman*, where Lyotard develops a series of essays that investigate the power of the sublime across many different areas. A more technical analysis of the sublime is given in the long study of Kant's *Critique of Judgement* in *Lessons on the Analytic of the Sublime*.

The work on the sublime is original and – whilst drawing heavily on Kant – Lyotard can be seen as having added a new chapter to this long-standing topic, which dates back at least to Longinus and takes in Burke and Schopenhauer, amongst others. The most significant divergence from Kant lies in the revaluation of the sublime over the beautiful and over taste. This reversal also involves a focus on the power of art to work through 'dissensus' rather than consensus. Where Kant sees the beautiful as the basis for the deduction of a *sensus communis* (a common sense underlying, though not determining, taste), Lyotard defines the sublime as a feeling that can reveal the limits and failures of any emergent taste or common sense. The most important essay on the difference between consensus and dissensus is Lyotard's much reproduced 'Sensus Communis'.

Lyotard's sublime has two main functions. First, it is an explanation for the way events stand beyond representation. The occurrence of feelings of the sublime depends on a failure of our powers of grasping and understanding an event. This is because the sublime involves a combination of pleasure and pain, where the pain comes from the frustration of our cognitive faculties. We are attracted to something (pleasure) but when we try to understand it, we fail (pain).

The second function of the sublime is to accompany a clash of ways of handling events (understanding and reason, for example). The feeling of the sublime shows how this clash is necessary and how different ways or regimes are incommensurable, that is, have no common measure and cannot justly be brought together in a wider narrative. Events do not only undo representation, they also undo hopes to reconcile different narratives. There is therefore a connection between the work on the sublime and Lyotard's earlier work in *Discours, figure*, his disbelief in meta-narratives from *The Postmodern Condition*, and his later work on the ungraspable materiality of a wide range of bodily sensations.

The work on the sublime is especially marked by two essays on the American abstract impressionist Barnett Newman ('Newman: The Instant' and 'The Sublime and the Avant-garde', both in *The Inhuman*). Lyotard's description of Newman's works makes a series of points that clarify the definition of the sublime. The paintings are ungraspable instants in themselves. They do not refer to another time or to heterogeneous times (something that Lyotard associates with his earlier libidinal work and Duchamp). Instead, the sublime work and sensation is the occurrence of an instant that calls to us and, at the same time, thwarts us. Lyotard calls this the event as *'Arrive-t-il?'*, translatable as 'Is it coming?'

As such, the sublime is also an obligation. Its occurrence obliges us to attempt to respond, despite our sense of the impossibility of finding a final just response – this is impossible because the instant cannot be grasped fully. Newman's painting therefore connects with the ethical turn of Lyotard's later works: to testify to events in their resistance to representation and resolution. To be ethical is to refuse to make claims to final understandings and Newman's works present us with events that guide us in this ethical stance. In Lyotard's words, this is to 'present the unpresentable'.

Whilst this ethical aspect of the sublime is not particularly new, Lyotard gives it a very original turn by breaking with the traditional subject-matter of sublime art. For him, Newman's works are not completely abstract, but neither do they take traditional figures of grand scale, of nature at its most powerful and terri-fying as their theme. Instead, the subject is the 'now', not in terms of what happens now, but in terms of the time in which something can happen, but prior to any identification. The sublime is the now as an event that has no fixed identifiable content. The sublime experience of Newman's painting is of some-thing that happens (the zip of light amidst the textured darkness of the back-ground) but of no particular something: 'What is sublime is the feeling that something will happen, despite everything, within this threatening void, that something will take "place" and will announce that everything is not over. That place is a mere "here", the most minimal occurrence.'[5]

There is also a religious aspect to Lyotard's work on the sublime, but it has little to do with organised religious doctrine and morality. Rather, in combin-ing an ethical obligation with an experience of a failure of representation, the sublime comes close to Judaism in its refusal to represent God. We are not called forth by an image, but by its absence. This absence is not pure, but conveyed by a minimal sense of matter in conjunction with feelings. Here, the sublime conjunction of pleasure and pain, taken from Kant, is supplemented by a terror and relief taken from Burke. The terror is that nothing might happen – the nihilistic sense of a void, time might stop. The relief is only partial – there is happening, but we know not what.

In many ways, however, the work on the sublime gives a skewed view of Lyotard's work on art, unless the material and unconscious aspects of that work are emphasised. In later essays, he retains the themes of the event and the idea that art is about moments beyond representation, but he also shows how artworks convey hidden and forgotten parts of experience. Following Freud, Lyotard describes art as a working-through or anamnesis. It triggers purely sensual experiences that bar the way for understanding and reason, but that let the unconscious flow through us in productive ways.

The later essay 'Painting, Anamnesis of the Visible' defends the capacity of art to speak for that which has been hidden and forgotten, or that which cannot be said in other ways. The holocaust is the most important event for this anamnesis. Art can bear testimony without betraying an unspeakable horror in mere figures or in representational narratives that flatten out any uniqueness. This capacity to witness stems from the connection between the sensual power of matter and its otherness.

Lyotard's later works on art return to his earlier ideas from *Discours, figure* to describe multiple, and sometimes minimal, experiences that remind us of otherness. We can never fully understand another's words or deeds, but we are destined to forget this. This forgetting can be worked through when art–events trigger a sensual awareness of an unbridgeable gap that is also a connection. This experience can be auditory, in the experience of the singular resonance of another's voice prior to language. We may use the same words, but the material vibrations that carry them are singular. In the throat and ear, we connect and disconnect at the same time.

In painting, colour is the material conductor for this experience of otherness and for the uncovering of an unconscious that cannot simply be recaptured and understood. Colours engulf and disturb what they fill. For Lyotard, this disconnection between colour and object reminds us of the fragility of objects and of our relation to them. As such, colour is not only something that brings an excessive intensity and life to things; it is also that which lends them a deathly aspect, because their known colour can fade, disappear, be distorted, or pass into others. There is still a relation to the work on the sublime in this later study. Colour comes out of nothing to fill a void, but also disturbs what we think we know and hold, drawing things closer to nothingness whilst giving them life.

This fusion of matter, emotion and thought sums up Lyotard's work on art. He follows and values artworks when they awaken what he calls the thought–body in us, that is, a soul in tune with something that holds reflection in suspense and that instead puts us in direct touch with events. Yet these events themselves undo our hold on them and teach us that matter is never to be captured because it always exceeds knowledge. The 'system' may exploit and repress desires and sensations, but matter and art can always reawaken them, so they may haunt us anew.

Notes

1. Lyotard, 'Anima Minima' in *Postmodern Fables*, p. 249.
2. Lyotard, *Discours, figure*, p. 277.
3. Ibid. p. 201.
4. Lyotard, 'En attendant Guiffrey', in *Des dispositifs pulsionnels*, p. 219.
5. Lyotard, 'Newman: The Instant', in *The Lyotard Reader and Guide*, p. 335.

Chapter 15

The Connivances of Desire with the Figural

The hypothesis which guides Freud in understanding the dreamwork is a radical connivance between the figure and desire. It allows him to establish a strong link between the order of desire and that of the figural through the category of transgression: the 'text' of the preconscious (day's residues, memory-traces) undergoes disruptions which make it unrecognizable, illegible; the deep matrix in which desire is caught thrives on this illegibility: it expresses itself in disordered forms and hallucinatory images.

Let us examine this machinery. Three kinds of components may be distinguished. The *image-figure* I see in hallucinations or dreams, the one paintings or films present, is an object set at a distance, a theme. It belongs to the visible order; it is a revealing 'trace'. The *form-figure* is present in the perceptible, it may even be visible, but is in general not seen: André Lhote calls it 'tracé régulateur,' the Gestalt of a configuration, the architecture of a painting, in short, the schema. The *matrix-figure* is invisible in principle, subject to primal repression, immediately intermixed with discourse, primal phantasy. It is nonetheless a figure, not a structure, because it consists in a violation of discursive order from the outset, in a violence done to the transformations that this order authorizes. It cannot be intelligibly apprehended, for this very apprehension would make its immersion in the unconscious unintelligible. This immersion attests, however, that what is in question is indeed the 'other' of discourse and intelligibility. To establish the *matrix-figure* in a textual, *a fortiori* systematic space would be to imagine it as an ἀρχή, to entertain a double phantasy: first that of an origin, and then that of an utterable origin. Far from being an origin, the phantasmatic matrix demonstrates to the contrary, that our origin is an absence of origin and that everything that appears as the object of a primal discourse is an hallucinatory *image-figure*, located precisely in this initial non-locus.

Image, form and matrix are figures inasmuch as each one of them belongs to the space of the figural according to a strict articulation specific to each one. Freud's energetic model of the reflex apparatus helps us understand this articulation. The economic hypothesis he derived from this was that all unpleasure is a charge, all pleasure a discharge. Pleasure obeys the principle according to which the discharge of energy is always sought through the most expeditious means: the aim is to return the psychical apparatus to a state of minimal excitation.[1] According to this principle, energy circulates freely within the psychical system, ready to be cathected into this or that zone, indifferently, as long as the zone offers the possibility of a discharge. This property of processes subject to the pleasure principle reveals the unbound character of the energy it uses. On the contrary, when the expenditure of energy is subordinated to the reality principle, the function it obeys is no longer to cancel all tension, but to maintain energy at a constant level: and more importantly still, the discharge cannot take place in just any zone of the psychical apparatus: some of these zones are open to others through facilitation but others are isolated by obstacles and the whole set of bindings regulating associations and exclusions is controlled by the Ego. The principle of this reality subordinates the possibility of a discharge to the transformation of the relationship between the apparatus and the external world, through the use of language, through motor activity, or both. Starting from perceptions and memory of perceptions, through word-presentations, the flow of energy moves toward the centers and organs of motor activity: Freud calls this the 'progressive' path.[2]

Guided by Fechner's psycho-analysis model as it might be, this description nevertheless already contains, metaphorically, a theme never to be disavowed and which is essential to the location of the figural. The space in which energy moves is qualitatively different, according as it is free or bound. The space of pleasure and that of reality are not the same. This already appears in Freud's analysis of the infantile condition — which is and remains the adult's condition. When faced by an 'internal' stimulus, before the secondary process is established and thus does not yet allow the modification of the outer world necessary for the discharge to occur, the subject is in a state of 'motorische Hilflosigkeit,' of motor helplessness:[3] in the absence of the specific action[4] whose performance would relieve the pressure of the need, the satisfaction of this need is entirely dependent on an external person. Three givens will thus be disassociated: the motor component of the reflex movement, e.g. the sucking accompanying the discharge: the affective component of satisfaction: the sensory component of the object whose intercession suppresses anxiety and permits the discharge. 'The first wishing seems to have been a hallucinatory cathecting of the memory of satisfaction.'[5] Desire thus is born through 'anaclisis' (attachment):[6] sexuality as a search for pleasure is buttressed by the instinct of self-preservation, which can be satisfied only through the specific action of a specific organ: it grasps the instinctual aim (satisfaction) and its object (the organ of the specific action) as the means of pleasure. Desire develops as a power for pleasure disconnected from the satisfaction of need.

Wish fulfillment (*Wunscherfüllung*) contains in itself the absence of its object. Essential to desire, this absence is constitutive of its relation to any object which claims to be *its* object. Likewise, one could say that the 'absence' of the organ is what characterizes desire's use of the body: organs are not seen by desire as a means to satisfy the need, but as erogenous zones whose excitation induces the staging of phantasy. The body is thus diverted. It is also fragmented: in self-preservation, the specific function is in principle subordinated to the survival of the organism as a whole: for desire, every organ is a possible erogenous zone, cathecting the organ becomes an end in itself if it provides for the production of the phantasies which fulfil desire. The disruption of realist and biological space which accompanies anaclisis is thus obvious.

Freud gives us an idea of this upheaval when he stresses the importance of regression.[7] Hallucinatory fulfillment is regressive in three ways: first, because it takes the retrogressive course of the psychical apparatus, contrary to what happens in specific action. Action starts from the excitation, goes through memory-traces, verbal traces, the motor zones, produces a transformation of reality and finally provides satisfaction as an outward discharge. In the fulfillment of desire, excitation passes through the different layers of the apparatus in the reverse direction and cathects perceptual memories with such an intensity that it induces the hallucination. The displacement of energy towards the perceptual end instead of the verbal-motor end is therefore regressive. This regression is the result of the principle of the immediate discharge at the lowest possible cost, or Nirvana principle. But regression also takes place in an historical sense, because the memory of the first satisfaction is reactivated like a return to the infantile experience. And above all, regression is characterized by the use of 'primitive methods of expression and representation in place of the usual ones;'[8] 'We call it regression when in a dream, an idea is turned back into the sensory image from which it was originally derived.'[9] There is an 'attraction which memories couched in visual form exert over thoughts separated from consciousness.'[10] Regression is produced as much by this as by the complementary action of censorship. What is at work is the elaboration of disfigured figures in place of recognizable figures, of rebuses in place of texts, is not only prohibition, but also desire's own force operating in its distinctive space and according to its specific relation with representation. Here, the figural is understood as the antipode of the verbal and the motor, i.e. of the reality principle with its two functions, language and action. To these two functions, desire turns its back.

This very 'otherness' is also the subject of an analysis subsequently carried out in order to characterize the unconscious;[11] Freud attempts to make the unconscious space intelligible by continually contrasting it with the space where processes under preconscious control are produced. The four characteristics he retains are: first of all, the absence of 'negations, of doubts, of degrees of certainty' or 'the absence of contradictions;'[12] unconscious 'judgements' have no modality and no quality, they are always assertive and positive. Secondly, 'the cathecting intensities (in the Ucs) are much more mobile:'[13] the unbound character of energy characterizes what Freud calls the primary process; the 'free' movements of this energy, he says, are displacement and condensation. These operations are explicitly held to impede the secondary process, i.e. perception, motility and *articulated language*. The third feature of the unconscious processes is that they are 'timeless; i.e. they are not ordered temporally, are not altered by the passing of time; they have no reference to time at all.'[14] Finally, the unconscious processes 'pay just as little regard to reality,' they are subject to the pleasure principle, to the 'substitution of psychical reality for external reality.'[15] As a result, these processes not only do not enter into the categories of judgement (modality, quality) but they do not even obey the fundamental constraints of discourse: condensation violates lexical constraints, displacement and the disregard for temporality violate the constraints of syntax. As for indifference to reality, it manifests both a refusal to consider (linguistic) reference and a disdain for the dimension of designation. Unconscious processes transgress the two spaces of discourse, i.e. that of the system and that of reference. The space which contains them and that they themselves produce is then another space, differing from that of the system in that it is incessant mobility and from that of reference in its treating words like things. Mobility in the systematic field of language and of the order of discourse short-circuits sense and introduces 'non-sense;' transgression of the referential distance leads back to magic, to 'the omnipotence of thought.' There is thus a violation of both negations; of the negativity which separates the terms of the system, and of that which keeps the object of discourse at a variable distance.

One can see that it is not enough to say that the unconscious is the introduction of the second negativity, as variability, into the first one. Such a reflection might lead us to contrast the philosophy of the system with the philosophy of phenomenological 'gesture,' of chiasma, of depth. But fundamentally, the unconscious space is no more that of gesture than it is that of the invariables. It is a topological space. If one can mistake its effects, it is because, from the point of view of language, transgression of the space of the system by displacements and condensations can be attributed as well to the characteristic mobility of the referential (sensory) space as to the mobility of the primary process. The overlapping of these two functions may not be itself innocent. The force moving at full speed within the wild space of the unbound can pass itself off as the gracious and spacious mobility of the gestating gesture of phenomenologies. What could cause confusion yet at the same time obliging us to be on our guard is that the dream operations comprise not only distortion, condensing and displacing the dream elements, but also the considerations of representability. Isn't this the proof that we have to deal with the dimension of designation? That this very dimension, mapped back into the course of discourse and onto the temperate and well-regulated space of communication, is what induces turbulences, sense effects which do not proceed from signification nor from syntax, but from vision?

If we stop here, we will perhaps develop a philosophy of the subject, we will become incapable of understanding dreams and the symptom in general. It is not the aesthetic space which comes to superimpose itself on the linguistic space in the dream: the bodily reach itself is, so to speak, enlarged beyond its worldly limits of the waking state. We must really take into consideration that we *sleep* while dreaming and that it is precisely the connaturality of the body and the world which is suspended by an immobility that not only eliminates the world, but also has the effect of mistaking the body for the world,[16] and, more importantly still, that the figures produced within this world which takes over the expanding stage of the body are not in the least governed by the rules of connaturality, by the directions of perceptual space, by the constitution of depth which makes 'real' things out of signs that afford one of their sides while masking the others. In dreams and neurotic symptoms, these properties of worldly figures disappear. When Freud teaches us that one of the essential operations of the dream is representation, let us therefore be on our guard: we must conclude from this that we have left the realm of language; but we must also assume – if it is true that the figure offered by the dream is not *bound* any more to the constraints of designation (which include both variability of the point of view and unilaterality of the visible), than it is to those of language – that we are no longer in the referential or worldly dimension. What we are dealing with is indeed a representation, but the rules of this scenic space are no longer those of sensory space. It is not only the author's text which is cut, superimposed, scrambled, it is also the face of the actors, the place where they stand, their clothing, their identity; as to the sets, they change in the middle of the action without warning. Action itself has no unity.

We can now come back to the classification of our figures and attempt to specify their respective connection with unconscious space. The *image-figure* is that made visible on the oneiric or quasi-oneiric stage. What is infringed here is the set of rules regulating the constitution of the perceived object. The *image-figure* deconstructs the percept, it produces itself within a space of difference. It can be precisely defined: deconstructing the outline of the silhouette, the *image-figure* is the transgression of the revealing trace.

This is conclusively illustrated in Picasso's sketch, *Etude de nu* (1941, Galerie Louise Leiris, graphite. Reproduced in Pierre Francastel, *Peinture et société*, Paris: Gallimard, 1965.), where the object of deconstruction is the edge, the line which shows that there is a single and reifying point of view; the coexistence of several contours implies the simultaneity of several points of view. The scene where this woman is sleeping does not belong to 'real' space, it allows several positions of the same body in the same place and at the same time. Erotic indifference to time, to reality, to exclusive poses. Similar examples of the deconstruction of values and colors could be found.

The *form-figure* is that which supports the visible without being seen, its nervure; it can itself be made visible, however. Its relation to unconscious space is given by the transgression of the *good form* (Gestalt). This 'good form' is the Pythagorean and neoplatonic form, grounded in a tradition of Euclidean geometry. A philosophy, nay a mystique, of the number and of its luminous, cosmic value depends upon it.[17] This form is Apollinian. Unlike it, the unconscious *form-figure*, form as a figural form, would be anti-Gestalt, a 'bad form.' We could call it Dionysian,[18] as an energetics indifferent to the unity of the whole.

It is certainly difficult to find examples of this in art, since art, we are told, demands that Apollo cooperate with Dionysius. Pollock's 'action painting,' at least in the works produced from 1946 to 1953, where the method of dripping (that we call 'passion painting') was uncompromisingly pushed to its limits, could give us an idea of what the 'bad form' might be like. A plastic screen entirely covered with chromatic flows, no stroke, not even a 'trace', no effects of echo or rhythm coming from the repetition or reentry of forms, values or colours on the surface of the painting, thus no recognizable figure; all of this suggests that we have passed over to the side of Bacchic delirium, descended unto the substratum where the plastic 'invariables,' the linear invariable at least, become a whirlwind, where energy circulates at top speed from one point of the pictorial space to another, prohibiting the eye from resting anywhere, from investing here or there, be it only for a second, its phantasmagoric charge.[19]

Finally, the *matrix-figure*. Not only is this not seen, it is no more visible than it is legible. It does not belong to plastic space any more than it does to textual space. It is difference itself, and as such, does not allow the minimal amount of structural polarity which its verbalization would require, or the minimal amount of construction without which its plastic expression as image or form cannot be obtained. Discourse, image and form are all unequal to it, for it resides in all three spaces together. Anyone's works are never but the derivatives of this matrix; we might perhaps catch a fleeting glimpse of it through their superimposition.[20] But the confusion of the spaces that prevails originally is such that words are being treated as things and as forms, things as forms or words, forms as words or as things, deconstruction bears no longer only on the textual trace as in the figural image, or on the regulating trace as in the figural form, but on the very locus of the matrix, which belongs at the same time to the space of the text, to that of the scenario, and to that of the stage: graphy, geometry, representation – each one deconstructed on account of the other two's unexpected mixture. Freud should be closely followed here.

Such are thus the fundamental modes of the connivance that desire establishes with figurality: transgression of the object, transgression of form, transgression of space.

Notes

1. It will be shown in *Beyond the Pleasure Principle* (1920; Standard Edition, XVIII, p. 7), that the functioning outlined here combines two principles: inertia or Nirvana and constancy, Eros being involved with the death instinct on one hand and reality on the other.
2. This very rough outline corresponds to *A Project for a Scientific Psychology* (1895; see *The Origins of Psycho-Analysis*. Standard Edition, I) and to *The Interpretation of Dreams* (1900; Standard Edition, IV-V), chapter VII, sections B and C.
3. *Inhibitions, Symptoms and Anxiety* (1926; Standard Edition, XX, p. 167).
4. *Three Essays on the Theory of Sexuality* (1905; Standard Edition, VII, p. 135).
5. *The Interpretation of Dreams*, p. 598.
6. *Anlehnung*. See mainly *Three Essays on the Theory of Sexuality*, pp. 181–82, 222–30. This concept was developed by Laplanche and Pontalis in the article 'Anaclisis', *The Language of Psycho-Analysis* (London: Hogarth Press and the Institute of Psycho-Analysis, 1973), translated from the French by Donald Nicholson Smith.
7. See in particular *The Interpretation of Dreams*, sec. B.
8. Ibid. p. 548.
9. Ibid. p. 544.
10. Ibid. p. 547.
11. *The Unconscious*, (1915: Standard Edition, XIV, p. 196).
12. Ibid. p. 186. In the same way, one finds in *New Introductory Lectures on Psycho-Analysis* the following: 'All the linguistic instruments by which we express the subtler relations of thought – the conjunction and prepositions, the changes in declension and conjugation – are dropped, because there are no means of representing them, just as in a primitive language without any grammar, only the raw material of thought is expressed and abstract terms are taken back to the concrete ones that are at their basis' (1932: Standard Edition XXII, p. 20).
13. Ibid. p. 186.
14. Ibid. p. 187.
15. Ibid. p. 187.
16. M. Sami-Ali, 'Préliminaire d'une théorie psychanalytique de l'espace imaginaire,' *Revue française de psychanalyse*. XXXIII (janvier/février 1969).
17. That which is found in Matila C. Ghyka's book, *Le nombre d'or*, Paris: Gallimard, 1931; and in Lhote's philosophy of plastic art.
18. See A. Ehrenzweig, *The Psycho-Analysis of Artistic Vision and Hearing, An Introduction to a Theory of Unconscious Perceptions* (London: Routledge and Kegan Paul, 1953), p. 57ff.
19. In saying this, I draw away from Italo Tomassoni's phenomenologico-existential interpretation of Pollock's work (*Pollock*, Florence: Sadea, 1968). I believe André

Breton's position was more accurate when he wrote about Arshile Gorky, an artist very close to Pollock from the very beginning of their respective works: 'I say that the eye is not *open* as long as it plays only the passive role of a mirror, even if the water of this mirror offers some interesting particularity: exceptionally limpid or sparkling, or bubbling or facetted; – that I deem this eye just as dead as that of slaughtered bulls if it is only capable of *reflecting*, whether it reflects the object under one or several of its angles, at rest or in motion, whether this object belongs to the waking world or to the realm of dreams. The eye's treasure is elsewhere: most artists are still turning the face of the watch in all directions; they have not the slightest idea of the spring hidden in the opacous case. The spring of the eye . . . Arshile Gorky is for me the first painter to whom this secret has been completely revealed. The eye's ultimate function cannot be to inventory as does the bailiff's visual organ, or to delight in the illusions of *fausse reconnaissance*, as does the oculus of maniacs.' (*Le surréalisme et la peinture*. Paris: Gallimard, 1965), pp. 196–197. One must note the total difference of function existing between a painting in which the *figural-form* is displayed and another that exhibits the *figural-image*. The two spaces are not compatible. The space of Picasso's sketch remains acceptable, even likable; it is the imaginary space, and although torn from the silence of the individual psyche and thrown under our collective eyes, it allows desire's fulfillment for the object (be it deconstructed) is still offered on the representational stage. Pollock's formal or rather anti-formal chromatic flows, on the other hand, reveal the movement of desire itself, instead of its hallucinatory object; they cannot be cathected by the pleasure principle for desire does not wish to see but to lose itself through a discharge upon and within the object. Pollock's space is one of maximal charge; no loss can be envisaged because there is no objectivist or gestaltist exit. From surrealism to the American lyric abstract trend that followed the war, what one witnesses is precisely a reversal of the *figural-image* into the *figural-form*; deconstructive activity ceases from attacking only visible outlines and superimposing visionary contours onto them, it attempts to break up the very space of mise-en-scène, the regulating trace, the spring of the eye. Dali embodies the obstinate preservation of scenic space, while with Matta, Gorky, Pollock, the probing and the exhibition of its substratum begin. A. Breton had foreseen this: 'Matta carries the disintegration of external aspects much further, for to those who can see, all these aspects are open, open not only as Cézanne's apple is to light, but to everything else, including *other opaque bodies*; they are always ready to fuse and only in this fusion can the golden key to life be forged [. . .]. It is also thus that he unceasingly invites us to a *new space*, deliberately wrenched from the old one, since the latter makes sense only insofar as it is distributive of elementary and closed bodies.' (*Le surréalisme et la peinture*, pp. 192–93).

20. This is the method advocated by Charles Mauron in *Des métaphores obsédantes au mythe personnel*, (Paris: Corti, 1963). Possibility of the incompossibles, occupation of a single space by several bodies or of a single body by several positions, simultaneity of the successive, consequently, approach of a timelessness which will be the chronical pendant of this 'topological' space. But in this particular case, Picasso is satisfied with deconstructing profiles, the revealing trace. Compare with Paul Klee's *Der L. Platz im Bau* (water-colour and ink on paper – G. David Thompson,

Pittsburgh), where the incompossibles are not of the same rank, some of them belonging, as here, to the *image-figure* (revealing traces) while others relate to the *form-figure* (regulating traces). The 'Zwischenwelt' takes place beyond the sketch. The sketch, as in Picasso's drawing, refers to the phenomenology of perception; Klee's sketches and watercolours bear upon the economics of sensory possibility.

Chapter 16

Painting as a Libidinal Set-up (Genre: Improvised Speech)

I. Propositions

1. On Two Desires

If it is possible to introduce desire into the consideration of painting, it is certainly not to make it the true content of painting, 'what' really would paint. It is not to make it the secret of its concept (the secret of the concept of painting – that would be desire!), nor the ultimate reference of all painting, all painting referring back to desire. It is not to make it the true content of painting, all painting having for its true content . . . libidinal signification, or whatever it may be. It is necessary to see immediately that it is not a matter of putting desire in the place of what the eighteenth century called 'nature' or even what Delacroix called 'sentiment'. It is not another term put in the same place. If we use it in this way – in the way many psychoanalysts do when they speak about painting, putting the unconscious in the place where, in the eighteenth century, one put nature – if we make this simple substitution without modifying the entire field upon which we work, then this substitution is useless.

Desire is a term borrowed from Freud. Yet in Freud's work itself there is a profound hesitation over the position and function of the term; a hesitation which is not merely circumstantial but probably decisive. There are two poles. One pole is that of *Wunsch-desire*, wish-desire. It entails negativity; it entails a dynamic; it entails teleology, a dynamic with an end; it entails an object, absence, a lost-object, and it also entails accomplishment, something like wish-fulfilment. All of this produces a set-up which requires us to consider meaning in desire. The other pole of the category of desire in Freud is libido-desire, process-desire, primary process. The great text of 1920, *Beyond the Pleasure Principle*, elaborates this; it will proffer the theory of the twofold regime of the processes, of Eros and the death drive. Without dwelling on these two regimes at the moment, what strikes me is that for both Eros and the death drive (but I repeat: it is not a matter of two drives, but of two regimes of the drive, two systems of energy), in both cases, it is a matter of a process of energetic fluxes and of the liquidation of these fluxes in what Freud calls a psychic apparatus, which is also the body, or even zones of the body, elements, organs, or partial organs, of the body.

With both Eros and the death drive (and thus always from the perspective of libido-desire), we are dealing with the repetitive rather than finalistic character of this process. When Freud speaks of repetition with regard to Eros and the *Todestrieb*, in both cases one finds repetition, but it is not repeated according to the same regime, and the category of repetition introduced at this moment is in 'contradiction', if this word makes any sense, with the category of finality implied in the *Wunsch*. Repetition at the level of the principle of constancy, at the level of the regulation of a particular apparatus, that is, repetition in terms of the referential unity (as the Cyberneticians say) of a particular system: this is Eros. Repetition according to the zero, according to the reference of the zero *or* the reference of the infinite (as we will put it), according to the reference of the absence of unity (you will say that here I reintroduce absence, but I will go on to explain this), but in any case repetition according to a reference to another thing than the apparatus of which we are speaking: this is what is called the death drive. The flows of energy entering into the apparatus are discharged without regard for the principle of constancy that rules the apparatus. In both cases, it is a matter of a positivity: just as much as when regulated in the apparatus as when deregulating the apparatus, desire is posed as transformable energy.

Here I will take desire in the second sense, desire in the sense of libido, in the sense of a process, desire as productive force, as energy open to transformations and metamorphoses, and as energy submitted to a double regime: first, the regime of the set-up or the system in which it is channelled, in which it is put to work, in which it produces certain effects, that is, in which it is transformed into something else. This is – to speak like Freud – the principle of constancy; the combination of what he calls Eros and the reality principle. (As an aside, you will note the profound congruence between such a consideration of the libido as process and what Marx calls power, labour power, as that which underlies the entire system. In Marx it is this same energy that operates, but according to Eros, inasmuch as it also is subordinated to a principle of constancy which, in the framework of capitalism, is the law of value, that is, the division into units and the commutability of these units according to an extremely simple category, which is the equality of values (or quantities of energy or work).)

And next, the libido according to the other regime; here we will call it a 'non-regime' because in this discussion we are speaking in a system of discourse which is also a regulated system, and we are consequently only able to speak negatively of this other regime (which is not regulated). We can only say that the energy which circulates according to this other regime is disordering, disorganised, deconstructing; we can only say it is dead (which is what Freud says). We can only say negative things about it, but this is because we are in a place from which this regulation by the zero or by the infinite of the drive can only appear as deregulation.

In fact, this energy is the same, and it is no less positive than that which is channelled in the networks of the system. We could think the excess of positivity in this 'regime' in the way that Nietzsche comes to speak of an 'excess of *jouissance*'. We could thematise it in terms of chemism in opposition to biologism; we could thematise it under the name of materialism or bestiality as in Bataille. The fact remains that it is necessary to impute to it – and for this reason we are obliged to make a hypothesis of it – return, repetition, dysfunctions, blockages, stases (according to Freud), crises (according to Marx), in the regime of constancy, where certain regions of the system appear as zones of suffering, of disorder, etc.

By introducing desire into the question of painting we in fact have recourse to a libidinal economy. And, by virtue of this fact, we also immediately have recourse to a political economy, because it is wholly impossible to take up one without taking up the other, wholly impossible to attempt to articulate one without articulating its connection with the other. It is necessary to think of desire as an energy that works (Freud is explicit about this: I have in mind the brief note at the end of the chapter on the dream work, where Freud reproaches other analysts with only paying attention to the manifest content and the latent thoughts, whereas the only important thing is the work, how one passes from the one to the other, how desire works). The important thing is energy insofar as it is metamorphic, metamorphosing and metamorphosed; for example, take the way in which the dream thoughts come to be transformed, manipulated, arranged, undone, broken, put back together, fiddled about with, squashed into manifest content; or again take the way in which energy comes to pass from a kinetic state of activity to a quiescent state.

And here you see that we find ourselves in close proximity to painting: how all of a sudden a gesture sets itself down in colour, spreads out in a particular way, on a particular support, or conversely, how a colour which is there, and that one has seen, comes anew to revive the energy of the one who looks at it, in the form of an affect or a dance or some such thing – if he is an honest man he will stand and dance, if he is a spiteful (occidental) man, he will stand and talk . . .

Thus, on the one hand, repeating itself, this energy infinitely repeating positions, investments, insofar as they are captured in its set-ups; but also, diluting the set-ups, diluting the arrangements, the investments of energy, putting everything back into play by way of excess, liquidating all this, confounding it: energy both as order and disorder, as Eros and death drive, and both always together.

2. On Lysis

If we take painting into consideration from the point of view of this economy, the first thing that we have to say is that in order to grasp its import, we must destroy the pictorial region as one of the fine arts, as an institution; that it is necessary to destroy its pseudo-autonomy, which is an ideological autonomy; and abandon methodically, from the outset, our ingrained habit of referring back to the 'act' of painting (with all the theology implicated in this 'act'), to the expressive or inexpressive 'intentions' of the painter, even to the 'unconscious' of the painter. I have in mind the work of Pierre Kaufman on 'emotional space', in which he notably says concerning Van Gogh that painting is a chromatic language, a language of colours, which retroactively comes to occupy the place left empty by the withdrawal of the discourse of the father (an excellent little metaphysical machinery: the father does not speak, this creates a vacuum, and in this vacuum I come to make colour speak). It is also necessary to renounce cheerfully the habit of thinking painting as a superstructure, and the so-called 'class' function of the pictorial institution; a function on which not much light has been shed.

Instead, it is necessary to begin by *diluting* the pictorial region, so as to proceed by a type of *lysis*, which is not an analysis because it is not at all certain, and because it does not even imply that we end up breaking something down to its basic constitutive elements. (We will only and always find energy.) And it is modern painting itself that effects this dilution. It is enough to open one's eyes, in order to receive the flow of energy that this painting emits from its entire surface, to perceive that it is precisely this dilution which is already underway, and that such painting carries out a dilution in the order of pictorial inscription which is analogous to the one which Marx discerns in what we call economic inscription, political economy; it is the same dilution, that is, a type of destruction of the codes that circumscribe regions, and the same passage of energetic flux across all forms. Marx said: everything is plunged in water, 'in the cold-waters of the egoistic calculus'; but first they are not so cold, and second: what is this ego? On the other hand, there is certainly calculation in capitalism since there is a law of exchange, which is that of the separation and substitution of units of energy (these being separated under the form of commodities).

The question *of* painting proceeds from the quite particular and peculiar set-up of modernity, of capitalism. Capitalism does not pose its problems in terms of meaning (Marx does not describe capitalism as a system of meaning). Capitalism poses its problems in terms of energy and the transformation of energy: transformation of matter, transformation of apparatus, production of apparatus, labour power, manual power, intellectual power, production, transformation of labour power, money . . . in terms of energy which circulates and which is exchanged, that is, which is metamorphosised. There is, then, a sort of polymorphism of this energy: from the moment that it is exchangeable, metamorphisable according to the law of value, the only requirement is that everything is fair game. Now, there is a polymorphism of modern painting which attests to an analogous dissolution of the objects, states, configurations, places, and modalities, which previously have circumscribed the institution that we call painting. It is necessary to begin from this fact, and to remain with it, to refrain from leaving it; it is necessary to dive into the waters in a kind of dissolution of the pictorial institution, a kind of dilution, a multiplication of the places and modalities of this inscription.

In a text by Alain Kirili, written alternately by him and by Philippe Sollers, called *Traces, inscriptions, marquages*, you will find the following note: 'the division of intellectual production: painting/literature is the very sign of the arbitrariness of the dominant occidental culture, because painting and writing belong to the same work of inscription'. We are fully in agreement with this, but it is necessary to go much further: it is not simply the splitting-up of painting/literature which is arbitrary, it is not simply the division of letter/line (Kirili later says: it is inscription which is the important thing, and thus pictography, because in pictography we find both literature and painting bound together before they are divided); it is necessary to say exactly the same for literature, painting and economics as well. Why hold in reserve economic inscription? Economy is a marking; production is an inscription, in a certain manner.

What is this dissolution of painting, then? We will never finish enumerating its traits: there are collages, there is the use of materials stuck on a canvas, scrap metal, photographs; you have the use of industrial paints; you have the use of new instruments of inscription like the spray gun; there are the new procedures in order to stretch the canvas; you have the silk-screen; and you have an unbelievable multiplication of 'scenographies': cubism, surrealism, neo-realism, realism, abstract expressionism . . . a type of explosion which goes in all directions and which is evidently a major challenge to the nomenclature fashioned according to the categories of art history. Such a dissolution, that is, the event of the divisions and the set-ups that regulate the places and the modalities of chromatic inscription becoming permeable, such an explosion should bring about effects – always in an energetic sense – at the level of our own language when we speak about painting. At the very least, this dissolution of chromatic inscription ought to lead to a dissolution of the theoretical inscription upon painting. One might expect that the theoretical set-up itself be shattered like the pictorial or economic set-up.

If you pick up Diderot's *Salons* or his *Essai sur la Peinture*, you find a discourse on painting that glosses painting, that is, one that attempts to produce in a linguistic order set-ups that are 'analogous' to the pictorial set-ups that Diderot describes as essentially representative. If you pick up the texts of Dezeuze and Cane, who are members of the 'Surface-support' group, here also you find a theoretical discourse, which is not a gloss but a sort of meta-language aiming to be the meta-language of painting. One could ask if wanting to continue producing a theoretical discourse on painting, wanting to elaborate a meta-language with its lexicon and syntax whose correspond-ing domain of interpretation would be painting, is not an anachronistic project; one could ask if it does not belong to a discursive model which no longer corresponds to anything in pictorial practice, since the set-ups which nowadays regulate pictorial inscription form, in their multiplicity, a sort of non-set-up. When painting is in the process of dissolving itself in energetic metamorphoses, in the same energetic metamorphoses that capitalism causes to pass through all institutions, is it not the case that producing a theoretical discourse based on an essentially linguistic model (as do Dezeuze and Cane) is as anachronistic as it would have been if in the face of capitalism Marx had wanted to produce – as his predecessors had – a meta-language of capitalism whose model would have been semantic? At bottom, what Marx in fact pro-duced is a kind of verbal equivalent of the 'frenzied' energetic procedures which constitute capitalism. It appears to me that producing a theoretical discourse on painting – theoretical in the sense that this word has today, that is, a meta-language whose model is inevitably linguistic (or more strictly language-like) – would be to reconstitute in the region of discourse a set-up that pictorial practice (here the interpretative domain that it is a question of understanding) is precisely in the process of liquidating or liquefying.

Rather than attempting to understand, what we have to do would be to transform the energy at stake in what we call painting, not in a theoretical set-up, but in a type of liquefaction, in a kind of aleatory production, in the sense intended by John Cage; rather than attempting to resolve the question of painting in the sense of arresting its meaning, we would have to dissolve the question, in the sense of undoing the stases, including theory as a 'stasis'. Here I feel much closer to Daniel Charles' analyses of music, or Daniel Buren's articles – although in Buren the critical dimension again remains marked. Dezeuze and Cane have grasped that it is necessary to criticise Freud by way of Cézanne, but they have not seen that it is also necessary to criticise Marxist theory by way of Pollock . . .

To paint then would be to inscribe colour, to inscribe pigments, to produce chromatic inscriptions. Kirili says: 'painting and writing come back to the same work, namely that of inscription'. This is true, but it says too much and too little. Swimming is also a work of inscription. It is therefore necessary, perhaps, to say that pictorial inscription has specifically to do with colour, that this is what is specific to it. To paint would be to make libidinal connections with colour, and above all, to bind the chromatised libido to a support; a work of inscription in this sense.

3. On Pictorial and Language-like Set-ups

These connections are compliant with the set-ups. There are investments, energetic blockages which conduct energy and which secure its transformation according to certain channels. The hand grasps the lipstick and it spreads colour across the lips. This is a pictorial inscription, a painting. It is obvious that we are dealing with an energetic set-up: the channelling of energy through the hand, the arms, the way in which colour is put on the lips, all this is regulated.

One hand holds a stencil; in the palm of the other there is a deposit of powdered iron oxide, and the mouth blows it: here is a set-up. This is how our ancestors painted their caves. This is painting according to a certain set-up.

A photographic apparatus captures light energy and inscribes it on film: is this painting? Why not? The eye apprehends the developed and projected photograph; the hand reproduces the photograph on a support on a scale of 10:1: is this painting? Many pop-art and hyperrealist canvases are made like this. This is a set-up; it works.

One hand dips a little brush into a liquid and applies it to the nails of the other hand: another set-up.

Two hands lift up a pot of paint, a man mounts a platform which is there, and pours the contents over the canvas on the ground. This is also a set-up. All this is pictorial and chromatic inscription.

A glass, a pane of glass (a description of a particularly mad set-up which is what we call 'painting' in the West between the fifteenth and nineteenth centuries) is placed between an object and the eye. The chin is locked in a metallic chin-strap which completely immobilises the head; the hand traces on the glass the outline of the object (without forgetting to close one eye); this tracing is then transferred onto a canvas; and then the outlined regions are filled with colour. Such is the set-up of Leonardo da Vinci and Albrecht Dürer. The latter went as far as to make engravings of these set-ups: what we have here, then, are repetitions of repetitions of repetitions.

The set-up is an organisation of connections: it is energy that channels and that regulates the influx and expenditure of energy in chromatic inscription.

Here is a simple model of a set-up according to a text written by Hans Bellmer, entitled *Petite anatomie de l'inconscient physique ou l'anatomie de l'image*:

> The different modes of expression: posture, gesture, act, sound, word, handwriting, creation of an object, all result from the same group of psycho-physiological mechanisms, all of them are subject to one and the same law of birth. Elementary expression, which does not have a preconceived communicative end, is a reflex. What need, what bodily impulse, does it respond to? For example, among the reflexes provoked

by extreme toothache we find a violent contraction of the muscles in the hand and fingers, which forces the nails into the skin of the palm. The clenched hand is an artificial focus of excitation, a virtual 'tooth' which, by way of attraction, diverts the flow of blood and nervous impulses away from the real centre of pain, finally diminishing its existence. Thus, to the cost of the hand, the toothache is halved; its expression, this 'logical pathos', being the visible result.

Is it necessary to conclude that both the most violent and the most imperceptible reflexive modification of the body, of a finger, a limb, the tongue, a muscle, consequently would be explicable as a tendency towards disorientation, towards the splitting of pain, in order to create a 'virtual' centre of excitation? This is certainly the case, and it commits us to conceiving the desired continuity of our expressive lives in the form of a series of deliberate movements which link the illness to its image. Expression, with the pleasure it contains, is a displaced pain, a relief.

The chapter from which this extract is taken has, as an exergue, a phrase from Paracelsus: 'The scorpion fights the scorpion'. Pain in one place fights pain in another. I have reservations concerning this text because it employs certain categories: 'expression'; the quite worrying category of 'the tendency to disorient pain'; 'to depreciate pain', 'relief', etc. But there remains in Bellmer both the comprehension and the description of what is important: the delocalisation of energy by its localisation elsewhere (energy flows away from the tooth: there is, then, displacement and a focus on another region, the palm for example). Here you have an energetic set-up, an operative transformer: in this case it is a transformer of the location of energy alone, and that is why it is 'simple'.

We could seek much more complex set-ups: the linguistic set-ups that Emile Benveniste describes under the names of 'narrative' and 'discourse', which refer to different levels of enunciation. (These come back to a particular linguistics, that of enunciation, and thus once again to a certain linguistic set-up, which is not only language-like but linguistic, or to a theoretical set-up concerning language, where language inscribes itself.) Benveniste brings the following traits into relief:

- In narrative, there is only the use of the third person, and the third person is not a person: from the point of view of enunciation, a person is the subject who speaks or who could speak here and now: *I* and *you*. *He* or *she* is the person who does not speak.
- For narrative, there is a selective grouping in the use of French tenses that Benveniste calls aoristic: the past simple, the imperfect, the pluperfect and the prospective (an example of the prospective: 'In the Mediterranean basin commercial warfare between the peoples of the North and the Semites *would not stop* [*ne devait pas cesser*] until the destruction of Carthage'. 'Would not stop': the prospective is the index of the future in narrative time). At the heart of the possibilities of the use of tenses in French there are, then, blocks, eliminations, filters; particular tenses are permitted, others not.

– On the side of discourse, in Benveniste's sense, there is, on the contrary, the use of the first and second person, and the tenses 'of discourse': the present, the perfect and the future.

Benveniste only elaborates the opposition of these 'modes of enunciation' from the point of view of tense and person. But implied in this are what linguists call 'aspects' and 'modalities'. Aspects and modalities are not marked on the surface in French, but they are traits relative to the relation of the subject of enunciation with the subject of the pronouncement and they are traits relative also to the relation of the tense of enunciation with the time of the utterance. Take a simple expression such as: 'he appeared' ['*il apparut*']: it is situated immediately in the narrative, in the 'mode of enunciation' of the narrative: we are in the third person, and we find the exemplary aoristic tense, the French past simple. But the following are implicated in this enunciation: (1) an aspect that concerns the enunciator-enunciated relation; when you say 'he appeared', it is not known if you, the enunciator, were or were not there: here there is a kind of occultation of the enunciator; (2) an aspect that marks the manner in which the process unfolds: 'he appeared' is punctual; (3) a modality which marks the mode of assertion: it is affirmative. And so on . . . If you take this group of modalities, you will see that what Benveniste calls 'the enunciative tenses' are more than a mere set of tenses – *they are veritable linguistic set-ups: they are arrangements controlling the direction of energetic fluxes on the inscriptive field of language, which thus determine the binding of the libido with language as a surface of inscription* (and it is this which produces the famous 'effects of meaning').

Here, then, you have the filtering of possibilities: there is a discursive set-up, narrative set-up, theoretical set-up. You have the circumscription of language-like modalities: for example, in the case of the narrative, you have a type of circumscription – the tale – into which myth, narration, a novel, a story, or a typical film scenario plug themselves. *You have a metamorphosis of libidinal energy into objects (here language), that is, concretions of quiescent energy*, what Marx called dead labour power, quiescent energy in the form of language-like set-ups, which, in turn, come to be transformed into affects, emotions, corporeal inscriptions; on hearing your narrative, people dream; or begin wars, revolts, semiotic or 'economic' glosses. This is to say that the energy lying here will set in motion certain effects, will come to be transformed into 'effects'.

In the narrative set-up, then, we effectively have an energetic transformer, but this time it is more complicated than the tooth and hand that we examined; here, there are displacements, modalities and surfaces of inscription. There are an immense number of possible pictorial set-ups. Dezeuze and Cane have attempted to produce a list of all those operative in 'painting'. They bring into relief categories of gesture, for example: gesture of the finger, of the wrist, the elbow, the shoulder, the overall gesture of the body (they forget the gesture of the mouth, of the feet), and the category of the tool: brush, bradawl, blade, knife, chisel, stamp, seal, press, compressor, vaporiser, spray-gun. A category of the medium: water, oil, spirit, resin, ink, adhesive, wax, etc. And then there is also pigment, which is not categorised. There is the support: paper, canvas, plastic, wood, stone, metal. Along with all of this, there is living labour power; how does it proceed? By way of stains, projection, vaporisation, by imprintation, impregnation, impression, compression (excluding scraping); by line: graphic, engraved, slit, tear, cut; by point: graphic point, perforation; by fold: creasing or cog. Each pictorial set-up is a combination of elements selected from different means of production.

Such combinations give us, for example, Yves Klein's prints (the large white canvases and the blue nudes imprinted on the canvas). Dezeuze and Cane speak of 'signifying practices' or of 'over-determined practices'; I am concerned that these are very much ideological borrowings. What is interesting, however, is the attempt to enumerate all the possible set-ups, all the possible energetic bindings that go to produce chromatic inscriptions. It would be necessary to supplement them. For example, why is it that skin is not listed among the supports? Tattooing is painting. It is not because our occidental set-up has eliminated the tattoo or has reserved it for the 'guys', that is, has devalued it and circumscribed it as a proof of savagery – that it is not considered to be painting. As Levinas would say, make-up is tattooing without risk, it is the temptation of the temptation of the tattoo. But even make-up is not admitted as painting because it is not 'noble', because it relates to the skin; and in our set-up, the support that is the skin is not 'noble'; but nevertheless the skin is a very good support upon which to paint. With someone like Klein, the occidental pictorial set-up breaks with its constraints, its proscriptions, because when he paints the naked body and when he makes a print of it on the canvas, then here the skin is taken seriously. It is not taken seriously as a support, but rather as a vehicle for making connections. Then there is also sand: the Pueblo-Indians paint on the sand; they get pigments and arrange them on the sand. If we do not consider sand to be a surface, it is because in the West there is a category of the *oeuvre*, the work; a work must endure, and it cannot endure in the sand. The Indians themselves care nothing for this conservative set-up of the West. Is it essential to painting that the energy deposited under the form of chromatic inscription remains as chromatic traces? The Indians consider it good if the painting is immediately dispersed in a wind of colour, as it proves that the inscription communicates with the general circuits of energy. One could paint on rocks, on water even (for the Vincennes biennial, an environmental artist proposed to dye the waters of New York port red).

We note that the places of inscription are narrowly circumscribed: paintings, pictorial inscriptions are placed in the interior of houses – specifically in uninhabited houses, in museums, galleries, exhibition spaces. Here also, it is a matter of an arrangement which regulates the *place* of pictorial inscription, and which is as strange as Dürer's chin-strap: placing pictorial inscriptions in kinds of refrigerators in order to be certain that the pictorial energy is conserved. This is an arrangement that remains to be analysed from an energetic point of view. If we seriously take pictorial inscription to be a form of chromatic inscription in general, then we must say that illustrated magazines, clothes, make-up, industrial design are also painting: here are things where energy is transformed everyday.

Insofar as modality is concerned, it is necessary to add another group of elements that are decisive in the set-up, namely the relation of the inscription to the support: is the chromatic inscription *tolerated*, as we say, by the support? Is it *occulted* by the support? Is it *revealed* by the support? I intentionally use these terms which are taken from a problematic of representation (Daniel Buren's). We could, however, keep the terms of the economic problematic, in saying: does the inscription *transmit* something to the support? Does it borrow its energy from the support? Is it not in communication with it from a libidinal point of view, and thus neutralising its energy? What I would like to do here is work on the variants of this last small part of the pictorial set-up, that is, the relation of the inscription to the support, along with the relation of the support to the place of inscription.

II. Analyses

You will recall the *1857 Introduction* where Marx says that it is with capitalism that work emerges as a category. This is not to say that previous societies did not work; they also worked: but it needed the empty universality of capitalist work – abstract, indifferent work – for us to grasp, *a contrario*, the set-ups for channelling and exploiting work in pre-capitalist economies. All things being equal, it takes the fluidity of energy in contemporary painting in order to understand that in previous pictorial set-ups it has always been a matter of energy, but that this energy was channelled in a certain manner which did not allow it to be revealed as energy, instead producing it under other set-ups. Recalling that painting does not exist as a separate region, we could very well imagine, for example, societies that do not libidinally *charge* chromatic inscription: we could imagine that colour served only to mark an object and that the entire libidinal charge bears upon the transportation of this object, upon its being-given or its destruction; it could make of colour merely a signal or a mark which 'says': here is an object which could be given in a potlatch, or: this is an object which must be conserved in memory. It is evident that in a set-up of this kind potential chromatic energy is repressed, disregarded, marginalised: colour is not the invested region, it marks the invested region (not flux, but circum-scription of flux).

I would like to show that even within the West there are types of variants in libidinal-plastic-political economy, that there are submersions and emergences of pictorial set-ups (which are not simply pictorial, but libidinal and political), mutations of energy which should be considered as ruptures of synchrony and not ruptures of diachronic history: at any given moment, many pictorial set-ups and many economic set-ups could very well co-exist near the surface, on the surface of a society; but there are, besides, moments when we see a new type of set-up appear on the surface, and first, the localisation of both pictor-ial and economic inscriptions. When in Flanders, in the middle of the four-teenth century, new organisations begin to harness the energy of labour power and then of raw materials, and the first manufacturers begin to operate, it is an entire set-up that emerges for the captivation, localisation and metamorphosis of energy, and it is new. In painting, there are also events of this type.

1. Towards the Political

Let us take a first group of four images:

1. The commentary of abbot Beatus of Liébana on the *Apocalypse of Saint John*, Saint-Sever (middle of the eleventh century).
2. Piero della Francesca (*circa* 1445; first generation of Italian perspectivists), *Flagellation* (Ducal Palace, Urbino).
3. Detail from a fresco by Ambrogio Lorenzetti (middle of the fourteenth century, Town (Pinacoteca Nazionale, Siena).
4. Francesco de Giorgio? (School of Piero della Francesca, *circa* 1465), *The Ideal City* (Ducal Palace, Urbino).

Each of these four images is supported by a different set-up, and yet, it is only a matter of miniscule variations in relation to the entirety of possible set-ups.

The Apocalypse of Saint-Sever

To begin, there is the formal approach: here the enumeration and characterisa-tion of the elements of pictorial inscription. First, there is what is properly called linear inscription. We have here what the linguists call frozen syntagms. Take the wing of the angel high on the right and the wing of the angel at the bottom on the left: it is the same contour, but reversed, the same procedure, the same inscription. Take the top part of the coat of the angel high on the right, and John's bolero at the bottom: they are the same. Take the Lord's feet (or hands) and those of the figures at the bottom, they are alike. Here you have units of linear inscription which are veritable syntagms, they are self-sufficient, they are major linear units. They are taken, compounded together and from them figures, in the everyday sense of the term, are fabricated. André Leroi-Gourhan makes the same observation about Palaeolithic paintings: he shows that the curve of the back of a horse, and the curve of the back of a bison are the same, and that consequently there is an impression of having a syntagm here, that is, a block linear set-up. You have what we could call a pictography in the strict sense, not only in the sense of drawing with colour, but in the sense of a type of linear writing, a writing with lines.

If you take another element of classical inscription, modelling or highlighting [*le modelé ou la valeur*], you see that there is nothing of them here. As we have seen in the cases of narrative and discourse, a set-up is always just as remarkable for what it excludes as it is for what it includes. Here there is neither modelling nor highlighting, there is no attempt to produce a thickness of the figures, there is no depth. We have a type of calligraphy.

If, for the time being, you now examine the actual chromatic set-up, you will observe a general opposition, a general system of oppositions of blue and red; you have here a bi-chromatic system with, nonetheless, a rose or very diluted red on the robes of the angel, on the throne or on the wings; and then you always have the same brown: the hairstyle, the hair. You will also notice an inversion of the line (because the lines are themselves chromatic elements: they are not linearities in black and white, but coloured lines), and so you have systems of lines that serve to compliment the surface colour: a red line on a blue background, blue line on a red background, red line on a white background, etc. Thus here you have a possible combinatory. We might also say that colour functions as a mark, but in this way we would take our leave from a properly formal analysis. We could show that the Lord is wearing a red robe and is wrapped in a blue cloak, which is the rule according to the Byzantine code, because he is both God and man.

If you now study the relation between the inscription, the support and the place – remember that it is a matter of an illustration in a sacred book, that this book is destined to circulate amongst clerics and to reside in consecrated places: the abbey, the treasury of the Abbey, the bishop's palace, etc.

The questions that we have to ask ourselves (following Daniel Buren, *Limites critiques*) are the following:

1. Do the medium and the pigment, the colour, cause us to forget that the image is inscribed on a page, by hiding the support? I would say not, for two reasons: first, there is a use of literal or scriptural inscription on the pictorial support itself: at the top you read a text which says '*Ubi angelus a domino librum accipit*' ('Where the angel receives the book from the Lord') and, at the bottom, 'John speaks with the angel'. Here you have an inscription in the contemporary sense. *Where* is it inscribed? When Philippe de Champaigne was going to make an *ex voto* to Port-Royal for the recovery of his daughter, he will write on a wall. What wall?

The wall of the cell where he pictures his daughter and Sister Agnes? Or on a plastic support, on a canvas? We might think that in the former case the writing is destined to show that *there is a* support, and that this support is the *real* place that (perspectival) painting *hides* (see Louis Marin). Here, we are in a place, on a support (the book of the Apocalypse) which prevents us from deriving the least illusionary impression from the chromatic inscription. And, moreover, there is also the ornamentation of the surrounding frame which sends us back to the written pages.

2. Does the surface hide the fact that there is a verso to the image? Is what is behind the painting, behind the plastic screen, given away or is it ignored, as is the case with an easel? Answer: in a manuscript, the back is also a page of writing; thus, as it is a matter of folios, which are written recto-verso, when the image is inscribed on a folio, it cannot give rise to illusion, it cannot hide the fact of its verso.

3. Does the support, the book with its chromatic inscriptions, hide the place in which they are found, in the same way that the museum disconnects the work from its context? No, the immediate place of the images is a book, this book is in a sacred place, and this sacred place is a place in society, in the circulation of energies and of objects that are depositories of energy in society. In the Christian society of the eleventh century all this is explicitly regulated. Consequently, in a system of this type, in response to the questions that modernity poses to representation, we can say every time, there is *no* occultation.

But what does sacred, consecrated mean, then? That the libido, with its ambivalence of Eros and the death drive, finds itself invested, channelled into stable set-ups, which are isomorphic with the set-ups of the society in question (eleventh-century Western society). On the one hand you find a language-like set-up which is exactly based on the model of the Christian narrative-myth. 'He appeared' is the nucleus of all mythic narrative, and it is exactly this that is at issue in Christianity: 'He appeared, he disappeared . . . and he was to reappear'. In parallel to this, you find a set-up which would be gestural, corporeal; this is the sacrificial set-up, the ritual set-up of the mass, which is a projection of the narrative set-up.

These two modalities of libidinal inscription are profoundly isomorphic (see Marcel Mauss). And then you have a feudal-clerical set-up, which is economic, a set-up of the gift and counter-gift, which is complex. On the one hand, there is *potlatch, expenditure, prestige*: if Abbot Grégoire himself pays for the luxury of supporting a monk to paint these images, it is because being in an economy of prestige, Saint-Sever Abbey actually draws an enormous benefit from the presence of this object in its treasury. And if, in addition, the abbey makes a donation of this object, then there is an operation of potlatch, of expenditure, in which the object enters into a highly libidinal circulation of charges and discharges, of transferences and counter-transferences; consequently, here you have an 'economic' set-up, with all the ambiguity that the word 'economic' carries. If the Abbey retains the book and the images, it is because we are no longer savages; we are already amidst conservation, hoarding, and perhaps already involved with economy in the sense of saving and no longer of expenditure. Both are ambivalently in play here. But in either case, our image inscribes itself in this economy.

I believe that there is a profound isomorphism between these different set-ups channelling energies into the different regions of inscription – language, the very corporeal region of flesh and blood that is at stake in sacrifice, and the economic region, that of 'goods' – and the pictorial set-up. On the image that you are looking at, it is possible to show how it is bound up with the other places of inscription: to say that it does not hide its support means that this image is dependent on a book that is itself bound up with a language-like set-up. For even if it only functions as a signal, this image can only function thus if it refers to the language-like set-up of the Christian myth, if it is recognisable by people who know the latter. It does not have this function or value if we do not attach it to it, if we do not bring it into communication with the sacrificial set-up of the mass or the ritual in general. It is a book that will find itself engaged at a certain point in the ritual; it will be on the altar, or on the pulpit of the brother-reader in the refectory. It is, in addition, impossible to understand this image if you do not insert it into the economic process of the gift. This means that the image is in fact a highly coded image wherein the energetic power of the colouration is restrained, repressed, circumscribed, kept in check: if this is the case, it is because the flow of libidinal charges and discharges pass into the Christian narrative myth, pass into the sacrifice of the mass, or the ritual of the meal, pass into the gifts and the counter-gifts of feudal-clerical society, and because within these other set-ups iconic plastic works only function as a mnemotechnic. Ultimately, this plasticity only works – and it is in this way that it will operate on walls, in frescos, when it is addressed to people who cannot read – it only works as a reference, as an object marked in a process, referring to this process.

If one wanted to articulate the connection of this object with the process in question, it would be necessary to show that it is not at all a representative connection, but rather a connection of a marking type: an object that bears chromatic inscriptions of this sort is signalled as an object able to circulate in Christian sacrifice, whose plastic elements (lines, colours, etc.) have their 'key' in myth, in the Christian language-like set-up, and whose support only functions through its relation to the gift and counter-gift economy of feudal Christianity. In comparing it to the small statuettes of the (supposed) Palaeolithic Venus, at whose high degree of abstraction we still marvel, we ought to think of what Leroi-Gourhan says of Palaeolithic art in general: that it is the first phase of this art that is the most abstract. We ought to be able to understand that if 'primitive' art is always highly 'abstract', then this is because it never functions for itself; it is not autonomous – like a separate region of inscription – for it belongs to a system of circulation and metamorphosis of energies that far exceeds pictorial inscription, and where the latter operates simply as a marking. Ultimately, it can simply be a signal, like the most archaic inscription: a notch on a stick. What is important in this case, then, is not the notch, but the circulation of the stick; it is the gift. *What is marked, is the very power of giving*, the potential gift; the libido is invested in the gift and not in the notch. The notch is there only to identify the gift, to refer to the gift. It seems to me that an image such as that of Saint-Sever belongs still, all things being equal, to a set-up functioning in this way.

The 'reading' by signaletic elements of an image composed in this manner and functioning according to such a set-up is in all likelihood legitimate: iconography and semiology as religious sciences . . .

A Fragment of The Town *by Ambrogio Lorenzetti*

We could marvel at the cavalier views in this image, but this would not be pertinent. In fact, it functions in exactly the same way as the preceding image, that is, simply as a reference. What do we see? It is a town. Is it representative? Not at all, for there is not the slightest attempt to produce an equivalent of what we can see with, as we say, the naked eye, or with the eye and a chin-strap. The image functions as a *signal*. In a fresco, it signals that there is a town. If you turn the image upside-down, it is still a town; the signal still works very well. The relation top-bottom, that is, the relation to the eye, to the subject looking at it – the relation that will be valorised in the set-up of representation – is not operative here. Even inverted the image still functions as a reference. It is still a town, and thus the eye is solicited as a power, not of seeing, but of remembering.

Piero della Francesca's Flagellation

If we first undertake, as we did before, a formal approach to the linear set-up, what is striking is that here there is a triple linear set-up, which is very different from what we saw in the Lorenzetti and in Saint-Sever's manuscript. The linear set-up, and more specifically the straight line, is enormously important. There is first of all a revelatory line; there are contours which allow us to recognise, to identify objects as if they were seen in three-dimensional extension: there are people, buildings, trees. There is thus a line that would be traced on the glass according to Leonardo's canon. There are, moreover, regulating lines of two sorts: a classic medieval line; if you observe the dimensions of this painting, it is possible to determine three principal elements in its width: one formed from four units, another formed from two, and then a third from three. The height is made up of four units. We have, therefore, a combinatory of four by nine and a rhythm that is from four to six, then from six to nine, if you 'sweep' from left to right.

This is a retrieval of Pythagoreanism; Pythagoreanism updated by the neo-Platonism of the Florentines, which is very marked in Piero, but all Romanesque building is constructed, musically, according to a rhythm of this sort. We have here harmonies of differences, equalities of differences that are wholly comparable to those of a musical scale. Piero invents nothing with this. But he introduces a completely different system, in which he invents every-thing: a perspectival system with a vanishing point. The vanishing point that is lost, submerged in the background of the wall, is also placed on a horizontal, which determines the horizon line. This vanishing point is constructed in a par-ticular manner; it will determine the place that we have to occupy to 'see prop-erly'. And to determine the rapidity with which the eye is drawn into it, a series of obliques have been constructed that converge at another point, the distance point; a series of obliques in relation to which all the tiling of the surface will be constructed. It is in bringing the two networks together, the vanishing point and the distance point, that it is possible to trace a trapezium, for example, that will be seen as a square in three-dimensional space.

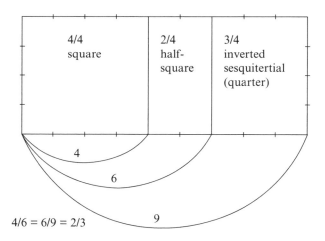

What is this distance point? It is the very distance at which you must place your eye in order to have a 'good point of view'; it is the orthogonal distance from this point to the surface of the painting, but after having under-gone a rotation through ninety degrees, it is now applied to the support, in such a way that the linear complex will not at all be seen as a trapezium, but as a square in perspective. This is indeed what happens here, inasmuch as the squaring on a quite remote distance point produces a considerable deepening, a very deep scene.

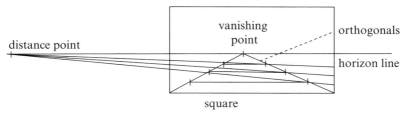

Therefore, there are three linear systems:

- a system of inscription of 'figures', profiles, contours of visible things;
- a harmonic system, which is traditional and makes the eye sweep musically across the plastic field;
- the perspectival system, which is not musical, which does not refer to an arithmetically regulated organisation of differences, but which is a predominantly visual geometrical system.

In a painting of this sort, we find at once an acoustic arithmetic of Pythagorean and neo-Platonic origin, and a revised and simplified Euclidean visual geometry. This is an unbelievably complex and constraining set-up for regulating linear inscription.

Concerning value now – and this is characteristic of Piero – the effects of modelling are obtained not by the heightening or lowering of tonality, but by changes of colour. We are not in a system of reinforcement, for example of pigmenting the same colour with black, for we have a different colour. Piero says that it is in this way that it is possible to obtain good modelling. The effects of modelling are produced by inscriptions of colours, for example of different blues. We owe the extraordinary luminosity of the work to this.

The chromatic system itself is highly ordered; on the outside (there is an 'outside' and an 'inside'), the dominant colour is towards the red end of the scale, and on the inside the dominant colour is towards green and blue, with some blue far on the right (in the heat), and red far on the left (in the cold) in chromatic counter-position. This is a relatively simple chromatic organisation, which is exceptionally harmonic and perhaps even highly codified.

And now, the relation inscription/support/place. What does it represent?. . . There is a flagellation. There is Christ with a Greek statue above him, which is strange. There is a foreground on the outside: it is supposed that – according to the local tradition – here, on the right, in the centre, stands Oddantonio, the brother of Frederic di Montefeltro, the then Duke of Urbino, surrounded by two advisers sent by Malatesta, who are supposed to have killed him. One particular episode in the sombre affairs of political struggle between principalities, between tyrannies. It is easy to imagine that the painting was requested by the Duke in commemoration of the murder of his brother. Piero sent him this *Flagellation*, which would thus have a metaphorical value. But how is the inscription made on the support? At first, the Italians said of perspectival technique: how amazing, it pierces the wall! It is a matter of what we ought strictly to call pictorial representation: this is to say, first of all, and before anything else, that the inscription *hides* itself. Medieval harmony guided vision, it guided the 'sweep' of the field, but perspectival construction is purely and simply effaced; of all the obliques, only the orthogonals will remain, and again, they will disappear, the painter dissimulating them in the scene. The references to the distance point will be completely effaced.

The Ideal City

This occultation, the occultation of a part of the inscription – which implies that one works gradually, inscribing and then rubbing it out, exactly as one does when writing an 'essay' – *is already an operation of staging* [*mise en scène*]. In these effacements, you have the essential element of the scenic set-up. Look at the (supposed) *Ideal City*; it is a scene, perhaps the plan for a scenic backdrop; it was perhaps one of the first backdrops to be painted according to Alberti's perspective, similar to those representations made in Ferrara. It is perhaps also a form of ornamentation for a chest, or a sketch for some marquetry. In any event, it is an experiment in perspective.

Here we have a set-up that can be schematically represented in the following way:

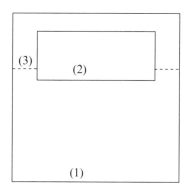

This enclosing set-up is in fact a set-up for the harnessing and circulation of libidinal energy in the case of representation: you have a first enclosure determining an outside and an inside – which is the theatre or museum building, a building belonging to those uninhabited, deserted places – that will determine the gap between 'reality' and what one could call, after the psychoanalysts, 'dis-reality', a place that would be a disreal space (the psychoanalyst's clinic is an dis-real place). Then one finds another place, a second limit internal to the first, and therefore *in* the theatre – the edge of the stage, the frame of the painting, the framework of the stage, something like a window, Leonardo's celebrated window, Dürer's perspective machines; and then, perhaps, there is a third invisible limit, which is what is below the stage, the wings, the machinery in the case of an Italian theatre – in the case of painting this will be construction according to a distance point – everything that will not be seen, but which itself makes visible. We have also to put all the scenography behind this limit. *All that effaces and is effaced, hides and is hidden at the same time.*

We have here a strong set-up for the channelling of energies. We can modify the relation auditorium/stage; for example, putting the stage in the centre, or on the periphery, or in a three-quarters arena, or even constructing a 'total theatre', a complex set-up with which an Italian stage can be obtained; the three-quarters arena, the annular stage, the central stage; the spectators either being placed in the middle, or being made to turn, or having the actors turn . . . In any event, it seems that we maintain what is essential to representation since we maintain limit (1), since we still have first of all the enclosure; and often also limit (2), but not necessarily, for one can imagine that on the inside, there is no longer a limit, and then one would have something like the socio-drama or revolution . . .

This representative set-up corresponds, in painting, to Brunelleschi's box, a small optical set-up, for representing the Baptistery as it is seen from the Dome of Florence.

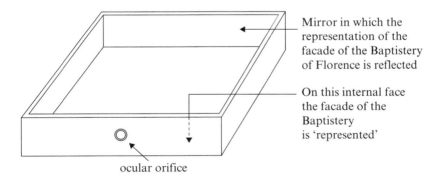

Mirror in which the representation of the facade of the Baptistery of Florence is reflected

On this internal face the facade of the Baptistery is 'represented'

ocular orifice

The mirror fulfils the same function as the cinema screen. The ocular orifice serves as a replacement for Dürer's chin-strap: immobilisation that permits disreality, that of the sleeper, of the spectator, of the person in analysis.

In this division and this enclosure, it seems to me that we have the conditions for seduction. I would rather say seduction than illusion, because the subject looking in the box, if he is not mad, knows quite well that he is not looking at the Baptistery itself. For those who have just sat down in a theatre, the same applies. We, who look at this scene from Piero's school, we well know that it is not of the order of *trompe-l'œil*, and it is not even illusory; it is seduction in the proper sense of the term: one is divided against oneself; there is scission.

To see how this set-up relates to what is not painting, with what occurs in what is called 'reality', it would be necessary to show how this set-up regulating the energetic transformations of pictorial inscription communicates with another set-up, which is the political set-up, in the proper sense of the term that is, the set-up regulating a certain number of inscriptions at the heart of the Greek *polis* or at the heart of the Italian city. Here also, in the set-up of the *politeia*, we have firstly the enclosure of a space: I am alluding to the works of Jean-Pierre Vernant, Pierre Vidal-Naquet and Marcel Détienne on the Greek city, and in particular on the fact that the city is closed in on itself like a circle, that it is a community of men who are gathered together in a circle closed in on themselves, that in the middle there is an empty space, and that this empty space is 'dis-reality'. There is therefore a first limit (1) in the city, which will circumscribe and filter the influxes of energy in the form of individuals (but not only this: in the form of goods also, and of language, of armed power). The influxes will be filtered exactly as one filters spectators at the entrance to a show. They will be filtered according to a certain number of criteria, whose totality defines what is called citizenship. On the inside, there is the central space; it is to be found in the communities of warriors in Homer, *ès mèson*, in the middle. When one speaks in politics, one speaks in the centre, and speaking in the centre is not the same thing as speaking anywhere else around it. When one speaks elsewhere, one says nothing, in certain respects. Who can speak in the centre? People who bear arms. We thus have another filtering set-up: women never carry arms, and consequently they never speak in the centre, and therefore they never say anything. Not everyone climbs onto the stage. And then we have also *processes of effacement*: in fact, wealth, cronyism, pressure groups, rhetoric, will be the means of being able to come to speak in the centre, all of them scenographies, but they will be effaced and must be effaced for the political scene to be constituted.

I believe that the modality of representative pictorial inscription is profoundly isomorphic with the modality of political inscription taken in the sense of the *politeia*. We have to say that the painter is like a prince and that the prince is like a painter; they are both *effaced effacers*, they are people working on the limit (3), and who efface themselves on the limit (2), on the stage; which does not mean that they cannot appear there; it is possible to paint princes and even painters, but whether they are on the stage as models or as orators, in the auditorium like spectators or like citizens, their power, strictly understood, is effaced. The limit (3), the scenography, the staging, the underpinnings of politics, never appears: the machinery remains hidden.

In a set-up of this sort, the libidinal charge is never on the subject, on the theme, on what is recounted; the representation can no longer recount anything. This set-up is no longer fixed to a language-like narrative set-up; for a very long time, certainly, one will continue to recount on the pictorial scene, but it is perfectly possible to paint a still life (a jug that is painted in order to be represented). Ultimately, this will be the elimination of the reference to the narrative, the decoding of what happens. On the stage, there is indifference: everything can be represented, everything can be staged, anybody can come to speak, and so on. Potentially, on the inside of a set-up of this sort, on the inside of the pictorial, theatrical, representative space, there is a sort of liquidation or liquefaction; many codes and constraining set-ups will explode (this is democracy), but what will not explode is (1). Only in (1) and (2) are there stable investments and counter-investments, and therefore constraints, repressions, and filtering of energy. On the inside, from the moment that there is a filtering in (1) and a scene, you can say or represent anything you want (like at University).

2. Towards the Energetic

It is now possible for us to approach the economics of the modern work. Let us take a group of five works:

1. Cézanne, *View of Gardanne*, 1885–6, oil on canvas (81 × 65), British Museum.
2. Cézanne, *Still Life with Onions*, 1895–1900, oil (66 × 81), Jeu de Paume.
3. Delaunay, *The Cardiff Team*, 1912–13, oil (196 × 130), private collection.
4. Delaunay, *Circular Forms*, 1912–23, oil on canvas (100 × 68), Musée National d'Art Moderne.
5. Klee, *Auserwählte Stätte*, 1927, watercolour on paper (46 × 30.5: sesquialtera), private collection.

Beginning with the *View*, we immediately observe a disordering of the axial representative relation. I mean that the problem for Cézanne here, with this disordering, is an extremely precise spatial problem, requiring the production of something very difficult: a descent and then an ascent of space, the ground descending and going up again, deepening and rising again. In this work, what is immediately striking is that the inscriptions on the support are visible as inscriptions. A significant part of the work of inscription, of the binding of colour on the support, is visible. There are traces of the tracing. What was previously simply effaced is no longer effaced. The strokes are visible. The support itself is visible, canvas appears, because Cézanne uses the support as an asset; in other words, the pigmented medium does not hide or occult the support; it does not repress it, if it makes sense to say such a thing. Not only does it tolerate it, but in certain respects, it reveals it as something that is also of the order of inscription; the hue of the canvas functions from the chromatic point of view, at the same time as the absence of lines in the entire lower right of the painting, lines circumscribing the painted surfaces – like the roofs or the facades of the houses, whose contours are strongly underlined – means that the canvas emerges in a misty space, a space of immobile tension, which will give an 'effect of meaning' to the space (warmth, silence).

In the *Still Life with Onions* there is also disordering, supposedly aberrant deconstructions, just as much relating to the orthogonals, the perspective lines of the table, which are perfectly incorrect, as to the oval of the glass which is not even closed, or the completely dismantled symmetry of the foot of the glass, which animates everything on the table with a movement to the left. We observe here effects of energy that are manifestly sought as such by Cézanne; I am speaking of the lines, but if we analysed the colours, which is infinitely more difficult and more significant, we would arrive at identical remarks. Beyond these 'deformations', note also the treatment of the background; it can only have an energetic value. If he aimed at representative ends, Cézanne would not put such a flat screen in the background; this background is already what one will call abstraction. Everything moves and is polarised in the direction indicated by the onions on the extreme left, at the same time as the enormous white mass – which is often to be found in Cézanne's still-lifes, and which is a fixation, a condensation of chromatic energy – falls, that is, anchors the composition towards the bottom. We note then, as we did before, an organisation in relation to a visual space; the subject remains placed in an always visual space, that is, in representation, but the scenography changes profoundly: the *support* is not treated as a transparent window giving onto a landscape, a spectacle, *but it is treated for properly energetic purposes*. It is absolutely impossible to approach Cézanne's work without considering energy and the economic; it involves a chromatic economy. There are still many traits belonging to representation, but things are beginning to become distorted, and there is no other 'reason' to be found for this than chromatic or linear circulation, fixation, polarisation, and exchange of fluxes.

Here is the very model of what Delaunay will term simultaneism or simultanism. It is a strictly chromatic inscription; there is not one line, not one pencil stroke, where the stroke, the attack of the brush is not perfectly visible; where, consequently, the work of labour power does not allow itself to be ignored, which indicates that this labour power is always there, always alive, always powerful. The distribution of the colours involves almost the whole spectrum. This is why the painting is extraordinary: it is close to being chromatically unselective; inscribing almost all colours on the same painting is absolutely forbidden by the Academy. And this chromatic abundance has strictly energetic purposes. In certain respects, something such as this completely fulfils the old desire of Cézanne, who always used to say: 'It has to turn [*tourne*]'. Indeed, here, it turns, and it turns without modelling, without perspective, without depth, without illusion; it turns like the sun. We also should note one extremely charged, violent point of contact that condenses the maximum contrast in the whole of the painting – this is the contact of the darkest edge with the lightest region. This is the place where all the chromatic energy is gathered together, and then redistributed at the same time in rays which burst forth, in cycles, and in envelopes. This is why it moves; the way in which the colours succeed one another is not arbitrary, it bears a relation to the spectrum. And then there is not even a single straight line preventing it from 'turning'.

In the *Cardiff Team*, there are still no lines. There is only colour, and a chromatic system that is perhaps less explosive, less diluted than the other, more subordinated to allusions. There is an allusion to the town, to the game in the town, an allusion to advertising, and there are 'quotations'; yet the cyclical figure of the big-wheel, of this sort of multicoloured target, and the use of the players' jerseys implies that the painting no longer functions initially as representative, even if still remains allusive. If you put it next to Cézanne's *Onions*, you see that what was still very representative there, here becomes allusive; it becomes autonomous as an object, that is, as a depository of chromatic energy that is distributed in a certain manner, and which is waiting for someone to look at it to take on this energy.

Here is Klee's *Auserwählte Stätte*. We have four colours spread out vertically in levels, with a montage that is partly *cut* (for example: the contact of the blue with the brown), partly melted; and there is an inverse contrast: on the one hand, a line that Klee calls the *medial* line, that is, a line that is closed in on itself, which is like a labyrinthine line emphasising the right angle, and where there are almost neutral colours; and on the other hand, large surfaces, large bands of intense colours. This very contrastive plastic set-up can have no other function than that of capturing and retaining chromatic and linear energy as potential libidinal energy.

3. Towards the Polymorphic

Here is a work by Yves Tanguy, which is called *Constructing, Destroying*. It is very allusive, very surrealist; it is a work on the idea of the scene; it is the end of representation in the sense of the completion of narrative. It recounts nothing immediately: what there is on the scene is indifferent, and it is this that is shown. There is multifaceted work on scenic lighting; the latter is so strong it is ironic, derisory; there are even intentional perspectival errors. But what is important here is that this scene without history is a scene without a background – there is no visible horizon. Representation persists as a set-up for visualisation, for seduction; it loses some of its traits.

In the Cézanne, Delaunay, Klee group, libidinal flows are captured in chromatic form, not – and this is the contrast with Tanguy – in the axial relation of representation, in the bringing of the eye and the thing onto an axis, the sort of relation that is a mirrored relation; but rather on the pictorial object itself, by the simple play of the plastic constituents. When we said that it became autonomous, we meant this: the object is no longer representative, and it is therefore made independent in relation to a supposed signified, represented or referent, etc. It has also become autonomous in relation to the place occupied by the eye; there is no 'right distance' from which to look at it, there is no privileged spectator; the energetic effect does not attain its paroxysm when the spectator is placed in a given point of the environing space.

This becoming-autonomous of the painting, from the energetic perspective, will give rise to a considerable number of ideological discourses: in Klee himself, to a cosmological ideology; in Kandinsky, to an ideology of language; in Delaunay, to an ideology of light. The musicalist ideology (of the Golden Triangle) will reappear, as will the arithmetical and geometrical ideology of cubism and constructivism, and finally that of semiology – all these discourses are attempts to produce an effect of channelling, of rationalisation on painting, at the very moment when what actually happens is a sort of sweeping and capturing of chromatic energy on the painting in itself and for itself, without finality, without justification, and without reference.

In this case, the inscription no longer hides anything and hence is not seductive. There is constitution of the pictorial object in the sense that one speaks of musical objects or of book-objects, etc., of something whose existence is not dependent either on a law, or on a meaning, but which functions simply as crystallised force.

Concerning the relation to *place*, this formation of the object is equivocal: whatever theories the modern object is referred to – the school of art to which it bears witness: conceptual, abstract, and so on – if we continue to say that it has in itself its own principle, that it is energy deposited in a chromatic form, the simple fact of saying that this energy is *deposited*, *conserved* as potential energy, implies that the problem of the work has not yet been posed. Of course, the support is no longer occulted, but what still remains so is libidinal energy itself; and it is because it remains occulted that numerous discursive ideologies are possible on this sort of object. The object as a conservable object and, therefore, the place of the work both remain intact. When Duchamp takes a urinal, signs it, puts it in a museum, then it becomes a 'work'. When Delaunay hangs his colours in a gallery, the chromatic and consequently libidinal potential of the painting is subordinated to a set-up that is no longer the scenographic set-up of the painting itself, but that of the gallery, that of the place of the painting. Once again filtering will occur that takes place at the entrance to the gallery, that is, on the limit (1).

A modern pictorial object is no longer coded – but is it really fluid, really fluctuating? Is it energy that is really free and potentially transformable at any moment? Much more, certainly, than Piero's *Flagellation*, but it is still a fetishised object; it is not a work as *good form*, connected with codes to which everybody is referred, which everybody possesses if they are to say: it is *good*, it is made correctly, rather it is an arbitrary object, libidinally charged and *placed under restrictions, with filtering*; at bottom this is what the fetish is, an object comparable to what Marx describes as the commodity, that is, anything able to be libinally charged and placed under the restrictions of the law of value, of property.

One can attempt to undo the framework of the privileged pictorial space. Here is a Tom Wesselmann: *Bathtub Collage* no. 3 (1963) (2.13m × 2.69m × 0.46 m): a real door against a wall, with a real towel-holder, a real towel (we should laugh in saying 'real'; you see that it's that famous reality or exteriority, *you can dry yourself* with this towel). Behind, there is a panel painted with fake tiling, a fake dressing-gown, and a fake towel. The use of intentionally industrial colours.

Here is a composition by Andy Warhol. There are tins of soup, four silk-screens overworked with oil; the blacks, and thus the values and distribution of the chromatic bands are achieved by serigraphy; they are absolutely identical from one tin to the other. A principle of repetition, which is absolutely essential in Warhol. He introduces objects that are objects of industrial reality (here, nevertheless, with a concession concerning the variety and the 'wild' richness of the colours), and he arranges them in four panels that form a series, and that are centred connotatively on the problem of repetition, of difference in identity, of indifference with a small difference, that is, at bottom centred on the problem of the very nature of industrial commodities, for it is always the same thing with a small difference, a singularity (here the pigmentation) which allows it to be exchanged and valorised. Even this composition, which is not without concessions on the chromatic level, remains, concerning the critique of the pictorial set-up, quite strong because it brings us close to what happens in commodity fetishism. (It would have helped here to have studied the complete environments of Oldenburg and Kienholz: you enter into a standard 'real' bedroom, but you perceive allusions to the fact of representation; in one bedroom, for example, the large bed is treated with perspective effects; it is a three-dimensional object, and therefore 'real', but it shrinks towards its most distant point. This offers a critique of representation, but one that is inverted, and that does not signify that representation is a commodity, but rather that the commodity is always representation, always fetishism).

We see clearly in all the pop artists a relation with the 'real' object outside the museum, and therefore with capitalist and industrial commodities; this is a very surprising relation because at the same time as they exhibit it, they accept it. It is not at all a critical attitude in the European sense of the term; it is something else entirely. Not only is the libidinally charged character of these objects shown, but also their obsolescent, exchangeable character, and the fact that they will disappear, be consumed, that they have no importance. And in showing that, it is indicated (but only negatively) that what is important is energy, fluidity, desire in its displaceability, and that these objects are concretions destined to disappear, just as what is important in a commodity for capital is not what it is, but what it can be transformed into; it is the metamorphosis that counts, and not the object itself. There are therefore elements of *de-conservation*, of liquidation in pop. Nevertheless, the painted objects remain works placed in museums, in galleries, and thus the limit (1) remains.

We are now in a polymorphous pictorial space, a polymorphous perverse space, a space in which all sorts of chromatic inscriptions are possible. I say 'polymorphous' and 'perverse' with reference to Freud and to the normal perversity of child-hood; the surface of the body is a region where all erotic inscriptions are possible (and this is the normal polymorphous perversity of childhood); I will say that the pictorial space tends to become analogous to that, the pictorial region tends to become a surface of the polymorphously perverse infantile body. We know now that the painter can make an inscription on anything, in any way, from the moment that libidinal energy, crystallised one instant in the form of chromatic inscription, can be metamorphosed into something else, and does not form a blockage. The same thing happens at the theatre: when the scenographer or the architect searches for a total theatre (Piscator), he searches for a perverse polymorphous theatrical space, where he can make all the inscrip-tions. In such buildings there is a heterogeneous surface of inscription, made of several regions able to be invested – at one moment here, at another there – in an aleatory fashion. This polymorphous trait is also profoundly congruent with the economic space of modern capitalism; a space in which supposedly eco-nomic inscription is potentially everywhere. There is, certainly, always an extremely precise limit (1) that is called property or law of value, but potentially capitalism sketches the possibility of taking anything and putting it into circu-lation according to certain minimal conditions, and first of all according to the condition that libidinal energy be crystallised in the thing, which Marx called labour power. There must be energy in the thing, and if this is the case, then it is metamorphosed into another object, another action, affect, anything. If you compare this with pre–capitalistic circulation, with that imposed, for example, by the medieval guilds, you will see a set-up wherein, on the contrary, the pro-duction of economic inscription and its circulation are meticulously regulated, with an obsessive attention to detail.

Hence by this very comparison we see that there is no solution to the problem of painting for as long as the segregation of the pictorial space is not lifted; and that now the only temptation-attempt is to make the limit (1) explode, to make painting come out from the walls, from uninhabited spaces. Here begins the problem of painting as a problem of non–painting; a problem of generalised libidinal inscription. If you paint on the walls of the subway, of houses, this is not OK; if you get hold of the public address system of *Saint Lazarre* station and play some Berio instead of a tape announcing the arrival of trains, it is not OK. The 'resolution' of the question of painting is the dissolution of the 'limit' (1). It is necessary to dissolve; we have to go in the direction of a generalised lysis. The objection is: we will never be able to eliminate the limit (1) because we cannot not be in representation. The most direct counter-question: when Freud poses the whole problem of the image in terms of representation, to what does he owe this? To his ignorance concerning contemporary painting and to the reactionary character of his aesthetics, to the fact that for him art is the Italian scene, in such a way that he will think the imaginary in this form, at the very moment of Cézanne's pictorial revolution that led to abstraction, in which he sees nothing of interest? Or else, does he owe it to the intrinsic impossibility of overcoming metaphysics, to the 'fact' that the meaning of A is in fact (in) B, and that we are always in a relation, in representation, in the representation of something else; that the attempt to realise energetic or economic description is in vain, and simply illusory; that one cannot do away with the problem of meaning as differed, and that the limit (1) is quite simply the gap constitutive of this difference, that is, constitutive of meaning?

Our hypothesis (and our conviction) here, based on the movement of polymorphism in contemporary painting and economy, has been that the force of what is painted does not reside in its referential power, in its seduction, its 'difference', in its status as signifier (or signified), and that is to say, in its lack, but in its plenitude of switchable libido.

Chapter 17

Newman: The Instant

The Angel

A distinction should be made between the time it takes the painter to paint the picture (time of 'production'), the time required to look at and understand the work (time of 'consumption'), the time to which the work refers (a moment, a scene, a situation, a sequence of events: the time of the diegetic referent, of the story told by the picture), the time it takes to reach the viewer once it has been created (the time of circulation) and finally, perhaps, the time the painting *is*. This principle, childish as its ambitions may be, should allow us to isolate different 'sites of time'.

What distinguishes the work of Newman from the corpus of the 'avant-gardes', and especially from that of American 'abstract expressionism' is not the fact that it is obsessed with the question of time – an obsession shared by many painters – but the fact that it gives an unexpected answer to that question: its answer is that time is the picture itself.

One acceptable way to locate and deploy this paradox is to compare Newman's site of time with that which governs two great works by Duchamp. *The Large Glass* and *Etant donnés* refer to events, to the 'stripping bare' of the Bride, and to the discovery of the obscene body. The event of femininity and the scandal of 'the opposite sex' are one and the same. Held back in the glass, the event has yet to occur; in the thicket, and in the judas-hold, the scandal has already occurred. The two works are two ways of representing the anachronism of the gaze with regard to the event of stripping bare. The 'subject' of the painting is that instant itself, the flash of light which dazzles the eye, an epiphany. But, according to Duchamp, the occurrence of 'femininity' cannot be taken into account *within* the time of the gaze of 'virility'.

It follows that the time it takes to 'consume' (experience, comment upon) these works is, so to speak, infinite: it is taken up by a search for *apparition* itself (the term is Duchamp's), and 'stripping bare' is the sacrilegious and sacred analogon of apparition. Apparition means that something that is other occurs. How can the other be figuratively represented? It would have to be identified, but that is contradictory. Duchamp organized the space of the *Bride* according to the principle of 'not yet' and that of *Etant donnés* according to that of 'no longer'. Anyone who looks at the Glass is waiting for Godot; the viewer pursues a fugitive Albertine behind the door of *Etant donnés*. These two works by Duchamp act as a hinge between Proust's impassioned anamnesis and Beckett's parody of looking to the future.

The purpose of a painting by Newman is not to show that duration is in excess of consciousness, but to be the occurrence, the moment which has arrived. There are two differences between Newman and Duchamp, one 'poetic', so to speak, and the other thematic. Duchamp's theme is related, however distantly, to a genre: that of *Vanitas*; Newman's belongs to the Annunciations, the Epiphanies. But the gap between the two plastic poetics is wider than that. A painting by Newman is an angel. It announces nothing; it is in itself an annunciation. Duchamp's great pieces are a plastic gamble, an attempt to outwit the gaze (and the mind) because he is trying to give an analogical representation of how time outwits consciousness. But Newman is not representing a non-representable annunciation; he allows it to present itself.

The time taken to 'consume' a painting by Newman is quite different from the time demanded by Duchamp's great works. One never finishes recounting *The Large Glass* and *Etant donnés*. The Bride is enveloped in the story, or stories, induced by the strange names sketched on the scraps of paper of the Boxes, etched on the glass, represented by commentators. In the instructions provided for the installation of *Etant donnés* narrativity is held back and almost disappears, but it governs the very space of the obscene creche. It tells the story of a nativity. And the baroque nature of the materials demands many a story.

A canvas by Newman draws a contrast between stories and its plastic nudity. Everything is there – dimensions, colours, lines – but there are no allusions. So much so that it is a problem for the commentator. What can one say that is not given? It is not difficult to describe, but the description is as flat as a paraphrase. The best gloss consists of the question: what can one say? Or of the exclamation 'Ah'. Of surprise: 'Look at that.' So many expressions of a feeling which does have a name in the modern aesthetic tradition (and in the work of Newman): the sublime. It is a feeling of 'there' (Voilà). There is almost nothing to 'consume', or if there is, I do not know what it is. One cannot consume an occurrence, but merely its meaning. The feeling of the instant is instantaneous.

Obligation

Newman's attempt to break with the space *vedute* affects its 'pragmatic' foundation. He is no longer a painter-prince, an 'I' who displays his glory (or poverty in the case of Duchamp) to a third party (including himself, of course) in accordance with the 'communication structure' which founded classical modernity. Duchamp works on this structure as best he can, notably by researching multidimensional space and all sorts of 'hinges'. His work as a whole is inscribed in the great temporal hinge between too early/too late. It is always a matter of 'too much', which is an index of poverty, whereas glory, like Cartesian *générosité* requires respectability. And yet Duchamp is working on a pictorial plastic message which is transmitted from a sender, the painter, to a receiver, the public, and which deals with a referent, a diegesis which the public has difficulty in seeing, but which it is called upon to try to see by the myriad ruses and paradoxes contrived by the painter. The eye explores under the regime of *Guess*.

Newman's space is no longer triadic in the sense of being organized around a sender, a receiver and a referent. The message 'speaks' of nothing; it emanates from no one. It is not Newman who is speaking, or who is using painting to show us something. The message (the painting) is the messenger; it 'says': '*Here I am*', in other words, '*I am yours*' or '*Be mine*'. Two non-substitutable agencies, which exist only in the urgency of the here and now: me, you. The referent (what the painting 'talks about') and the sender (its 'author') have no pertinence, not even a negative pertinence or an allusion to an impossible presence. The message is the presentation, but it presents nothing; it is, that is, presence. This 'pragmatic' organization is much closer to an ethics than to any aesthetics or poetics. Newman is concerned with giving colour, line or rhythm the force of an obligation within a face to face relationship, in the second person, and his model cannot be *Look at this (over there)*; it must be *Look at me* or, to be more accurate, *Listen to me*. For obligation is a modality of time rather than of space and its organ is the ear rather than the eye. Newman thus takes to extremes the refutation of the *distinguo* introduced by Lessing's *Laocoon*, a refutation which has of course been the central concern of avant-garde research since, say, Delaunay or Malevitch.

Subject-matter

Subject-matter is not, however, eliminated from Newman's painting in any strict sense. In a monologue entitled *The Plasmic Image* (1943–5), Newman stresses the importance of subject-matter in painting. In the absence of subject-matter, he writes, painting becomes 'ornamental'. Moribund as it may be, surrealism has to be given credit for having maintained the need for subject-matter, and for thus preventing the new generation of American painters (Rothko, Gottlieb, Gorky, Pollock, Baziotes) from being seduced by the empty abstraction to which the European schools succumbed after 1910.

If we accept the views of Thomas B. Hess, the 'subject-matter' of Newman's work is 'artistic creation' itself, a symbol of Creation itself, of the Creation story of *Genesis*. One might agree insofar as one can accept that there is a mystery or at least an enigma. In the same monologue Newman writes: 'The subject matter of creation is chaos.' The titles of many of his paintings suggest that they should be interpreted in terms of a (paradoxical) idea of *beginning*. Like a flash of lightning in the darkness or a line on an empty surface, the Word separates, divides, institutes a difference, makes tangible because of that difference, minimal though it may be, and therefore inaugurates a sensible world. This beginning is an antinomy. It takes place in the world as its initial difference, as the beginning of its history. It does not belong to this world because it begets it, it falls from a prehistory, or from an a–history. The paradox is that of performance, or occurrence. Occurrence is the instant which 'happens', which 'comes' unexpectedly but which, once it is there, takes its place in the network of what has happened. Any instant can be the beginning, provided that it is grasped in terms of its *quod* rather than its *quid*. Without this flash, there would be nothing, or there would be chaos. The flash (like the instant) is always there, and never there. The world never stops beginning. For Newman, creation is not an act performed by someone; it is what happens (this) in the midst of the indeterminate.

If, then, there is any 'subject-matter', it is immediacy. It happens here and now. What (*quid*) happens comes later. The beginning is that there is . . . (*quod*); the world, what there is.

Duchamp took as his subject-matter the imperceptibility of the instant, which he tried to represent by using spatial artifices. From *Onement I* (1948) onwards, Newman's work ceases to refer, as though through a screen, to a history which is situated on the other side, even if that history were as stripped down and as supremely symbolic as is for Duchamp, the discovery, invention or vision of the other (sex). Take the sequence of 'early' paintings (in which Newman becomes Newman), that come after *Onement I: Galaxy, Abraham, The Name, Onement II* (1949), *Joshua, The Name II, Vir Heroicus Sublimis* (1950–1) or the series of five *Untitled* paintings (1950), which ends with *The Wild*, and each of which measures between one and two metres in height and four to five centimetres in breadth; we can see that these works do not 'recount' any event, that they do not refer figuratively to scenes taken from narratives known to the viewer, or which he can reconstitute. No doubt they do symbolize events, as their titles suggest. And to a certain extent the titles do lend credence to Hess's Kabbalistic commentaries, as does Newman's known interest in reading the Torah and the Talmud. Yet Hess himself admits that Newman never used his paintings to transmit a message to the viewer, and never illustrated an idea or painted an allegory. Any commentary must be guided by the principle that these works are non-figurative, even in a symbolic sense.

If we examine only the plastic presentation which offers itself to our gaze without the help of the connotations suggested by the titles, we feel not only that we are being held back from giving any interpretation, but that we are being held back from deciphering the painting itself; identifying it on the basis of line, colour, rhythm, format, scale, materials (medium and pigment), and support seems to be easy, almost immediate. It obviously hides no technical secrets, no cleverness that might delay the understanding of our gaze, or that might therefore arouse our curiosity. It is neither seductive nor equivocal; it is clear, 'direct', open and 'poor'.

It has to be admitted that none of these canvases, even if it does belong to a series, has any purpose other than to be a visual event in itself (and this is also true, if not more so, of the fourteen *Stations* of 1958–66). The time of what is recounted (the flash of the knife raised against Isaac) and the time taken to recount that time (the corresponding verses of Genesis) cease to be dissociated. They are condensed into the plastic (linear, chromatic, rhythmic) instant that *is* the painting. Hess would say that the painting rises up (*se dresse*), like the appeal from the Lord that stays the hand of Abraham. One might say that, but one might also say in more sober terms that it arises, just as an occurrence arises. The picture presents the presentation, being offers itself up in the here and now. No one, and especially not Newman, makes me see it in the sense of recounting or interpreting what I see. I (the viewer) am no more than an ear open to the sound which comes to it from out of the silence; the painting is that sound, an accord. Arising (*se dresser*), which is a constant theme in Newman, must be understood in the sense of pricking up one's ears (*dresser son oreille*), of listening.

The Sublime

The work of Newman belongs to the aesthetic of the sublime, which Boileau introduced via his translation of Longinus, which was slowly elaborated from the end of the eighteenth century onwards in Europe, of which Kant and Burke were the most scrupulous analysts, and which the German idealism of Fichte and Hegel in particular subsumed – thereby misrecognizing it – under the principle that all thought and all reality forms a system. Newman had read Burke. He found him 'a bit surrealist' (cf. the Monologue entitled *The Sublime is Now*). And yet in his own way Burke put his finger on an essential feature of Newman's project.

Delight, or the negative pleasure which in contradictory, almost neurotic fashion, characterizes the feeling of the sublime, arises from the removal of the threat of pain. Certain 'objects' and certain 'sensations' are pregnant with a threat to our self-preservation, and Burke refers to that threat as *terror*: shadows, solitude, silence, and the approach of death may be 'terrible' in that they announce that the gaze, the other, language or life will soon be extinguished. One feels that it is possible that soon nothing more will take place. What is sublime is the feeling that something will happen, despite everything, within this threatening void, that something will take 'place' and will announce that everything is not over. That place is mere 'here', the most minimal occurrence.

Now Burke attributes to *poetry*, or to what we would now call writing, the twofold and thwarted finality of inspiring terror (or threatening that language will cease, as we would put it) and of meeting the challenge posed by this failure of the word by provoking or accepting the advent of an 'unheard of' phrase. He deems painting incapable of fulfilling this sublime office in its own order. Literature is free to combine words and to experiment with sentences; it has within it an unlimited power, the power of language in all its sufficiency, but in Burke's view the art of painting is hampered by the constraints of figurative representation. With a simple expression like 'The Angel of the Lord', he writes, the poet opens up an infinite number of associations for the mind; no painted image can equal that treasure; it can never be in excess of what the eye can recognize.

We know that surrealist painting tries to get around this inadequacy. It includes the infinite in its compositions. Figurative elements, which are at least defined if not always recognizable, are arranged together in paradoxical fashion (the model is the dream-work). This 'solution' is, however, still vulnerable to Burke's objection that painting has no potential for sublimity: residual fragments of 'perceptive reality' are simply being assembled in a different manner. And Newman finds Burke 'a bit surrealist' because, as a painter, he sees only too well that this condemnation can only apply to an art which insists upon representing, upon making recognizable.

In his *Critique of Aesthetic Judgement* Kant outlines, rapidly and almost without realizing it, another solution to the problem of sublime painting. One cannot, he writes, represent the power of infinite might or absolute magnitude within space and time because they are pure Ideas. But one can at least allude to them, or 'evoke' them by means of what he baptizes a 'negative presentation'. As an example of this paradox of a representation which represents nothing, Kant cites the Mosaic law which forbids the making of graven images. This is only an indication, but it prefigures the minimalist and abstractionist solutions painting will use to try to escape the figurative prison.

For Newman, the escape does not take the form of transgressing the limits established for figurative space by Renaissance and Baroque art, but of reducing the event-bound time (*temps événementiel*) in which the legendary or historical scene took place to a presentation of the pictorial object itself. It is chromatic matter alone, and its relationship with the material (the canvas, which is sometimes left unprimed) and the lay-out (scale, format, proportions), which must inspire the wonderful surprise, the wonder that there should be something rather than nothing. Chaos threatens, but the flash of the tzimtzum, the zip, takes places, divides the shadows, breaks down the light into colours like a prism, and arranges them across the surface like a universe. Newman said that he was primarily a draughtsman. There is something holy about line in itself.

Place

'My paintings are concerned neither with the manipulation of space nor with the image, but with the sensation of time,' writes Newman in *Prologue for a New Aesthetic*, an unfinished monologue dating from 1949. He adds: 'Not the *sense* of time, which has been the underlying subject matter of painting, which involves feelings of nostalgia or high drama; it is always associative and historical . . .' The manuscript of the *Prologue* breaks off here. But some earlier lines allow us to elaborate further on the time in question.

Newman describes how, in August 1949, he visited the mounds built by the Miami Indians in south-west Ohio, and the Indian fortifications at Newark, Ohio. 'Standing before the Miamisburg mound – surrounded by these simple walls of mud – I was confounded by the absoluteness of the sensation, by their self-evident simplicity.' In a subsequent conversation with Hess, he comments on the event of the sacred site. 'Looking at the site you feel, Here I am, *here* . . . and out beyond there (beyond the limits of the site) there is chaos, nature, rivers, landscapes . . . but here you get a sense of your own presence . . . I became involved with the idea of making the viewer present: the idea that "Man is present".' Hess compares this statement with the text written by Newman in 1963 to introduce a maquette for a synagogue which he designed and built together with Robert Murray for the Recent American Synagogue Architecture exhibition. The synagogue is a 'perfect' subject for the architect; he is not constrained by any spatial organization except insofar as he is required to reinstate as best he can the commandment: 'Know before whom you stand.'

> It is a place, Makom, where each man may be called up to stand before the Torah to read his portion . . . My purpose is to create a place, not an environment; to deny the contemplation of the objects of ritual . . . Here in this synagogue, each man sits, private and secluded in the dugouts, waiting to be called, not to ascend a stage, but to go up to the mound where, under the tension of that 'Tzim-tzum' that created light and the world, he can experience a total sense of his own personality before the Torah and His Name.

On both the sketches and the plan, the place where the Torah is read is inscribed 'mound'.

This condensation of Indian space and Jewish space has its source and its end in an attempt to capture 'presence'. Presence is the instant which interrupts the chaos of history and which recalls, or simply calls out that 'there is', even before that which is has any signification. It is permissible to call this idea 'mystical', given that it does concern the mystery of being. But being is not meaning. If Newman is to be believed, being procures 'personality' a 'total meaning' by revealing itself instantaneously. An unfortunate expression, in two senses. It so happens that neither signification, totality or personality are at stake. Those instances come 'after' something has happened, and they do so in order to be situated within that something. *Makom* means place, but that 'place' is also the Biblical name for the Lord. It has to be understood in the sense of 'taking place', in the sense of 'advent'.

Passion

In 1966 Newman exhibited the fourteen *Stations of the Cross* at the Guggenheim. He gave them the subtitle: *Lama Sabachthani*, the cry of despair uttered by Jesus on the cross: *My God, why hast thou forsaken me?* In a text written to accompany the exhibition, Newman writes: 'This question that has no answer has been with us so long – since Jesus – since Abraham – the original question.' This is the Hebrew version of the Passion: the conciliation of existence (and therefore of death) and signification does not take place. We are still waiting for the Messiah who will bring meaning. The only response to the question of the abandoned that has ever been heard is not '*Know why*', but *Be*. Newman entitled a canvas *Be* and in 1970, the year in which he died, he reworked it as *Be I (Second Version)*. A second canvas, which was entitled *Resurrection* by the dealer who exhibited it in New York in 1962, was shown together with the *Stations* at the Guggenheim in 1966 under the title *Be II* (it was begun in 1961). In Hess's book, the reproduction of this work bears the legend *First Station, Be II*.

It has to be understood that *Be* is not concerned with the resurrection in the sense of the Christian mystery, but with the recurrence of a prescription emanating from silence or from the void, and which perpetuates the passion by reiterating it from its beginnings. When we have been abandoned by meaning, the artist has a professional duty to bear witness that *there is*, to respond to the order to be. The painting becomes evidence, and it is fitting that it should not offer anything that has to be deciphered, still less interpreted. Hence the use of flat tints, of non-modulated colours and then the so-called elementary colours of

Who's Afraid of Red Yellow and Blue? (1966–7). The question mark of the title is that in '*Is it happening?*', and the *afraid* must, I think, be taken as an allusion to Burke's terror, to the terror that surrounds the event, the relief that *there is*.

Being announces itself in the imperative. Art is not a genre defined in terms of an end (the pleasure of the addressee), and still less is it a game whose rules have to be discovered; it accomplishes an ontological task, that is, a 'chronological task'. It accomplishes it without completing it. It must constantly begin to testify anew to the occurrence by letting the occurrence be. In Newman's first sculptures of 1963–6, which are entitled *Here I, Here II,* and *Here III* and in the *Broken Obelisk* he completed in 1961, we find so many three-dimensional versions of the zip which strikes through all the paintings in a rectilinear slash, ineluctably, but never in the same place. In Newman verticality does not simply connote elation, or being torn away from a land that has been abandoned and from non-meaning. It does not merely rise up; it descends like a thunderbolt. The tip of the inverted obelisk touches the apex of the pyramid, 'just as' the finger of God touches that of Adam on the ceiling of the Sistine Chapel. The work rises up *(se dresse)* in an instant, but the flash of the instant strikes it like a minimal command: *Be.*[1]

Note

1. I will break off this study here. A lot remains to be said. In the meantime, it is time to state my debt to the memory of Thomas B. Hess for his *Barnett Newman* (New York: Museum of Modern Art, 1971), which is the source for all direct quotations from Newman.

Chapter 18

On What Is 'Art'

My intent will be to defend the thesis whereby the sentence 'This is art' is consistent by its very inconsistency.

I shall begin by analyzing the sentence's properties. It is simple to show that the sentence is not consistent (in the ordinary logical and epistemological sense) when taken literally, without concern for the connotations that the history of modern art attaches to art's 'creation' and 'reception' (what Paul Valéry terms, respectively, 'production' and 'consumption').

I shall then attempt to show that one's motives for detecting the inconsistency in the sentence 'This is art' are quite possibly traits characteristic of the reflexive status in the artistic operation (for example, writing) and of its reception (for example, reading). In this second step I will tacitly seek help from Kant, but also, especially, from Valéry (even though his angle may seem altogether different).

Finally, it would be appropriate to draw from these brief analyses a few observations relative to disorder and order, nothingness and the witnessing of nothingness, singularity and consensus. These observations will only be provisionally sketched.

1. Inconsistency

Here, I use the term *consistency* for the properties expected of a sentence claiming to state what is true or false. I use the term *cognitive* simply for this family of sentences claiming to state that something (obviously) is true or false. I do so knowing, like everyone else, that this claim is not the same as to verify or falsify a mathematical statement or, let us say, a 'physical' one (that is, one possessing a referent reputed to be real, which is not the case for mathematics). I will limit myself here to taking a cognitive physical utterance for a term of comparison by supposing that the sentence 'This is art' applies to a real object (referent).

'This is art' appears, at the very least, to be a partial determination if not a definition (defined as a complete description). The sentence attributes a predicate 'art') to a propositional subject ('this'). (This could be expressed otherwise, for example, as Noam Chomsky's noun phrase ['this'] and verb phrase ['is art']. Linguistically this would be more interesting, but, for that very reason, less enlightening logically or epistemologically. It could also be expressed in Frege-Russell notation.) What is usually called knowledge resides in this attribution of a predicate to a subject. Knowledge is the recognition that an object (referent), named by the propositional subject, belongs to the class named by the predicate. The object named 'this' belongs to the class 'what is art'.

There are, in the vocabulary of *The Differend*,[1] three operations that appear to me indispensable to cognition and recognition. I will not bother to expand upon the problematic that led me to these conclusions: suffice it to say that, considered within a language-like perspective, it is the very problematic of the possibility of knowing a *reality*.

In order for a sentence to be cognitive, that is, capable of indicating the truth or falsity of what it signifies concerning its referent.

1. It must first be endowed with meaning. In other words, it must connect one term with another, and this connection must take place by means of connective (Kant called them synthetic) operators that are reputed to be rational, or at least reasonable. These are the operators that Aristotle, and Kant after him, called categories. In modern logic (which is extensional), the symbol of inclusion ($\supset$) designates the connection of one term with another; the nature of this connection is specified in the play of symbols of quantity, quality, and relationship (parentheses, equals signs, and so on). The existential 'this' belongs to the universal class of 'what is art'.

2. The second (properly physical) condition for a cognition is that the logically conceived sentence must be confronted with 'reality'. Practically speaking, this means that cases must be presented that appear to verify the meaning of the sentence in question (or at least to falsify the sentence that contradicts it).

I stress the term *case*, and here is how we find it glossed in contemporary logic: '*there is* a certain *x*' and this *x* belongs to *y* (for example, it belongs to what is art). This *there is* obviously eludes the capacity for signification. It belongs to the capacity for showing or indicating. It presupposes that 'something' particular is given, here and now, to the locutor (and to the allocutor, who must be able to ascertain that there is, really, this).

The cognitive procedure thus demands that deictics ('here,' 'now,' 'this,' 'that,' 'I,' 'you,' and so on) be used. In the sentence under question, *this* is precisely such a deictic.

3. For the third condition, you may notice, the deictic 'this' only refers to a 'there is something' to the extent that it is currently indicated by the current sentence.

The question of this current moment needs to be studied in depth. It is enough, for now, to say that this moment is the *in actu* or the *actu* of performance artists; the *in situ* or the *situ* of performance arts. This raises difficult problems concerning space-time, or, more precisely, concerning not the time in which the sentence is localized, but the time which is marked by the sentence – a marking often effected by the sentence's presence alone and sometimes by its presentation. When we find the term *now* (or any of the deictics adjacent to this term: 'here,' 'you,' and so on) in a sentence, it indicates the instant that is contemporaneous with the time in which the current sentence takes place; contemporaneous, but measured (if I may express it this way) from the time of this sentence. To say 'today' (a case analogous to 'now') is not the same as saying '2 February 1989.' In the latter case, the measurement of time is carried out by means of a calendar (years, months, days).

A calendar is an evenly divided grid of proper nouns that allows us to indicate all of the 'nows' in a solar year by making them independent of their current designation. When I say '2 February 1989,' I am not saying that it is 'now' or yesterday or tomorrow. And if it happens that it is in fact 'now,' the indication of this 'now' by its date detaches it from the current moment of the deictic sentence and fixes it on a grid of proper nouns whose interrelationships are ordered in a fixed manner independent of the deictics.

Like all proper nouns, dates are and only are designations (that is, they have no meaning). But, unlike deictics, the designators that dates are fall under the category of what Saul Kripke terms 'rigid designators,' which I understand to mean that the designated is only designated (and not signified), but that it is identical to itself no matter what the current sentence designating it is.

Thus proper nouns keep their designative value from one sentence to another and from one speaker to another.

Each of the nouns and symbols used by science are such rigid designators and thus proper nouns. Examples of these nouns would be those designating units of length, intensity, weight, mass and velocity.

Without this 'rigidity' in designation, it could not be proved that *this* (a simple deictic) confirms the assertion that *x is y* or that 'this is art.' For we must be able to place 'this' in a world (a grid, for the calendar, but this goes for all tables of designative regularities) of nouns independent of 'performances' (sentences insofar as they are current), in order to be certain that both the current sentence P_0 and the *later* sentence P_1 still have the same referent.

It is now obvious what makes the sentence 'This is art' inconsistent. To be precise:

1. It is not inconsistent because it presupposes the class of 'objects that are art.' Recognition must take place: a logically inclusive relationship must be established between the object under examination and a class to which it is reckoned to belong. This class is thus defined beforehand. We may accept that from this point of view the sentence is consistent, provided that the class of 'what is art' be known.

When the receiver (the public) protests that 'this is not art,' he is holding to an explicit or implicit definition of the class of 'what is art.'

He cannot be accused of being wrong unless we accept that the definition of this class may change, or, in a case of major importance, if we accept that the 'this' in question can contribute to a modification in the definition of this class.

In themselves, neither of these presuppositions (neither a modification of art's definition nor a modifying role played by a certain 'this') leads to an inconsistency. A model analogous (but only analogous) to this modification and this modifier may be readily located in the history and epistemology of science. In science, the definition of classes (what is electric, what is dense, what is interactive, and so on) may be enlarged as well. In science, too, it is 'this,' a designated (and also, of course, named, that is, communicable) reality that may be the modifier of it. This is called discovery and/or invention.

2. Where inconsistency with respect to our sentence's truth or falsity intervenes is in that it lacks the name of 'this.' It is inconsistent, in this sense, because it is incomplete. It should be linked to another sentence like 'The Venus de Milo [name] or the Large Glass [name] is *this* [deictic], and this is art.' Without the so-called proper nomination, that is, the exclusive nomination that localizes 'this' on a grid of regularities (for example, the nominal catalogue of works belonging to the class of what is art), we do not know *what* we are talking about when we say, simply, 'this.' Nothing ensures that the speaker of the sentence P_0 (mine) indicates by 'this' the same referent as his allocutor. And if they carry on a conversation with each of them, in turn, from sentence to sentence, becoming the locutor and then the allocutor, they will never know if it is of the same referent that they are speaking.

3. Yet this defect is only such within the framework of the exigencies of a cognitive sentence (one whose purpose is to tell the truth concerning a referent). My thinking (following many others) is that the question as to whether this is or is not art (assuming that 'this' is named) can only be settled cognitively to the extent that 'this' (under its name) is submitted as an object to know or recognize, that is, as a referent either belonging to or not belonging to the class of 'what is art.'

Under this supposition, 'this' (under its name) is submitted as a thing (and this positional operator is called 'modality') – that is, as a material object, a 'physical' object in the sense discussed above, a 'sensible' object if one prefers – to be classified in a set.

Now, there is no doubt that artworks may thus be taken as things to be recognized and placed in known and defined sets. A major portion of literary and art criticism is engaged in this project. This is also the main concern of museum curators and librarians.

Let us examine what Valéry has to say about this procedure in his *Introduction to Poetics:*

> There remains the artwork itself, insofar as it is a sensible thing. This is a third consideration quite different from the previous two.
>
> We thus look upon an artwork as an *object*, purely as an object, that is, without adding any part of ourself to it than that which can be applied without distinction to all objects. This is an attitude marked rather distinctly by the absence of any production of value.
>
> What can we do with this object which, this time, can do nothing with us? We surely can do something. We can measure it according to its spatial or temporal nature; we can count the words in a text or the syllables in a line of poetry; we can note that such-and-such a book was published at such-and-such a time, that the composition of some painting is a copy of some other, that a hemistich of Lamartine's may be found in St Thomas, and that some page of Victor Hugo's belongs, as early as 1645, to an obscure Father Francis. We can point out that such-and-such a reasoning is a paralogism, that this sonnet is incorrect, that the rendering of this subject's arm defies anatomy, and that some use of words is bizarre. All of this is the result of operations which one may assimilate to purely material ones, since they are reducible to superpositions of the artwork (or fragments thereof) to some model.
>
> This treatment of works of the mind does not distinguish them from all other possible works: it places and maintains them at the rank of things imposing a *definable* existence upon them. Here is the point to be remembered:
>
> *Everything that we can define is immediately distinguishable from the producing mind and stands in opposition to it.* In the same stroke, the mind turns it into the equivalent of a material upon which or an instrument by which it can perform.
>
> The mind thus places that for which it has determined a definition outside its reach and, in this, it shows that it knows itself and only trusts what is not it.[2]

Valéry suggests that the definitional (which is also referential) procedure stands in opposition to what he calls the 'producing mind,' that is, the mind insofar as it 'creates' (to use that old term), and that opposition, according to Valéry, is as present in the 'consumer' (the receiver) as in the producer (the writer, the artist).

To the extent that the mind is concerned with art (or, rather, with making art), that it is so little motivated by definition, reference, or conceptual determination, Valéry further suggests in this passage, if it comes to suppose or to apprehend artworks as things, to place them 'outside its reach,' it is because 'it knows itself,' because 'it only trusts what is not it.'

To put it another way, 'this' is directed to the cognition of things because 'this' is neither a known nor a knowable nor even a recognizable thing to the mind that 'produced' 'this.' Moreover, we may yet ask ourselves whether 'what is art' is only established precisely at the instant when 'production' (or what Valéry also calls 'poetics' – I would say 'writing') ceases and makes way for classification.

2. Consistency

My punctual and awkward recourse to Valéry already causes us to enter the area of consistencies attributable to our inconsistent sentence.

That sentence, 'This is art,' is not, I repeat, consistent from a cognitive point of view. It therefore is not even classifiable within the sort of critique that Valéry represents in the above text. The unnamed 'this' is the point at which it fails vis-à-vis cognitive consistency. And it is beginning with this point that I will ascend once again toward its 'poetic' or written consistency.

1. To accomplish this anabasis, I will seek help once again from Valéry, for the insistence of 'this' in our sentence appears entirely congruent with the stress Valéry puts on what he calls *act* or *in-act*. I have remarked that a deictic only refers to an element of situation (for example, a person, time, space, object) by placing it in relation to the actuality of the sentence in which that deictic itself appears, in other words, in relation to the current or in-act sentence. On this point, Valéry writes:

> Everything that I have said thus far can be reduced to these few words: *the work of the mind exists only in-act*. Outside of this act, what remains is but an object with no particular relationship with the mind. Bring the statue that you admire to a people sufficiently different from ours: it will be but an insignificant stone; a Parthenon but a small marble quarry. And when a poet's text is used as a collection of grammatical difficulties or examples, it immediately ceases to be a *work of the mind*, since the use to which it is put is altogether foreign to the conditions of its origin, and since a consumption value that would give this work a sense is denied it. (40; italics in original)

It is pointless to belabor what is clearly understood here: this (passably enigmatic) *act* or *in-act*, this act *of the mind* (a no less obscure entity that is properly 'the work of the mind') is (negatively) circumscribed at the outset as what is not the artwork as object or thing. The artwork as act is not the artwork as object.

As object, the artwork is named and signified or signifiable. Conditions are placed on it; it is governed by rules of the cognitive belonging to either one or several sets.

The mind that recognizes or strives to recognize it ('Is it art?') is not the mind, the poetic mind that makes it. The poetic mind is only in-act, that is, here and now: the mind has neither permanent sights nor a permanent grip on it, because the mind does not possess a defined and constant identity for it.

Valéry expresses it even better in the following passage which may be considered a definition of undefinable actuality or presence:

> However clear, obvious, strong or beautiful is the spiritual event that concludes our expectation, that completes our thought or raises our doubt, nothing is yet

irrevocable. Here, the next moment has absolute power over the product of the preceding one. This is because the mind, reduced to its substance alone, does not have the finite at its disposal and is absolutely incapable of linking itself to itself. (48)

According to Valéry, the state of the poetic mind affects the consumer as well as the producer. That poetic state is not, properly speaking, a state, but a mode of temporality remarkable for its discontinuity and discreteness. It is a sort of spasm in which what has been done does not govern what is yet to be done. 'The mind . . . is absolutely incapable of linking itself to itself.' Neither the linkages, nor the connections between one word and another, nor the connections between one part of a visual or sonorous figure to another are fixed, and, at each moment, there is a 'decision' to be made as to how to create linkages. Forming a form (for there will be, in the end, a form) is not bound to a project.

2. The use of the terms *expectation* and *doubt* should be noted in the above passage from Valéry. I have argued that a 'decision' had to be made. In the uncertainty in which the disconnection of moments throws the mind – a disconnection that is, thus, a proliferation of possible linkages between one moment and the next – the mind waits for a decision. A decision one waits for is not a decision one makes.

The *act* or the *in-act* thus takes on a meaning that is not immediately a temporal one, but one of *exis*, of being-there, or perhaps even of *ethos*, of availability. Let's say a manner of being, of being with respect to time, of course, but, for this reason, of a manner of being with respect to the linkage. (And I stress that this is not a manner of being with respect to being.) And it is assuredly not a manner of being with respect to the object (even a future, anticipated, or projected object): there is no object in this *exis* or *ethos*.

What the writer, composer, painter, or filmmaker (or even the reader, listener, or spectator) waits for is for 'it to come along' What is waited for is the event of the 'decision' that serves as act for and end to the infinity of possibles. It should be recalled that: 'the mind, reduced to its substance alone, does not have the finite at its disposal.' It desires or waits for it, but does not have it at its disposal. The mind will not complete the form.

For it is the case that the mind is nondefinitiveness and the non-ending of linkages, indetermination, and what Valéry, in short, calls disorder:

> Wherever the mind is at stake, everything is at stake. Everything is disorder and any reaction against disorder is of the same nature, for disorder is, further, the condition of its own fecundity: it harbors that promise since its fecundity is contingent upon the unexpected rather than the expected, and upon that of which we are ignorant (and because we are ignorant of it) rather than what we know. (59–60)

This disorder is also the mind's 'freedom.' Others have referred to free association or *aura*.

The act that decides is not an *action* in the strict sense of the term – it is an event. Valéry writes: 'clear, obvious, strong . . . beautiful is the spiritual *event* that concludes our expectation.'

We may 'lower the degree of freedom in the system of the mind' (strange system), but, Valéry adds,

> as for the rest, I mean as for the modifications and substitutions that this constraint leaves open, we simply wait for what we desire to be produced. For we can do nothing but wait for it. *We have no means by which to reach precisely what it is within us that we wish to obtain.* (49; italics in original)

I believe I recognize in this 'freedom' or this 'disorder' what I, for my part, call passibility; a disseizure.

'Instability, incoherence, inconsequence constitute,' writes Valéry, 'the most common regime [of the mind when it gives itself over to] its substance alone' (46).

3. Yet this is a disseizure and a passibility in expectation of their end result. Something is wished for in this expectation. Not something from the regime of voluntary action in which it is 'I' who wishes. Something is wished that is not 'I,' something that is not the completed object, which immediately turns into the simple referent of possible cognitions or interpretations.

These are cognitions or interpretations that only pay indirect homage to inexplicable indetermination through an indefinite proliferation of their determinations and explanations: in one sense, this is or is not art; in some other sense also, this is or is not art. Commentary would be interminable and, more important, futile (incapable of accumulating a patrimony, a capital of clear judgments). This is an eminent difference between the history of commentary on poetic works and that on natural effects.

What, then, is wished for at the heart of uncertainty, in the proliferation of imaginary possibilities? What is desired? Simply the event of an end. In a sense, a death. Yet is it a death of what is simply possible, or a death in order to give birth to the artwork?

Here we must introduce the necessarily concomitant *topos* of the expectation of the act at the heart of disorder, the *topos* of fatigue.

Valéry discerns two kinds of fatigue through art and poetics:

> If I link myself to the page that I must write or to the page I wish to understand, I enter, in both cases, into a phase of lesser freedom. But in the two cases, my freedom may have two opposite appearances. My very task may urge me to pursue my freedom and, far from experiencing it as a displeasure, as a divergence from my mind's most natural course, I might give myself over entirely to it, advancing with so much life in the way paved by my design that the feeling of fatigue is diminished. This may go on until, in truth, fatigue suddenly clouds over my thought, confusing the play of ideas, reconstituting the disorder of normal short-term exchanges and the dispersive, restful state of indifference.

> Then again, constraint may be at the first level, work may become more noticeable than its effect, the means goes against the end result, and the mind's tension must be nourished by increasingly precarious resources – resources increasingly estranged from the ideal object whose power and action must be maintained at the cost of a fatigue that quickly becomes unbearable. There is indeed a great contrast between two applications of our mind. (50–1)

Not being able to give this text the commentary it deserves, I will merely stress that good disorder does not fatigue; weariness falls upon you. It's a way of ending on a happy note. But the specter of the act that we try to bring on through endless rule- and constraint-making is a fatigue of drying-out and desertification, a fatigue caused by the will and an obstinacy that moves us toward sterility. This is a fatigue effected by rules and perhaps by the breathlessness caused by having to produce an artwork just the same. It is a fatigue caused by being required.

4. Let us pause at this term, *sterility*. In any 'this,' is it not, at bottom, a question of a banal analogy with the pain of childbirth and with the impatience to give birth.

'This can all be summed up by the following formula: in the production of the artwork, *action comes into contact with the undefinable*' (57; italics in original). Is he stating anything other than that the phallus touches that which lacks it?

And by this touch, assuredly killing the hysterical agitation of renewed beginnings to be forgotten, that of disorders to be misread, of the panic before virtual linkages, a child, too, is engendered: the artwork. As soon as he is born, the child can be subsumed under the rule of knowledge. But at that cost, he will remain misconceived like a child born of inconsistency, as long as he himself has not engendered upon the 'consumer' this very same agitation and this very same expectancy of the end of agitation from which the artwork is born.

Besides his *Cahiers (Notebooks)*,[3] many texts, starting with *La soirée de M. Teste*,[4] demonstrate how this sexual difference (let us call it sexual for the sake of convenience) occupies and undoubtedly preoccupies Valéry's thought. We know his perplexity before femininity and aversion to the possibility of disorder (a male, cognitive term) in his house, the mind.

I shall not develop this point here, but simply state that as much could be said, although in another fashion, of the Kantian preoccupation, the Kantian division between the imagination and reason. With the beautiful, it lies in a division or an emulation, tempered by a marriage [*fiançailles*], and with the sublime, it lies in a conflict brought to the point of rupture where the proliferating network of imaginary possibles becomes shredded and the act or comprehension appears as it truly is in its princely principle: not the rule of knowledge but the law of transcendence and the unknowable, the event itself and the act that is incomparable to any regularity.

I am not particularly beholden to this division of tasks between imaginary and symbolic under the regime of the real, as Lacan would have said, and that Valéry, a bit naively but consistently, calls desire.

I simply state this: 'this is art,' a cognitively inconsistent sentence, is consistent with regard to the double inconsistency of art (or of writing). There is an 'initial' (a poor term) inconsistency in the indetermination of possible linkages that is nevertheless not just hysteria, itself unfelicitously determined in its repetition (here, one would have to explore the area of *unlinking*). And there is a 'final' inconsistency of a determinant work-producing event, one that produces it 'from time to time,' that is, not as an object, but as an occasion, a case, a 'this,' here and now, the occasion for reiterating the same conflict (which may be sweet or furious) in the said 'consumer.'

3. Reflection

I promised to approach at one point the question of reflection. I lack the moment of reflection, as I always do.

As always, because reflection (which I mean here in the Kantian sense) is of the order of a time in relation to which what we call time, 'physical' time, clock time, also called (by antiphrasis, I suppose) 'real' time, never ceases being insufficient. The time of reflection, in the wide acception that Kant lends the word (under the rubric of reflecting judgment), is exactly what I have discussed in reference to Valéry under the name of artwork's time.

I repeat that determining an object supposes that we already possess the rule of its signification: the class to which it belongs and the categories of that belonging.

Reflection supposes that we do not possess that rule. Consequently, we do not even possess the object since we are not yet in a position to signify or name it. We can just barely indicate it as 'this,' as a case or an occasion. This is what Kant says of the object from an aesthetic point of view: it is only occasion.

We do not yet, therefore, possess the rule; we are waiting for it. Actually, in Kantian orthodoxy, it is not the rule of comprehension that we are waiting for, but, where art is concerned, the form imagination might take. But the case (if it may be called such) of reflection being uncertain, expectation and uncontrolled senselessness, is, for this reason, no less pertinent. No less pertinent because it is poorer for the fact that what will serve as act is not even the concept, but the form.

In Kant's *First Critique* there are strange, nearly impenetrable, but decisive pages on the amphibology of the concepts of reflection. I would have liked to lend them some commentary, because they are so enlightening, but I will forgo that wish.

Rather, I would like to focus briefly on the following: reflection is a disposition of the mind by which it judges without concept. To judge, that is, to settle [*trancher*], to decide, to discern: the strength to discern, *Urteilskraft*, is also the strength to bring together, to synthesize. What Valéry calls *act*.

And if this takes place without concept it is because previously, before the advent of a decision, nothing occurs but the senseless flow of every linkage possible – Valéry's 'disorder,' to which would correspond the comparison with Kant.

We see that this reflection is not a bending of thought back upon itself, but rather a bending within thought of something that seems to not be itself since thought cannot determine it. Yet it is the bending of something that is possibly more 'inside' thought than itself.

This further inside is nothing other than feeling, *Empfindung*, or, as we say today, affect. Valéry writes:

> A poem on paper is nothing other than a writing subjected to everything one can do to a writing. But among all of its possibilities, there is one and only one that places this text under the conditions where it will take on the strength and form of action. A poem is a discourse demanding and bringing forth a continuous link between the *voice that is* and the *voice that is coming* and *which must come*. And this voice must be such that it imposes itself and inspires the affective state of which the text is the unique verbal expression. Remove the voice and the required voice and all becomes arbitrary, the poem is transformed into a series of signs linked only by the fact that they are traced materially one after the other.[5]

Inspiration of the affective state. I will not insist: we are indeed speaking of the same thing, of a 'this' that is in no way a thing, but rather an occasion for a 'pure' feeling in the Kantian sense, pure in that it is not motivated by anything. The voice, the double voice, the one that declares that this is beautiful and the one that calls for others to share this feeling–judgment, that voice may also be found in the Kantian analytic.

Again, and to conclude, Valéry: 'the works of the mind, poems and others, refer to nothing other than what engenders what engendered them themselves and absolutely nothing else.'[6]

A sentence understood clearly as follows: this is art if 'this' engenders the pure feeling (disorder, the expectation of its end, and the hope of its transfer to a receiver) from which 'this' itself was born.

Such is the resistance of art – a resistance in which all of its consistency consists: determination should never exhaust birth.

Notes

1. Translator's note. Cf. J. F. Lyotard, *The Differend: Phrases in Dispute*.
2. P. Valéry, *Introduction à la poétique* (Paris: Gallimard, 1938), pp. 38–9; italics in the original. The volume contains two texts : 'De l'enseignement de la poétique au collège de France' (February 1937), an outline of the course Valéry gave beginning in December 1937, and 'Première leçon', the inaugural lecture of that course, given on 10 December 1937. Unless otherwise noted, all references are to this work.
3. P. Valéry, *Cahiers* (Paris: Gallimard, 1987).
4. P. Valéry, *La soirée de Monsieur Teste* (Paris: Nouvelle Revue Française, 1927).
5. P. Valéry, *Introduction à la poétique*, pp. 40–1.
6. Ibid. p. 42.

Select Bibliography

The best bibliography of works by and on Lyotard is available on the Internet at http://sun3.lib.uci.edu/indiv/scctr/wellek/lyotard/index.html

English Editions of Lyotard's Work

Lyotard, Jean-François (1984), *Driftworks*, ed. R. McKeon, New York: Semiotext(e).

Lyotard, Jean-François (1984), *The Postmodern Condition: A Report on Knowledge*, trans. G. Bennington and B. Massumi, Manchester: Manchester University Press.

Lyotard, Jean-François and Thébaud, Jean-Luc (1985), *Just Gaming*, trans. W. Godzich, Minneapolis: University of Minnesota Press.

Lyotard, Jean-François (1988), *The Differend: Phrases in Dispute*, trans. G. Van Den Abbeele, Manchester: Manchester University Press.

Lyotard, Jean-François (1988), *Peregrinations: Law, Form, Event*, New York: Columbia University Press.

Lyotard, Jean-François (1989), *The Lyotard Reader*, ed. A. Benjamin, Oxford: Blackwell.

Lyotard, Jean-François (1990), *Duchamp's TRANS/formers*, Venice, CA: Lapis Press.

Lyotard, Jean-François (1990), *Heidegger and 'the jews'*, trans. A. Michel and M. Roberts, Minneapolis: University of Minnesota Press.

Lyotard, Jean-François (1990), *Pacific Wall*, trans. B. Boone, Venice, CA: Lapis Press.

Lyotard, Jean-François (1991), *The Inhuman: Reflections on Time*, trans. G. Bennington and R. Bowlby, Cambridge: Polity Press.

Lyotard, Jean-François (1991), *Phenomenology*, trans. B. Beakley, Albany, NY: State University of New York Press.

Lyotard, Jean-François (1992), *The Postmodern Explained to Children: Correspondence 1982–1985*, trans. D. Barry, et. al., Minneapolis: University of Minnesota Press.

Lyotard, Jean-François (1993), *Libidinal Economy*, trans. I. Hamilton-Grant, London: Athlone Press.

Lyotard, Jean-François (1993), *Political Writings*, trans. and ed. B. Readings and K. P. Geiman, London: University College London Press.

Lyotard, Jean-François (1993), *Toward the Postmodern*, ed. R. Harvey and M. S. Roberts, NJ: Humanities Press.

Lyotard, Jean-François (1994), *Lessons on the Analytic of the Sublime*, trans. E. Rottenberg, Stanford, CA: Stanford University Press.

Lyotard, Jean-François (1997), *Postmodern Fables*, trans. G. Van Den Abbeele, Minneapolis: University of Minnesota Press.

Lyotard, Jean-François (1998), *The Assassination of Experience by Painting – Monory*, trans. R. Bowlby, London: Black Dog.

Lyotard, Jean-François and Gruber, Eberhard (1999), *The Hyphen: Between Judaism and Christianity*, trans. P. -A. Brault and M. Nass, New York: Humanity Books.

Lyotard, Jean-François (1999), *Signed, Malraux*, trans. R. Harvey, Minneapolis: University of Minnesota Press.

Lyotard, Jean-François (2000), *The Confession of Augustine*, trans. R. Beardsworth, Stanford, CA: Stanford University Press.

Lyotard, Jean-François (2001), *Soundproof Room: Malraux's Anti-aesthetics*, trans. R. Harvey Stanford, CA: Stanford University Press.

French Editions of Lyotard's Work

Lyotard, Jean-François (1954), *La Phénoménologie*, Paris: Presses Universitaires de France.

Lyotard, Jean-François (1971), *Discours, figure*, Paris: Klincksieck.

Lyotard, Jean-François (1973), *Dérive à partir Marx et Freud*, Paris: Union générale d'éditions.

Lyotard, Jean-François (1973), *Des dispositifs pulsionnels*, Paris: Union générale d'éditions.

Lyotard, Jean-François (1974), *Économie libidinale*, Paris: Minuit.

Lyotard, Jean-François (1975), *Le Mur du Pacifique*, Paris: Christian Bourgois.

Lyotard, Jean-François (1976), *Sur cinq peintures de René Guiffrey*, Paris: Galerie Stevenson and Palluel.

Lyotard, Jean-François (1977), *Instructions païennes*, Paris: Galilée.

Lyotard, Jean-François (1977), *Récits tremblants*, Paris: Galilée.

Lyotard, Jean-François (1977), *Rudiments païens: genre dissertatif*, Paris: Unions générale d'éditions.

Lyotard, Jean-François (1977), *Les Transformateurs Duchamp*, Paris: Galilée.

Lyotard, Jean-François and Thébaud, Jean-Luc (1979), *Au juste: conversations*, Paris: Christian Bourgois.

Lyotard, Jean-François (1979), *La Condition postmoderne*, Paris: Minuit.

Lyotard, Jean-François (1980), *La Partie de peinture*, illustrated by H. Maccheroni, Cannes: Maryse Candela.

Lyotard, Jean-François (1980), *Sur la constitution du temps par la couleur dans les œuvres récentes d'Albert Aymé*, Paris: Traversière.

Lyotard, Jean-François (1981), *Daniel Buren, les couleurs, sculptures, les formes, peintures*, Paris: Centre Georges Pompidou (with B. H. D. Buchloh and J. -H. Martin).

Lyotard, Jean-François (1981), *La Ligne*, Paris: Adami Catalogue, Galerie Maeght.

Lyotard, Jean-François (1981), *Monory. Ciels: Nébuleuses et galaxies: Les Confines d'un dandysme*, Paris: Galerie Maeght.

Lyotard, Jean-François (1982), *Monogrammes/Loin du doux*, Paris: Catalogue Barchello, Galerie de dessin.

Lyotard, Jean-François (1982), *Le Travail et l'écrit chez Daniel Buren: Une introduction à la philosophie des arts contemporains*, Limoges: NDLR.

Lyotard, Jean-François (1983), *Le Différend*, Paris: Minuit.

Lyotard, Jean-François (1984), *L'Assassinat de l'expérience par la peinture, Monory*, Talence: Le Castor Astral.

Lyotard, Jean-François (1984), *La Peinture du sacré à l'ère postmoderne*, Paris: Centre Georges Pompidou.

Lyotard, Jean-François (1984), *Tombeau de l'intellectuel et autres papiers*, Paris: Galilée.

Lyotard, Jean-François (1985), *Les Immatériaux*, Paris: Centre Georges Pompidou.

Lyotard, Jean-François (1986), *L'enthousiasme: La critique kantienne de l'histoire*, Paris: Galilée.

Lyotard, Jean-François (1986), *Le Postmoderne expliqué aux enfants*, Paris: Galilée.

Lyotard, Jean-François (1987), *Que peindre? Adami, Arakawa, Buren*, Paris: Éditions de la Différence.

Lyotard, Jean-François (1988), *Heidegger et 'les juifs'*, Paris: Galilée.

Lyotard, Jean-François (1988), *L'Inhumain: Causeries sur le temps*, Paris: Galilée.

Lyotard, Jean-François (1989), *Les Guerre des Algériens: Écrits, 1956–1963*, ed. M. Ramdami, Paris: Galilée.

Lyotard, Jean-François (1991), *Leçons sur l'analytique du sublime*, Paris: Galilée.

Lyotard, Jean-Francois (1991), *Lectures d'enfance*, Paris: Galilée.

Lyotard, Jean-François (1993), *Moralités postmodernes*, Paris: Galilée.

Lyotard, Jean-François (1996), *Signé Malraux*, Paris: Grasset.

Lyotard, Jean-François (1997), *Flora danica: La sécession du geste dans la peinture de Stig Brøgger*, Paris: Galilée.

Lyotard, Jean-François (1998), *Chambre sourde: L'antiesthétique de Malraux*, Paris: Galilée.

Lyotard, Jean-François (1998), *La Confession d'Augustin*, Paris: Galilée.

Lyotard, Jean-François (2000), *Misère de la philosophie*, ed. D. Lyotard, Paris: Galilée.

Editions of Journals on Lyotard

L'Arc: Lyotard (1976), no. 64.

Diacritics (1984), vol. 14, no. 3.

L'Ecrit du Temps: Questions de Judaïsme (1984), 5.

Les Cahiers de Philosophie: Jean-François Lyotard: Réécrire la modernité (1988), 5.

L'Esprit Créateur: Passages, Genres, Differends: Jean-François Lyotard (1991), 31(1).

Philosophy Today (1992), vol. 36, no. 4.

Journal of the British Society for Phenomenology (2001), vol. 32, no. 3.

Parallax (2001), vol. 6, no. 4.

Yale French Studies: Jean-François Lyotard: Time and Judgement (2001), 99.

Interviews with Lyotard

Lyotard, Jean-François, 'Nietzsche and the Inhuman: Interview with Jean-François Lyotard', trans. R. Beardsworth, in *Journal of Nietzsche Studies*, Issue 7, Spring, 1994, 67–130.
Lyotard, Jean-François and G. Larochelle, 'That which resists, after all' in *Philosophy Today*, vol. 36:4, Winter 1992, 402–17.

Books on Lyotard

Benjamin, Andrew (ed.), (1992), *Judging Lyotard*, London: Routledge.
Bennington, Geoffrey (1988), *Lyotard: Writing the Event*, Manchester: Manchester University Press.
Billouet, Pierre (1999), *Paganisme et postmodernité: J. -F. Lyotard*, Paris: Ellipses.
Browning, Gary (2000), *Lyotard and the End of Grand Narratives*, Cardiff: University of Wales Press.
Carroll, David (1987), *Paraesthetics: Foucault, Lyotard, Derrida*, London: Methuen.
Crome, Keith (2004): *Lyotard and Greek Thought: Sophistry*, Basingstoke: Palgrave Macmillan.
Derrida, J. et al. (1985) *La Faculté de juger*, Paris: Minuit.
Harvey, Robert (ed.), (2000), *Afterwords: Essays in Memory of Jean-François Lyotard*, Occasional papers of the Humanities Institute at Stony Brook, Stony Brook, NY: Humanities Institute.
Lyotard, Dolorès et al. (2001), *Jean-François Lyotard: L'exercice du différend*, Paris: Presses Universitaires de France.
Malpas, Simon (2003), *Jean-François Lyotard*, London: Routledge.
Readings, Bill (1991), *Introducing Lyotard: Art and Politics*, London: Routledge.
Sfez, Gérald (2000), *Jean-François Lyotard: la faculté d'une phrase*, Paris: Galilée.
Silverman, Hugh (2002), *Lyotard: Philosophy, Politics and Sublime*, London: Routledge.
Sim, Stuart (1996), *Jean-François Lyotard*, Hemel Hempstead: Prentice Hall and Harvester Wheatsheaf.
Sim, Stuart (2001), *Lyotard and the Inhuman*, Cambridge: Icon Books.
Williams, James (1998), *Lyotard: Towards a Postmodern Philosophy*, Cambridge: Polity Press.
Williams, James (2000), *Lyotard and the Political*, London: Routledge.

Index